NACHITUTI'S GIFT

AFRICA AND THE DIASPORA
History, Politics, Culture

SERIES EDITORS

Thomas Spear
David Henige
Michael Schatzberg

NACHITUTI'S GIFT

ECONOMY, SOCIETY, AND ENVIRONMENT IN CENTRAL AFRICA

David M. Gordon

THE UNIVERSITY OF WISCONSIN PRESS

The University of Wisconsin Press
1930 Monroe Street
Madison, Wisconsin 53711

www.wisc.edu/wisconsinpress/

3 Henrietta Street
London WC2E 8LU, England

1   3   5   4   2

Printed in the United States of America

Library of Congress Cataloging-in-Publication Data
Gordon, David M., 1970–
Nachituti's gift: economy, society, and environment in central Africa / David M. Gordon.
        p.   cm.—(Africa and the diaspora)
Includes bibliographical references and index.
ISBN 0-299-21360-9 (hardcover: alk. paper)—
ISBN 0-299-21364-1 (pbk.: alk. paper)
    1. Luapula River Valley (Zambia and Congo)—Social life and customs.
    2. Luapula River Valley (Zambia and Congo)—Economic conditions.
    3. Luapula River Valley (Zambia and Congo)—Environmental conditions.
    4. Fisheries—Economic aspects—Luapula River Valley (Zambia and Congo).
    5. Fish trade—Luapula River Valley (Zambia and Congo).
    6. Bemba (African people)—Economic conditions.
        I. Title.   II. Series.
        DT3140.L83G67   2005
            968.94—dc22

CONTENTS

ILLUSTRATIONS

Figures

Photographs

Maps

PREFACE AND ACKNOWLEDGMENTS

When I first arrived in Mweru-Luapula, the fertile floodplains, rivers, and lakes that form part of the political boundary between Zambia and the Democratic Republic of Congo (DRC), I planned to investigate how chiefs, businesspeople, and politicians had secured power and profit during the colonial and postcolonial periods. In graduate school, after reading the work of scholars like Janet MacGaffey, Jane Guyer, and Sara Berry, I had decided to study informal political and economic networks that rested on unrecorded or illicit economic activities. It took more than a few visits to the fish markets to change my mind. While bargaining over my evening meal, I practiced my Bemba language skills by asking about the fishery. Who caught the fish? Where were different species found? How were they caught, processed, and traded? As some of my questions were answered, I came to realize how crucial the fishery was to the subsistence and commercial economy of the Luapula Valley—it seemed to be the full-time occupation of nearly one-quarter of those who lived in the densely populated valley and a significant source of revenue and food for all. A study of the fishery posed questions key to understanding central Africa's political economy, most notably how corporate groups controlled access to scarce resources and translated this access into forms of wealth.

I was uncertain about this realignment of interests. A pioneer in the writing of Luapula's history, Mwelwa C. Musambachime, had already written an excellent doctoral dissertation about the rise of the fishery during the colonial period. Perhaps an investigation of a fishery put too literal an interpretation on Jean-François Bayart's "politics of the belly"? Yet if, as the popular African saying goes, a goat eats where he is tethered, my food for thought—and my food!—was Luapula's fish. Patterns of wealth, patronage, and political power in Luapula revolved around the fishery; fish are to Luapula what cocoa is to parts of West Africa. The questions I had asked about rural elites in the abstract became grounded in the fishery. How had forms of ownership and control in the fishery been transformed during the colonial period? What cultural underpinnings helped to define and legitimize those who controlled access to the fishery? Had the insertion of the fishery into a colonial market economy in the hinterland of central Africa's Copperbelt transformed older and more established meanings and manifestations of wealth, community, and identity?

The fishery also rekindled an older interest that had been put on the back burner while I planned my doctoral research—environmental history, the changing relationships between people and natural resources. Before fish are hauled out of the river and lake, they have biological features not necessarily connected to human society. Why do some fish prosper in certain areas and not others? What are the feeding and breeding patterns of the fish? I would discover that such breeding and feeding habits held economic, social, and political implications. When economy and ecology were considered together, a more complete picture of historical change would emerge.

While I would have to search farther than the fish markets for answers, source material for a contested arena of activity crucial to both everyday welfare and extraordinary wealth was not difficult to come by. The collection of oral testimony and songs formed a central component of my research. Over a fifteen-month period, between June 1997 and July 1998, I interviewed more than one hundred individuals in Mweru-Luapula, Lusaka, and Lubumbashi. I followed up this research with interviews in Luapula in December 2000 and January 2001 and in June and July 2002. I had learned rudimentary Bemba at the Ilondola mission near Chinsali (Zambia); however, to minimize errors in translation most of the interviews conducted in Bemba were transcribed with the help of a research assistant into either English or French. Of equal importance to formal interviews was participant observation; eating fish, trying my hand at catching them, and casual conversations with fishers and traders.

There is a vast collection of written material generated over the last century by officials concerned with the fishery. I consulted the reports and correspondence of several colonial government departments at the National Archives in Lusaka, the Special Collections at the University of Zambia, the Public Record Office in London, and the Archives Africaines in Brussels. Postcolonial fisheries departments and aid agencies have continued to produce a number of reports not yet archived. I consulted such material at the headquarters of the Department of Fisheries in Chilanga and Nchelenge (Zambia), the *Service de l'environnement et conservation* in Lubumbashi and Kipushi (DRC), and at several local district offices in Zambia and DRC. While the archives covering Katanga in southern DRC were destroyed during the war of 1996–97, I was able to consult the University of Lubumbashi's student *mémoires,* many of which are based on local archival collections. At the Zambia National Broadcasting Corporation in Lusaka I made use of a wonderful collection of old Bemba songs, dating back to the 1950s. I taped the relevant songs, and with the help of a research assistant, transcribed and translated them. They provide a unique perspective on the everyday folklore of socioeconomic, cultural, and political change.

A variety of scholarly works guided this project from its inception. Mwelwa C. Musambachime's unpublished doctoral dissertation on the development and growth of the fishery in the colonial period provided a foundation for my research. Two anthropologists have published ethnographies based on their fieldwork in the area. Ian Cunnison's studies of kin, clan, and kingdom based on research conducted in the late 1940s informed my understanding of Luapula's corporate groups and provided a basis to measure change over the next fifty years. Based on fieldwork conducted in the 1970s, Karla Poewe has published several studies on women, religion, matrilineal relationships, and economic development; her work directed my attention to the gendered dimensions of commerce. With the exception of Cunnison's occasional forays, the precolonial history of Luapula and the Kingdom of Kazembe was relatively underdeveloped at the time of my research. However, even as I embarked on my study, Giacomo Macola was researching and writing *The Kingdom of Kazembe;* Macola's work and numerous discussions with him have corrected and guided my understanding of Luapula's precolonial history.

This book would never have taken its final form without the help of scholars based in the United States, South Africa, and Zambia. Robert Tignor and Emmanuel Kreike of Princeton University directed the early stages of conceptualization and writing. Their respective interests in the history of business and the environment are evident throughout this study. Jeff Guy, Keith Breckenridge, Cathy Burns, and Marijke du Toit helped me rework a clumsy doctoral dissertation into a far sleeker manuscript during a very productive year at the University of Natal in South Africa. History departments at the University of Zambia and the University of Lubumbashi offered opportunities to present my work and exchange ideas with faculty and students. At the University of Maryland, Paul Landau offered valuable commentary on finer details, and Leslie Rowland provided skilled editorial advice. Catherine Hays,

Julia Skory, and Jason Kneas helped to refine the maps, photos, and figures. Giacomo Macola, Mwelwa C. Musambachime, Jane Parpart, Bizeck J. Phiri, Debra Spitulnik, Walima Kalusa, and Robert Cancel inspired me with their own scholarship and offered advice, comments, and criticism. Jan Vansina's detailed reading of the manuscript alerted me to errors in fact and interpretation. Chapter 2 is based on an article, "Owners of the Land and Lunda Lords: Colonial Chiefs in the Borderlands of Northern Rhodesia and the Belgian Congo," published in the *International Journal of African Historical Studies* 34.2 (2001): 315–37. It appears in the book with the permission of the editor.

I have inflicted my ideas and, on occasion, the rough manuscript on friends and family. James Lee, Mike Goldblatt, Caryn Harris, my mother, Adele Gordon, and my father, Hiliard Gordon, have discussed half-baked ideas and read parts of the manuscript. My partner, Lesley Brown, displayed exceptional care, support, and sensitivity in her focused reading and advice. But special gratitude must go to the fishers, farmers, traders, friends, research assistants, and informants in the Luapula Valley. There are too many to name all of them. Mike Kolala, Bruce Mubita, André Kabaso, and Mary Benkali welcomed me into their homes and lives. Mwata Kazembe XVIII Munona Chinyanta and Mwata Kazembe XIX Mpemba Kanyembo facilitated the research. My friend and research assistant, Andrew Billing Chalawila, passed away before the completion of this book; he labored with patience, care, and friendship to educate a rather ignorant *umusungu*.

TRANSLATION AND ORTHOGRAPHY

Over the last two centuries, several related Bantu languages have been spoken in the Luapula Valley. Nowadays, the people of the Luapula Valley speak a distinctive dialect of Bemba (or Chibemba), one of Zambia's more important national languages; in the DRC, Bemba is combined with a Swahili dialect. These languages differ substantially from the older languages of the valley, which are now in the process of disappearing. These were also Bantu languages, which include what early observers termed "Chishila" (after the Shila—fishers—who lived in the valley) and the language of Kazembe's court, which many Luapulans now identify as "Lunda" even while it had only a distant relationship to Ruund. Where possible I have tried to remain faithful to the Luapula Valley's dialect and for clarification have included the vernacular in the notes. A glossary at the end of the book includes important vernacular terminology. When using Bemba nouns, the initial vowel is retained where appropriate, for example *abantu* not *bantu*, unless the noun is in its definite form, in which case the initial vowel is excluded. Most translations have been conducted with the help of first-language Bemba speakers familiar with the Luapula Valley's vernacular. The final translations are my own, as are any errors that may appear.

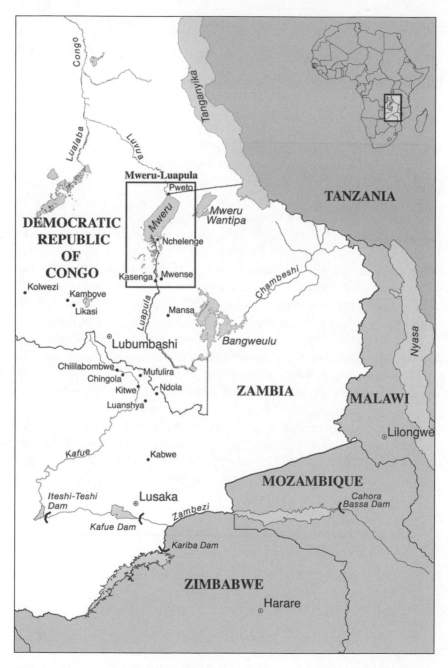

Map 1. Mweru-Luapula and the region.

NACHITUTI'S GIFT

Introduction

Tenure, Wealth, and Environment

Fishmongers, mostly women, lay bundles of fish bought or bartered from fishers early that morning on tables roughly hewn from sticks and planks. There is no ice to cool the fish; only a tablecloth of flies shields them from the tropical sun. Animated buyers haggle over prices with sellers who become more accommodating as the day wears on and the flesh of their fish begins to soften. Near the fresh fish stalls, rows of dried fish retailers sit patiently behind their neat piles of salted bream, smoked barbel, and sun-dried sardines. Buyers inspect the dried fish and ensure that there is adequate flesh and no maggots, sand, or other signs of bad processing. A few women and young men stroll through the market interested only in fish for the evening meal; but those who want to buy large quantities—usually of small dried fish that are well preserved and easy to carry back to the faraway urban centers—attract the attention of the marketers. These entrepreneurs gather up their piles of fish, stuff them into sacks, and load them on buses and trucks headed for the Copperbelt's towns, where the fish will adorn the urban market stalls. Customers will again pass by, carefully picking out the bundles of fish that attract their eye, and take them to their modest urban homes, where the fish will be cooked with care over charcoal braziers and made into enticing relish to accompany a plate of thick maize or cassava polenta.

This book details the history of an African fishery—its peoples, economy, and environment. It explores three interconnected themes germane to the continent and to the underdeveloped (or developing?) world: tenure, wealth, and environment. The first, tenure rights, is the most important and overarching theme: the book considers struggles to gain access to, control, and secure rent from resources that have ill-defined and contested rules of ownership. The theme of contested tenure rights is an unresolved arena of debate and policy formulation recognized by social scientists to be of key concern to the world's poorest peoples. The book points out that in Mweru-Luapula, resources were never "common property"; before colonialism, complex tenure systems linked to clan groups governed the use of lands, lakes, and lagoons. Precolonial tenure rights were undermined by colonial and postcolonial states that declared the fishery to be a form of common property governed by state-enforced regulations. Informally, however, new or changed corporate groups contested these regulations and enforced different forms of tenure. Rights in resources were always a matter of power, exerted and enforced through available cultural, social, political, and economic means.

The problem of tenure is linked to that of wealth. European measures of wealth have long been tied to rights in things or property. However, historians and anthropologists of Africa recognize that wealth is a subjective and social phenomenon that varies across societies and political economies. Many African societies, prior to colonization by European powers, relied on measures of wealth tied directly to social relationships rather than the accumulation of bullion, currency, rights in property, or "things" in general. With the onset of colonial capitalism, new forms of wealth and new opportunities to accumulate such wealth appeared. "How—exactly and in slow motion—have African and European changing systems of wealth acted, and continue to act, upon one another?" Jane Guyer has asked.[1] The Luapula Valley's lucrative fishing economy, conflicting tenure systems, and rich sets of social relationships embedded in its families, clans, and economic corporations provide an ideal opportunity to explore the intersection of these different forms of wealth and their transformation over the last century. No single form of wealth came to dictate patterns of economic activity in the Luapula Valley, as the linear trajectories of development theory predict. Fishers and traders continued to invest in social relationships alongside their engagement with a regional market economy; clans and corporations valued both people and things. Indeed, since tenure relations were always contested, people continued to choose investments in direct social relationships rather than abstract property. The accumulation of these varied forms of wealth would have implications for states and organs of civil society, the structure and shape of corporate groups, and more generally the workings of capitalism.

A third theme, or underlying assumption, of the book is that tenure, wealth, and political economy in rural Africa, as in the rest of the world, cannot be divorced from environmental context. Africa's biological diversity has provided the backdrop for a number of environmental studies that seldom view humans as participating members of their natural environments, with the exception of several works in the growing subfield of African environmental history.[2] Economic and agrarian studies, on the other hand, often ignore or downplay environmental context. While scholars have recognized the need for connections across disciplinary boundaries, the lack of integration of economic and ecological studies has led to an incomplete appreciation of how environmental contexts structure human economies.[3] This book demonstrates that different tenure rules applied to different environmental systems found in a single fishery. For example, the tenure rules of lagoon areas where a number of fish spawned were far more precisely defined than those of the open lake.

The book is divided into two parts, each with three chapters. Part 1 focuses on tenure and economy in the change from precolonial polities to colonial states. The first chapter describes how forms of corporate organization defined ownership and control over both fishery and farmlands in the precolonial era. Such relationships were represented and legitimized by stories like that of Nachituti's gift of the land and lakes to the eastern Lunda paramount, Mwata Kazembe, who conquered much of the lower Luapula Valley in the eighteenth century but recognized autochthonous "owners" of the land. The second and third chapters turn to the nature and consequences of colonialism. They examine the rising importance of colonial chiefs drawn from the Kazembe Kingdom as resource managers and the spread of new meanings of wealth and networks of economic power through exchanges of labor and produce with the nascent mining economies. Part 2 of the book explores the fishery in the late colonial and postcolonial period by devoting a chapter to the political economy and distinctive tenure relationships that emerged around the exploitation of each of the three most important species of commercial fish—mpumbu, pale, and chisense. The book illustrates how particular industries based on natural commodities with distinct biological qualities affected patterns of ownership and wealth and held wide-ranging political and social implications.

The Problem of Common Resources

The economic problem and environmental threat of a fishery—what economists term the "fisherman's problem"—stems from the lack of incentive to limit exploitation of common property resources. Since a fishery cannot easily be transformed into exclusive property, there is little incentive to limit exploitation—any one fisher cannot rely on others to do the same or be sure that more fishers will not arrive. An increasing number of fishers or an increasing effort by existing fishers will lead to economically and biologically unsustainable fishing. As the total catch rises beyond the point at which fish can reproduce at the level required to sustain their maximum yield, marginal returns from the fishery become negative; increasing fishing effort beyond the maximum sustainable yield will actually decrease the total catch. However, if entry is unlimited, the arrival of still additional fishers will occur until total costs equal total yields, well beyond the maximum sustainable yield—an outcome that is both unprofitable and environmentally deleterious. H. Scott Gordon first identified this problem in his seminal article on the economics of a fishery.[4] Garrett Hardin, who was more concerned with the environmental fate of the commons in general, used the principles of Gordon's model to describe natural resource collapse caused by the combined forces of increased population and opportunistic economic agents in pursuit of individual gain; he called it "the tragedy of the commons."[5]

Followers of so-called common property theory, which developed from the insights of Gordon and Hardin, have promoted forms of private property to ensure that people have an interest in the preservation, sustainability, and profitability of their resource base; they view the privatization of a resource as essential to its survival. Unless the value of a resource can be determined and made to mean something for those who exploit it, the inexorable logic of the "tragedy of the commons" will kick in. In the case of a fishery, they argue, fishing effort can be limited to economically and environmentally optimum levels by establishing legal "stakeholders." Moreover, the degree of stability that such a system of fishing rights brings would allow fishers to borrow against future catches, invest in labor-saving technology, and even embark on the road to capitalist development.[6]

Anthropologists, who tend to focus on more informal types of ownership and property relationships than resource economists, often offer a different perspective. They defend the commons from a welfare perspective, since livelihoods of poor indigenous communities rest on continued access to natural resources that are not declared private property, and they further argue that any "commons" has a regulatory apparatus or at least sets of values that ensure communities do not overexploit their resource. Since most commons are not "open access," they are not subject to endless increases in exploitation by resource users and newcomers.

Moreover, they question the essentialist assumptions of economically utilitarian human behavior and Malthusian crises that informed Hardin's "tragedy of the commons" model.[7] Scholars of Africa's rangelands, for example, argue that communal resources were for the most part successfully managed and only became prone to forms of environmental "degradation" with conquest and authoritarian colonial measures.[8] Lucrative fisheries in Africa and elsewhere were rarely open-access common property. Some such "anti-tragedy" arguments follow up with the contention that privatizing nature exposes it to forces of production and exploitation that result in degradation.[9] Communal property, according to such arguments, should be defended against capitalism (or private property) for the welfare of poor communities and for environmental preservation. While correcting certain presuppositions made by Gordon and Hardin, these arguments also introduce essentialist and ahistorical notions of their own. Not all indigenous communities have rules that strictly regulate access, and even if they had in the past, many of these rules changed or were eroded or ignored as trade connected previously remote areas, enforcement mechanisms were undermined, and new migrants arrived to exploit increasingly scarce resources.

Resource economists have made some concessions to these critiques; in particular, few resources are still described as open access, and formal rights to resources are recognized to be only one of a collection of mechanisms that define ownership. Randy Simmons and Peregrine Schwartz-Shea, for example, find that endogenous collective institutions often linked to group identities have evolved to shape rights in common resources.[10] Economic associations, from clans to corporations, played a significant role in defining tenure rights in such "common" resources. Scholars now agree that ownership rights are embedded in social institutions rather than legalistic contractual relationships (even while policy prescriptions are still often based on this rather naïve view). An illustration of this growing consensus in an African setting is Sara Berry's argument for "property as social process." Berry argues that forms of ownership and the enforcement of rights in property are always embedded in social relationships. Hence, the dichotomy between public and private ownership is false. Property is about power; rights in property, whether public or private, have to be enforced, and the agencies of enforcement are always located in social contexts. Individuals who claim ownership of resources cannot act autonomously; their claims rely on social networks that act to support resource rights. Thus property is a "social process, in which negotiations over ownership and use of resources inform and are influenced by relations of authority and obligation."[11]

This book develops these insights by considering the changing conceptualization and institutionalization of rights in Mweru-Luapula's fishing resources over the last 150 years. It explores how societal groups like patronage networks, clans, families, religious congregations, and ethnic and national communities mobilized to challenge or to secure and strengthen resource claims. The argument begins by emphasizing that the precolonial fishery cannot be described as an open-access commons; not only were there restrictions on access, but there were oral traditions that delineated forms of ownership, or at least certain rights in resources. Colonial states did not recognize these forms of tenure and declared resources like the fishery to be public property controlled by colonial chiefs—in other words, they created a legal "commons." Instead of incorporating established forms of tenure into a legal realm, colonial regimes attempted to impose an array of regulatory measures on newly created common resources. In the postcolonial period, legal formulations were inherited from the colonial period, but state capacity was eroded and an emergent civil society began to reformulate its own regulations and tenure arrangements.

Tenure in Precolonial Africa

The opposition between "traditional" commons and "modern" private property offered by versions of common property theory is a way of clarifying our present-day relationships to resources rather than an accurate portrayal of the past. According to this rather simplified opposition, the open-access commons is typical of those societies not yet "dynamised" by capitalist relations of production in contrast to societies subjected to the commodity fetish of capitalism, most developed in the United States, where in the words of one historian of U.S. environmental law, "the natural world has been everywhere, relentlessly, transformed into property."[12] In fact, the complex system of ownership and control of water and land resources in precolonial Africa (and much of precapitalist Europe) cannot be described adequately by opposed notions of "commons" and "private property."

A "commons" implies that certain people in a community have *rights* to resources as defined by accepted but often unwritten rules. Daniel Bromley and Michael Cernea acknowledge as much when they argue that property of any form should not be viewed as an object but as "a right to a benefit stream."[13] Rights to benefits from resources can, of course, be much weaker in certain societies than private property rights are in a capitalist and legalistic society. Nevertheless, communal rights do imply the inclusion of some and exclusion of others from limited resources, even if such rights are not as fully fledged or "complete" as private property rights. Such broad theoretical reflections are confirmed by close historical examination. Access to the English "commons," such as woodlands and pastures, rested on social responsibilities, restraints, and obligations that constituted a system of rights to limited resources, often supervised or enforced by seignorial officers.[14] In the case of medieval Europe's inland fisheries, certain tenure rights had been defined by the thirteenth century: "Private control over access to fisheries . . . became a twig in the bundle of remunerative rights being assembled into lordship over land and men."[15] In his study of customary rights in early modern England, E. P. Thompson emphasizes that "[c]ommon right is a subtle and sometimes complex vocabulary of usages, of claims to property, of hierarchy and of preferential access to resources, of the adjustment of needs, which, being *lex loci*, must be pursued in each locality and can never be taken as 'typical.'"[16] The "commons" took on a more vague and general meaning only with the rise of legalistic states and capitalism; property was enclosed and inscribed in law and rules of exchange, thereby developing what we recognize to be private ownership and freehold tenure in opposition to rather romanticized views of the open-access "commons."

As E. P. Thompson has noticed, it is problematic to "explain the commons in capitalist categories."[17] The task is even more difficult for those societies that have left few written records. What, then, were the forms of communal tenure and resource ownership in noncapitalist and oral societies? A romantic tradition in Western thought associates non-Western and noncapitalist tenure arrangements with the core idea of the allegedly fabricated speech of Chief Seattle in which he compared a market in land to buying and selling the sky: "The idea is strange to us. The earth does not belong to man. Man belongs to the earth."[18] Scholars of Africa have also indulged in this line of thought. Anthropologists have argued that in precolonial Africa, with its plentiful land and limited technology, control over people, or rights-in-persons, were more important than ownership of land and other productive resources.[19] With the exception of a few parts of Africa, anthropologist Elizabeth Colson has argued, "Africans were concerned to use the land, not to hold it. They saw themselves as dealing with the earth as a sacred entity which existed independently of men. A claim to control the earth might very well amount to sacrilege."[20] For historian John Thornton, the importance of rights-in-persons resulted less from limited technology and low population density than from "African law," which did not recognize the "fiction of landownership."[21]

Anthropologists have, however, also realized that simple models of "communal" tenure do little justice to the interlocking networks of economic obligation that define access to productive property in a variety of noncapitalist and non-Western societies. In his classic studies, Bronislaw Malinowski explicitly pointed out that among Melanasian fishing communities, "There is a strict distinction and definition in the rights of every one and this makes ownership anything but communistic."[22] Indeed, even African lineage societies, which invested in social relationships and had complex transactions dealing with rights-in-people, negotiated rights to the land and other resources through earth priests, often the heads of clans, who were actually known as "guardians" or "owners of the land" (in Bemba, *umwine wa mpanga*).

I have spent some time considering what the title "owner of the land" means in the African context. It is a term familiar to many sub-Saharan African societies, and yet, clearly, "ownership" did not imply a fully fledged system of private property and freehold tenure. The title "owner" as employed in Mweru-Luapula will be further explored in the next section of this introduction and in chapter 1; here, a few general observations are in order to clarify the nature of ownership and the role of these precolonial owners of the land. First, the "title-deeds," or charters of ownership, were not conveyed in written documents but in narrative. Oral charters supported fluid types of wealth and ownership; encoded laws, by contrast, could support far stronger forms of ownership and ultimately, if the resource allowed and enforcement agencies were strong enough, types of private property. Nevertheless, the importance of such narrative charters, referred to by Jane Guyer and Samuel Eno Belinga as "wealth-in-knowledge," in defining access to resource rent has often been underestimated.[23] Second, this ownership was often legitimized by a relationship between the owner and ancestral or nature spirits, which in turn expressed their pleasure or displeasure through their control over nature. Third, these owners were often subordinated to rulers who at some point had conquered the land but still recognized autochthonous rulers as owners who could control or at least mediate with the spirits that controlled nature. Conquerors were thought of as owners of the people, while the conquered became owners of the land.

Even taking into account the characteristics of such forms of ownership, certain resource owners mediated rights to resources. Underlying these property rights were not only the material structures of land and technology but also the cultural agency of oral tradition. Property rights were inscribed in stories; the more contested the resources, such as those of Mweru-Luapula's fishery, the more important and contested the stories. Oral traditions were charters to the control of natural resources like the land, lakes, and rivers. And those who claimed rights over them did so through the retention and retelling of these narratives. Since oral traditions are an aspect of collective memories and collective memories assume identities, memory and identity being closely entwined, we arrive at one of the central challenges that our study poses for resource economics: the way in which corporate identities inform ownership of and control over resources.[24] To further explore how forms of social memory and identity informed ownership and resource rights, we need to focus our attention on the land, lakes, and peoples of Mweru-Luapula.

Land, Lakes, and People

Mweru-Luapula is part of the vast Congo River drainage basin. The Luapula River begins in the shallow Lake Bangweulu, which is fed by the Chambeshi River with its source on the Muchinga Plateau, home to the Bemba peoples. After leaving Lake Bangweulu, the wide swamplike Luapula flows south. Then as it hits the curving plateau, it turns around, flowing north and forming a river a few hundred feet wide. As it meanders north, it becomes narrower and faster flowing, and after a hundred miles, the Luapula descends in a series of rapids called Mambilima Falls. Here the Luapula Valley begins. From Mambilima, the Luapula River continues northward for about one hundred miles, rushing through the valley, until it widens out into a series of lagoons and marshes, eventually forming Lake Mweru. The lake itself is some eighty miles long and twenty-five to thirty miles wide. It reaches a maximum depth of about fifty feet near its rocky northern edges and is far shallower in the south, where sandy beaches are found along its shoreline. Near the entrance of the Luapula River, there are several small islands, including Chisenga, Isokwe, and Nkole, and farther out into the lake a large settled island called Kilwa. To the east of the Luapula's entrance, another major river, the Kalungwishi, also feeds the lake. At its northern tip, the lake is drained by the Luvua River (locally known as the Lualaba), which continues until it reaches the Lualaba and eventually the Congo River.

The Muchinga Plateau to the east and the Kundelungu Mountains to the west, both highlands of mixed savannah woodlands known in Bemba as Miombo (trees of mostly the *Brachystegia* genus), surround the Luapula Valley. Although the highland soils are generally low in nutrients, when combined with fertilizer, usually supplied by burning branches cut from trees (a well-known system of agriculture found across the central African highlands; in Bemba, *chitemene*), the land provides opportunity for prosperous farms of staple crops like millet, sorghum, maize, and to a lesser extent, cassava, as well as vegetable gardens consisting of groundnuts, pumpkins, cabbage, and a variety of squashes and spinaches. The lower reaches of the Luapula Valley, which the colonial geographer C. G. Trapnell called the Luapula Lake Basin System (in Bemba, Chipya), is characterized by high grass, shrubs, and few *Brachystegia* trees. Here, the cultivation of cassava mixed with groundnuts is preferred.[25] Cassava can be grown in soils with varying levels of nutrients, and its adaptability explains its spread across much of central Africa. However, in the fertile Chipya and floodplains of the Luapula Valley, where maize and millet can be grown without much fertilizer, there is no straightforward environmental reason for cassava's cultivation. Luapulans link their preference for cassava to culture and history; they are proud cultivators and consumers of cassava, which they claim to have farmed at least since the arrival of the eastern Lunda some two hundred years ago.

Oral traditions tell of four groups of settlers and conquerors that converged on the resource-rich valley before the onset of colonialism. While apparently providing the Luapula Valley with a chronological history, such oral traditions rely on narrative compression and should be treated as palimpsests of social memories that describe the rights of conquerors and autochthones rather than a factual account of waves of settlement. According to these traditions, the first settlers were the Abatwa. Then Kaponto's people arrived and killed the Abatwa by burning the land. In the wake of a vast fire, a long period of rain and flooding led to the formation of *Mwelu mukata mukandanshe*—the great expanse of water that even the locusts cannot cross. The third significant group is said to have migrated via the Bemba Plateau (Lubemba) and achieved a level of centralization previously unknown in the Valley. They were led by Nkuba and called Shila, meaning fishers, but perhaps also referring to rituals and taboos relating to fishing and hunting *(imishila*, sing. *umushila)*. They named the previous inhabitants of Luapula "Bwilile," those who eat their own, because they paid no tribute and had no chiefs.[26] A ruler who had the title of "Mwata Kazembe" led the last conquerors, thought by historians to have arrived by the mid-eighteenth century. The conquerors called themselves "Lunda" (referred to by historians as eastern Lunda), and adopted certain Lunda oral traditions, insignia, and political institutions. They occasionally sent tribute and emissaries to the central Lunda court of Mwaant Yaav. "Lundahood," however, remained a political office rather than an ethnic identity.[27] Although such oral traditions should be treated with circumspection, they do attest to a long history of encounters between old settlers and new migrants and demonstrate one of the central narrative clichés of Luapulan historical narratives.

In addition to its history of migrants and settlers, the Luapula Valley has been a center for regional and even global commerce at least since the eighteenth century. The oral tradition of the eastern Lunda refers to the trade and production of high-quality salt in the valley—perhaps valued for trade or for its use as a preservative. Our first eyewitness records of the eastern Lunda date back to Portuguese traders who sought to purchase ivory and slaves from the Kazembes. In 1798, the governor of Sena Rivers Province of Mozambique, José Maria de Lacerda e Almeida, visited the Kazembe Kingdom and reported that Mwata Kazembe had forged trade contacts with the Portuguese on both the East and West African coasts. Although many more trading expeditions might have occurred, we have records of only two more encounters between Portuguese traders and Kazembe's court. In 1806–10, the so-called Angolan *pombeiros* (traveling merchants) P. Baptista and Anastacia José described how Kazembe insisted that subordinate chiefs keep trade routes open with the coast. And in 1831–32, José Monteiro and Antonio Gamitto's expedition spent a frustrating few months at Kazembe's court, where they attempted to forge a trading alliance with him. By then it seems likely that Kazembe had a number of other trading partners, especially Swahili merchants who provided him with cloth and guns in exchange for ivory and slaves.[28] Trade with the Indian Ocean increased through the nineteenth century when the Nyamwezi trader Msiri married into Luba royalty and established his capital Bunkeya to the west of the Luapula Valley. Msiri was renowned for trade in ivory and slaves with Swahili traders from the East African coast.[29] Long before the rise of a lucrative fish trade during the early colonial period, the peoples of the Luapula Valley had exchanged a variety of commodities in diverse trading networks.

Multiple encounters with the outside world led the peoples of the valley to distinguish between autochthones and conquerors, those who "owned" the land and lakes and those who came as conquerors and traders. Stories, associations, and shrines marked the physical landscape with a symbolism understood only by those elders who "belonged" to the land and thereby "owned" it.[30] This local shrine system was a type of environmental management that stretched from the Luba confederation on the upper Congo River, across the Zambezi watershed, southward to the rain shrines of the Shona ancestral traditions on the dry Zimbabwean plateau, east to the Mbona cult of the Shire Valley, and west to the flood traditions of the Lozi.[31] Thomas Reefe describes these "owners" as earth priests who "propitiated the founding ancestral spirits to ensure the fertility of the land and the bounty of the hunt. . . . [T]hey fulfilled well-defined regulatory roles where there was competition for specific territory and limited resources. . . . [T]hey supervised the hereditary rights of lineage heads to regulate access to hunting land, to fishing streams and to wild fruit trees."[32] While these networks of earth priests resembled forms of environmental management in East Africa, best described by Steven Feierman's work on the Shambaa Kingdom, where local rulers had the ability to "heal" or "harm" the land, the system south of the equatorial rain forest had certain distinctive cultural and linguistic features—in particular a conceptual separation between the "original" owners of the land and the rulers of the people.[33] This separation of owners from rulers, when in fact they were often joined together in alliance, bears remarkable resemblance to networks of ownership and control over people and lands found in West African conquest states, where as Jean-Loup Amselle observes, a "category of first settlers is an intellectually convenient fiction that allows one to formulate the theme of alliance between the landowners and the possessors of spiritual power on the one hand and the possessors of physical power on the other."[34]

The character of rulership and ownership depended largely on the history of the encounters between conquerors and autochthones and on the resources available. By adopting indigenous ancestral religions and shrine systems, the conquerors, generally affiliated to the Lunda or Luba polities, came to rule the people while recognizing that the autochthones owned the land or were at least custodians of it. For example, in Zimbabwe, the conquering Ndebele adopted the ancient Mwali cult's shrines and guardians, with their rainmaking functions, which helped to legitimize their rule;[35] in western Zambia (Lozi) the Kololo ruler adopted the indigenous Nyambe shrine responsible for the flooding and hence fertility of agricultural fields;[36] in Malawi, the Maravi adopted and adapted the Banda/Chipeta earth cults;[37] and closer to the

Luapula Valley, the royal Crocodile Clan fused with the older rites of nature to define Bemba culture.[38] The conquered owners were organized in what anthropologist J. M. Schoffeleers refers to as ecological cults "concerned with man's role as a transformer and recipient from his natural environment."[39] Owners were often associated with animals, particularly snakes or crocodiles, indicated either through clan names or the frequent physical manifestations of the animal.[40] Such ecological cults contained the lore and the laws of the land; they were the way conquerors and conquered defined rights to the land, just as the peoples of Eurasia inscribed such tenure agreements on tablets and parchments. In Mweru-Luapula, where water and fish needed management, the most important cults, rituals, and shrines revolved around the river and lakes.

The first conquerors of the Luapula Valley to encounter local shrines and ecological cults were the followers of Nkuba around the late seventeenth century, although the stories of conquest and the mechanisms of incorporation seem beyond recovery.[41] More recent and comparatively clear was the rise of territorial ecological cults linked to conquest by the eastern Lunda under Mwata Kazembe. The conquest of the autochthones by Mwata Kazembe is told in the story of Nachituti's gift, a narrative that defines the reciprocal relationships between rulers of the people and owners of the land. Nachituti gave the land and lakes to the eastern Lunda; but while the gift allowed the Lunda to rule the people, Lunda reciprocation meant that Nachituti's people, autochthonous clans that took on the generic "Shila" ethnic label, would be recognized as owners of the land and lagoons. The oral tradition of Nachituti's gift defined and legitimized relationships between political rulers, resource managers, and the land, river, and lakes.

Nachituti's story begins with a cruel deed committed by her brother, Nkuba, who killed Nachituti's son, whom he accused of committing adultery with his favorite wife. Nkuba placed the skin of his dead nephew under the royal throne to ensure his eternal submission. But when Nachituti found her son's skin after a drunken party in the royal enclave, she fled to Mwata Kazembe, king of the eastern Lunda, and pleaded for him to avenge her son's murder. Kazembe sent his most trusted generals to capture Nkuba. After a protracted expedition, the Lunda generals conquered and subjugated the Shila and Bwilile, found Nkuba, and executed him. When the generals returned with Nkuba's head, Nachituti gave Mwata Kazembe a basket of earth representing the land and a pot of water representing the lake and rivers. Since her brother was dead, she agreed to marry Mwata Kazembe.

Nachituti's gift of the lands and rivers became the charter of Lunda rule over some of the most prosperous parts of the Luapula Valley. In return, the Lunda recognized the Shila ruler, Nkuba, as owner of the land and lagoons around Chisenga Island. The story of Nachituti's gift divided authority over the fishery into a realm of control over people on the one hand and ownership of the land and lakes on the other. It offered a foundational myth that described the basis of economic and political life prior to colonialism—the networks of dependence between rulers and producers, kings and clans. The story of Nachituti's gift ensured that conquerors remained indebted to the conquered.

Tenure and Colonialism

At the end of the nineteenth century, another wave of conquerors descended upon the Luapula Valley. They proved to be a decisive force in Luapula's history, reconceptualizing the river and lake as an international border, inscribing resources in written laws, and promoting certain precolonial rulers above others. The onset of Belgian and British colonialism and the arrival of colonial capitalism redefined the way resources and people were perceived and ruled. Colonial officials, as Elizabeth Colson argues, brought to Africa "European concepts of legal tenure which they were prone to interpret as universal legal principles applicable everywhere; these became basic to the land law of each territory."[42] The most influential and transformative colonial idea was that resources—from the land to the lakes—were communal property. Africans did not have strict forms of tenure and title; oral traditions were not a basis for modern property rights. Instead, resources were defined as a form of "common property," mostly administered by colonial chiefs on behalf of their "tribal" subjects. In general, the owners of the land and lagoons were sidelined and their charters of ownership ignored; control over resources instead fell to the new "traditional" rulers, colonial chiefs. The newly developed system of "tribal" tenure in turn inhibited the development of individual rights in land.[43]

During the 1890s, two colonial powers occupied the Luapula Valley. To the west it became part of King Leopold's Congo Free State, taken over by Belgium in 1908; to the east, the colonial entrepreneur Cecil John Rhodes's British South Africa Company (BSAC) was granted concession over the colonial territory named North-Eastern Rhodesia (it became part of Northern Rhodesia in 1911). The British Colonial Office took control of the territory from the BSAC in 1924. The Belgian colonial state felt it could not rely on African fishers and traders to supply the copper mines with fish rations; they therefore invited Europeans, mostly Greeks from Rhodes Island, to exploit the waters of Mweru-Luapula. Luapula's fishery was more marginal to the food supply of Northern Rhodesia's mines, and British colonial officials allowed African control under the direction of colonial chiefs. Both colonial administrations subordinated precolonial systems of ownership to colonial visions of a common resource administered by a combination of district officers and colonial chiefs.

Such "common resources" were to become entangled in an array of colonial regulations that designated environmentally and economically correct ways to exploit them. Colonial chiefs were charged with the implementation and enforcement of new laws and regulations. Colonial commercial ventures provided opportunities for Mweru-Luapula's chiefs to intervene in the allocation of resource rights and benefit from them, much as they had for the Asante chiefs discussed by Sara Berry.[44] In colonial Zambia, chiefs had control over local courts, tax collection, and the allocation of licenses and permits, leading to what Samuel Chipungu termed a *boma* class.[45] In Mweru-Luapula's fishery, chiefs had exceptional opportunities to secure resource rent since they collected funds from fishing permits and net licenses and were responsible for the enforcement of fishing regulations. However, chiefs often suffered from a lack of local legitimacy; while they had self-proclaimed "traditional" sanction, there were few historical precedents for enforcing regulations. Because the colonial and postcolonial states, the self-proclaimed modernizing forces, rested on these "traditional" rulers (whose authority in turn rested on, or was challenged by, diverse social networks), a confusing array of formal and informal mechanisms, which were enmeshed in both modern and traditional rationales, arose to define, legitimize, and enforce access to resources.

Rights in resources can only be as strong as the agencies that enforce them. And colonial states, despite their ambitious plans, did not establish autonomous agencies of enforcement. Colonialism in Africa was, for the most part, conducted on the cheap, with colonial administrations struggling to balance their budgets. Sara Berry describes the precarious nature of colonial authority in the countryside as "hegemony on a shoe string";[46] colonial states had to rely on a system of "decentralized despotism" based on collaborating chiefs.[47] And these decentralized chiefs were often unreliable in the enforcement of regulations that came to govern newly declared common property.[48] For this reason, informal mechanisms like group identities and a variety of associations became more important enforcers and protectors of rights than formal regulations. The lack of autonomous enforcement agencies contributed to continued investment in social networks as opposed to abstract property. These general features of tenure were given precise form by the particular environmental characteristics of the resource. In the case of the mpumbu fishery, where fish were mostly caught for a few weeks in the upper reaches of the Luapula River after an arduous spawning event, forms of clan-based tenure were most developed; they were undermined in the colonial period when expatriate fishers used new fishing technologies to catch mpumbu before they spawned. For the pale fishery, the lagoons where spawning occurred provided the best fishing grounds; access to the lagoons had been under the control of clans and would be the subject of many struggles in the colonial and postcolonial periods. Pelagic fisheries such as the sardine-like chisense, by contrast, were relatively open access and provided opportunities for migrant entrepreneurs and others without established resource rights.

Claims to resources in Mweru-Luapula and indeed in much of postcolonial Africa take on multiple forms. For no matter what the rulings of the state—whether land and resources are declared "Native Trust," nationalized as the property of the state, or proclaimed to be under a system of private property and freehold tenure—official legal realms tend to legitimize themselves (or not) through "traditional" authorities and other social networks. In Mweru-Luapula, rules of ownership and property rights were only as strong as the agencies that enforced them; and these agencies in turn depended on sets of social relationships. Rights to resources came to rest on multiple and diffuse sets of mobilizations that involved clans, chiefs, states, and commercial corporations.

The Meanings of Wealth

A second claim made by resource economists is that only through mechanisms that limit ownership can individuals or corporations manage to collect rent from resources, invest it, and in turn contribute to a growth in wealth. As has been pointed out, this model rests on a narrow definition of wealth, whereas wealth is a subjective phenomenon that rests, like property, on social relationships (even if this is rarely acknowledged in the obfuscations of exchange-based political economies). So what needs to be explored is how rights in resources were converted into appropriate forms of wealth. Only then can we understand the dynamic social processes and associations that ensured wealth was continually being made.

In his study of west central Africa during the Atlantic slave trade, Joseph Miller considered how the political economy of use values engaged with an Atlantic exchange economy. According to Miller, the value of a good in west central Africa was measured in terms of its productive potential, that is, in terms of the potential labor—the dependents—that such goods were able to mobilize. The commodity boom in nineteenth-century west central Africa, according to Miller, was a result of the desperate need for more goods to create and sustain dependencies that had been undermined by the greater availability of goods and their corresponding devaluation.[49]

Miller's dynamic model is a good way to begin to understand the changing meanings and manifestations of wealth in the Luapula Valley. In the precolonial period, the Kazembe Kingdom also relied on the distribution of goods, mostly cloth acquired through the trade in ivory and slaves, to ensure dependents. These dependents, of which the owners of the land and lagoons were one group, were valuable in terms of their potential labor, which was actualized when their followings supplied the Kazembe Kingdom with produce like millet, cassava, and fish. Through the late nineteenth century, in a fashion similar to a slightly earlier period in west central Africa, the increase in the number of traders and an increase in the available goods led to a decline in the Kazembe Kingdom's monopoly over trade goods, contributing to the centrifugal forces that led to the partial disintegration of the kingdom.

The rise of the colonial economies further disrupted a political economy that had rested on monopoly control over the trade in ivory and slaves. From the 1910s and increasingly through the 1920s, the rise of the copper mining towns led to demand for workers and for produce to feed the workers. Where the previous political economy had revolved around cloth, protection, and other services and rare goods provided by the Kazembe Kingdom, money now lubricated the circuits of exchange. Money as medium of exchange and a measure of wealth differed in at least one significant way: it was far more fungible. The Kazembe Kingdom could not control the spread of money through the valley, which occurred primarily through remittances of urban wages and the sale of fish to European traders or directly to urban areas. The accumulation of money would result in the emergence of new fishing entrepreneurs, who engaged with both the colonial economy and with Luapula's local political economy, which still placed a premium on investment in human relationships. Established patterns of credit and interdependency engaged with these new instruments of credit; clan and corporation were sometimes reconciled, while at other times business associations created very different networks of dependents.

New strategies to accumulate wealth spread across the valley along with the new political economy. Money itself was an instrument of credit, exchange, and investment, *par excellence*. It could secure dependents, but it could also become capital and be invested in other goods or in technology such as improved nets, boats, or motor vehicles, all of which held the potential to secure increased returns from the fishery. The emergence of commodity exchange at first relied on Congolese francs, since the closest urban area was the copper-mining center of Elisabethville (present-day Lubumbashi). By the 1910s, African traders had begun to sell fish to the burgeoning working class in Elisabethville; however, a more powerful class of expatriate, predominantly Greek, traders based in the Belgian Congo emerged. They traveled on motorized boats to remote fishing villages where they purchased fish and helped to build patronage networks based on credit for urban goods and fishing gear. After the colonial period, Africans replaced the expatriates but kept the same system of business organization. Some Luapulans who began as small-scale fishers and traders became "big men," *abakankâla* merchants, with their own motorized boats, vehicles, and access to currencies and goods that could act as instruments of credit.

In the precolonial period, patronage networks had extended outward from the Kazembe Kingdom, through the owners of the land and lagoons, to the fishers and farmers of Luapula. The monopoly that a few traders or trading lords had over imports from the Indian Ocean helped to sustain their privileged positions. Patronage networks that rested on the distribution of goods in exchange for the promise of future labor remained a feature of the colonial and postcolonial economy through a new class of fish traders. In the pale fishery, which relied on the export of fresh fish to the urban areas, patronage extended from wealthy traders who had negotiated lucrative contracts with mining corporations for the supply of fish. They supplied fishers with nets and other goods and thereby created indebted dependents, who promised them their catch. Copper replaced ivory and slaves as southern central Africa's most important international export, and those traders with connections to the copper mines replaced the agents of the Kazembe Kingdom as patrons with indebted networks of fishers. Some traders, like the Congolese businessman Katebe Katoto, would use their fishing businesses as a base from which to expand their ventures and become heads of the most powerful political and economic networks in the subregion.

So while the colonial and postcolonial periods brought radically new forms of wealth and opportunities for securing economic power, the spread of dependencies remained an important aspect of social relationships. Large-scale and extensive patronage networks surrounded the wealthiest of entrepreneurs, who mediated access to the mining economies and held enough capital to invest in the means to transport fish to the urban areas. Yet from the 1970s entrepreneurs on a smaller scale, often women who specialized in the exploitation and trade of the small chisense fish, also invested in social relationships, in particular in their own families *(ulupwa)*. Women who managed to secure economic autonomy from husbands and boyfriends through the chisense fishery invested in their own children: they consolidated control over their households and kin networks. These small-scale enterprises sustained social relationships, defying the expectations of some development theorists, who tend to ignore the ongoing importance of social networks and family relationships in market economies.[50] The chisense fishery, an underappreciated industry ignored or derided by states and many aid organizations, became a source of livelihood to several thousand people and ensured that social relationships remained a sought-after form of wealth.

Conflicts brought about through economic change and rising levels of inequality were expressed in familiar cultural idioms, often presented as "traditional"; through their articulation, we are able to trace the contours of struggles surrounding economic change. Cultural narratives proliferated with economic and environmental change in a fashion similar to the moral economies of Meru and Arusha mountain farmers, where, as Thomas Spear puts it, "concepts of moral community revolved around ideals of economic justice and social responsibility, in which purposeful moral actions linked social behavior and natural phenomena."[51] For example, the most lucrative of Mweru-Luapula's fisheries had been the mpumbu, which gathered in massive spawning events after the first floods of the rainy season. When European fishers monopolized and overexploited the mpumbu fishery, African fishers drew on discourses of witchcraft and tradition to implicate Europeans, their patrons in the colonial states, and unfair and useless conservation regulations for the end of the mpumbu's spawning events and their eventual disappearance from the waters of Mweru-Luapula. Changes in wealth and its distribution would continue to be explained through invented tradition, witchcraft, and evangelical Christian churches. Such cultural realms linked the way people perceived the world to the way they acted in it; they constituted and protected a sense of moral community that was the bedrock of economic association.

Conclusions

This historical study confirms sociologist Jean Philippe Platteau's argument that fisheries in the Third World do not follow a pattern of institutional evolution from small-scale subsistence operations to large-scale capitalist businesses.[52] The lack of institutional evolution toward economies of scale found in such fisheries is in marked contrast to the combined emergence of economic scale and legalistic framework in some large-scale fisheries, for example in California, Japan, or the North Atlantic, where fishing industries provided a basis for capitalist forms of business (even taking into account their deleterious long-term environmental consequences).[53] On the other hand, there are examples of fisheries in the developed world's economic hinterlands, like the lobster gangs of Maine, where small-scale informal rights continue to proliferate.[54]

The economic structure of Third World fisheries (and their economies in general) was an outcome of their particular histories, especially the colonial impact and the nature of colonial capitalism. Despite the increasing value of fish and their progressive commoditization, ownership and fishing rights did not develop in Mweru-Luapula because of the legal regime imposed by colonialism. Precolonial rights in resources held by owners of the land and owners of the lagoons were not formalized; instead they were abolished in favor of a form of regulated public property. This led to a bifurcation in tenure rights between formal and informal realms, with investments in social relationships remaining crucial to securing informal access to the fishery.

The nature of economic association depended on both the local fishing economy and ties to the regional mining economy. In the pale fishery, traders provided credit in the form of goods and fishing gear in exchange for future catches. Indebted fishers surrounded these trading patrons, who could acquire credit and capital through states or mining companies. In the chisense fishery, where it was more difficult to monopolize rural-urban trade, small-scale operations based on family ties persisted and proliferated. Smaller-scale fishers and traders, who lacked both capital and instruments of credit, relied on the labor that their families, especially their children, provided. Patronage networks, families, and clans—all held together by moral economies, trust, and credit—remained a core feature of the fishing economy.

Since fisheries in Africa are such distinctive and underappreciated economic activities, their histories tend to challenge some of the central tenets of development theory. In Mweru-Luapula, rules of tenure and ownership over lagoons well stocked with fish and fertile floodplains weakened with the arrival of colonial states. The lagoons became common property, governed by a mix of colonial chiefs and officials and exploited by an array of autochthonous and migrant Africans and Europeans. However, informal tenure arrangements persisted and revolved around social networks linked to "traditional" authorities, rural-urban traders, clans, and families. This historical trajectory challenges one of the central economic expectations of modernity[55]—that private property, freehold tenure, individualism, and concomitant forms of investment will accompany and promote economic development and commercial expansion. Economic development and growth have not contributed to more formalized tenure arrangements; instead, Mweru-Luapula's fishery has witnessed an array of layered claims to increasingly scarce resources. Contrary to the expected trajectories of capitalist development, wealth accrued from the fishery has been devoted to consolidating and expanding social networks. Rights-in-persons remain a respectable and rational way to invest and display wealth.

PART ONE

STORIES OF CONQUEST

1

Nachituti's Gift

The Kazembe Kingdom and Owners of the Land

My first encounter with the story of Nachituti was in October 1997, during a visit to Lunde, the royal graveyard of the Kazembe rulers. Mwata Kazembe XVIII Munona Chinyanta, who died less than one year later, invited me to a ceremony to introduce me to Lunda customs; he also wanted me to photograph the ceremony and to transport dignitaries in my vehicle. The ceremony was unprecedented. Before his imminent death, Munona wanted to pay respect to his ancestors and ensure that the graveyard was clean and well maintained. En route to the graveyard, situated in Chief Kanyembo's area about five miles off the main road that runs through the valley, our trucks stopped at streams and termite mounds, which signified past boundaries and sacred places of rest. Lunda aristocrats fired muzzle-loading guns at each stop, and the Mwata requested permission from the gravekeepers and owners of the land to pass through their lands. When we finally reached the graveyard, the rough dirt track, which resembled no more than a footpath, ceased at a wooden barrier beyond which lay a field recently cleared of bush scrub and trees. We climbed out of our trucks, took off our shoes, and tied white cloth on our arms, for we were about to enter the burial place of chiefs and needed to show respect and protect ourselves from their spirits. We proceeded from one grave to the next with the keeper of Lunde reciting the praises of the dead kings and, together with the Mwata, giving libations of millet beer and throwing white earth called *impemba* (or *ulupemba*). Munona then placed copper plaques on the twelve previously unmarked mounds (five kings are buried outside the royal graveyard). After a drenching thunderstorm, we trudged in the mud for about one hundred feet to another grave on the outskirts of Lunde, where the Mwata began to give offerings. There was no copper plaque for this grave, so I asked my research assistant to whom it belonged. "Nachituti," I was told, "the queen of the Lunda."

His answer was unexpected. Although I knew that the people of Luapula had strong matrilineal affiliations and women had often attained positions of political significance, I thought that royal and aristocratic descent in Kazembe's eastern Lunda kingdom was patrifilial, with women playing a relatively minor role in the affairs of state. Yet here was a woman important enough to be buried next to the royal graveyard, the highest honor for anyone associated with the eastern Lunda kingdom. During that research trip, I heard more about Nachituti, especially from the elders in their stories of how the Lunda came to rule Luapula. I re-read the classic ethnographic and missionary texts about the Luapula Valley and indeed found that Nachituti featured in the idiosyncratic narratives of the missionary Dan Crawford, the articles and book by the Rhodes-Livingstone anthropologist Ian Cunnison, and the oral history of the Lunda written down by a collection of elders under the direction of Mwata Kazembe XIV Chinyanta Nankula.[1] Yet her importance, and that of the valley's matrilinealages in general, were always submerged under the history of the eastern Lunda kingdom and the Kazembes patrifilial descent, first drawn by Ian Cunnison and since then frequently reproduced and much discussed (for an updated version see figure 1).[2]

I returned to the Luapula Valley two years later, convinced that my previous study had underestimated the importance of the stories of the valley, and especially that of Nachituti. I suspected that the people of Luapula explained the elusive rules that governed the politics of access to their resources—the land, rivers, and lakes of the valley—and articulated relationships between owners of the land and lagoons and the Kazembe Kingdom through such oral traditions. To further explore these stories and their political impacts, I extended a study of patterns of production to consider how productive resources were embedded within cultural narratives. Specifically, I examined how narratives provided a "constitution" that explained and legitimized resource access at least until the coming of the colonial states in the early 1890s, and even afterward.

Historians and anthropologists have long noted that narratives, especially those that describe traditions of "genesis," are ways of describing contemporary culture, society, and political struggles rather than historical facts. Even Jan Vansina, who defends the historical validity of oral tradition against the many critiques of structural anthropologists, admits that such traditions "are expressions of present and past world views, that may reflect past events but do not necessarily do so."[3] Vansina describes oral traditions as "palimpsests" that do not "reflect exactly and necessarily the world view held now, but still incorporates elements of different ages."[4] Used with care, the intellectual or cultural historian can employ an oral tradition to explore the relationship between cosmologies and sociocultural and political change.

A bourgeoning field in historical anthropology has been the exploration of how hegemonic fictional narratives articulate with and impose themselves on existing cosmologies, especially in processes of conversion, where biblical narrative sequences influence the representation of everyday life and hence quotidian agency in social, political, and economic realms. John and Jean Comaroff, for example, argue that missionary narratives replaced southern Tswana forms of representation and became instruments of cultural hegemony; J. D. Y. Peel has offered a more dialogical approach whereby biblical narratives appear persuasive to potential converts when they adapted to existing, vernacular narratives. It is because of the strength of previous narrative traditions—rather than their weakness, as argued by the Comaroffs—that biblical narratives became so influential.[5] In the case of northeast Zambia, Robert Cancel has demonstrated a narrative tradition rich in allegory.[6]

The Nachituti narrative provides an opportunity to explore the relationship between narrative and social agency in a precolonial setting. In telling and interpreting Nachituti's story, I am less concerned with historical accuracy than with the fiction that has provided the idiom and ideology that structured political relationships between the peoples of the valley and allotted "charters" of rule and ownership over the land and lakes. Rather than verify the story of Nachituti's gift, this chapter explores how the story came to define Lunda political control and Shila ownership over the land and lakes. The purpose is not to deny or prove the historical validity of oral traditions but rather, following J. M. Schoffeleers, to demonstrate some historical dimensions to the ideological confrontations found within oral traditions.[7] In doing so, this chapter will not provide a historical reconstruction of the Kazembe Kingdom; those interested in a detailed history of the kingdom should consult the work of Giacomo Macola.[8] However, we will locate the emergence of the Nachituti narrative in the early nineteenth century and follow its spread as a charter of rule and ownership in the latter half of the century when the Kazembe Kingdom weakened and came to rely on the agency of dispersed aristocrats and owners of the land and owners of the lagoons *(abêne ba mpanga/kabanda,* sing. *umwine wa mpanga/kabanda).*

In the Luapula Valley, a story about the past was an integral part of the present. Characters in historical narratives were not ossified in the past; ancestral personae were adopted in the present through "positional succession" and old kin relations kept alive by what Ian Cunnison called "perpetual kinship."[9] Historical narratives defined political titles or offices, which would have an ongoing historical presence. Thus, the stories of the characters in Nachituti's narrative, like "Mwata Kazembe," "Nkuba," "Kalandala," and "Nachituti" herself, could refer to the activities of a number of different individuals who occupied that title at different times (with the partial exception of the Kazembes, who have distinct historical personae due to praise poems for each "Kazembe" combined with a chronological king list, an invention of the twentieth century).[10] If the dynamics of this system are not well understood, attempts at historical reconstruction will be flawed; on the other hand, historians possess raw material in the form of living political relationships that are the articulation of past kin ties. Details about identities and relationships between lineages were preserved as political offices as long as the ancestors continued to be inherited by the living. Past kin relations thereby had ongoing implications for contemporary life. This was a two-way process: contemporary conflicts also impacted on the history that was told. For example, a fight between perpetual relatives, say an uncle and nephew, might have transformed the emphasis of a story or superimposed another narrative on the original. Once we understand the dialectical interplay of past and present in Luapula, we can begin to explore the web of relationships between the narration of a story, the politics of the narrators, and the making of history.

The story of Nachituti's gift is a story of two gifts, both of which describe relationships of economic and political reciprocity between giver and recipient.[11] The first gift is the head of Nachituti's brother, Nkuba, which the Lunda aristocrats, Kalandala and Nswana Ntambo, gave to Kazembe. By doing so, Kazembe was indebted to the Lunda aristocrats for his first bride, Nachituti, freed from her dead brother, Nkuba. The giving of this gift was reenacted through the continued giving of aristocrats' sisters and sisters' daughters as the Kazembes' brides *(ntombo)*. Kazembe thereby remained obligated to his aristocrats, who described themselves as "owners" of the king. The second is Nachituti's gift of the land and lakes to Kazembe; this ensured that Kazembe was indebted to Nachituti and recognized her people, the autochthones of the valley, as owners of the land and lagoons. Nachituti's people continued to give Kazembe produce from the lands and lakes—cassava, millet, game meat, fish, and other wild produce—and in return Kazembe bestowed on their leaders the titles of owner of the land or owner of the lagoon.

The Narration

Eastern Lunda oral traditions link the beginnings of the Kazembe Kingdom in the Luapula Valley to a series of encounters between emissaries of Mwaant Yaav, the central Lunda paramount, and southern Luba lineage heads. Chinyanta, a warrior who had previously surrendered to Mwaant Yaav, led an expedition to Luapula to find the Lunda blacksmith Lubanda, who had fled some years earlier. Instead, Chinyanta found salt pans. When he attempted to inform Mwaant Yaav of his lucrative discovery, Mutanda, the owner of the salt, murdered Chinyanta by drowning him. Mwaant Yaav appointed Chinyanta's son, Ng'anga Bilonda, as "Kazembe" and told him to avenge the death of his father by killing Mutanda.[12]

These are the murky tales of the beginnings of eastern Lunda rule on the Mukelweji and Luapula Rivers. We know with some certainty that Kazembe conquered and settled in the Luapula Valley toward the middle of the eighteenth century.[13] The Kazembe or eastern Lunda entourage called those whom they conquered "AbaShila," meaning fishers; this became a generic term for Luapula's autochthones. The most famous and common story of eastern Lunda conquest of the Shila, which is still told in the valley and has become part of the "universal" history of the valley accepted by both Shila and Lunda narrators, is related to a period of Lunda expansion under Mwata Kazembe I Ng'anga Bilonda's son, Mwata Kazembe III Ilunga.[14] In the first part of this chapter, I will concentrate on the telling of the story in the late twentieth century and suggest some reasons for its particular emphasis. The remainder of the chapter will locate the emergence of the story in the mid to late nineteenth century.

> It was during the reign of Mwata Kazembe III "Ilunga" [approx. 1760 to 1805]. The Lunda capital was at Kasankila near Mofwe Lagoon. At that time, the Lunda did not cultivate land, they did not even catch fish. This is why they had to be in the middle of the Luapula Valley, where the Shila people could bring them food.
>
> Nachituti and Nkuba lived on Chisenga Island. Nkuba had many wives and among them he loved one greatly. One day he found his nephew, the son of Nachituti, with this most beloved

wife. In a jealous rage, he killed his nephew, skinned him, carefully
dried the skin, and kept it under his mat.

Nachituti didn't know what had become of her son. She asked,
"Where's my son?"

One day a man came to her and said: "I will tell you where your
son is if you promise not to tell who informed you."

"I promise," Nachituti replied.

"In the palace where your brother sits you will find the skin of
your son."

Nachituti did not know how to verify this old man's words since
her brother Nkuba was always in his palace, sitting on his mat.
Then one day there was a party in the palace with much drinking.
While her brother was drunk, Nachituti looked under the mat and
there she found the skin of her son. Upon finding the skin, she decided to go to Mwata Kazembe, who she knew to be a fierce warrior. At that time there was little water, so Nachituti could walk
from Chisenga to Kasankila. There was only a little stream *(Ka-
bunda)*, which she had to cross. The rest of the land was a forest
where they dug caterpillars to eat.

When Nachituti arrived at the stream, the Lunda helped her
across. Then when people in the *ichipango* palace saw a woman, they
reported her to Mwata Kazembe. He told the guards to let her in.
She went up to Mwata Kazembe, took her menstruation cloth and
threw it in his face. She said: "If you are a man, you will avenge the
death of my son. I want you to kill this man, my brother Nkuba."

On hearing this Mwata Kazembe instructed his warriors Kalandala and Nswana Ntambo to find Nkuba and to bring him back
alive. They went to Chisenga, but upon arrival found that Nkuba
had fled to his brother Mulumbwa's village. Since Kalandala
couldn't find Nkuba at Chisenga, he was angry and started killing
people. He killed many people, even the Abena Bwilile who
couldn't run from Chisenga because they wanted to die in their
own country. The Bwilile made porridge and slept under animal
skins to escape Kalandala. They thought that when the Lunda
found the porridge they would eat it and burn themselves. But the
porridge cooled down by the time the Lunda arrived. While eating
the porridge the Lunda pierced one of the animal skins with a
spear and someone cried out. The Lunda thus knew that there
were people under the animal skins and they killed them all.

After killing the Bwilile, they found other people who belonged
to Nkuba and fought them but still could not find Nkuba. They returned to Chisenga Island and were told that Nkuba had fled but
that his people came to fetch food for him. They were told to wait

for them and then would be led to Nkuba. Nkuba's people came and rang bells to tell people to come with food. Kalandala heard the bells and captured them. "Please don't kill us," they pleaded. "We'll show you where to find Nkuba."

They led Kalandala to Nkuba. When they arrived at Nkuba's hiding place, they rang bells to tell Nkuba that food had arrived. Upon hearing the bells, Nkuba came to collect the food. Kalandala caught Nkuba, and since he was angry with Nkuba for all the trouble he had put him through, he disregarded Mwata Kazembe's instructions and killed him. He decapitated Nkuba, put his head in the boat, and returned to Mwata Kazembe. On their way the head of Nkuba jumped out of the boat and into the river. The place where Nkuba's head jumped out is called *Pacalala Nkuba* [the place where Nkuba lies] and is still known by that name today.

When they arrived at Mwata Kazembe, they explained how the head had jumped out of the boat. But Nachituti knew her brother was dead and wanted to reward Mwata Kazembe. She took a basket, filled it with soil, and a pot, and filled it with water. She gave the basket to Mwata Kazembe and said, "I give you the land"; and she gave the pot and said, "I give you all the water; the rivers and lagoons this side and the other side of the Luapula are yours." Mwata Kazembe told her that since she had instructed him to kill her brother, she should stay with him. Mwata Kazembe looked after Nachituti. When she died she was regarded as a chief and buried next to the royal graveyard, Lunde. Even if a chief is dead, upon his burial, the procession must stop and pay respect at the grave of Nachituti.[15]

Those familiar with the oral traditions of south central Africa will immediately identify several "mythic" elements, some of which will be further explored in the next section. Nkuba is a variation on "the drunken king," explicated by Luc de Heusch, while Nachituti fits into a pattern of unmarried women who surrender the political realm to a conquering patriarch, as found in the famous Lunda epic of the seduction of Ruwej or the less studied but common story of Kipimpi and Nakutola.[16] These narratives fit into even more widespread genres of disempowerment from sisters as lineage members to wives as subordinates.[17] "Nkuba" is a title common to many different stories about the founding of polities on the frontiers of Lunda expansion.[18] The meaning of their names also reveals the symbolic nature of the narrative; "Nkuba" means "lightning," while "Nachituti" could be derived from "tûta," to pull down or destroy.[19]

Despite these generic tropes, the story of Nachituti has particular elements that tied it to the Luapula Valley and the eastern Lunda kingdom of Kazembe. I have heard the story from more than twenty different elders and read several more versions recorded by missionaries and researchers over the last century. The literate usually recite a story similar to the one written down in Mwata Kazembe XIV Chinyanta Nankula's *Ifikolwe Fyandi na Bantu Bandi* (My ancestors and my people), which is a popular book in the valley and was once read as a school textbook.[20] The story of Nachituti has thus been exposed to the much-discussed problem of feedback in oral traditions influenced by written versions, which change the form and often the content of oral narrations.[21] However, as Luise White points out, feedback can also be "manipulated for specific impact."[22] Even with the dissemination of a written version, a single, authoritative story has not appeared. There is a clear generic story and then several variations in detail depending on the teller. The generic features of the story are clear. Nkuba killed his nephew. The mother of the murdered nephew, Nachituti, fled to Kazembe and pleaded for revenge. Kazembe sent his aristocrats, Kalandala and Nswana Ntombo, to capture or kill Nkuba; after they returned and reported that they had decapitated Nkuba, Nachituti gave Kazembe a basket of earth representing the land and a pot of water representing the river and lakes. This core narrative is found in the versions recorded before and after the publication of *Ifikolwe Fyandi*.

Prince Dyulu Kabeya, nowadays an important Lunda aristocrat, told the above detailed version of the story to me. He is literate and has read *Ifikolwe Fyandi*. Still, there are several variations in detail. In the written, official version, Nachituti prostrates naked in front of the chief but there is no mention of a menstruation cloth. And the head of Nkuba did not jump out of the boat; *Pacalala Nkuba* is simply named as the place where Nkuba was decapitated (other versions claim that Nkuba continued to speak after his head was cut off). The variation that struck me as most significant was that in Prince Dyulu Kabeya's version, Kazembe instructed Kalandala to bring Nkuba back alive, whereas in *Ifikolwe Fyandi*, and most other versions, Kazembe's explicit instructions were to kill Nkuba and bring back his head.[23]

Why did Prince Dyulu Kabeya change the story? It was possible that he wanted Kazembe to appear merciful, concerned with the lives of those he conquered, compared to the brutal Nkuba. Yet this explanation was unconvincing. Prince Dyulu Kabeya told many stories of Kazembe conquering the land by force and killing those he

conquered. The praise sung by Kazembe during his dance of conquest, the *Mutomboko*,[24] when he received the land and lakes from
Nachituti, is:

> I love to seize the country by force
> I who am given lands and peoples
> While others are given goats and sheep.[25]

Why, then, did Prince Dyulu Kabeya insist that Kazembe told Kalandala not to kill Nkuba? After several hours of discussing more recent
political events, a possible answer emerged. Two years prior, after the
death of Mwata Kazembe XVIII Munona Chinyanta in June 1998,
there had been a succession dispute. The details need not concern us;
however, the end result was that certain Lunda aristocrats asserted their
authority and appointed a new Kazembe against the accepted rules of
succession. There had been much discontent with this decision and
even an attempted coup. Nevertheless, the decision of certain aristocrats was respected and supported by the Zambian government.

The point of the altered story was not that Kazembe told Kalandala
not to kill Nkuba, but that Kalandala *did* kill Nkuba. This demonstrated
Kalandala's independence of action and that an aristocrat, not a Kazembe, conquered the land and lakes. During the entire interview, Dyulu
Kabeya was at pains to emphasize that Kazembe was powerless without
the Lunda aristocrats, of which Kalandala was one of the most important members. The Lunda throne did not belong to Kazembe but to the
aristocrats who were the owners of the king *(umwine wa mfumu)*. Despite
Kazembe's contrary instructions, it was Kalandala who killed Nkuba.
After he returned with Nkuba's head, Kalandala danced the Mutomboko dance of conquest and sang:

> I am the only Kalandala . . .
> I who killed Nkuba and all his children
> Nkuba, the Owner of Chisenga Island
> Together with his own brother.[26]

Other versions of the story told by the aristocrats emphasize their
agency in different ways. For example, the aristocrats frequently claim
that Kalandala actually found Nachituti and brought her to Kazembe.[27] Whether Kalandala brought Nachituti to Kazembe or Nkuba's head, the effect is the same: Kazembe is indebted to Kalandala and
by implication to the aristocrats in general for killing Nkuba and thereby
freeing Nachituti from her brother.

The Aristocrats

The different emphases of Nachituti's story have thus far been related to tensions between Lunda aristocrats and the king, Kazembe, in the late twentieth century. Like ancestral spirits, stories arose in response to the politics of an era; that they were part of popular memory in the late twentieth century indicates their continued relevance for the peoples of Luapula. Nevertheless, this oral tradition does not only represent concerns of the late twentieth century. Oral traditions are palimpsests that incorporated the views of past generations and superimposed them in new versions. Deeply embedded in the story of Nachituti's gift are conflicts between autochthonous clans, kings, and aristocrats for control over the people, lands, and resources of the valley.[28]

In the early nineteenth century the Kazembe Kingdom was at its most powerful. The testimony of several Portuguese travelers and traders describe the kingdom, with its western and eastern peripheries stretching for at least one hundred miles in either direction, as the most significant and centralized state in the eastern portion of south central Africa. Based on the estimates of Gamitto in 1831–32 as well as later accounts, Giacomo Macola reckons that its capital, the *musumba,* must have numbered at least ten thousand, an extraordinary and probably unprecedented number for this area, leading to a unique system of urban administration.[29] Political control in the peripheries was facilitated by the distribution of Lunda insignia, lineage power brokering, and the collection of tribute. In the heartland of the Luapula Valley, Kazembe appointed aristocrats as territorial governors *(bachilolo,* sing. *chilolo)* to ensure the payment of tribute and recognition of his rule.[30]

Yet even in the early nineteenth century, there were signs that the authority of the Kazembe Kingdom was challenged at its peripheries. Luba titleholders to the northwest competed with the Kazembe Kingdom over local resources and long-distance trade routes.[31] Toward the east, Bisa traders blocked attempts to establish a permanent trading relationship with the Portuguese colonial outposts on the Zambezi. Moreover, Lunda aristocrats were not always willing to bear arms for Kazembe. For example, the Portuguese *pombeiros* were detained for up to four years at Kazembe's court because of the danger of travel to the Zambezi. When Kazembe eventually sent them along with his chief aristocrat, Mwinempanda, a superior Bisa force bribed Mwinempanda into abandoning the expedition and robbed the *pombeiros* of Kazembe's trading merchandise of slaves, ivory, and copper.[32] After 1850, it seems that Kazembe Kingdom weakened even further. Conflict then spread to the heartland and capital itself as Swahili traders and the Nyamwezi trader, Msiri, adopted eastern Lunda tactics of lineage power brokering and competed for control over the lucrative slave and ivory trades. A series of internal wars linked to succession disputes limited the political authority of the kingdom in the Luapula Valley and checked its reach and influence in its western and eastern peripheries.[33]

Before 1850, at the height of the kingdom's authority, aristocratic appointments extended the rule of the Kazembe and collected tribute. In the late eighteenth and early nineteenth century, Portuguese traders and emissaries witnessed the role of aristocrats like Mwinempanda, Kanyembo, Kalandala, and Chibwidi.[34] "The court of Mwata Kazembe is composed of Chilolos . . . who constitute a nobility," Gamitto reported in 1831–32, "and these are respected by the people in the same way as they themselves respect Kazembe."[35] A series of practices and narratives linked the king to dispersed aristocrats, the most notable being the giving of close kinswomen to the king as *ntombo* wives (from the Ruund word, *ntombw,* a political pawn). This ensured that the kingdom was tied to its more dispersed representatives through family relations that were then perpetuated. The influence of aristocrats increased if their *ntombo* kinswomen gave birth to a prince. Since royal descent was patrifilial (see figure 1), only the sons of kings *(umwana wa mfumu)* could become princes. Clan and lineage membership, however, were generally passed on from the mother. Thus, if an aristocrat ensured that the chief was married to his sister or sister's daughter, he stood a good chance of securing a prince as close avuncular relative, preferably as sister's son *(mwipwa).* If this prince became king, the wife giver's clan would form the *abacanuma,* literally those who stand behind (the throne), and gain status through their privileged access to royalty.[36] The giving of *ntombo* is described by the Nachituti story. Nachituti, freed from her brother by Kalandala and Nswana Ntambo, became the wife of Kazembe. Kazembe was indebted to the aristocrats for bringing him Nachituti, and their marriage tied Kazembe to Kalandala.

This type of lineage power brokering extended from the level of aristocrat and king to that of clan and aristocrat. While aristocrats had probably received title from their father, they also belonged to a matrilineal clan *(umukowa,* pl. *imikowa),* or more precisely a particular lineage *(ichikota,* pl. *ifikota)* within a clan, a variation on a system of matrilineal institutions common to the south central African savanna in precolonial times.[37] There is some disagreement on the importance and persistence

of these clan groups among Bemba-speaking peoples. Andrew Roberts
has argued that on the Bemba plateau, clan identities were ephemeral
and had "limited importance as corporate groups."[38] A White Father
missionary with more than twenty-five years of experience on the
Bemba Plateau has questioned this assertion and maintains a greater
corporate presence and continuity for Bemba clans.[39] Certainly, in the
Luapula Valley, due to the association of certain clans with fertile farming lands and lucrative fishing lagoons, clan identities had greater continuity and held greater political sway, at least in the precolonial period.
Unlike more transitory Bemba villages reliant on shifting *chitemene* agriculture, several clans established claims over the land and lagoons.
Moreover, as Ian Cunnison noticed, clans on the Luapula attained
greater historical depth through their attachment to the Kazembe lineage, as will be further illustrated by the history of Luapula's Goat
Clan.[40]

Clan identity was matrilineal; it was traced through the mother
(although a secondary clan could be that of one's father). This did not,
however, make Luapula into a matrilineal society, or part of what is
sometimes misleadingly referred to as the "matrilineal belt" of central
Africa.[41] In Mweru-Luapula, clan identity was primarily political; it described relationships to resources and to other allied or "joking" clans
(like the Leopard Clan for the Goat Clan). However, the perpetual kinship system upon which the Kazembe Kingdom rested was bilateral,
perhaps mimicking the primary kin unit found in Mweru-Luapula, the
bilateral family *(ulupwa)*. Several old Luapulan proverbs attest to the importance of bilateral descent: "The child of a hippo plays in all waters"
(Mwana wa mfubu angala matenge yonse) or "the offspring of the mother is
the offspring of the father" *(Bwana ku kanyina, bwana ku kawishi)*.[42] In
many ways, as demonstrated in chapters 3 and 6, the *ulupwa* family was
a more lasting form of social organization that allowed for the emergence of big men and big women in the colonial and postcolonial periods. There was no definite system that related kin to lineage, lineage to
clan, and clan to ruler. Ian Cunnison's informants emphasized that in
the Luapula Valley, "people behave among themselves in a certain way
and therefore are related in a certain way: not that people are related in
a certain way and therefore behave in a certain way."[43] The strength of
constructed or fictive kinship seems to have been equally true in the precolonial period. Nevertheless, while actual kin or clan ties may have
been tenuous, the idiom of kin and clan helped to define relationships to
valued resources and to the Kazembe Kingdom.

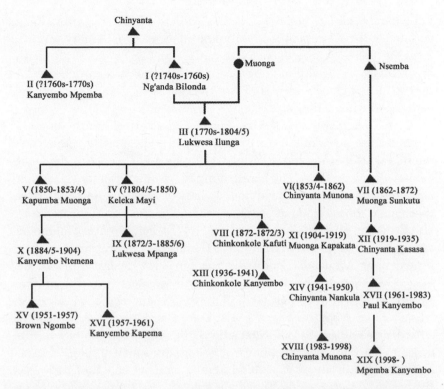

Figure 1. Genealogy of the Kazembes. From Macola, *Kingdom of Kazembe*, xxvi, 231, and author interviews.

Clan leaders *(bachikolwe)* who wished to ally themselves with prestigious Lunda rulers gave sisters or nieces to titleholders as wives to gain influence over future inheritors of the title. Patrilineal identity was Lunda; the matrilineal, an autochthonous clan.[44] Based on research conducted in the late 1940s, Ian Cunnison claimed that around the mid-nineteenth century, Kalandala was sent to oversee Nkuba on Chisenga Island and married one of Nkuba's sisters.[45] The son from this marriage inherited Lunda identity from his father and Nkuba's identity from his mother (since Nkuba was Kalandala's son's mother's brother). This relationship was perpetuated; henceforth, Nkuba would always be Kalandala's son. The same relationship developed between the Lunda aristocrat Nswana Ntambo and Nkuba's brother, Mulumbwa. Luapula's clan members maintained their influence over Lunda titles by encouraging their sisters' sons to retain their mother's clan identities, thereby perpetuating a matrilineal clan system. On the other hand, the Kazembe

Kingdom became rooted in local clans, thereby contributing to its local legitimacy. This combination of Lunda title with clan identity was the basis for the emergence of the Nachituti story. The narrative rested on an exchange in "wealth-in-knowledge" between the legitimating narratives of Lunda titleholders and local clans. Such narratives held together political relationships.[46]

Clans under eastern Lunda rule possessed a distinct history that tied them to Kazembe's kingship and to the broader episodes of Lunda conquest. Take, for example, the history of the Luapula lineage of the Goat Clan, which is an important clan among the aristocrats and is common among the minor chiefs, headmen, owners of the land, and owners of the lagoons throughout the Luapula Valley. The story of the Goat Clan, like all of Luapula's stories, depends upon the teller. Most clan members agree that the most senior ancestor is Chibwidi, who was the owner of the salt pans of Lualaba conquered by Chinyanta, the father of Mwata Kazembe I Ng'anga Bilonda. Chibwidi was the first to give Bilonda an *ntombo* bride from the Goat Clan. The bride, Muonga, bore the child who became Mwata Kazembe III Lukwesa Ilunga (1770s–1804/5). After his investiture, Mwata Kazembe III Ilunga asked his mother, Muonga, to leave her ancestral home and come to stay with him. She arrived with her brothers, Koni and Nsemba, and her daughter, Mpanga. By then, Mwata Kazembe III had already fathered a son who would become Mwata Kazembe IV Keleka Mayi (1804/5–1850). Since Mwata Kazembe III Ilunga wanted the kingship to remain within his mother's family, he insisted that his son, Keleka Mayi, marry his sister, Mpanga. Keleka Mayi and Mpanga conceived another Goat Clan prince who became Mwata Kazembe IX Lukwesa Mpanga (1872/73–1885/86). Mwata Kazembe III Ilunga also married two other Goat Clan wives, Kasau and Munona, who gave birth to two more princes, who became Mwata Kazembe V Muonga Kapumba (1850–1853/54) and Mwata Kazembe VI Chinyanta Munona (1853/54–1862). This is how the matrilineal Goat Clan became a force behind the patrilineal Lunda kingship and how the Goat Clan attained its historic depth and corporate complexity.[47]

By giving birth to kings or princes, the Goat Clan ensured that their matrilineal members were appointed to important positions in the Lunda hierarchy and government through much of the nineteenth century; the Goat Clan would stand behind the throne *(abacanuma)* and become an influential set of aristocratic appointments. Important Goat Clan ancestors like Chibwidi, Koni, Kasau, Mpemba, Nsemba,

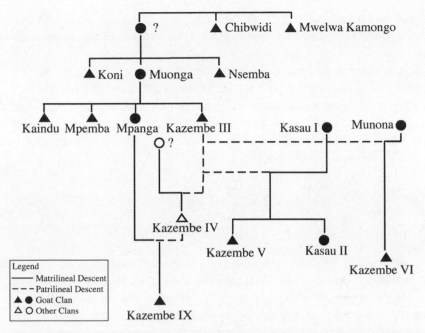

Figure 2. The Goat Clan and the Kazembes. From author interviews.

Kanyemba, Shanyemba, Kaindu, and Chilalo became *bachilolo* aristo-crats who were awarded with portions of land and lakes, *amayanga* (sing. *iyanga*) colonies, scattered across the southern Luapula Valley (see map 2). Political relations between members of the Goat Clan were main-tained even while actual kin relationships diverged. Thus, for example, the present-day Koni calls himself Chibwidi's nephew (sister's son: *mwipwa*), even though this relationship probably refers to the nineteenth century. Either men or women could inherit the positions. Chibwidi is presently a woman and Kasau a man. Nevertheless, Chibwidi remains Kasau's "uncle" (two generations are generally compressed into one).

Praises *(amalumbo,* sing. *ilumbo)* celebrated the stories of the Goat Clan that linked the clan to the king and to the land and lakes. A clan had a generic praise, but each clan head *(chikolwe,* pl. *bachikolwe)* inno-vated; they adopted a phrase from the generic praise and then added lines that referred to their specific lineage section within the clan. For example, a common phrase found throughout the Goat Clan praised the contribution of the Goat Clan to the kingship by boasting that the goat provides the leather for the belt *(inshipo/ulukanga)* worn by Ka-zembe.[48] Chibwidi's praise begins "Chibwidi, the belt worn by royalty"

(Chibwidi lukanga ulufwele abakata). Others made reference to the belt in a more oblique fashion. The praise of Kaindu, which is incorporated into many of the Goat Clan praises, is "Kaindu who watches the cow" *(Kaindu akamutamba ngombe)*. (Presumably, Kaindu watches the cow because its leather can be used for Kazembe's belt instead of the goat's leather.)[49] The praise then celebrates particular ancestors within a clan lineage. For example, Chilalo, the Goat Clan elder appointed to guard the harbor on the Luapula by Kazembe (owner of the harbor: *umwine wa cabu*), praised himself:

> We belong to Kaindu who watches the cattle
> While others watch an empty place
> Ilunga who can reach far with hands
> Mwata Kazembe found him
> I am the sleep that can attack even the cunning.[50]

Ilunga was the name of the first Chilalo, the direct matrilineal ancestor of the current Chilalo. He boasted of his calling to guard the harbor and of his prowess in doing his duty with his magic and his long hands that reach his enemies. Lunda aristocrats and appointments like Chilalo were part of the royal network; they considered themselves "true" Lunda, the descendents of the conquerors of the valley, even while they maintained their autochthonous clan identities. Their stories of conquest provided a stage upon which the politics of resource access could be articulated; they wove the fabric of authority, the charters that secured Lunda rule over *amayanga* colonies.

The Owners

Toward the end of 1867, when David Livingstone visited a much weakened kingdom, he reported on the authority of autochthonous owners of the land and lagoons: "An old man named Pérémbé [Mpelembe] is the owner of the land on which Casembe has built. They always keep up the traditional ownership. Munongo [Mununga] is a brother of Pérémbé, and he owns the country east of Kalongosi [Kalungwishi]: if any one wished to cultivate land he would apply to these aboriginal chiefs for it."[51] Early nineteenth century Portuguese travelers left little account of these "owners," despite the Portuguese testimony of the kingdom and the *bachilolo* aristocrats being more detailed than that of Livingstone. By contrast, Livingstone was unimpressed by the *chilolo* aristocrat, Mwinempanda, who was indebted to the Swahili traders and "showed no inclination to get out of it [his debt]. . . . Casembe rose in the esteem of all of us as Moenempanda [Mwinempanda] sank."[52] It seems likely that the role of the owners increased through the nineteenth century as the influence of eastern Lunda conquerors and aristocrats declined, at least in matters concerning land and resource management. As the authority of the kingship was challenged, the Kazembes relied on local rulers rather than aristocratic appointments. This gave decentralized rulers significant agency vis-à-vis the central kingdom. In the nineteenth century, the owners of the land and lagoons asserted their relationship to the land, to their clan identities, and to a set of ostensibly pre-Lunda political institutions and oral traditions.

A clan was linked to the land or lakes through the *umwine wa mpanga* or *kabanda,* the owner of the land or the lagoon, who supervised and had ritual duties over a portion of land called an *akatongo* (pl. *ututongo*). This was the most local and tangible level of land ownership. The conquering king, Kazembe, owned the country *(calo);* his representatives, the aristocrats, governed *amayanga* colonies in the country; finally, owners of the land had the closest ties to *ututongo* lands. "The poor man has an akatongo, a king has a country" *(Akatongo ka mulandu, calo ca mfumu),* as on old Luapula proverb puts it.[53] *Ine,* the root of the term *umwine,* which has been translated as "owner," expresses a relationship of identity, an extension of the self. The title "owner of the land" or "owner of the lagoon," *umwine wa mpanga* or *umwine wa kabanda,* closely identified lands or lakes and the ritual duties of these lands with an individual and his or her clan.[54]

I have expressed these relationships in abstract and rather academic terms. On the Luapula, they were expressed through oral traditions that compressed several narratives defining the roles of clan leaders in relation to the land on the one hand and to conquerors on the other. The Nachituti narrative combines several stories, all of which connect clans and titleholders, from the owners of the land through the Lunda aristocrats to the king, Kazembe. The characters, Nkuba and Nachituti, are a core component of Luapulan oral traditions that predate eastern Lunda conquest. According to testimony collected from Shila elders by Edouard Labrecque in the 1940s, Nkuba and Nachituti left their Bemba homeland for the Luapula Valley after a pregnant Nachituti threw a fertility doll of her husband's daughter, Muchinda, into the river. Muchinda claimed that Nachituti had thereby rendered her infertile and demanded Nachituti's child in payment. Nkuba, rather than surrendering his sister's child, decided to fall, like lightning *(nkuba),* on a country far away. They left for Luapula.[55] Besides the similarity in characters, this narrative seems quite different to that of Nachituti's gift. However, certain generic and symbolic elements of the story of Nachituti's gift that are emphasized by the Shila bear a remarkable resemblance. According to Shila narrators, the murder of Chituti, the son of Nachituti, by Nkuba was justified since Chituti was allegedly practicing witchcraft and killing women.[56] Thus, in both stories Nachituti and her child are guilty of a form of witchcraft leading to infertility; Nachituti is the destroyer of the family and her child needs to be sacrificed to restore order. Her refusal to accept this fate leads to migration and contributes to a new polity. By giving the land and lakes and marrying Kazembe, Nachituti invited Lunda to stay; the Shila praise her as *Nachituti uwaobwele uLuunda,* Nachituti who invited the Lunda to stay.[57] In a similar fashion, according to the Shila testimony about Nkuba's migration to Luapula, it was Nachituti who brewed the beer that was exchanged with the autochthonous Bwilile for the ivory that formed the basis of Nkuba's pre-Lunda state.[58] In both stories, Nachituti first destroys and then helps to create a new polity.

The account of Nkuba leaving the Bemba heartland because of the doll that Nachituti threw away is probably the result of yet another narrative compression. Ian Cunnison recorded the same story, except the daughter of Matanda, a lord found to the south of the Luapula Valley, accused the daughter of Kaponto of losing her doll and hence making her infertile. When Matanda demanded Kaponto's daughter in payment, Kaponto left for the Luapula, where he conquered the Abatwa pygmies and established the Bwilile (those that eat themselves [since they have no chiefs]) villages.[59] West of the Luapula River, the Abena Mumba (Clay Clan) have told a story similar to our original Nachituti story, except Nachituti is the sister of Matanda, and Matanda is praised as the one who invited the Lunda *(Matanda uwaobwele Luunda).*[60] Finally, there is an even more generic aspect of the story, which is found in many clan histories west of the Luapula River and especially in the story of Kipimpi, an unmarried hunter, who comes across a wandering woman and calls her "Nakutola," literally, "I pick you up." The Nakutola story is the founding history of several clans west of the Luapula.[61]

In the context of all these competing stories and charters located across the valley and toward the Copperbelt, our original story of Nachituti's gift becomes all the more interesting. The analysis confirms Giacomo Macola's contention that the story of Nachituti's gift probably emerged in the nineteenth century as the "standard aetiological explanation of Lunda-Shila relations." However, the "archetypical form of the cliché" does not, as he suspects, stem from Lunda narrators.[62] Rather, it is a cliché embedded in the autochthonous clan histories of the wider region, many of which do not even reference the eastern Lunda (a wider study of clan histories might reveal other influences on the core history of the eastern Lunda). All of these clan histories refer to the role of particular titleholders and their tenure over precisely defined lands and lakes, rather than generic "Lunda-Shila" relations. This is why each story, while similar in generic elements and symbolism, makes specific references to places, like islands, streams, rivers, or lagoons. The meaning of these narrations emerged out of both their abstract and symbolic content and their precise geographic and historical contexts.

Nachituti's gift explicates the relationships between Nkuba, Kalandala, and Kazembe, all in reference to Chisenga Island, which has fertile farmland and is a productive fishing area. There are several geographic specifics in the narration, such as Chisenga Island, Kasankila, certain streams, or the place where Nkuba's head jumped out of the boat (Pacalala Nkuba).[63] These designate boundaries of the lands and lagoons to which the story refers and over which the titleholders claim control. The narration specifies titleholders and their roles: Kalandala delivers Nkuba (and hence Nachituti's gift) to Mwata Kazembe; he is entitled to rule Chisenga Island as his colony *(iyanga)* but must ensure that tribute is paid. After giving the land and lakes to him, Kazembe requested that Nachituti stay and marry him. The title "Nkuba," the brother of Nachituti and former political chief, became Kazembe's perpetual "Mwadi," the principal wife responsible for ensuring that Kazembe was well fed. Like a responsible "wife," he had to bring Kazembe tribute from Chisenga Island, which became Kazembe's storehouse *(ubutala bwakwa Kazembe)*. In return Nkuba was recognized as an owner of the lagoon by Kazembe and Kalandala; Chisenga Island was Nkuba's *akatongo* land.[64] Kalandala married Nkuba's sister, and the title of Nkuba passed on to Kalandala's son. Thus Kalandala became the perpetual father to Nkuba.[65] The Shila became, as Gamitto wrote in 1832, "the pure descendents of the conquered chief" of Chisenga Island.[66] A set of political offices that defined tribute obligations, identity, and ownership over the land was articulated in the narrative.

The narrative developed some time in the early nineteenth century when Kalandala was sent to rule Chisenga Island. He probably married Nkuba's sister, as Cunnison records.[67] This relationship gave birth to a story couched in local—and hence convincing—clichés that emphasized

Nkuba's ties to the land and Kazembe's rule through conquest. Eyewitness accounts would confirm this approximate dating: the story in its complete form was not recorded by early nineteenth century Portuguese traders (except by Gamitto's above-mentioned oblique reference), but was recognized by the missionary Dan Crawford some sixty years later as a core rationale for patterns of land ownership.[68] Thus, from about the middle of the nineteenth century, the story was manipulated to emphasize the role of certain titleholders and the obligations of others. Kazembe's court, seeking to minimize obligations to the ruler and owner of Chisenga Island, claimed that the gift was of little significance since the Lunda had already conquered the Shila. The version recorded in *Ifikolwe Fyandi*, which was written by Mwata Kazembe XIV Chinyanta Nankula in collaboration with Lunda elders, dismisses Nachituti's gift because "the whole land was already conquered by their [the Lunda's] own might, and they did not care for her words."[69] Kalandala and his "son," Nkuba, on the other hand, have stressed the importance of Nachituti's gift. If Nachituti had not given Chisenga Island to Kazembe, he would not rule the entire country. Nachituti did not surrender the lands and lakes; she *gave* them to Kazembe and thus ensured a role for Nkuba and his people as owners of the land and lagoons. The story of Chituti's infidelity and witchcraft, Nkuba's cruelty, and Nachituti's gift defined ties to the land and to the Kazembe Kingdom.[70]

There is symbolic content to the story that is common to south central Africa. The story of Nachituti warns of how jealousy between an uncle and nephew can alienate the brother-sister ties so important to matrilineal relationships. And, as a result, the sister may choose to leave the family and ally herself with rivals—a bitter and alienated Nachituti went to live with and marry Kazembe. In this sense, the cruel brother, Nkuba, resembled Frazer's scapegoat king, whose social and political failures enhanced his sacred virtues.[71] The onset of Kazembe's rule due to Nkuba's failure to adequately manage political affairs did not deny Nkuba's prior ties to the land and lakes; instead, a new form of ownership was recognized, affirmed, and institutionalized through sets of rituals dealing with the land. The term "Shila," while meaning "fisher," might also be derived from the sets of rites *(imishila,* sing. *umushila)* related to fishing and hunting.[72] Kazembe ruled the people; the Shila rulers engaged with the spirits linked to the land and lagoons.

The rites linked to Nkuba's ownership of the lands and lakes were communicated in an association called Ubutwa. Mwelwa C. Musambachime contends that Ubutwa originated among the Abatwa pygmies,

spread to the Bwilile inhabitants of Luapula, who called themselves
Mbolela Pano (I rot here), and was later adopted and spread by the Shila
of Nkuba. While the early origins of Ubutwa remain obscure, there is
sufficient evidence to indicate that by the nineteenth century it had
taken the form of an association of villages that recognized and articulated the ritual duties of owners of the land and lagoons, especially
those related to Nkuba. A father or mother of spirits *(Shingulu* or *Nangulu)* led the association's meetings and was responsible for the communication of the rites of the land and lakes and their spirits to its members.[73] The few informants who were prepared to talk to me about
Ubutwa insisted that the organization was called Ubutwa because of
the verb *twa* (to pound), since members would dance while pounding a
mortar, perhaps a performed reference to the mutuality between male
and female; or, as Musambachime points out, it could mean a "sharp"
point, perhaps referring to the qualities of rulership. According to Plymouth Brethren missionary, Dugald Campbell, who described Ubutwa
ceremonies in 1914, Ubutwa members were taught secrets of the cult
and learned an esoteric language called *Lubendo.* During Ubutwa festivals, initiated members constructed temples, prayed to local *ingulu* spirits, drank beer, gave libations, and sang. The association forged cohesive
bonds across clan and gender boundaries and promoted "wife swapping," a form of mutual support during harvest time called *ubwafwano.* It
also might have, as Musambachime argues, structured political relationships between Shila rulers allied to Nkuba. According to the oral evidence of Musambachime and the testimony of Campbell, Nkuba, the
failed king, was praised as a magician in Ubutwa songs.[74] Defeat deprived Nkuba of his secular power but not his ritual duties.

The institution of owners of the lands or owners of the lagoons
seems to be an adaptation of far more widespread Luba political traditions that incorporated local house or village heads into the Luba
confederation as earth priests.[75] In the case of dispersed Luba rulers,
Mary and Allen Roberts have argued that the "center" was a mythical
construct that legitimized rulers on the "periphery."[76] For the eastern
Lunda, we have some evidence of a more stable center, the capital of
the Kazembe Kingdom, situated next to Mofwe Lagoon; however, the
idea of the center was still an attractive legitimating device for peripheral rulers. Owners of the land and lagoons acquired status through
their connections to the Kazembe Kingdom, often signified by the distribution of Lunda insignia. Kazembe recognized the defeated chiefs as
owners of the land *(mpanga)* or of the lagoons *(kabanda)*, depending on

whether their area fell next to the river or toward the plateau. The owner had responsibilities to the land and "owned" the story or charter that reiterated ties to the Kazembe Kingdom. Relationships like those between Nkuba, Kalandala, and Kazembe on Chisenga Island were articulated in other stories that referenced lands stretching outward from the residence of Kazembe. Mununga, Nkuba's perpetual "nephew" (sister's son: *mwipwa*), who lived to the north of the Lunda heartland, surrendered to the Lunda and agreed to pay tribute to the aristocrat, Kasumpa. As Livingstone recounts in 1867, he was also recognized as an owner of the land.[77] And to the south, the Rat Clan rulers (Abena Mbeba) Mulundu, Malebe, and Lubunda offered tribute to Kazembe through Kashiba.[78]

While these owners were conquered and paid tribute to Kazembe and his representatives, they retained their autonomy. Kazembe and the Lunda governors did not choose their successors, had little influence over the allocation of their lands, and recognized their ritual duties over the land. In exchange for their tribute, Kazembe recognized the owners as arbitrators in conflicts over the land and lagoons. In times of drought or other natural misfortunes, Kazembe would call on the owners to request the intervention of the spirits. Farmers and fishers had to seek the permission of the owners and pay an appropriate amount of tribute or tax, some of which would find its way to Kazembe, often by way of his aristocratic governors.[79]

The conquest of the land and the establishment of the titles of owners of the land and lagoons was rehearsed in rituals that surrounded the flow of tribute from the owners to Kazembe. In the same way that the Lunda aristocrats gave Kazembe wives, the owners of the land and lagoons gave Kazembe the produce of the land and fed him. A set of rituals, an extension of gendered household relations to the level of king and subject, dictated Kazembe's eating habits.[80] He had a special kitchen *(mbala)* where a virgin *(mwadyambalala)* prepared his food. No one was allowed to eat with him or observe him eating, just as no wife should view her husband eating. There was one exception to this rule, indicating Lunda-Shila reciprocity, when the former ruler and owner of the lagoon, Mukamba, came to the palace with the first sweet papyrus, *iminkono.* He washed his hands, peeled the *umunkono,* and placed it in Kazembe's mouth. After eating, Kazembe said, "I have tasted *umunkono.* Now, let your people eat."[81] The owners had to be careful to bring food to the palace at night, for if it was brought during the day Kazembe would have to share it with the aristocrats and any other important

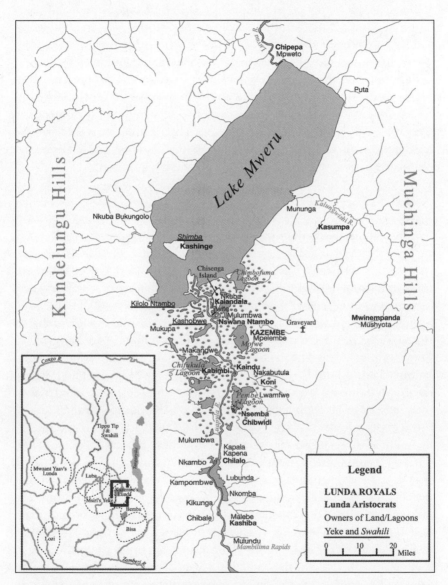

Map 2. Mweru-Luapula, 1860s–1880s. Select Lunda aristocrats, owners of the land/lagoons, Yeke, and Swahili. Note the pairing of aristocratic representatives and the owners.

functionaries.[82] These rituals, like the raising of a flag for a nation-state, provided an opportunity for the performance and articulation of the political alliances that constituted the Kazembe Kingdom.

By the middle of the nineteenth century, stories like that of Nachituti's gift expressed the reciprocal relations between Lunda rulers and owners of the land and lagoons. They indicated political failures, a collapse of matrilineal relationships and succession, and the arrival of fierce conquerors. Together with the Ubutwa association, the stories functioned to give cohesion to the owners of the land and lagoons, who were once rulers of the country. What remains is to see how these stories and rites of rule were connected to the social relationships that emerged out of the exploitation of Luapula's physical environment.

The Fishery

The heartland of the late-nineteenth-century Kazembe Kingdom extended from Mambilima Falls in the south, home to the Rat Clan ruler, Mulundu, northward, past the colonies of the loyal Goat Clan aristocrats who stood behind the king to Mofwe Lagoon, where the Lunda established their capital and buried their kings. Luapulans called the area around Mofwe Lagoon, Kanaya, from the verb *ukunaya,* meaning to make porridge, since it provided the people with food. As the river flows north it passes "Kazembe's storehouse," Chisenga Island, where Nkuba had lived and where his head still rested (Pacalala Nkuba). Then, where the Luapula opens out into Lake Mweru, a large island called Kilwa (meaning dry place) appears.[83] According to Kaponto's oral tradition, this had been home to some of the original Abatwa before Kaponto settled here and drove them away.[84] It is also where Nkuba Bukongolo fled after the Lunda defeated his brother, Nkuba Kawama. On the eastern shores of the lake, near the mouth of the Kalungwishi River, Nkuba's perpetual nephew, Mununga, ruled and paid tribute to Kazembe. And on the northern and northeastern shores, Mpweto and his brothers settled. They called themselves "Bwile," dark place, after the land, since when they arrived it was night.[85] Here the lake empties into the Luvua River, known locally as the Lualaba. Describing the Luapula Valley in this way is somewhat misleading; I have conflated a number of separate stories, all of which referred to local relationships between the Kazembe Kingdom, aristocrats, and owners of the land. These stories defined physical boundaries and actual duties for rulers and owners. By considering all of the stories together, however, we get an idea of the number of charters that entrenched the Kazembe Kingdom in Mweru-Luapula and provided local leaders with the rules of tenure and governance.

The value of the land and lakes rested on the sweat of human labor. The story of Nachituti's gift also relates how people learned to cultivate the land and catch fish, to harvest the wealth of the land and lakes. Before Nachituti gave the land and lakes to Kazembe, people lived on the caterpillars they found in the forest. It was only after Nachituti's gift that the Lunda planted their gardens, laid their nets, and set their fish traps. The land and the lakes present two interconnected but distinct productive spheres, the farm and the fishery. Each had distinct gendered relations of production and each interacted in a particular way with the local political and cultural landscape.

The length of the river, from the Mambilima Falls to the lagoons where Lake Mweru begins, is about one hundred miles and extends in width from a few hundred feet in the dry season to a few miles during the annual rainy season between November and March. The lake itself is eighty miles long from north to south and between twenty-five and thirty miles wide. This expanse of river, lagoon, and lake contained distinct but interconnected ecologies that provided different bounties to villagers. Parts of the deep, open waters of the lake were inaccessible to fishers with limited equipment, while the lagoons offered rich and accessible fishing grounds. Moreover, the ecology of the lake changed with season, year, and human intervention. During the annual floods certain fish species migrated to lagoon areas like Mofwe and Chimbofuma; during the dry season they retreated to the deep waters of the lake.

There are three general ecological zones that provided opportunities for different levels and types of human resource extraction and corresponding differences in political authority and tenure arrangements. The first zone, the relatively deep (forty to fifty feet) open waters of the lake, especially off the rocky northern shores, provides an ideal habitat for large adult fish like pale and mpumbu before they spawned (see the appendix for a list of fish). From their canoes, fishers employed floating nets and lines with hooks. It was particularly dangerous on the open lake; before they commenced fishing, fishers boasted of their bravery in praises that challenged the spirits.[86] The vast open areas of the lake were only lightly exploited.

The second zone is the lake's sandy shores, generally around the Kalungwishi River, toward the east and southwest of the lake. This area supports a diverse range of adult and juvenile fish and acts as a spawning ground for many of them, especially pale. Fishermen used nets made from the fibers of local plants, called *kaboko*. They either left them overnight *(amalalika)* or chased fish into them by the beating of surrounding water *(ukutumpula)*.[87] On the beaches, women caught small sardinelike fish called nshipo (later known as chisense) by dragging long pieces of cloth through the shallows.[88] According to Livingstone, a number of fish ascended the Kalungwishi River at different times of the year to spawn. He described a system of weirs used to catch fish in the river: "Fish in great numbers are caught when ascending to spawn: they are secured by weirs, nets, hooks. Large strong baskets are placed in the rapids, and filled with stones, when the water rises these baskets are standing-places for the fishermen to angle or throw their nets."[89] Owners like Mununga controlled access to the fishery. Where the Kalungwishi River flows into the lake, Mununga conducted an annual ceremony to "open" the fishery at the beginning of the most significant spawning events.[90]

The third zone runs from the lake upstream for about one hundred miles through a series of lagoons and swamps and islands, most notably Chisenga Island, the Pembe, Chifukula, and Mofwe Lagoons, to the village of Mulundu at the Mambilima rapids. A few months into the rainy season, the Luapula floods its banks, and the width of the river extends from a few hundred feet to a few miles. These nutrient-rich floodplains provide fertile feeding grounds for young fish; adult fish regularly spawn during this time. The villagers took advantage of the inundation. Fishermen in canoes caught spawning fish with floating nets in the river. Nearer the rapids and falls of Mambilima, villagers built dams and weirs *(amâmba*, sing. *ubwâmba)* and installed traps *(imyôno*, sing. *umôno)* to catch fish as they spawned or as the floodwaters receded. Through the careful construction of such dams and weirs, villagers continued to catch fish well into the dry season.

In the swamps and lagoons south of Lake Mweru, political and spiritual authority over control of the fishery was most defined. Most of this area fell within the heartland of the Kazembe Kingdom, where old rulers like Nkuba, Malebe, and Mulundu had been incorporated into the Lunda political structure as owners of the lagoons. With increased competition over these lucrative fishing areas, owners of the lagoons developed significant tenure rights; they controlled access to fishing areas, ruled over the setting of nets and weirs, and adjudicated over conflicts. Their control over lucrative fishing grounds in turn contributed to the migration of families to their villages and an increase in people under their control, in many ways similar to the Nunu water lords described by Robert Harms.[91]

In Mweru-Luapula, the owners of the lagoon legitimized their political role through ritual duties. They made offerings like millet meal, the old food of the valley, to the ancestors *(imipashi,* sing. *umupashi)* or to nature spirits *(ingulu)*. Sometimes they visited the graveyards of the ancestors and offered beer and white clay. The ritual duties, perhaps communicated through the Ubutwa or similar associations, were connected to more widespread beliefs about the role of nature spirits in ensuring good catches. Fishers placed charms on their nets to attract fish and to protect themselves and their nets from crocodiles. In song, they asked nature spirits *(ingulu)* like the mermaid, Akankubunkubu, to chase catfish from their hiding places and the python, Winkonkelela, to lead the mpumbu on their spawning runs. The owners of the lagoons, with their privileged access to ancestral power, were responsible for placating these spirits, thus ensuring the success of the catch and the safety of the fishers.[92]

The most important duty of an owner of the lagoon was the annual opening of the fishery *(ukufungule sabi)*.[93] A typical example was the Rat Clan leader, Mulundu, who, together with other clan elders, was responsible for the mpumbu fish that spawned every year after the first heavy floods (see chapter 4). During the mpumbu's spawning season, fish were caught in abundance, smoked and stored, given as tribute to Kazembe's representatives, and exported to the plateau areas. Before catching commenced, Mulundu made a pilgrimage to a shrine or house of spirits *(nganda ya imipashi)* that housed a relic called Masombwe. Here he prayed and offered beer and white clay to the ancestral spirits: "We have rested. Now permit us to catch fish. Give us relish, you spirits."[94] Masombwe then informed him if the ancestral spirits had accepted the gifts; if they had, the mpumbu would follow the Winkonkelela nature spirit and spawn in the nearby Mambilima rapids. Mulundu then went with his villagers to the river and speared the first fish. Women ululated and the catching began.[95] According to Cunnison, when the fishery was opened on the Pembe Lagoon, north of Mulundu's village, live fish were tied onto women who danced with them to the ancestral graves.[96] Although the opening of the fishery on the correct date was of economic and ecological significance, the primary duty of the owners was not control of people's fishing effort but the control of nature facilitated by their long-standing connections to the lagoons. The objective of these rites was specific—a successful spawning system. Yet the form that the prayers took was common to the Luapula Valley and to most Bemba-speaking areas.[97] Generic cultural forms, stories, or praises were applied to site-specific resources and spirits.

In the catching of fish, there was little moderation. A song compares
a fishing net to a village hen:

> You are the hen who searches in the rubbish pits
> look from one side to the other.
> You are the pecking beak of a hen
> that leaves nothing in the way.[98]

The mother hen pecks at every last scrap of food left in the village, just as
the net should catch all fish that came across its path. (Fishermen even attached parts of a hen to their nets to invoke the spirit of a hungry hen.)
Although fishermen caught as much as they could, certain technological
limitations and ecological conditions checked levels of exploitation. The
kaboko fibers out of which nets were made were not very durable and
easily broke. Crocodiles and hippos often destroyed nets that had taken
weeks to manufacture. Despite the high levels of exploitation, fishing remained sustainable and seemed to have had little impact on the diversity
of fish species. In 1867, Livingstone claimed there were thirty-nine species of fish; in the early 1940s, prior to a severe decrease in species diversity due to targeted fishing practices (see chapter 4), Shila elders listed
some thirty-four types of fish with their own distinct praises and twenty-
two without any praises, all found in Lake Mweru or the Luapula River.[99]
    In precolonial times, location was more important than capital-
intensive fishing technology in ensuring large catches. Control exerted
by established clans over lucrative fishing areas limited and constrained
the rise of precolonial "big men," who would become more widespread
in the colonial period, with the decline of clan-based tenure rules, the
rise of capital-intensive forms of exploitation, and new markets.[100] Prior
to colonialism, fish were part of an important local exchange system,
but there were limited markets, at least compared to the future markets
of the urban Copperbelt (although fish were important for exchanges
with slave and ivory trading caravans). This meant that there was little
incentive for an individual to invest heavily in ensuring exclusive access
to the resource. Fish only translated into significant forms of wealth-
in-people through clan-based controls over fishing grounds and labor-
intensive investments like intricately constructed weirs that rested on
collective village labor rather than the capital of any single fisher or
trader.[101] Clan-based controls and labor-intensive fishing techniques
worked against the accumulation of wealth by ambitious individuals.
Slaves, ivory, and to a lesser extent salt were more important commodities than fish in the rise of trading lords across the region. This would

change with new technologies and new markets. As catches became concentrated in a few large nets and traded with urban markets, a class of big men would accumulate new types of wealth from the fishery. The established relationship between tenure, clan, and religious systems would rupture; successful fishers would be considered witches who had killed their relatives to chase fish into their nets.

Let us not preempt our story; before the arrival of the colonial regimes, a dynamic ancestral tradition dictated patterns of authority and resource management in the fishery. The nature of this authority depended on the type of incorporation into the Kazembe Kingdom, the local ecology, and levels of exploitation. From the rapids of Mambilima where the mpumbu spawned to the lagoon areas of Mofwe and Chimbofuma where the pale bred, fishers competed for the most prosperous fishing grounds. Conquered village leaders were integrated into the Kazembe Kingdom as owners of the lagoon who developed systems of ownership and control over contested fishing resources. However, even in the lagoons, villagers could not live on fish alone; agricultural production on the land also contributed to distinct types of village authority.

The Farm

As one ascends the plateau to the east of the valley, where most of the farms are located, a hill called Nakafwaya appears. Nakafwaya, meaning "the one who desires," was another famous woman in Lunda stories of conquest. She is praised as "Nakafwaya who wants to marry many different men" *(Nakafwaya uwafwaya ukupwa kubaume milongo)* because she married three successive Kazembes. Yet, unlike Nachituti, we are able to record the emergence of the Nakafwaya title in the nineteenth century and give her a historical presence that goes beyond that of a mythic charter. During the reign of Mwata Kazembe VI Chinyanta Munona (1853/54–62), Kazembe's brother, Kabwebwe, married a young woman called Yamfwa Kafuti. When the Mwata saw his sister-in-law, he decided to marry her and give his brother land as compensation. When Chinyanta died, Kafuti married Mwata Kazembe VII Muonga Sunkutu (1862–72), only to abandon him for the challenger to the throne, Mwata Kazembe VIII Chinkonkole (1872–72/73). Yamfwa Kafuti then became known as "Nakafwaya"; her name became a title succeeded by her younger sisters and sisters' daughters.[102] So important was Nakafwaya to the Lunda of the late nineteenth century that she is often associated with Nachituti. Indeed, the Kanyemba titleholder claims that

Nachituti and Nakfwaya were the same person.[103] This would explain
the final unanswered question behind the Nachituti story: Who is actually buried next to the Lunde graveyard for the kings? It seems likely
that someone of Nakafwaya's political influence and sway would be
buried near Lunde; she would then be called "Nachituti," as the story of
Nachituti's gift became more popular in the late nineteenth century.
The royal court of the twentieth century, sanctioned by Christianity,
would thereby avoid the improper sexual connotations of the title Nakafwaya and prevent any other queen *(mwadi)* or Nakafwaya titleholder
from laying claim to a burial near the royal graveyard. It could have
also been an attempt to hide the grave of Nakafwaya from "witches"—
according to testimony collected by Campbell, the dead bodies of Nakafwaya and Kazembe had been "stripped" by members of the Luba
"Buyembe" society.[104] Luapula's Lunda historians, however, insist that
the grave on the outskirts of Lunde is indeed that of Nachituti.

Luapulans are unsure why the hill toward the plateau is named after
Nakafwaya. According to Dyulu Kabeya, when Kazembe went on his
tours of the countryside he would rest at a place on this hill prepared by
Nakafwaya.[105] Yet on another level, Nakafwaya is associated with the favorite food of the valley, cassava or *tute*.[106] The original Nakafwaya
was reputed to have been proud of her cassava fields; in 1867, Livingstone
observed six to twelve men carrying Nakafwaya to her garden, where
she was "very attentive" to her cassava crop: "A number of men run
before her, brandishing swords and battle axes, and one beats a hollow
instrument, giving warning to passengers to clear the way: she has two
enormous pipes ready filled for her smoking. She is very attentive to her
agriculture; cassava is the chief product; sweet potatoes, maize, sorghum, pinesetum, millet, ground-nuts, cotton."[107] The richest lagoon
area, known as Kanaya, meaning the making of porridge, is also known
as Nakafwaya because of its fertile floodplains. Naming the hill Nakafwaya was a reminder that the cultivation of the land that emerges from
the swamps was the task of woman and that its produce, cassava, was
the gift of this very prominent Lunda woman.

Luapulans claim that cassava first arrived with the Lunda and took
over from the older staples, sorghum, millet, yam, and sweet potato.[108]
Cassava spread along the trade routes stretching from the Portuguese
bases in Angola on the west coast to the Kazembe Kingdom. In Mweru-
Luapula, it began as a food for trading elites and the royal Lunda court.
Gradually, through the nineteenth century, it became more popular
among the ordinary inhabitants.[109] When Lacerda's expedition visited

the valley in 1798, cassava was an important food for trading elites. The *pombeiros* in 1806–10 also reported cultivation and consumption in the main trading centers; but they both make clear that millet and sorghum were popular, especially for the production of beer.[110] When Livingstone visited the valley, however, it seems that cassava was the crop of both the elite and commoners. "Cassava is very extensively cultivated indeed," he reported in 1867, "so generally is this plant grown that it is impossible to know which is town and which is country: every hut has a plantation around it."[111] The cultivation of cassava differed from the finger millet still found on the Bemba plateau by the end of the nineteenth century, which lends credence to local claims that cassava came with migrants or traders from the west.[112]

While lacking in nutritional value, cassava was high in calorie yield and offered certain advantages as a crop. Cassava cultivated on prepared mounds *(mputa)* did not require the *chitemene* system common to the plateau cultivation of millet and could withstand the heavy rainy season.[113] The fertile soils of the valley floor combined with the lack of trees meant that *chitemene* agriculture had not been widespread, which could have made the cultivation of cassava easier to introduce. Outside of the fertile floodplains, the roots could grow without much fertilizer and were relatively drought resistant.[114] Moreover, the root could remain in the ground for up to four years, to be harvested only when needed, thus eliminating the need for storage and minimizing the risks associated with roaming war parties who pillaged stores of food. Finally, in addition to the calorie yield of the root, women used the leaves of young cassava plants to make a spinach-like dish *(katapa)*.

The advantages of cassava production were not evident to all farmers. At least fifty years or more after it was introduced to the Bemba Plateau, it had yet to gain widespread use, despite the fact that the plateau soils are less fertile than the valley soils and the plateau inhabitants could have taken advantage of this crop, or at least diversified their crops. Why, then, did cassava gain dominance in Luapula but not on the plateau? The advantages of cassava only become clear if the gendered division of labor and the respective costs of male and female labor are considered. Millet and sorghum farming required more involvement by men in the preparation of the *chitemene* fields, in particular in cutting and burning the branches. By contrast, cassava did not require new *chitemene* fields and the burden of production fell on women, who cultivated, harvested, and prepared the root. Cassava was easier to plant and harvest than millet and sorghum, but intensive labor was needed to prepare the

mounds and transform the root into an edible food. This involved soak-
ing and drying the root for several days before it could be pounded into
the flour used for making thick porridge called *ubwali*.

On the Bemba Plateau, cassava replaced millet cultivation only
when men migrated to the copper mines, withdrew from farming, and
left cultivation in the hands of women.[115] The withdrawal of male labor
from agriculture in the Luapula Valley, by contrast, occurred long before the onset of migration to the copper mines. Close to the fishery and
the eastern Lunda heartland, men were involved in a variety of nonag-
ricultural tasks. Men set the nets, constructed weirs and traps, and fished
in canoes on the river and lake (although women undertook certain
forms of trap and chisense fishing).[116] Besides fishing, capturing hippos
for their delicious meat was an especially popular pursuit. The Shila
gave names to individual hippos and thought of them as their "goats."[117]
When the mud flats of the lagoons became inundated, men killed big
game, like elephants and buffalo, trapped in the mud, in part to secure
the ivory that Kazembe required for export in the nineteenth century.[118]
Men were also involved in warfare, either conscripted by the Lunda or
defended their own villages.

As men in the Luapula Valley took to other tasks, women cultivated
and processed the necessary crops. The relative benefit of cassava for
women is the subject of some debate. Achim van Oppen argues that the
western Lunda adoption of cassava allowed women opportunities for
greater economic autonomy from men by trading cassava with the slave
and ivory traders. Anita Spring and Art Hansen, on the other hand
have argued that in general cassava increased burdens of women in the
fields and in processing the crop.[119] Of course, greater autonomy and
greater labor burdens for women are by no means mutually exclusive. A
less benign view of the intensification of female agricultural labor in the
nineteenth century would be the rise of a more established slave mode
of production that generally revolved around female slaves. But cassava
also provided opportunities for elite women.[120] In Luapula, elite women
had so much status and autonomy that toward the end of the nineteenth century, the Victorian-minded missionary Dan Crawford termed
them "Black Suffragettes." He also recorded the existence of a powerful
women's association, perhaps similar to Ubutwa, called *Ubulinda*.[121]
Whatever their relative economic and political status, instead of crops
that required male labor to prepare *chitemene* fields, Luapula's women
planted cassava in mounds, harvested it, and prepared it when needed.
The cultivation of cassava was suited to Mweru-Luapula's environment

and its gendered division of labor, which it tended to reinforce. In the nineteenth century, the fishermen and hunters contributed to the tribute required by the Kazembe; women labored in the fields and plantations.

In the same way as owners of the lagoon mediated access to the fishery, owners of the land supervised access to limited land. In the valley, fertile areas near the river's edge were limited and highly sought after by the nineteenth century.[122] The relatively high population density in the valley contributed to the importance of owners of the land. Koni, the Goat Clan elder who combined the duties of a Lunda aristocrat and the role of an owner of the land, looked after the area that surrounded the sacred waterfall described as *ichitutawile* (music without rhythm) and Nakafwaya's hill.[123] He paid tribute to Kazembe with natural produce like honey and mushrooms as well as millet and cassava and would bring thatch or timber on the Mwata's request. There were ritual obligations to the land; each year he would cover himself in white cloth and clay and go to the sacred waterfall to offer a sacrifice of goats and chickens to the ancestral spirits.[124] Such ceremonies were duties to the ancestors who had lived and died on the land and to the nature spirits who would ensure a fruitful harvest. Like the rituals that opened the fishery, the rites of the owners of the land ensured that the spirits of the bush rewarded the labor of people.[125]

Unlike the sparsely populated plateau areas, the people of the valley had to secure access to limited land. There was not much uninhabited, forested land that could be used for *chitemene* agriculture. Combined with limited land was a shortage of male labor and an intensification of female agricultural labor. These factors led to the popularity of cassava, which could be cultivated and prepared without men and without forests. The shortage of land further contributed to the importance of clans and owners of the land, who were responsible for assigning land for cultivation and for mediation with the spirits of the bush. The duties of the owners of the land vis-à-vis the land and the Kazembe Kingdom were articulated in stories of conquest that placed them within a network of perpetual kin and made them part of the Kazembe Kingdom.

Conclusions

When I first arrived in the valley, an old respected businessman, Paul Chisakula, tried to explain to me how Kazembe's people came to Luapula. "The Lunda conquered us by marrying our women."[126] It took me several years to fully appreciate this lucid refrain at the heart of the

Nachituti narrative. The Shila elders provided the missionary Edouard Labrecque with a similar explanation in the early 1940s: "The Lunda inherited the Shila's country when they married Shila women. The Shila were many, the Lunda few."[127] Not only did Kazembe marry Nachituti, in the archetypical story of conquest, but clan heads gave *ntombo* brides to aristocrats and to Kazembe to secure influence. They became Lunda and the Lunda came to belong to Luapula. Kazembe recognized the autochthonous clans as "Shila," the fishers who owned the land and lakes. Conquerors and conquered negotiated and defined their roles through the telling of stories of conquest. Identity was embedded in this narrative landscape.

On Chisenga Island, in the heart of the valley, Nachituti's betrayal of her brother Nkuba was a linchpin of relations between conquerors and conquered, between those who owned people and those who owned the land and lakes. The story also suggests the autonomy and political agency of women. "To this day," the missionary Dan Crawford reported in 1889, "the common ruse of a crushed wife is to make a gracefully turned allusion to that revolutionary deed of a negress long ago, the covert threat in her hint being that what woman has done, woman can and will do."[128] Nachituti's gift explained reciprocal relationships between the Kazembe Kingdom, aristocrats, and owners of the land and lagoons. But these relationships were not without exploitation and force. The Shila elders continued to tell Labrecque that "all paid tribute to the fierce messengers of Mwata Kazembe, the great chief of the Lunda."[129]

Stories of conquest translated ancestral rights over the land and its resources into the present. "Certes," Dan Crawford wrote, "nothing can move a drowsy old African like a jag from past history."[130] Ian Cunnison also emphasized the importance of stories of the past: "History and interest in the past are here so all-pervading that they merit a somewhat wider treatment than they normally receive."[131] Stories of the past were like constitutions that governed the present. However, observers like Crawford and Cunnison underestimated the dynamism of a historiography that formed new stories and changed or forgot old ones. New stories would be incorporated into the present; the people of the valley even included Cunnison and Crawford, respectively nicknamed *kalanda imikowa* (one who talks of clans) and *konga abantu* (the enticer of people), in new narratives that wove the fabric of local authority.

In the 1890s, the officials of King Leopold II and the BSAC descended on the valley in increasing numbers and with unmatched firepower. The new conquerors of Luapula did not respect the old stories of conquest and the oral titles of the owners of the land and lagoons. They attempted to establish administrations that functioned according to the exigencies of their world and an increasingly global capitalist economy. Missionaries came to convert the people, administrators to civilize, and anthropologists to study them. Ichthyologists instructed fishers on rules that accorded with new, scientific discourses. As colonialism became entrenched, older stories of conquest would become entwined with colonial fables. The remainder of the book shall consider how the people of the valley, with their stories, political traditions, and resources confronted and incorporated the new conquerors and their coterie of commercial, religious, and scientific agents to remake the political ecology and economy of the valley.

2

The Colonial Net

Chiefs on a Colonial Border

A global ecological history might be written, one central epi-
sode of which turned upon the mis-match between English and
alien notions of property in land and the imperialist essays in
translation.

E. P. Thompson, *Customs in Common*

From the boardrooms of the European capitals, where in the 1880s
European diplomats and rulers shared what King Leopold II once
termed the "*magnifique gâteau africain,*" the Luapula Valley must have
seemed a tiny morsel.[1] Avid readers of missionaries and explorers like
David Livingstone and Henry Morton Stanley probably knew the
names of Lake Mweru and the Luapula River. After all, in 1873 Livingstone had died near the Luapula, which he believed to be the source of
the Nile. It was also home to "King Kazembe," described by occasional
Portuguese expeditions into the interior.[2] Yet it was hardly a focus of the
negotiations between the European diplomat-entrepreneurs at the series of conferences responsible for the division of Africa. Only several
years later, when the conquerors "pacified" local rulers and surveyed the
land, did the colonists gain an idea of their proclaimed possessions.[3]

In Mweru-Luapula, the nature of conquest led to the disintegration
of some of the more powerful precolonial polities. Msiri, the most prominent Katangan ruler in the late nineteenth century, was the first to fall to
Belgian mercenary forces. By the late nineteenth century, Msiri was involved in several conflicts; he had to quell frequent revolts by clients, and
his army was drained by an ongoing war with the Swahili trader Shimba
on Kilwa Island. He dealt with the increasing number of Europeans by
playing them off against one another and negotiating different treaties

with the Congo Free State and the BSAC. After an altercation during negotiations, one of King Leopold's mercenaries, Captain Bodson, shot and killed Msiri, leading to the collapse and disintegration of his tribute and trade polity. In King Leopold's Congo Free State, there was no Luapulan leader who remained powerful enough to take advantage of colonial conquest and reconstitute a following. Instead, Plymouth Brethren missionary Dan Crawford created a community of converts out of some of Msiri's former subjects and slaves; others fled and took refuge in their clans' villages.[4]

On the other side of the Luapula River, the conquest and incorporation of Mwata Kazembe's eastern Lunda kingdom into the colonial state went more smoothly and gave shape to local colonial institutions. Mwata Kazembe X Kanyembo Ntemena (reigned from 1884/5–1904) held back the agents of the BSAC for a number of years. In 1892, Ntemena paid tribute to the BSAC representative, Alfred Sharpe. Over the next few years Ntemena had contacts with Europeans, including Dan Crawford, who visited his capital, and a rubber trader whom he had permitted to build a house nearby. However, after the BSAC administrator Dr. Blair Watson established a post on the Kalungwishi River, near Lake Mweru, Ntemena became more antagonistic. In 1897 he refused to accept European rule and did not allow a British flag to be raised in his kingdom. He successfully repelled a group of local and Swahili soldiers led by Watson. Two years later, in 1899, Alfred Sharpe, then the governor of Nyasaland, returned with a company of Sikhs and Nyasaland armed forces. The colonial forces burned the Lunda capital to the ground. Ntemena escaped with his most important notables by crossing the Luapula. A few weeks later, a missionary escorted him back via Mambilima, where Henry J. Pomoroy had established the Johnston Falls mission in 1897–98. Ntemena agreed to BSAC suzerainty, and he rebuilt his capital at Mwansabombwe.[5]

The conquest of the Luapula Valley ruptured and then recreated the terrain of resource politics. Tenure rights, forms of ownership, and control over resources that developed during colonialism grew out of the engagement between colonial officers, the Kazembe Kingdom, Lunda aristocrats, and owners of the land and lagoons. In the Belgian Congo and Northern Rhodesia, as in most of colonial Africa, colonial authority rested on African "chiefs." In the Luapula Valley, the Kazembe royal family allied themselves with the British colonial regime and displaced Lunda aristocrats and owners of the land and lagoons as managers of what colonial officers thought was "tribal" property. The

Kazembes proved more able to adapt to conquest and more adept at manipulating the structures of colonial rule than the aristocrats and owners of the land and lagoons. Moreover, tenure systems that were defined through oral traditions like Nachituti's gift were far more difficult for colonial rulers to understand and appreciate than the Kazembes' rule by "tribal" right. Colonialism contributed to the consolidation and centralization of chiefly authority over the land and water resources of the valley while undermining tenure rights vested in owners of the land and lagoons.

On the plateau region directly east of the Luapula Valley, we see a similar process of consolidation by central chiefs and the divestment of local village and clan elders. Henrietta Moore and Megan Vaughan have argued that the association between Bemba identity, Bemba chiefship, and *chitemene* agriculture was not a vestige of a precolonial past, as Audrey Richards argued in the 1930s, but rather an outcome of the colonial encounter when a collaborating male elite engaged with an emergent colonial state. Bemba chiefship under Paramount Chief Chitimukulu became more closely allied to rituals of the land and the cutting of trees in the early twentieth century as raiding and slave trading declined as a source of authority and power. And as the BSAC grappled for control in this labor- and food-producing hinterland, they encouraged the adaptation and transformation of Chitimukulu's Bemba chiefship, which could provide them with greater political and economic leverage.[6] In the Luapula Valley, in a fashion similar to Chitimukulu's chiefship, the Kazembes redefined their political roles by securing control over resources and resource rent—in this case, access to the fishery and scarce riparian farmland.

In King Leopold's Congo Free State, following the cruel chaos of conquest and concessionaire exploitation, a few owners of the land and lagoons and Shila clan rulers were able to escape Kazembe's authority and become colonial chiefs. For example, in 1908, after BSAC authorities set fire to his canoes for not obeying colonial regulations regarding sleeping sickness, Nkuba fled Chisenga Island and became a chief on the western banks of the Luapula.[7] The Belgian colonial state, which succeeded the Congo Free State in 1908, placed resources under a formal state structure allied closely to colonial commercial interests rather than allocating them to chiefs. No chief with the same authority and power as Kazembe emerged to take control and redefine the rules of access to the fishery and farmlands. Instead, less influential chiefs were subordinated to Belgian officials attached to the colonial service. The colonial state closely supervised chiefs who were selected according to a combination of colonial pragmatism and hereditary principles. Even though some of these chiefs had previously held titles as owners, they had different and generally reduced powers and duties.[8]

In both Northern Rhodesia and the Belgian Congo, fragile colonial structures of governance undermined and replaced precolonial forms of resource ownership and management. Where the Lunda became chiefs, their rule depended less on the reciprocal forms of governance of the precolonial period than on a careful negotiation of interests between resentful and rebellious villagers on the one hand and modernizing colonial bureaucrats on the other. On both the Belgian- and British-ruled banks of the Luapula, precolonial forms of ownership were subordinated to a system of public or "tribal" property controlled by colonial chiefs and officials.

Copper and Fish in the Belgian Congo

In the Belgian Congo, the relationship of the colonial state to mining interests was a significant force in the making of local forms of authority, including control over the fishery. After the cruel abuses that led to the collapse of King Leopold's Congo Free State, the Belgian administration worked with expatriate capital to take responsibility for the *mise en valeur* of the colony. In the Katangan province of the Belgian Congo, large-scale expatriate capitalists played an important role in all sectors of the economy; the Belgian colonial state viewed its primary responsibility as the mediation between mining interests and rural African society. The "marriage of iron and rye" in Prussia, or perhaps more accurately the "uneasy union of maize and gold" in South Africa, found its counterpart in the early colonial world of Katanga with the growth of the copper industry and its insatiable appetite for Luapula's labor and fish.[9] Demand for labor in the Katangan copper mines and for fish to feed the workers were the economic forces that brought colonial capitalism to the Luapula Valley. Rural administrative policy conformed to these needs and attempted to oversee all economic and political activity in the villages.

An oft-cited summation of the Belgian colonial policy, officially termed "paternalism," refers to it as *dominer pour servir*, according to the term coined by the Belgian proconsul, Pierre Ryckmans: authoritarian colonial rule was justified by the rapid social and economic development of the colony.[10] Yet Belgian colonial policy, especially prior to

World War II, was a mélange of ideas that differed from one official to the next. Although policy was not strictly divided along ethnic lines, Flemish administrators like Louis Franck, colonial minister between 1918 and 1924, had more sympathy for "national autonomy" and favored a type of indirect rule, while Walloon administrators followed a more centralized policy. Moreover, Catholic missionaries advocated assimilation to wipe out any vestige of "paganism."[11] To appease all, colonial legislation combined features of direct and indirect rule. In addition to the prevarications in policy was the uneven application of any particular policy; in the end, the nature of colonial rule depended largely upon local conditions. In those areas crucial to the smooth running of the colonial economy, administrators played a heavy hand in the running of daily affairs. This was especially the case where precolonial political structures were thoroughly destroyed during "pacification." While the notorious early period of concessionaire exploitation, termed "red rubber," was not as devastating to Luapula's population as in other parts of the Congo Free State, colonial administrators, ivory traders, and labor recruitment agencies eroded precolonial forms of governance.

At first, colonial chiefs emerged through ongoing encounters between villagers and the nascent colonial state. Immediately after colonial conquest, local leaders feared contact with the colonial regime; many decided to appoint individuals to deal with the colonizers rather than risk personal engagement. After the benefits of colonial chieftaincy became evident, however, ambitious individuals who might have held marginal political positions collaborated with the colonial regime.[12] In 1906 King Leopold, concerned with revelations of abuses in the Congo Free State, formalized the position of colonial chiefs when he decreed that all Congolese must have a chief who would be partly responsible for judicial and administrative duties. King Leopold's officials began to invest so-called *chefs médailles* with authority to govern the surrounding villages.[13] That such colonial chiefs had rarely held the lion's share of political authority in precolonial villages would contribute to their limited authority in future years.

After the takeover of King Leopold's Congo Free State by Belgium in 1908, the relationship between an expatriate-staffed colonial state and collaborating chiefs was further formalized into an organized state structure. In 1910, the Comité Spécial du Katanga, the quasi-state agency that administered private and public holdings in Katanga since 1900, handed over governmental duties to the Belgian Congo; in 1914, Katanga became one of four provinces of the Belgian Congo. Katanga was further divided into four districts supervised by *commissaires* and these districts parceled into *territoires* ruled by *administrateurs*. Mweru-Luapula (the Belgians named it Luapula-Moëro) was in the *district du Haut Luapula* and the *district du Tanganyika Moëro*.[14] At the level of the *territoire, chefs médailles* would exercise certain administrative powers. If the *territoire* was considered too "ethnically diverse," as was the case in the lower Luapula Valley, it was further divided into *secteurs* and administered by chiefs representative of this assumed diversity. While the selection of chiefs was supposedly only made after lengthy local enquiries, in Mweru-Luapula most of the chiefs remained the same as those originally appointed by officials of the Congo Free State.[15]

From the 1920s, as part of ongoing attempts to consolidate and strengthen geographically dispersed colonial chiefs and officials, the administration embarked on a reorganization of rural government. This coincided with a wider colonial reorganization of provincial and district administration as part of a general drive toward greater administrative efficiency. In 1933, the colony was divided into six provinces, and Katanga Province was renamed Elisabethville Province, after its capital, and consisted of three instead of four districts, effectively further centralizing government.[16] Mweru-Luapula fell under a single district administration, which included much of the Copperbelt, the *district du Haut Katanga*.[17] These territorial adjustments reduced the size and influence of the district administration and, according to historian John Higginson, coincided with a growing power of the provincial secret police. Many more liberal administrators, including the *commissaire de district* responsible for Mweru-Luapula, Fernand Grevisse, left their posts.[18] At the same time as these provincewide reorganizations, chieftaincies were consolidated in an attempt to make them run on a more efficient basis, partly to increase rural production and tax revenues. By 1926, chiefs had formal judicial power in a local native tribunal, and in 1933 each chief or *secteur* head was put in charge of a "Native Treasury" or *caisse administratif des circonscriptions indigène*. These were but landmark provincial measures in what were constant and ongoing attempts to reorganize courts, treasuries, and the vagaries of chiefly rule.

During the first twenty years of Belgian colonialism, reforms were unevenly implemented and enforced. In Luapula, the number and diversity of precolonial rulers, including the direct vassals of Msiri and Kazembe's polities, owners of the land and lagoons, and ambitious aspirants made it difficult to unite the fishers behind single *chefferies*. Instead, owners of the land and lagoons and other chiefs were combined into centralized *secteurs* under the authority of a chief selected primarily for his loyalty to the government. These chiefs, even if they had not ruled in precolonial times, were not necessarily hated or even distrusted by villagers who recognized the need for a mediator with the colonial regimes. A popular song recorded in Chief Nkuba's new area proclaimed, "We have chiefs who are clever enough to speak in front of a white."[19] During tax collection, the most onerous task of a chief, the people fled into the bush and the chief would be left to offer an explanation to the district official. According to one villager, upon the arrival of the administrator, the chief's heart would "palpitate" with fear.[20]

On the other hand, colonial chiefs could be, and in many cases were, cruel toward their subjects. A Belgian colonial report praised Nkambo, a chief on the banks of the Luapula River, for his excellent performance even though he was "sometimes brutal, always despotic."[21] In another chiefdom adjacent to Nkambo, two men accused Chief Sapwe of whipping another to death; however, the *commissaire de district* ruled that the men only brought charges up because of "hatred of their chief."[22] Underlying these outbursts of cruelty and violence was the precarious authority of illegitimate chiefs who could not be relied on to implement and enforce colonial policy. Instead, the administration emphasized that their dispersed officials needed to make their presence felt. So in Kasenga, the territory under which most of the lower Luapula Valley fell, the *commissaire de district* rallied administrators and colonial officials to play a more active role in the running of everyday affairs. He complained that if all was well and peaceful, it was a result of favorable conditions, not administrative initiative.[23] In fact, colonial authority in the rural areas relied on the influence of Belgian colonial officials rather than chiefs—hence the constant appeal for greater colonial supervision.[24] In the Belgian Congo, colonial officials and not chiefs had the most influence over ownership, control, and allocation of land and water resources.

World War II increased the demand for copper and consequently for fish to feed the copper miners. The success of the mining industry depended on a stable fish supply to meet the food needs of the workforce, and the administration set out to further organize and commercialize the fishery. They taxed commercial fishers and traders; with the funds, they established a *fonds poisson*, which aimed to invest in technological innovation and develop regulations concerning fisheries. The administration made better quality nets available to fishers and tried to encourage the rise of larger-scale fishing ventures by establishing a fishing school and training boat builders. The *fonds poisson* also funded the *mission pisci-cole*, which conducted research, advised on legislation, and implemented regulations concerning the fisheries. Mweru-Luapula, as the most important fishery in the Belgian Congo, became their main focus.[25] Of the three distinct branches of the *mission piscicole*—research, economy, and propaganda/police—the last proved the most significant. Fish guards *(gardes-pêche* and *moniteurs-pêche)* were meant to educate local fishers about more efficient fishing techniques and prevent illegal fishing, but in fact the policing role became far more important than the pedagogic one.[26]

Although customary forms of resource control were acknowledged, and to a certain extent encouraged, the administration relied on its own agents and did not consider chiefs and local headmen trustworthy figures in establishing rules over access to the fishery and riparian farmlands. "Tradition" and traditional authorities could not be relied on to manage valuable resources. In 1948, a colonial official reported that even though colonial legislation conformed to some aspects of traditional fishing customs, there was an "intentional lack of comprehension" by chiefs and their subjects regarding new legislation.[27] And there was little incentive for chiefs to follow new rules, for unlike in neighboring Northern Rhodesia, the funds from taxing and licensing fishers did not contribute to a chief's *caisse administratif des circonscriptions indigène* (Native Treasury). Instead, state funds generated by the fishery remained in the *fonds poisson*, administered for the most part by Belgian colonial officials.

The Belgian administration in Mweru-Luapula was an uncomfortable and explosive mix of Belgian officials, roaming police forces, and sometimes brutal but ultimately politically and economically weak chiefs. Even while formal policy gave rights in resources to communal representatives like chiefs, these rights were firmly subordinated to the whims of colonial officials.[28] Chiefs, even if they were the historic owners of the land and lagoons, did not represent any significant source of village authority. The Belgian colonial state had ignored or at best undermined exclusionary rights held by owners of the land and lagoons and vested authority over what they considered to be economically strategic common resources in colonial officials.

Chiefs and Tenure Rights in Northern Rhodesia

Mwata Kazembe X Kanyembo Ntemena surrendered to the British in 1900. He immediately embarked on securing his political future in the new colonial state and convinced officials of the BSAC like Alfred

Sharpe, Blair Watson, and H. T. Harrington (nicknamed *Bwana Kijana,* or young master) to choose members of the royal family as chiefs and thus keep his network of authority intact.[29] However, the spread of the formal colonial state to the Luapula Valley was gradual. Although the first BSAC bases were near Lake Mweru, by 1908, Kawambwa had become the district headquarters, or "Boma," for the entire valley. The Kawambwa Boma was on the plateau. It took a day to journey to the valley and then several days to travel from one chief's village to the next. Compared to the Belgian Congo, with its administrative center on a navigable portion of the Luapula and joined by road to Elisabethville, Mweru-Luapula was a remote outpost for Northern Rhodesian officials. There was no all-weather road through the valley until 1947, and it was not a crucial labor-supply hinterland for the Northern Rhodesian Copperbelt. Most men from Luapula, even on the Northern Rhodesian side of the river, looked, or were recruited, for waged work on the Copperbelt of the Belgian Congo, which was nearer and more accessible than the Northern Rhodesian Copperbelt.

Greater intervention in the valley's affairs began when the BSAC implemented a series of ambitious and detested measures to combat sleeping sickness, which was detected in the lower Luapula Valley and on the shore of Lake Mweru. From 1908 to 1910, riparian villages were re-located to higher ground and labor recruitment by Union Minière du Haut Katanga (UMHK) suspended until 1911. Luapulans resisted these measures, and many of them, like Nkuba, relocated to the Belgian Congo, where anti-sleeping-sickness measures were not in place.[30] Kazembe took advantage of these disruptions and replaced the owners who fled to the Congo with loyal headmen, like Kashulwe, who came to rule Chisenga Island in Nkuba's place.[31] This burst of repressive administrative activity did not, however, herald longer and sustained administrative interest and development in the Luapula Valley. Even after the takeover of the colony by the Colonial Office from the BSAC in 1924, established patterns of administrative disinterest persisted. When the copper industry in Northern Rhodesia expanded in the late 1920s, fish were not considered an essential item in workers' rations, as they were in the Belgian Congo, since beef was more readily available. Thus, the colonial administration had little reason to pay attention to the region. As late as 1929, the Kawambwa district commissioner admitted in his report on a tour of the valley that "the close proximity of Elisabethville and the road system in connection therewith completely debar the possibility of competition with the Belgians."[32]

By then, owners of the land and lagoons and those aristocrats out of favor with the central court found that they had been subordinated to the authority of colonial chiefs generally drawn from Kazembe's own clan or family. During the reign of Mwata Kazembe XI Muonga Kapakata (1904–19), the aristocrats Kashiba and Mwinempanda and members of the royal family, Kambwali, Chiboshi, and Mukwampa, all secured large tracts of land and riparian villages to administer as chiefs.[33] Muonga ensured that his sons, like Mukwampa, or members of his own Rain Clan, like Chiboshi, received chieftaincies or headmenships.[34] Even where colonial officials gave non-Lunda rulers, like the Rat Clan's Mulundu and Lubunda, positions as chiefs, they were still subordinated to Kazembe.[35] The official colonial tenure arrangement of the Luapula Valley gave a centralized chief authority over the allocation of land and other natural resources to his "tribal" subjects. If land was relatively plentiful, as on the Bemba Plateau, this did not necessarily ratchet up the power of individual chiefs; however, in the Luapula Valley, with its limited fertile land and lucrative fishery, control by tribal chiefs consolidated and centralized authority under the eastern Lunda royal family.

Commercial changes in the 1930s began to set the pace for greater administrative interest in the valley. Colonial officials complained that the spread of the commercial economy due to trade with the Belgian Congo diminished the tenuous control of colonial officials and chiefs; the fishing villages were, according to the district commissioner, aggregations of "uncontrolled and detribalized natives concentrated for the sole purpose of making money."[36] And chiefs on the plateau complained that all their subjects had deserted their villages to exploit commercial possibilities in the fishery; the Chishinga chief, Mushota, was allegedly very "bitter about the steady migration of his people to the Luapula."[37] Colonial officers were especially concerned about the concentration of fishers and traders in Mulundu's village near the rapids of Mambilima.

Mulundu was the leader of the Rat Clan who, according to his oral tradition, had adopted the Lunda blacksmith Lubunda and was thus considered his perpetual "father." After the conquest of the valley by the Lunda in the eighteenth century, Mulundu paid tribute to Kazembe, who in turn recognized Mulundu as an autonomous ruler who could choose his own line of successors drawn from his matrilineage. Mulundu maintained his authority over the land through a series of rituals, many of which were connected to the Masombwe relic. After colonial conquest, however, the Northern Rhodesian administration paid little attention to the matrilineal succession of the Rat Clan and instead recognized the authority of Kazembe as the ruler of the entire valley. In 1932, when the administration required a local representative in Mulundu's area, they appointed Chief Nshinka Mulundu as a subordinate to Kazembe. This altered previous understandings of the relationship between Mulundu and Kazembe and tied both to the hierarchical chain of authority established by the colonial state.[38]

As the colonial administration began to consolidate Native Authorities and provide them with greater benefits, Nshinka Mulundu became increasingly concerned with his status as a subordinate chief within Kazembe's Lunda Native Authority. He contended that this subordinate status was not historically accurate; as the head of the Rat Clan he should be entitled to be the head of an independent Native Authority with its own Native Treasury. The colonial administration disagreed. For them the issue concerned the practical needs of local government. They argued that the profusion of small, independent chiefs undermined the Native Authorities' ability to work as viable units of local government under an "enlightened" elite.[39] Relations between Mulundu and the administration deteriorated, and in 1939 the district commissioner identified him as "very unstable." "Chief Mulundu," the district commissioner complained, "is far from the influence of the Boma and even from the enlightened members of the Lunda Native Authority. . . . A more prolonged and constant form of supervision and advice must be made available."[40]

Yet colonial doctrine and officials were not the only influences on the making of chiefs; village politics also played a decisive role. As Karen Fields points out, the position of a colonial chief was always tenuous, subject to a "double articulation" between chief and colonial officials on the one hand and chiefs and village subjects on the other.[41] Prior to the 1930s, Mulundu was not the sole authority in his village. He ruled with a changing alliance of clan and village elders. For example, the head of another matrilinealage, the Rain Clan, was charged with preserving the Masombwe relic, which Mulundu could only consult in the presence of the heads of five other clans.[42] In the early 1940s, the villagers found that the apparatus of political power had changed. When the colonial administration placed Mulundu under the authority of Kazembe many of the clan elders, some women, were deprived of their political roles. For the villagers the most important task of a ruler was the protection of people from crocodiles, lions, and witchcraft and the preservation of local resources. Mulundu had not protected the position of other clan leaders; moreover, he was now a servant of Kazembe and

African and European traders. Rumors circulated that Mulundu was a *munyama*, a vampire-man, who sold human meat and hearts to the Kaboko hospital or to the Catholic priests in Kasenga. The priests used the meat for magic or sold it to businessmen who canned it to sell to the people of the valley.[43] "They [the *bamunyama*] could do business through him by paying him something," claimed one village elder.[44] New commercial elites in tandem with the colonial authorities had bought the loyalty of Mulundu, the protector of the lands and lakes. If we consider Karen Field's "double articulation" between a chief and his subjects and a chief and the colonial administrators, the chief-subject side of the articulation was on the verge of collapse by the 1940s.

When the colonial authorities deposed Nshinka Mulundu in 1946, it was obvious that the other side of the double articulation had also collapsed. Local administrators had long complained of Mulundu's "ineffectiveness" and his lack of control over his people. For example, in 1944 unknown arsonists burnt down Johnston Falls mission (Mambilima), and Mulundu had little success in bringing the culprits to book.[45] In 1946, an opportunity arose to replace him. The chief accused a villager of committing "adultery" with one of his wives. He imposed a sentence of a £5 fine, locked the man up, and then put him to work for several days (in precolonial times illicit sexual intercourse with the wife of a ruler was one of the few crimes that justified death, as illustrated by the Shila version of Nkuba's killing of Chituti).[46] The man complained of his treatment to the district commissioner, who accused Nshinka Mulundu of misusing his judicial powers to rid himself of a romantic rival. The district commissioner, with the consent of Kazembe, recommended Mulundu's dethronement and expulsion to the governor. Given the *bamunyama* accusations, no villager opposed his dismissal. The governor forced Nshinka Mulundu to hand over his position to a colonial appointment, Chimambi Mulundu. Nshinka Mulundu conceded defeat, but in an act of defiance, refused to hand over the sacred Masombwe relic to his successor.[47]

It was easy enough for colonial officials to depose Nshinka Mulundu, especially with the support of Kazembe, who had become the linchpin of colonial rule in Luapula; however, Kazembe could also be a fragile link in the colonial chain of authority. Mwata Kazembe XI Muonga Kapakata had already alienated many of the more important aristocrats because of his preference for his own children and clan for positions in the colonial state. In 1920, Mwata Kazembe XII Chinyanta Kasasa, who had succeeded Muonga one year earlier, was found guilty

of "indecent assault" and "false imprisonment" of the wives of rebellious Shila subjects who refused to pay increased taxes.[48] Given that the
Kazembes often had to rely on force to collect tribute from Shila subjects
in precolonial times, this Shila rebellion was perhaps not as surprising as
the fact that Kazembe was brought to book and fined for his behavior.
Colonial officials were increasingly dissatisfied with the "despotic" rule
of the Kazembes.

Colonial officials continued to emphasize the urgency of administrative reform in Mweru-Luapula due to its growing commercial significance.[49] From the late 1920s, an array of legislation and directives facilitated colonial efforts to push chiefs along a "modernizing" track. The
Native Authorities and Native Courts Ordinance (1929) was followed by
the Native Treasury Ordinance (1936), which gave the Native Authorities that surrounded chiefs powers of revenue collection and made
them responsible for the payment of staff. However, in Mweru-Luapula,
this legislation either confirmed the appointments of the first two decades of colonial rule or further enhanced Kazembe's rule over lesser
chieftaincies.[50]

In 1935 Chinyanta Kasasa died and Mwata Kazembe XIII Chinkonkole, who would reign for the next five years succeeded the throne. Chinkonkole hardly measured up to colonial expectations of an enlightened
indirect ruler. The district commissioner, while on a joint tour of the villages with Chinkonkole, noted that nobody volunteered to carry Kazembe's *machila* (traveling hammock); for the district commissioner this
signaled a lack of respect for the Kazembe.[51] Chinkonkole was, according to the district commissioner, "an amiable old gentleman whose men-
tal condition is open to question."[52] He insisted, "The time has come for
a more progressive refinement of indirect rule which is based not entirely
on the traditional tribal institutions of the Lunda chiefs but has in it the
more democratic element of district councils on an elective basis."[53]

In the 1940s, as part of the drive toward political modernization, new
reforms were aimed at consolidating smaller subchieftaincies into Native
Authorities and subordinating them to Superior Native Authorities. Ex-
pert councilors were to guide the Native Authorities in what the administration considered to be a progressive and modern direction.[54] The reforms did not, however, involve the introduction of more democratic or
representative political structures; they "modernized" the administration by introducing "progressive" elements without undermining chiefs.
The changes were still built on the colonial chieftaincies created before
the indirect rule legislation had even been passed. Moreover, the control

of resources by "tribal" chiefs was further enhanced in 1947 with Native Trust legislation that placed local resources under the control of Native Authorities. The most important Native Authority in the valley remained the Lunda Native Authority presided over by Kazembe.

Kazembe accrued extra income from the Native Treasuries established in 1936. The Lunda Native Authority collected a portion of the fish licensing fee and a tax of a fish levy of 1/4d. per pound of fish paid by the traders. [55] The funds were supposed to be disbursed by the Native Authority to "develop" the fishery; yet the meanings of "development" for Native Authority chiefs and colonial administrators did not always coincide. According to anthropologist James Pritchett, for the Lunda-Ndembu of northwestern Zambia, development meant a strategic directing of funds to local individuals rather than any change in economic organization or surplus extraction.[56] In Luapula, the Native Authority funds intended for development enriched the chief and his retinue. The Lunda Native Treasury became one of the wealthiest across the entire territory of Northern Rhodesia and attracted a significant following.[57] By 1954, the Native Authority was given effective control over the implementation of fishing regulations and the collection of fishing-related revenues. Kazembe and his subchiefs and headmen became the most important resource managers and bureaucratic beneficiaries.

The connection of the lucrative Lunda Native Authority treasury to the fishing industry began to place a premium on a Lunda "tribal" identity. In 1937, before the real effect of the Native Treasury could be felt, colonial officers reported that Kazembe had little authority over the Luapula Valley's "absentee population of mine labour and a mixed collection of fish traders." For example, in Mulundu's and Lukwesa's chieftaincies, colonial officers reported that "[t]he village as a social unit does not really exist."[58] One year later, in 1938, the effects of the new Native Treasuries were evident. Colonial officers and Native Authorities could identify outsiders who did not belong to the area: "Natives who displayed a lack of manners, unusual in Native areas, were interrogated and in every case it was found that they were members of other tribes."[59] The importance of showing deference to the Lunda Native Authority and being a "tribal" subject of Kazembe increased as the Lunda chiefs gained funds from the fishery.

Fortunately for the colonial reformers, in 1941 Mwata Kazembe XIII Chinkonkole died and Shadreck Chinyanta became Mwata Kazembe XIV. Villagers and colonial officials remembered his nine-year reign as a highpoint for the Kazembe chieftaincy. Previously educated and employed in Elisabethville, Mwata Kazembe XIV Chinyanta could write and speak English and French fluently. Upon coming to the throne he appointed young men drawn from the educated elite to act as his advisors. He wrote the first history of the eastern Lunda in Bemba, entitled *Ifikolwe Fyandi na Bantu Bandi* (My ancestors and my people), which emphasized and laid down in writing the history of the Lunda conquest of Luapula, a history that colonial authorities could surely understand and appreciate as justification for Kazembe's rule.[60] Chinyanta created the Lunda National Association, perhaps to replace the colonial Lunda Native Authority, where representatives chosen from the region discussed policy and counseled the chief on issues pertaining to the fishery and to village life in general. A secretary kept minutes of the meetings and sent them to the local district official. The association constructed schools, offices, a clinic, and roads in the Lunda capital, Mwansabombwe. Chinyanta encouraged parents to send their children to school and visited many of the schools himself. Indeed, the leadership of Chinyanta set an important precedent for future inheritors to the throne.[61]

Colonial administrators supported Chinyanta's modernizing influences; they were less sanguine about his democratic reforms and alleged that some of his "ministerial" appointments had a "history of opposition to Europeans."[62] Nevertheless, Chinyanta was someone with whom colonial officials could work. Unlike his predecessors, he had worked in the urban towns of the Copperbelt. And to bring his modern and progressive vision for the valley to fruition he was prepared to deal with both colonial officials and with a progressive group of educated Africans. Luminaries like the future nationalist leader Dauti L. Yamba and the businessman Benjamin Kapapula were "ministers" in his National Association's "cabinet." Chinyanta thus straddled the "modern" worlds of colonial officials and urban African nationalists. In this sense, he proved an ideal collaborator. His son, the late Mwata Kazembe XVIII Munona Chinyanta, who grew up in the palace during his father's reign, described his father as "no less than a European because he was moving with time, planning ahead. When he took up the chieftainship people suspected that he was going to get married to a white lady because of what he was doing. He was a big planner, he was a developer . . . he was brown and fat . . . like a whiteman; that's why he was friends with the colonial administrators both in Congo and here in Kawambwa."[63]

Chinyanta managed to further strengthen his hold over the chiefs of the valley. Lunda subordinate chiefs—Kanyembo, Kambwali, Lukwesa, and Kashiba—were promoted above autonomous owners of the land

and aristocrats, and Kazembe's authority over them was tightened. Chinyanta became responsible for the selection and appointment of the Lunda chiefs, and his approval was required for the appointment of the Rat Clan chiefs Mulundu, Lubunda, and Katuta Kampemba.[64] In the south of the valley, the most loyal Lunda aristocrat, Kashiba, gained formal authority over the owners of the lagoon, Malebe and Nkomba.[65] By the 1950s, Chinyanta had succeeded in manipulating the levers of colonial power to ensure that most colonial chieftaincies were in the hands of the royal family or loyal aristocrats.

Chinyanta's rule also led to the decline of the reciprocal relationships brought about by the giving of *ntombo* brides. As a Christian, he refused to marry extensively and thereby deprived the aristocrats and clan elders of an important avenue of influence in the central court. He made some concessions to the aristocrats who had lost their *amayanga* lands; he allowed them to retain positions in the Native Court, a source of some income, even while the new, educated elite circumscribed their positions in the Lunda Native Authority.[66] At the installation of the successor to Chinyanta, Mwata Kazembe XV Brown Ngombe (reigned from 1951–57), Kalandala appealed to Brown Ngombe by referring to the time he had caught Nkuba and thereby brought Nachituti to Kazembe. "You see," Kalandala told Brown Ngombe, "it is Kashiba and I who set you in your place. Amongst the Lunda there is none greater than us. It is we who grant you the position of Kazembe, it is we who put you in daylight. Now you will give preference to others. Simply because we cannot write, can you deny us, the representatives of your ancestors, a living? If a European has children, some may go to school and earn money, others may not go to school; but will these for that reason be discarded by their parents? They will not. Their father will give them work with him and they will enjoy money. . . . I, who caught Nkuba, have nothing now."[67]

Even at the height of colonialism, the Kazembes did not exert absolute power over their subjects. Elements of local power loosely related to aristocrats, the owners of the land and lagoons, Shila clans in the valley, and the Chishinga clans toward the plateau, contested the new colonial networks of authority. The circulation of witchcraft allegations that accompanied the consolidation of political power by the Kazembes and their families best illustrates the complex mélange of sacred and secular political forces. A popular mourning song, a type of Luapula blues sung to a guitar, recorded in 1961 and still heard in the valley in the 1990s, laments the death of two successive Kazembes, Chinyanta (died 1950) and Mwata Kazembe XV Brown Ngombe (died 1957). The song combines issues of rivalry between chiefs during colonialism, rural-urban migrancy, growing rural wealth, and witchcraft. Sung by a migrant worker who was on the Copperbelt when he "heard the news" of Kazembe's death, it warns the succeeding Mwata Kazembe XVI Kanyembo Kapema (reigned from 1957–61), who was nicknamed "Hitler" because he gave the British such a hard time, that he will not live long for witchcraft abounds in Luapula. Two Kazembes are already dead as the Shila and Chishinga chiefs, Mulundu and Mushyota respectively, vie for authority and desire Kazembe's wealth, the "upstairs" house and "suit and tie."

> Mourners of Chibongo
> When Kazembe died
> I was not present
> The day I heard the news
> I heard Kazembe died in his palace
> In his suit and tie
>
> He died in one day and did not rot
> When Kabumbu heard
> He took leave
> Before he rotted and was buried
> Kabumbu arrived here
> Alas, he landed in death
>
> You bewitchers of the chiefs in the land of the Lunda
> Go and succeed
> Mwata Kabumbu is dead
> If it is the house you fight for in the land of the Lunda
> Upstairs with a corrugated iron roof
>
> Mulundu and Mushyota
> They fight to succeed Mwata
> We told Mulundu not to succeed
>
> Even though you have succeeded
> Kanyembo you won't last
> Because you do not know what killed Mwata
>
> Now we have Kanyembo
> Kanyembo is our chief in the land of the Lunda
> We have also heard at Musangu, brother
> That Kanyembo is about to die

The suit left by Kabumbu
Cannot be worn for he is sick

Even though you have succeeded
Kanyembo you won't last long
Because you don't know what killed Mwata

You people, enthrone a white person
They won't kill him
Because he is government.[68]

Colonialism had entrenched the Kazembes' formal authority, but memories of autochthonous charters of ownership challenged colonial chiefs and acted as informal forms of ownership and title. These threats were a rehashing of old rivalries recorded in the stories of conquest over the local owners of the land and lagoons that responded to new social and political realities. The Kazembes managed to dominate the owners of the land and lagoons by forging close ties with the colonial state, changing the previous balance of power between Lunda rulers and owners. However, the Shila owners resented their subordination to Mwata Kazembe's Native Authority and the Chishinga were jealous of Kazembe's newfound wealth and the fact that many of their previous subjects, plateau dwellers, had migrated to the valley to take advantage of the fishery, thus further decreasing their followings and their tax base. According to such songs, the Shila and Chishinga avenged themselves by using their "magic"—the privileged ties that the owners of the land and lagoons had to the natural and ancestral spirits of the valley.[69] Since Kazembe was vulnerable to the jealousy of such rulers, the chieftaincy might as well be given to a white person who cannot be killed by witchcraft "because he is the government."

The Lunda chiefs had managed to secure appointments in the colonial state apparatus at the expense of the owners and the aristocrats. Nevertheless, villagers warned that the accumulation of political power came with a price: the Kazembes should beware of the intrigue and jealousy of those left out by colonial arrangements of power and authority. The owners of the land and lagoons could still employ their ties to the land and lakes to harm the Kazembes. Colonialism in Northern Rhodesia had restructured the politics of resource tenure from oral forms of title held by the heads of clans to the rule of colonial chiefs and officials. However, chiefs still had to contend with challenges from their rivals and subjects.

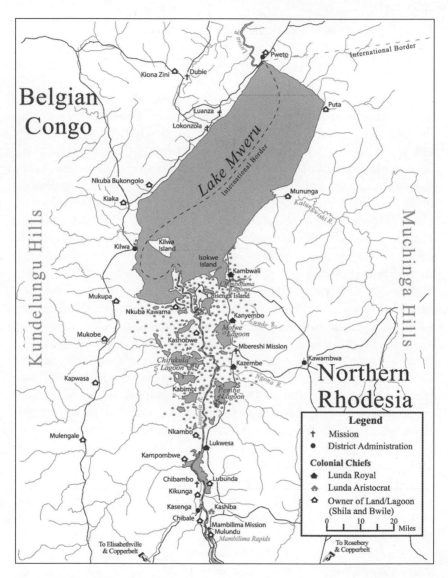

Map 3. Colonial Mweru-Luapula, 1940s–1950s.

Owners of the Land and Chiefs of Tribes

During my visits to the Luapula Valley, I frequently discussed what had happened to the spirits of the land with clan elders and those who still called themselves owners of the land or owners of the lagoons. In one village, next to the floodplains of the Luapula River, I was told of an old shrine, a spring called Chishima. Privileged elders had performed rituals to satisfy spirits *(ingulu)* who took the form of two pythons and guaranteed the miracles of nature, a role commonly played by snakes across the region.[70] According to this owner of the lagoon, the pythons ensured that the water from the spring was clear and delicious to drink. A lush tree provided shade over the spring and it was a favorite place to gather, collect water, and bathe. About fifty years ago, at the height of colonialism, anthropologist Ian Cunnison, nicknamed the one who talks of clans *(Kalanda mikowa),* came to study the people of the valley and their clan traditions. The nature spirit shrines intrigued him, especially the spring, which was only a few hundred feet from the mobile home where he stayed. He allegedly asked whether he could perform the rituals. "After Kalanda Mikowa [Ian Cunnison] came to the Chishima fountain to perform rituals, the snakes disappeared," claimed Moses Mwelwa Kasau, a boy at the time of Cunnison's visit. "Kalanda Mikowa had asked Chibulwa, the village headman at Chishima, if he could perform the rituals. People agreed and he performed the prayers. But the spirits *[ingulu]* disagreed and instead of water coming from the spring, only mud came, and the snakes disappeared from the spring. So you Europeans caused the disappearance of our rituals. No more miracles occur since the culture of the Europeans *[ulutambi wa umusungu]* is different to ours."[71] Perhaps cultural conflict and the interventions of skeptical anthropologists did not lead to the disappearance of the snakes; but colonial officers and chiefs displaced or at least challenged the authority and tenure rights of the owners of the land and lagoons.

The change was not simply a reorientation of political authority from owners to Lunda chiefs but involved a different form of resource management. In a comparable case study of the Nunu fishers on the lower Zaire River, Robert Harms has argued that "[t]he bureaucratic activities of colonial chiefs bore little resemblance to the largely ritual activities of the precolonial Nunu guardians."[72] In Mweru-Luapula, one way of gauging the change is to consider the differences between agents of the chiefs responsible for enforcing laws called village headmen *(umwine mushi)* and the owners of the land and lagoons.[73] With the augmentation of chiefly power during colonialism, colonial officials insisted that chiefs have local representatives in all the villages. Previously such representatives were the aristocrats such as Kalandala or the owners of the land and lagoons such as Nkuba. However, since the colonial demand for village representatives did not match the existing geography and given duties of owners and Lunda aristocrats, networks of headmen under the chiefs were established. William Katwe, an owner of the lagoon appointed by Mwata Kazembe, explained the difference between the chief's network of headmen and an owner of the lagoon: "A *mwinemushi* [headman] deals with the government and is registered by the Boma [government offices], while a *mwinekabanda* [owner of the lagoon] just works with the chief."[74] Owners of the lagoon were awarded with Lunda relics called *akatasa* and were responsible for praying to the spirits and throwing white clay *(ulupemba)* and red dye *(inkula)* into the river before fish could be caught. A headman had none of these ritual duties.[75] Or, as the Goat Clan elder Chibwidi put it, "*Mwinekabanda* are responsible for the rivers and produce; *mwinemushi* looks after the people in the village."[76]

While I recorded these descriptions well into the postcolonial period, they reveal two different systems of authority at work: Headmen looked after people while owners of the land and lagoons were responsible for the land, lakes, rivers, and their produce. The genesis of this bifurcated form of authority, control over people on the one hand and land and water resources on the other, dates back to the conquest of the Luapula Valley by Kazembe. As argued in the previous chapter, it was rehearsed in the story of Nachituti's gift of the land and lakes to Mwata Kazembe, which recognized local forms of ownership as distinct from the rule of conquerors. Mwata Kazembe praised himself as one who was given "lands and people" to rule while others ruled only goats and sheep (but "owned" the land and lakes).[77]

The bifurcation between rulers and owners was further accentuated and transformed in the colonial period as the Kazembes managed to assert control through colonial chieftaincies. According to colonial ideas, property belonged to a "tribe" and was vested in the colonial chief. Local headmen enforced a chief's rules and regulations through the control over people—for example, enforcing restrictions on fishing or, in other parts of Africa, cattle dipping or anti-erosion regulations. For Kazembe and for his village headmen, people, conceived of in terms of "tribal" affiliation, were the object of authority. The owners of the land

and lagoons, by contrast, had owned the land and lakes through their relationships with ancestral and nature spirits. They could not prevent fishers from fishing—only those who control people could do that—but they could ensure a good catch by performing the appropriate rituals before fishing commenced. This was what the "opening of the fishery" *(ukufungule isabi)* by the owners of the lagoons was about; performing the correct rituals to satisfy nature and the ancestors. Such ownership of resources was tied to the welfare of people; as Schoffeleers points out, a primary feature of "ecological religion" was a "social interpretation of the environmental process."[78] If the fish did not spawn, for example, the problems were linked to both societal imbalances and the ancestral world. Owners ensured, or at least encouraged, the harmony of ecological, spiritual, and societal forces.

Environmental and economic regulations over "tribal" property under colonialism came to rest on an entirely different principle: the regulation of people considered to be members of a tribe. Colonialism vested authority in a "tribal" chief who could prohibit people from fishing in certain areas or during certain times of the year; they acted through their control over their subjects.[79] Unsurprisingly, those rulers who had previously held positions of power over people rather than natural resources, like the Kazembes, were most able to work with this new system of governance. Rules over people replaced the rules of the land and lakes. This led to the marginalization of an ecological ideology that had integrated discourses about society with those about nature. The new chiefly bureaucracy and colonial government separated people and nature; nature became an object acted on by people, rather than an integral part of societal forces.

The distancing of political authority over the lands and lakes from the owners of the land and lagoons meant that stories like that of Nachituti's gift no longer represented formal charters or rights to the land and lakes. Prior to colonialism, the integration of people and their environments through such stories vested natural resources in local representatives who belonged to the lands. Under such a system the "commons" was not open access but had certain charters and forms of ownership. Colonial laws did not recognize such autochthonous charters as acceptable statements of ownership or even control over the land and lakes. Henceforth, access would be tied to the authority of the state and its local agents, whether expatriate officials or chiefs. This facilitated the creation of a "commons," exploited by individuals who justified their rights to resources by their "tribal" affiliations.

Conclusions

For precolonial rulers, the profits and pitfalls of colonialism were un-evenly spread. The Kazembes managed to negotiate the contours of the colonial political terrain; they collaborated on their own terms and gained what benefits they could from alliance with the colonial adminis-tration while attempting to maintain respect and legitimacy within their communities. The Kazembes reconstituted a network of Lunda chiefs related to them—the Lunda "family" did not perish with colonialism. Moreover, within the colonial state structure, the Kazembes managed to subordinate aristocrats and owners of the land and lagoons to their Lunda Native Authority. After 1941, the Kazembes and their retinue became the dominant political force in the Luapula Valley, controlling access to the fishery by allocating fishing licenses and enforcing regu-lations. In response to this, villagers challenged the authority of the Ka-zembes by mobilizing around local leaders such as the owners of the land and lagoons.

On the other side of the river, in the Belgian Congo, despite escap-ing the authority of the Kazembe Kingdom, owners of the land and lagoons had little success in maintaining charters of ownership during the early colonial period due to the combined power of concessionaire interests and the colonial state. Instead of chiefs, colonial bureaucracies staffed by Belgian officials managed the affairs of the fishery. They col-lected tax from traders, encouraged large-scale fishing ventures, con-ducted research, and policed the fishery. In both Northern Rhodesia and the Belgian Congo, a colonial net of authority spread across the valley. It was different from precolonial forms of governance, which were legitimized by stories that defined ancestral ties to the land, river, and lake. Instead of rulers who managed resources through ritual inter-ventions that ensured autochthones the privilege to farm on the land and fish in the lakes, colonial officials and chiefs decided on rules of ac-cess to the fishery and to the land; they governed over people conceived of in terms of tribal units.

The authority of colonial chiefs and bureaucrats was precarious due to their limited capacity to police fishers and traders: the fibers of the colonial net were too flimsy to control the fishers, traders, and farmers. Older rules of access to the wealth of the fishery had been transformed, but not eradicated. The people of the valley still remembered the stories of the clans that "owned" the land and lakes and articulated them as a challenge and an alternative to rule by colonial chiefs. But from below, new corporate groups were also replacing the clan system of ownership. Social networks based on entrepreneurial big men and their families and evangelical Christian churches had begun to challenge the authority of both colonial chiefs and owners.

3

The Meanings of Wealth

People and Things

Mike Kolala, a prosperous farmer and politician in the Luapula Valley in the 1990s, was proud to describe his grandfather's entrepreneurial endeavors:

> My grandfather was a businessman. He used to buy fish caught on Lake Mweru and take them to sell on the Copperbelt in Mufulira or Luanshya. After some time, he bought his first vehicle, and in 1953 he bought a shop along the Kazembe-Kashiba road . . . with the help of his friend, Mulewambola, who heard that a white man was selling because of the Federation issue [1953]. Mulewambola went to my grandmother and told her what was happening. At that time there was only £7 in the house and that £7 was paid for the shop. When grandfather came he was very pleased with Mulewambola, so he entrusted him as shopkeeper. They succeeded as traders; they were known throughout Luapula, and earned a lot of money.[1]

Life stories of the men of Mweru-Luapula like that of Kolala's grandfather, Charles Harrington, one of the many sons left behind in the valley by the colonial official H. T. Harrington *(Bwana Kijana)*, celebrate entrepreneurship and the accumulation of monetary wealth. The stories usually emphasize the ties of friendship and family that enabled the rise of their businesses. Success is then measured by the spread of the businesses' reputations and the amount of money that the entrepreneurs managed to accumulate.

The several terms that indicate "wealth" in present-day Luapula Valley testify to its past meanings, manifestations, and strategies for accumulation. *Ubukankâla* means the wealth of a "big man" *(umukankâla,* pl. *abakankâla).*[2] Its most traditional usage indicates wealth represented by the number of followers, children, or other dependents that an individual managed to attract, maintain, and work for him or her. On the other hand, there is *ubunonshi*, which means commerce or wealth through commerce, and those who participate in it are *abanonshi* (sing. *umunonshi*). Wealth of any type, through trade or labor, allows for accumulation; of money, *ulupiya* (perhaps from *lupa*, the palm of the hand) or *ndalama* (perhaps from *ndâla*, that which waits overnight or a season until its value is realized), of treasures *(chuma)*, and of commodities *(ifintu)*.[3] Those who attain wealth can then extend credit *(nkongole)*, which may be paid back in farm produce or fish.

This chapter explores the strategies to accumulate things, people, and money (or other instruments of credit) in Luapula's predominantly "marketable but not bankable" economy during the colonial period.[4] In the first half of the twentieth century, the valley's political economy incorporated fishers' and traders' commercial networks that stretched from the fishing camps of Mweru-Luapula to the growing urban areas of the central African Copperbelt. Predominantly male villagers began businesses through credit extended by expatriate traders or with limited capital acquired from fishing, trading, or working in the nearby mining towns. Traders exported fish to the urban areas and imported urban goods into the valley. Many of these entrepreneurs attempted to expand their business ventures, but only a few managed to become wealthy and powerful individuals, big men. Others remained with their small-scale, capital-starved businesses, weathering the storms of political, ecological, and economic change.

The people of the valley identified several different agents within this emergent rural elite. Fishers sold their produce to Congolese-based expatriate *commerçants*,[5] who supplied the copper mines in Elisabethville (present-day Lubumbashi) with workers' fish rations. Africans also traded significant amounts of rural produce with the Copperbelt towns. Luapulans termed those involved in either urban trade or wage labor *abanonshi* (sing. *umunonshi:* a person receiving remuneration through commerce). The *abanonshi* earned a salary or traded rural produce in the mining towns of the Belgian Congo or Northern Rhodesia; they benefited from the urban markets' demand for produce and labor, and by mobilizing village labor they expanded the rural economy. The opposite flow of urban goods into the valley led to the rise of even smaller-scale traders who sold their wares in the villages (these traders were often called *komelesa*, after *commerçant*). While they traded urban goods, these itinerant traders were dependent on limited rural markets. Deprived of capital, they relied on credit from the wealthier expatriate *commerçants* who owned stores on the Congolese side of the Luapula.[6]

Local trade in salt, fish, and agricultural products and long-distance trade in slaves, ivory, copper, and textiles with the Lunda heartland, central Tanzania and the Swahili coast, and Portuguese outposts on the Zambezi had been a feature of Luapula's political economy at least since the mid-eighteenth century and probably much earlier. Commodities like copper, iron, and textiles were precolonial currencies.[7] From the 1910s however, the diversity of goods offered as wealth that could be distributed to dependents far surpassed that of the precolonial period. Textiles were still important, but fashionable clothes and shoes were more desirable. Building materials like brick, glass, and corrugated iron roofing, tinned food items, soap, boats built of planks instead of dugout canoes, and nets made of durable nylon or used truck tires all became sought-after items that could be distributed in exchange for money or on credit. So money, in particular Congolese francs, became a sign of wealth, in addition to a necessity to pay colonial tax. Many of the goods were acquired on credit, not for the promise of future payment, but for the recognition of dependency and the promise of future labor that accompanied such dependency. Fish traders would distribute nets and other urban goods in exchange for a promised share of the fishers' future catches. In this sense, the new exchange economy of the Luapula Valley was articulated with a political economy of use values. For entrepreneurs in the Luapula Valley, the value of a good was still measured by the labor that they could expect from its distribution to their fishing and farming clients. Profits were measured by the difference between the cost of rural labor in terms of the bundles of goods demanded by fishers and farmers and the exchange value of fish in the urban markets.

During the early colonial period, men controlled the profits of the fishery and rural-urban trade. Rural businesses drew on the labor of women—wives and unmarried, divorced, or widowed sisters—but profits remained in the hands of men who tried to restrict distribution to their wives and affinal kin. Big men used these commercial opportunities to consolidate control over their children and bilateral ties within their own family *(ulupwa)*, while undermining the claims of their wives' matrikin, in particular their brothers and mothers' brothers. Men attempted to use colonial structures such as Native Authorities to further protect their wealth and insulate themselves from claims by wives and their families. By the 1940s, an increasing number of women made inroads into the fish trade, and a few of them managed to become rural-urban traders independent of husbands, leading the way for the emergence of a class of "big women," able to exert influence over their own children and matrikin. Thus, while commerce and a monetized economy initially consolidated the position of men over their families—as Audrey Richards observed on the Bemba Plateau[8]—a few women were able to use the fish trade to carve out a commercial role for themselves.

Historians of Africa have often underestimated how closely intertwined economic and social developments were with cultural and religious change. In part, this oversight is due to reliance on colonial records, which separated and often opposed religious and economic spheres. "In the Luapula Valley, as elsewhere," a Northern Rhodesian colonial official claimed, "the villagers' ruling passion is not religion but money."[9] However, entrepreneurship and the accumulation of money were not an alternative to religion, a kind of sublimation of religious desires, as hoped by colonial administrators concerned with the influence of evangelical churches. Wealth fed directly into rank and status. Big men purchased status and influence in established corporate groups or developed hierarchies of rank and status in new associations like churches. In a similar fashion to the conversion of wealth from Atlantic commerce into rank in Igbo associations illustrated by Jane Guyer, Luapula's commercial networks contributed to the rise of a multilayered civil society organized by evangelical churches and witchcraft purification associations.[10] Moreover, the meanings of wealth and money were symbolically powerful and tied to religious belief. Conflicts between the new entrepreneurs and their families took the form of witchcraft accusations and counteraccusations, with chiefs, churches, and rulers mobilizing support for their patrons and clients. Underlying these conflicts was the rise of an *abankankâla* trading elite that sought to extricate itself from systems of wealth based on obligations toward numerous permanent indebted dependents to one based on the accumulation of more fungible instruments of credit, most notably money.

European *Commerçants* and African Fishers

Colonial officials in the Belgian Congo and Northern Rhodesia had different visions for the economic development of Mweru-Luapula. In the Belgian Congo, Mweru-Luapula was a close and crucial hinterland for the copper mines; colonial administrators invited expatriate fishermen and entrepreneurs to exploit Mweru-Lupaula's fishery, primarily to provide cheap food for urban Copperbelt workers. On the Northern Rhodesian side of the river, the BSAC, which ruled Northern Rhodesia until 1924, was less concerned with the development of Luapula's remote fishery and left it to African exploitation. Ultimately, however, commercial activities proved more important than state doctrine. African businessmen prospered in the Congo despite colonial restrictions; and in Northern Rhodesia, expatriate businessmen gained a foothold despite Native Trust legislation that attempted to constrain their economic activities. Toward the end of the colonial period, big businessmen— *commerçants* and *abakankâla*—stood at the helm of numerous cross-border networks of small-scale traders and producers.

The lucrative fish trade began with rising demand for food by workers on Katanga's copper mines. When the Belgians built a road from Elisabethville to Kasenga on the banks of the Luapula in 1918 and began to organize the trade according to the exigencies of the mining economy, the number and influence of expatriate *commerçants* grew.[11] Greeks based at Kasenga built large charcoal-driven boats, called *ifyombo* (sing. *ichombo*), to reach the remote fishing villages on the shores of Lake Mweru. Employing goods, food, or money *(franca)*, they purchased dried and smoked fish and returned to Kasenga where they loaded their produce on to trucks headed for Elisabethville.[12] In the 1930s, following the construction of several ice plants on the Congolese side of the Luapula, European traders monopolized the fresh fish trade. At this point, African traders were not competitive in the fresh fish trade because they lacked the capital required at all stages of marketing and did not have reliable customers like the chief mining company, UMHK.[13]

The Congolese authorities regarded the African itinerant trader *(commerçant ambulant)* as an irritating economic parasite. Ten years after the Belgians took the colony from King Leopold II and reformed the concessionaire system that had resulted in "red rubber," colonial officials still feared that uncontrolled small-scale traders would charge exorbitant prices for rural produce and thus deprive the larger colonial trading firms of their profits.[14] In Katanga, expensive rural produce would cut into the profits of mining companies who were reliant on cheap food for mine workers. If rural producers or traders earned too much, recruitment of cheap labor would be difficult; itinerant traders were *"une véritable nuisance."*[15] From 1917, the Belgians increased surveillance of these traders and began restricting their activities. In Mweru-Luapula, Kilwa's *commissaire de district* identified 3,768 traders who could earn several hundred francs from a single voyage between the rural and urban areas. Not only did these traders represent lost labor for the production of rural produce, the *commissaire de district* argued, they decreased the amount of labor available to European firms.[16] In response to these concerns, the

Belgians constructed a barrage of obstacles to small-scale traders, including measures that combated vagrancy, enforced mandatory trading licenses in 1925, and restricted trade to commercial centers that discouraged small-scale entrepreneurs by charging high rental fees.[17]

Although the administration united in opposition against what they considered to be unregulated commercialism by independent traders, their attitude toward African business in general was divided and fluctuated over time. The Great Depression and labor unrests in the early 1930s had substantially weakened UMHK and Katanga's colonial economy as well as threatened stable food supplies to the mines.[18] The administration became more willing to work with what it termed a "responsible" African commercial elite. In Mweru-Luapula, local administrators sought to cultivate a class of commercial African fishermen and a few wealthy African traders. Over the next decade, the effects of this would become apparent; in 1949, according to estimates submitted by the Congolese to Northern Rhodesian colonial officials, an estimated four thousand Congolese African fishermen earned a combined £100,000 per annum, or £25 per capita (the total earnings included several wealthy fishermen based on the islands of Isokwe and Kilwa who earned up to £900 each).[19] Two Congolese Africans each owned two trucks and a boat. Aroon Ngwashi, the best known, had three shops, two Chevrolet trucks, and a thirty-ton boat called *kwesha*, which means "to attempt." He succeeded, and by the 1950s his business had become one of the most prosperous on the Congolese side of the valley (in 1953 his Elisabethville bank account held the considerable sum of 17,746 francs).[20] The Belgian administration, although remaining concerned, had supported these businessmen. They began a credit scheme for African businessmen in 1938, and probably as a result of this scheme, the number of African businesses jumped from seven in 1940 to twenty in 1944 and twenty-seven in 1947.[21] However, expatriate businesses still had significantly more outlets per firm and were more numerous.

The expatriate fishers and traders generally came from Mediterranean fishing areas; many of them were Jewish or Greek, especially those from Rhodes Island, occupied by Italy from 1912 to 1943. Nissim Soriano arrived in Kasenga with his two sisters around 1938. He began to trade in fish, then opened a shop at Kashobwe, on the other side of the river from Mwata Kazembe's capital. He befriended the renowned Mwata Kazembe XIV Chinyanta Nankula and married his daughter. The sons from this marriage would become the most powerful businessmen on the Congolese side of the Luapula, if not in the entire Katangan

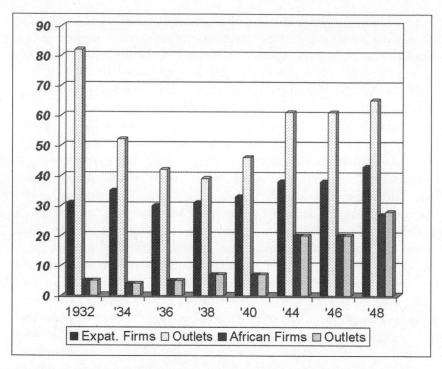

Figure 3. Expatriate and African firms and outlets in Kasenga, 1932–1948. Source: *Rapport Economique Annuel*, 1932–1949. From Kadiebwe Kapambu-Kabaswa-Kutuswa, "Monographie socio-économique du Territoire de Kasenga, 1933–1958." Mémoire, UNILU, 1976–1977, p. 83, based on records from the *Conseil de Province du Katanga*, *1932–1950*.

province (for more details on this influential family see, chapter 5).[22] Benson Leon arrived in the 1940s, began his business ventures by loaning goods to local African businessmen who would sell them on his behalf, before turning to the fish trade and opening a large shop in Kasenga.[23] The Greek Paraskevas brothers arrived in the 1930s and constructed three large boats for transporting fish to Kasenga. The fish were trucked to Elisabethville, where they were kept in large depots next to the railway line on route Munama (or *ndjandja* as it became known in Lubumbashi).[24] Vassili Malexenis, one of the best known and wealthiest Greeks in the area, began his fishing business during World War II when the Belgian administration encouraged Greek immigration so as to secure food supplies for the strategic copper mines. Later, he became known for his diesel-powered *ichombo*, the *Astride*, that plied the lake and collected fish.[25] Another Greek who came during the war years, Hadzi

Phillip, spread his long *kapopela* nets across the river to catch tons of mpumbu fish, transported on ice to Elisabethville. Like Nissim Soriano, many of these traders married in Luapula and had several sons who would become prominent businessmen.[26] Not all of the Europeans attained commercial success; Ian Cunnison recorded meeting several Europeans in the Congo, identified by the colonial authorities as "degenerates," who lived on the economic margins.[27]

Success for the *commerçants* often rested on the benefits that a white skin provided in a colonial context; they fostered contacts with the local administration, negotiated contracts with the mining companies, and mobilized capital through bank loans. In the rural areas, cheap African labor was always available in exchange for manufactured goods. A Belgian colonial administrator reported it comforting to hear the Greeks praise the wealth of the Congo and their resultant lifestyle: "The Congo is rich; for us it was good fortune to come here, and we never want to return to Greece or leave your colony. . . . It is rare to find a country where we can live as peacefully as in the Congo."[28] The alliance between the *commerçants* and the colonial state affected village perceptions of the European traders. Trade with an *umusungu* (white) meant interacting with a colonial state that had created an economic infrastructure for European traders. Unlike trade between Africans, which was arbitrated by village rulers and chiefs, complaints about dishonest trade or the nonpayment of salaries were lodged with the colonial administration for arbitration.[29] Indeed, their collaboration with the colonial regimes and the fish and money that they accumulated made many of the Greek traders seem far too fortunate to be ordinary men. Wealthy Greeks became targets for *bamunyama* vampire-men accusations.

In contrast to the Belgians, the Northern Rhodesian administration discouraged expatriate traders and fishermen. In the 1930s, they rejected requests by Europeans to fish in the waters of the Mweru-Luapula.[30] Since the fishery fell under the control of chiefs, the administration demanded that any fishing receive the prior approval of the relevant Native Authorities, which was unlikely.[31] Nevertheless, expatriates in the Congo and Africans in Northern Rhodesia forged business relationships. Since Mweru-Luapula consisted of hundreds of miles of remote territory, the Northern Rhodesian administration found it difficult to prevent expatriates crossing over into its territory to trade with African fishers in Northern Rhodesia and vice versa.[32] Many Africans worked as fish buyers or middlemen for Congolese-based expatriate traders. Others sold goods on behalf of expatriates and received a commission.

A credit *(nkongole)* system enabled *commerçants* to loan trusted itinerant traders goods that they could sell in inaccessible villages. In this manner, African traders occasionally earned enough to establish their own trading businesses and transport goods to and from the urban areas.

African traders who dealt with the Congolese-based *commerçants* were initially reticent about the opening of European stores in Northern Rhodesia, but came to welcome them if the stores were oriented toward the wholesale market and did not sell directly to the villagers. African traders worked with European store owners in the same way as they did with the *commerçants* on the other side of the river; the store owners gave them goods on credit that could then be sold or exchanged for fish in the villages. Traders gained their initial capital and experience from working in the European stores and began their careers in the employ of European or, later, Indian traders.[33] A Jewish trader with headquarters in Luanshya, I. Zlotnik, exported bananas and owned several stores along the valley. Villagers appreciated his prices and named him *macipisha* (he sells cheaply). Others like Harold Booth (Booth Ltd.) and the African Lakes Corporation (Madala stores) owned several outlets (these were sold in about 1955 to the Central African Marketing Company).[34]

Cash, Credit, and Business Networks

Trade helped to form new economic allegiances that rested on the extension of credit. Expatriate traders loaned African traders goods, and these goods would be distributed to fishers and farmers in exchange for their produce, which could in turn be exchanged by the African traders for cash, either in the urban areas or through other expatriate traders. Cash and credit thus facilitated the extension of commercial ties through villages and fishing camps. "Business during colonial days was done on credit," according to Booker Kapapula, the son of one of the more important businessmen, Benjamin Kapapula, "All you needed was a few trustworthy people. . . . The Greeks used to bring secondhand goods and these were given to people they trusted. They collected their money at the end of the month. When the English came they brought their goods from England to sell, they trusted people, the shops were all over, the shops were flooded with goods."[35] The return on capital for expatriate traders in this capital-starved economy was lucrative. Through these networks of trust and credit, wealthy expatriate traders constructed linkages to the business networks of Mweru-Luapula, the foundation of the Luapulan economy. New consumer goods followed the lines of *nkongole* credit into the valley. Trade and credit brought new prosperity. Glass windows let light into homes built from clay bricks as new building techniques and materials spread across the valley. Men and women wore new factory-manufactured clothes. The trade fueled a desire for goods offered by the European world; the fishing villagers composed a song to celebrate the coming of these traders and their goods:

> Sale, Sale
> If you who have fish
> Here is some salt
> Here is some money
> Here are some clothes.[36]

It was boom time. In the late 1940s, the anthropologist Ian Cunnison reported that he often heard it said, "It is the Copperbelt here."[37]

The prosperity of Mweru-Luapula and the spread of money as an exchange instrument was linked to the rise of the Copperbelt, where Luapula's produce could be sold and where many of the valley's men found waged work. Those *abanonshi* employed in the mining towns could invest their urban earnings in rural enterprises. Biston Katongola worked as a cook in Elisabethville. He returned to Chief Mulundu's village in 1926 when he had enough money to begin his own fishing business that he hoped would earn more than his cooking job. With the money earned from selling fish to the Greeks, he bought secondhand clothes *(kombo)* and other goods to sell—a common starting point for the secondhand clothing trade according to Karen Tranberg Hansen.[38] Soon he was able to establish a small shop in his home area where he sold clothes, soap, oil, and a variety of other new commodities. It was the beginning of a profitable family venture; by the 1960s his business, together with that of his brother Jim Kapesha and his missionary-educated sons, would become one of the largest trading ventures in the valley.[39]

The Mwenso brothers, cousins of Jim Kapesha and Biston Katongola, also began their business in the 1920s. The Mwensos traced their descent back to the original Shila clans of the valley and also had their own village in Chief Mulundu's area. The founder of the business, Jameson B. Mwenso, attended the nearby Johnston Falls (Mambilima) mission school. After finishing primary school, Jameson Mwenso's mother gave him two shillings to begin a business. He bought fish and departed on his bicycle for Elisabethville on the dusty road from Kasenga, along which the European traders transported fish in their large trucks. With money earned in Elisabethville he bought secondhand *kombo* clothes, loaded them into a canoe, and traveled up and down the Luapula River selling them to, or trading them with, prosperous fishermen. After a few years, he managed to buy five bicycles that family members rode to Elisabethville with fish and returned with clothes, soap, and other urban luxuries.[40] These were the modest beginnings of a family business that forty years later was large enough to make the Mwenso brothers a household name in Zambia.

The story of Benjamin Chabalala Kapapula, the father of one of Luapula's most powerful families and son of Mwata Kazembe XII Chinyanta Kasasa, demonstrates the importance of relationships with *commerçants* for capital-starved African businessmen. Because he was born outside the palace, Benjamin Kapapula was not in line for the position of Kazembe. Instead, he took advantage of a missionary education in the Belgian Congo and underwent further training in Southern Rhodesia (present-day Zimbabwe). His father recalled him from Southern Rhodesia to take the place of an ailing lesser chief and enter into a profitable position in the Lunda Native Authority. But the ailing chief lived many more years, and Benjamin Kapapula decided to become a businessman. He had no capital, but taking advantage of his Congolese education and knowledge of French, he found employment as a middleman. Using a canoe, he went from village to village, buying fish with money provided by the Greeks and earning a four franc profit for each kilogram load he carried to the large *ifyombo* boats. Benjamin Kapapula sent all seven of his children to school, for he realized how education, especially learning English and French, had benefited his business by enabling him to secure the trust of European buyers.[41]

Labor for these businesses often came from a home village and engendered networks of obligation to several families. The Nkomba brothers heralded from a prominent autochthonous clan and at their peak owned several shops along the valley road. The Nkomba village, established in 1922 after the colonial authorities lifted the sleeping sickness regulations and villagers were allowed to return to the southern part of the valley, was about three miles north of Johnston Falls (Mambilima) mission, in the area administered by Chief Kashiba (although the Nkombas were themselves owners of the lagoon). Nkomba Kakoka, the founder of the village, traded fish caught in the nearby Luapula with the *commerçants* and, with the money earned, bought *kombo* clothes. The women of the village—sisters, wives, and daughters—ironed and repaired the clothes, and then other family members delivered them by bicycle and canoe to villages across the valley. After a few years, the

Nkombas began to concentrate on the sale of luxury commodities, especially clothes. They bought cloth in Fort Rosebery (present-day Mansa) to manufacture clothes and bought other goods such as sugar, salt, and cooking oil in the Congo to sell or trade in their shop.[42]

Nkomba Kakoka passed on the control of the business to his sister's son *(mwipwa)*, Titus Chiputa, according to the rules of succession and inheritance of his matrilineal clan. Such matrilineal rules did not mean that women enjoyed control over the business; on the contrary, the system remained patriarchal and men controlled the profits extracted from the labor of women. Wives, who lived with their husbands as part of a virilocal residential section far from their own family, remained especially vulnerable to exploitation.[43] Nevertheless, the beneficiaries of a man's business also included the extended matrilineal family, often sisters and their children, who might choose to remain with their wealthy brothers and mother's brothers rather than their poor husbands.[44] Such obligations meant that a business had to contribute to the households of several families. The advantage of this arrangement was that a business drew on the labor of more than one household—the Nkombas could rely on their entire village. As long as labor could easily be turned into profit, as in the early development of the fishery, it was a profitable arrangement; but the persistent shortage of capital made the arrangement unstable. When money was needed to pay for tax, clothes, school fees and supplies, or funerals, the clamoring for meager profits could undermine a business and diminish its ability to invest in more capital-intensive activities.[45]

The tensions created by abundant labor and scarce capital were most evident in fishing ventures. The major obstacle faced by fishers was mobilizing enough capital to acquire better boats and improve their nets and fishing gear, which would increase catches and profits—for this reason, many fishers relied on nets distributed by wealthy fish traders and remained indebted to them. Initial capital and labor was needed to make durable nets, including gill or seine nets, woven from material far stronger than the traditionally used *kaboko* plant fiber. The best material was nylon purchased in the Congo. A nylon net cost about £12 and its life of approximately one season of intensive fishing earned between £40 and £50. The next best choice was thread made from a motor tire. It cost about 35 cents plus several extra weeks of labor to make the thread and had an earning potential of £20 over four months (half the season) after which it began to disintegrate.[46] Most fishers who could secure enough labor used these old tires to make nets. Nkomba Kakoka, who as a headman could rely on the labor of his village, began to fish with nets made from motor tires purchased in the Congo, where they were made available to the local fishers by the administration.[47] The chosen fishing technology corresponded to capital-starved but labor-abundant village resources. The fishers did not accumulate money; when it was made available, fishing families frequently spent it on the purchase of goods for distribution to secure dependents and laborers who would work for them. Ensuring networks of indebted dependents was a more rational investment choice than hoarding money, which could be raided by colonial tax collectors or family members before it was converted into capital.

From *Abanonshi* Traders to *Abakankâla* Capitalists

From the late 1940s, an increasing number of small-scale, capital-starved entrepreneurs managed to transform themselves into capitalist *abakankâla* who either specialized in trading fresh fish, more profitable than dried, or in providing transport for other traders.[48] Prior to 1955, Europeans transported more than 65 percent of the fresh fish that went to the Copperbelt. The trade in fresh fish was risky and required a certain capital outlay. Moreover, although fresh fish were a popular commodity, the few consumers who had refrigeration facilities limited the urban market. A fresh fish trader had to work with retailers with large refrigeration facilities rather than selling fish directly to the consumer. This benefited European traders, who could negotiate contracts with urban retailers and mining companies. The construction of the ice plant at Kashikishi in 1955–56 was a turning point. Northern Rhodesian traders no longer had to transport ice from the Copperbelt, and the risks and capital outlay decreased.[49] From 1955 to 1956, the share of fresh fish traded by Africans increased from less than 35 percent to approximately 70 percent of the total.[50] African traders like Jim Kapesha, the brother of the fisherman and trader Biston Katongola, made three trips in a single month, June 1956, and transported 11,431 pounds of fresh fish out of a total of 195,880 pounds transported by African traders on the Northern Rhodesian side of the border over the same period.[51]

Abakankâla success was also linked to rising wages of, and increased remittances from, urban workers. By the 1940s, there was so much wealth to be made in Luapula that many of the migrant workers who had labored in the mines of Elisabethville and the Northern Rhodesian Copperbelt began to return to their villages.[52] These *abanonshi* invested their urban earnings in new rural businesses. During the 1930s, in the wake of the depression, Northern Rhodesian mine management had been intent on instituting new measures to control and cheapen labor costs, especially after the Copperbelt strike of 1935. To combat "detribalization," which they thought partly responsible for the strike of 1935, and reduce workers' repatriation costs, management initiated "voluntary savings schemes" in 1939.[53] Although not the intention of mine management, the schemes allowed workers from Luapula, who generally worked in Mufulira, to invest savings in rural businesses. Paul Kapasa Chisakula grew up in Lukwesa's village in the center of the valley where he watched his father do business with the Greeks from Kasenga. He left for school in Mufulira and there became an underground supervisor and chairman of the Mufulira mine workers union. During the strike of 1940 he acted as go-between for the determined workers and the rigid mine management. After the strike, he decided that the Copperbelt was "too hectic" and returned to his home village, Lukwesa, where he joined his brother, Moses, to launch a small trading venture. The Chisakulas bought goods in the Congo and traveled by canoe to isolated fishing villages, where they sold their goods and purchased fish. Soon they were able to buy an outboard engine and reach even more remote villages and fishing camps. Eventually, in 1952, they opened a permanent shop in Lukwesa where they earned between £250 and £300 per month.[54]

In the late 1950s, transport surpassed fresh fish as the most profitable enterprise and attracted the wealthiest *abakankâla*. A road through the Northern Rhodesian side of the valley built in 1947 allowed traders to bus, instead of cycle, their goods to the Copperbelt towns. Luka Mumba was one of the earliest and best-known African transporters. After being imprisoned in the Congo for belonging to the Jehovah's Witnesses—or the "Watchtower," as it was known across southern central Africa— he traded fish and sold secondhand *kombo* clothes in the town of Samfya on Lake Bangweulu. He then began to organize water transport on Lake Bangweulu and road transport between Samfya and Mansa. Luka Mumba's lake and road transport system transformed the trade routes between Lake Bangweulu and the fish markets of the Copperbelt and led to the rise of a wealthy new depot village, Mwamfuli. A few years later, with the help of some European traders, he purchased a number of buses and trucks that he used for transport in the Luapula Valley, revolutionizing the trade in a similar fashion.[55] Others followed Mumba's lead: the Mwenso brothers, Jim Kapesha, and later, the Kapapulas all established transport businesses. Each small truck transported about ten traders with 3,000 pounds of dried fish, and a bus-truck combination carried as many as sixty traders with 30,000 pounds of dried fish.[56]

Initially colonial policies had influenced the growth of entrepreneurial activities in Mweru-Luapula; however, by the 1950s patterns of economic activity on both sides of the Luapula looked similar. Networks of African and expatriate traders and fishers were based on a combination of capitalist and capital-starved entrepreneurs who managed to escape, shield themselves from, or rapidly adjust to changes in colonial policies. A few small-scale traders became *abakankâla* through the profits of the transport or fresh fish business. Luka Mumba, the Mwenso brothers, and Jim Kapesha graduated from being small-scale fishermen to large-scale transporters. Aroon Ngwashi's various businesses competed with the Congolese *commerçants*. Others like Paul Chisakula and the Nkomba brothers set up retail shops along the valley. Benjamin Kapapula invested his meager fish-trading profits in education for his children, who managed to launch their own trading and transport businesses. Many of the wealthier fishers and traders who sought to emulate these *abakankâla* left their nets to their sons, younger brothers, and nephews: Dodge vans and Bedford trucks replaced fishing nets as the most profitable investment.

These were the celebrated success stories of the valley. For the most part, however, overcoming the forces of instability still patterned the expansion of African rural-based businesses. The most durable businesses could draw on cheap village labor through networks of credit and trust and could convert labor into a variety of forms of wealth by investing it in a range of activities. However, a business had to delicately balance its labor needs with the networks of obligation that such needs created. Without sufficient labor and instruments of credit, a business could not be launched; but with too extensive networks of obligation, profits would be quickly consumed by hungry families.

Gender and Commerce

The expanding fishing economy and the rise of a rural elite transformed families, clans, and gender relations. Men in certain clan-based businesses, like the Nkombas, adapted older matrilineal practices of inheritance and engaged their sisters and wives in business activities, especially with tasks like sowing or fish processing that could be performed in the village. Although most itinerant traders in the early colonial period were men, commercial village networks involved women who farmed cassava and processed fish. The women of Nkomba village collected firewood to smoke the fish to be sold, processed and packaged fish, tailored clothes, and occasionally worked as shopkeepers.[57] Even while women's labor was exploited, men were the main beneficiaries of the fish trade; such big men used opportunities provided by the cash economy to consolidate bilateral ties over their families, frequently to the detriment of their wives and in-laws. However, the injection of fungible wealth into gendered village networks also helped to transform the role of some women and slowly enabled them to become small-scale traders and enter the male-dominated world of rural-urban commerce.

When migrant men established fishing camps, women from the nearby villages provided cassava in exchange for fish or other goods, perhaps in a similar fashion to their provision of cassava rations for the caravan trade before colonialism. Much of the fish bartered was destined for the family pot, although some could be dried and sold in turn to urban traders. The cassava-fish trade linked fish prices to cassava prices; thus, a boom in the fish industry meant benefits for cassava farmers, mostly women. When fish prices increased due to the relaxation of fixed prices in 1950, there was an immediate impact on the local village economy. Due to the rise in fish prices, women found it impossible to purchase fish for their daily needs and small-scale trade; they reacted by increasing the price of cassava eight-fold. Fishermen refused to accept the new prices and a conflict ensued between male fishermen and female farmers. Finally, Mwata Kazembe persuaded the women to reduce the price of cassava and requested that the colonial authorities lower the fish prices. Notwithstanding such setbacks for cassava producers, the booming fishing economy allowed women access to cash and to a degree of financial autonomy.[58]

In such profitable times, women began to diversify their economic activities and made headway in the male-dominated fish trade. A few women established more substantial businesses. The best example is the daughter of Benjamin Kapapula, Anna Kapapula, who became a renowned fish trader in the valley. After high school at Mbereshi Girls School, Anna undertook a teacher-training course and got a job at a local school. While teaching, she made dresses for sale and then became a sales assistant for the European-owned Booth stores. She decided to use the money she earned from this job to trade in fish, for she had seven children and needed extra income to keep them in school. With money and a few barter goods she went up to Kashikishi fishing camp and bought a box of fresh fish, which she then sold for a profit in the nearby town of Mansa. Mabel Shaw, the founding headmistress of the Mbereshi Girls

School, visited her former pupil, Anna Kapapula, in 1959. She found a young, ambitious businesswoman with a van and two stores in Luapula. Anna shocked the valley's male inhabitants—and her old teacher it seems—by her scandalous dress (jeans and a bright red blouse) and the fact that she drove her own van to transport fish and other goods between the lake and the Copperbelt. Her brothers flocked around her to gain some access to her wealth; she controlled her own *ulupwa* family, a faithful husband and dutiful children.[59] At this time Anna Kapapula was an exception. Indeed, she reached almost legendary status in the valley, much like Nachituti in the Shila oral tradition. In later years many others would follow her lead and become big women.

Change in the relative wealth of men and women and gendered patterns of household organization were not the result of modernity and commerce liberating women from "tradition." While some women were subjected to enslavement and forced to work in agricultural fields in the precolonial Luapula Valley, free women who belonged to families with strong matrilineal ties had a significant degree of economic autonomy with respect to their husbands and, through their brothers, control over their children. This autonomy was threatened as men began to acquire wealth in the form of money. Men hoped to translate this new wealth into new followings, which included greater control over their wives and their children, and to sever cumbersome and costly ties to their in-laws. Audrey Richards observed the same phenomenon among the plateau Bemba; men who had money tightened their hold over their children.[60]

Men also exploited the new political structures to achieve greater control over family and followings: patriarchs took independent-minded wives to Lunda Native Authority courts to sever their attachments to their families and to restrict the obligations of husbands to wives' families. The Lunda Native Authority court heard many cases of wives who sought to leave husbands because they did not provide sufficiently for their families. In precolonial times, women often abandoned or "divorced" poor providers, taking their children with them; colonial Native Authority courts attempted to curtail this avenue of female autonomy.[61] The Native Authority tried to stem the exodus of women to urban areas by introducing fines of £2 for women found on the Copperbelt without a Native Authority pass—although with limited success, judging by the number of women who made it to the Copperbelt.[62] On the other side of the Luapula, chiefs complained to the Belgian administration that the rate of divorce was on the increase and that young women refused to get married.[63] Male colonial officers agreed: the *commissaire de district* argued that traditional judges did not have sufficient legal mechanisms or willpower to halt the increasing liberty of Luapula's women.[64] In fact, such complaints probably reflected new attempts by men to restrict the mobility of their wives and secure control over their children.

Popular songs warned young men of women who only wanted money:

> Women are thieves
> Their treachery is unimaginable
> They love money
> Young men, beware of these devils
> In truth, they're prostitutes.[65]

For the men of Luapula who told the story of Nachituti's betrayal, there was an old lesson contained in such a song; yet as a money economy spread across the valley, its message became more acute. But the change was not due to the growing liberty of women, as the colonial authorities imagined and patriarchs proclaimed, but rather newly acquired wealth that allowed men to challenge women and emphasize their own kinship ties within their *ulupwa* families. The "treachery" of women was in fact a discourse drawn on by men to protect their wealth from their wives and their in-laws. As they did throughout much of southern central Africa, men drew on invented tradition to justify dominance over women, especially in marriage; they circumscribed sisters' rights as members of matrilineages and made them into dependent and exploitable wives.[66] Rural-urban business networks gave men greater purchase over the liberty of Luapula's women and their children. Trade and money bound the heroine Nachituti more closely to the will of Kazembe; from being the sister to the owner of the land, she became the wife of a wealthy big man. But commerce was a double-edged sword; a few women did manage to tap into the new commercial realm, and in future years their role in the fishery and in rural-urban trade would grow.

The Spirits of Capitalism

Commerce swept away established hierarchies of political power, kinship patterns, and forms of social organization. In its wake, Christianity emerged as a revolutionary ideology, introduced from the outside, but rapidly diffused by social movements that developed a language of conflict linked to the Bible and to witchcraft. This language was an expression of the moral economy of the valley, which valued ties between people as an important measure of wealth, threatened and transformed by the changing economic landscape. New forms of fungible wealth could be invested as economic capital or converted into social rank in the hierarchies of rural religious associations like churches.

A popular Zambian song first recorded by the renowned musician Bartolomeo Bwalya in the early 1960s complains of witches in Mununga, a prosperous fishing town on the southeastern shores of Lake Mweru, and mourns those they have killed:

> Too many people die here, mother
> Because this country is very bad
> Ala, there are many witches
> They will burn in God's place.[67]

The above version, recorded in 1963, warns visitors, probably itinerant traders, that witches who kill many people in Mununga are agents of Satan and will burn in "God's place." It rests on a combination of two related religious forces that swept across the valley in the first half of the twentieth century—Christianity and witchfinding movements. European missionaries introduced Christianity, but by the 1930s the most powerful church, the Jehovah's Witnesses, or Watchtower, was led and controlled by Africans. Witchfinders, by contrast, adopted Christian idioms but heralded from Nyanja-speaking lands to the east and not Europe. They latched onto local experiences and vernacular ideas about ancestral spirits to help villagers explain and attempt to exorcise the changes brought about by colonial commerce.

The endeavors of Dan Crawford and the Plymouth Brethren missionaries illustrate the process of imposition of fundamentalist Christianity from above. In 1886 Frederick Stanley Arnot of the Plymouth Brethren arrived at the Bayeke leader Msiri's capital, Bunkeya. Dan Crawford followed in 1890 and was present at Msiri's assassination; for creating a community of converts out of Msiri's dispersed subjects and slaves, he was named him *Konga Abantu,* the Enticer of People.[68] A few years later in 1894, Crawford relocated to Luanza on the western shores of Lake Mweru where he built a mission station and spread his particularly fervent Christian doctrines. In 1897, Crawford and Henry J. Pomoroy established the Johnston Falls mission next to Mulundu's village. After a precarious first few years due to threats from Kazembe, Dugald Campbell took over the mission in 1901, and Willie Lammond after him in 1905. Other missions followed: in 1900 the London Missionary Society established the Mbereshi mission on a hill overlooking the valley, near Kazembe's rebuilt capital, Mwansabombe. And on the Congolese side of the river Catholics opened missions at Pweto (the White Fathers) and at Kasenga (Benedictines).[69]

Christianity began to alter the religious dimensions of the local authority of owners of the land and lagoons. Christian believers challenged owners of the land and their ancestral and nature spirits. God began to replace ancestors as the provider of fish and game; worship at the spirit shrines became associated with magic. "Before the Lammonds came this is where they used to have magic. It was quite a normal thing. Now when the missionaries came people started hiding, fearing. . . . So somehow there was a change," explained a Christian village elder from Mulundu.[70] Encouraged by the missionaries, the villagers increasingly identified the spiritual authority of the ancestors as a subterranean force called witchcraft, which had to be combated. Crawford presented himself as a crusader against the power of witchcraft. In his published diaries, he boasts of the gospel's power over Satan's many hidden forms and manifestations.[71]

One of the primary objects of the missionary attacks was the Ubutwa association that had defined the parameters of ownership and rulership for Shila elders and the owners of the land and lagoons vis-à-vis the Lunda rulers. However, the cross-lineage associational life promoted by Ubutwa did not simply disappear. Other social and spiritual associations would replace Ubutwa as new deities appeared, new stories were introduced, and new political authorities developed. While Christian missionaries condemned and attempted to eradicate African religious beliefs, believers managed to incorporate and transform Christianity from a colonizing force imposed from above to a revolutionary force from below. Dan Crawford delighted in observing that "[w]ith the converted African, Christ's mercy, like the water in a vase, takes on the shape of the vessel that holds it. Your constant joy is to hear in a foreign lingo some simple act of faith taking a new meaning by one twist of the Negro tongue."[72] Crawford knew that a Christianity imposed from above would never truly transform African rites and religions; that would be left to the spread of Christianity from below.

The Watchtower Church first spread to Luapula from the mines of Southern Rhodesia. Perhaps, as one historian suggests, it was colonial exactions during World War I that catalyzed African opposition to colonial rule and created a receptive audience for Watchtower's millenarian message.[73] Indeed, social historians have celebrated the movement as an "avatar of colonial revolt," or in the subtle synthesis of Karen Fields, as revival *and* rebellion.[74] Even before the war, there is evidence that the Africanist preaching of the missionary Joseph Booth was received with enthusiasm.[75] And in 1924 one of the movement's most famous leaders, Jacob Napoleon Mumbwa, proselytized in the Luapula Valley. Villagers adopted his radical "truth"—that they would soon be liberated from colonial rule by African-Americans—with enthusiasm and *en masse* conversions. While at first the movement had only spread in spurts of fervor, by the early 1930s, in the wake of the depression when thousands of urban *abanonshi* workers returned to the villages of Luapula, its millenarian message could be heard across the valley.[76]

During his fieldwork in the late 1940s, Ian Cunnison estimated that roughly half of all the lower Luapula Valley's Christians belonged to the Jehovah's Witnesses, an outgrowth of the original Watchtower movement.[77] He also noted that people of Luapula associated the Watchtower Church of the 1920s and 1930s with Ubutwa. Watchtower had its own esoteric language and held similar celebrations with distinctive dances and songs. Men and women could hold equal positions in the church and become officers. Moreover, allegiance to the church was more important than to clan and kin; identity was primarily determined by church membership. But most significantly, Watchtower members were known for the same type of mutual help as Ubutwa, by allowing wives to work for others, or *ubwafwano*, referred to by those who denigrated the custom as "wife swapping."[78] While Ubutwa had provided a model for the spread of cross-clan and kin associations, the church changed such associations from secretive and selective to public and commonplace. Social identities that transcended clan and kin through voluntary self-help associations were found in Ubutwa; however, Watchtower allied such cross-clan identities to an open and universal doctrine of faith.

Through the 1930s and 1940s in Northern Rhodesia, a tone of political moderation reverberated throughout the Christian movement. By the 1940s European Jehovah's Witnesses and their African supporters had taken over the movement and alienated it from some of its more African forms.[79] Mutual aid through "wife swapping" no longer took place, an established church hierarchy was put in place, and women were denied important positions like preachers. The movement established working districts and each district selected a leading preacher. Then, each church selected a chairman and several elders.[80] Still, every year thousands of members gathered in huge district assemblies, where members discussed questions of faith, self-help, and their distinctive relationship to chiefs, government, and politics in general.[81] Alongside these reformed Jehovah's Witnesses congregations, the more moderate Seventh-day Adventist Church gained in popularity. In the 1920s two American missionaries established the first mission at Chimpempe, near Kawambwa on the plateau overlooking the valley. And through the 1930s and 1940s a number of converts formed African-run Seventh-day Adventist congregations on the Northern Rhodesian side of the valley.[82] While some of the radical millenarian messages were diluted, the new faith provided a basis for a social identity independent from the taxing financial obligations of clan and kin. It also offered opportunity for new forms of status not linked to either clans or chiefs—perfect for young entrepreneurial upstarts.

In the Belgian Congo, the Watchtower doctrine retained its radical focus. Colonial officials, backed by Catholic missionaries, would have no ties with evangelical Protestants, who, they thought, only encouraged independent sects that challenged colonial authority. In the 1930s, they identified a number of "mystical and superstitious" sects encouraged by the "xenophobic tendencies" of their colonial subjects.[83] If the administration found Watchtower members, they imprisoned them for several months. In fact, the Congolese administration identified and punished Watchtower members whenever villagers or workers defied colonial authority. When villagers attacked Chief Kashobwe, north of Kasenga, for allegedly being a *bamunyama* merchant in human flesh, the administration blamed Watchtower and "évangélistes protestants" who came from Northern Rhodesia.[84] Despite the prohibition, Watchtower prospered, especially near the Northern Rhodesian border and in Elisabethville's urban areas where church members learned to avoid detection by colonial officials and smuggled church-related literature from Northern Rhodesia. In 1952 colonial officials in Katanga admitted that Watchtower was so firmly entrenched that they could not hope to eradicate it.[85]

Church members in rural areas were migrant laborers, traders, and entrepreneurs who, upon returning to the village, found that they could not be easily incorporated into the colonial apparatus of village authority and were too ambitious to accept their lot as ordinary members of their lineage groups. The church offered opportunity for the conversion of wealth into positions of authority and power. Most wealthy entrepreneurs, especially in Northern Rhodesia, were members of either Watchtower or the Seventh-day Adventist Church. In Kashikishi, Paul Chisakula was an elder of the Seventh-day Adventists; his brother, Moses, established the church in Lukwesa. In Kashiba, the *abakankâla* traders, Charles Harrington and Gerald Chisenga, were elders of the

Seventh-day Adventist Church. In the Mwense district, businessmen such as Jonathan Kabaso, Joshua Katongola, and Jim Kapesha were all prominent Watchtower members.[86] Self-styled "civilized" *abanonshi* migrants joined the ranks of the church and accepted their *abakankâla* counterparts as elders.[87] In the prosperous fishing camps, like those found in Mofwc Lagoon, branches of Watchtower proliferated.[88] African independent churches formed cross-clan bonds among a new entrepreneurial class and provided associational support, *ubwafwano*, for their members.

The church's appeal extended beyond those involved directly in rural-urban trade and wage labor to a spectrum of people in the village. Although denied more prominent positions like preachers, women constituted their own groups within the church. By the 1940s, Watchtower had disavowed "wife swapping" and insisted on new types of marital relations. Both Seventh-day Adventists and Watchtower prohibited divorce (except in the case of a woman's adultery) and expelled male members if caught in an adulterous relationship. In Luapula divorces and extramarital liaisons were common and sought-after by women, especially if husbands were poor providers. In this sense, the church could further consolidate the position of men who wanted to restrain the autonomy of their wives. But, conversely, if a husband was wealthy, a wife wanted protection against a potential divorce that would rob her of everything including her children, who might choose to ally themselves with their wealthy father rather than their poor matrikin. The church was the most effective weapon against abandonment. From its initial encouragement of mutual help through "wife swapping" to prohibitions on divorce and the encouragement of paternal rights in *ulupwa* families, Watchtower and the Seventh-day Adventists gave expression, and even contributed, to changing household gender relations, helping to consolidate the family of big men and limit the tendency of women to leave selfish husbands.[89]

In addition to detachment from affinal kin, Watchtower members sought to divorce themselves from the affairs of "Rome": they refused to participate in any form of "government" like chiefs or political parties. Although tension between political parties and Watchtower would emerge during and after decolonization, the lines of conflict during colonialism were generally between chiefs and Watchtower members. Watchtower members considered obeisance to chiefs as idolatrous. At first the Northern Rhodesian administration permitted chiefs to punish disrespectful Watchtower members; however, in the 1940s, as the administration became less concerned with Watchtower as a source of political opposition, they refused to support repression by the chiefs.[90] In 1950, Mwata Kazembe XIV Chinyanta Nankula, a member of the London Missionary Society, prohibited a Watchtower assembly next to his capital. The provincial commissioner overruled the Mwata's decision and gave permission for the assembly, which resulted in some seven thousand of Luapula's members congregating at the Lunda capital. When Nankula died three weeks later, many believed it was due to bewitchment by a European missionary who was angry that the Mwata had relented to colonial pressures and permitted the Watchtower assembly.[91]

While chiefs opposed Watchtower, they accepted witchfinding as a means to informally tax the new big men of the fish trade. The first widespread case of witchfinding in the colonial period occurred in the early 1930s, perhaps related to the depression. Young men dressed in European clothes, typical urban *abanonshi*, went from village to village to identify witches. Despite the Witchcraft Ordinance of 1914, Northern Rhodesian colonial authorities permitted the *bamuchapi* (from the verb *capa* [to clean] in Nyanja) and chiefs to play an active role in their witchfinding ordeals. Upon arrival in a village, the chief or headman slaughtered a chicken or goat and prepared a ritual meal. Then he summoned the villagers and lined them up for inspection. Each person looked into a mirror that revealed the witches. The witchfinders, or *bamuchapi*, made the witches drink a purification potion that would kill them should they continue to bewitch people or cure those who had inadvertently bewitched others. The *bamuchapi* did not charge for their services, but they sold magical powders and amulets for protection against further evil magic.[92]

Although the fervor of the *bamuchapi* witchfinding movement subsided in the late 1930s, it further encouraged a vocabulary and practice for the detection and punishment of witches. According to the early missionaries like Dugald Campbell, such forms of witchcraft *(ubuloshi)* had previously been associated with the Ubutwa society.[93] After the *bamuchapi*, they became far more open. In the Luapula Valley, chiefs set up branches of their Native Courts called traditional courts (or *ichilye chaa ntambi*), supervised by the Lunda aristocrats, who would judge matters related to witchcraft. While the initial *bamuchapi* movement was led by witchfinders who occasionally visited the villages, the process became institutionalized under the chiefs. Unlike the itinerant *bamuchapi*, a professional class of witchfinders *(abashinganga)*, who charged a fee for their services, began to emerge. The traditional court called on these witchfinders to find the magic *(ubwanga)* in the homestead of the accused witch during a cleansing ritual called *uluboko* (or *ukubuka*). If someone was found guilty of witchcraft they were given medicine called *kalolo* to neutralize the witchcraft. The accuser and accused would have to pay the fees to the court and the witchfinder, and should the alleged witch refuse to acknowledge his or her guilt, there would be an additional fine, corporal punishment, or, at worst, banishment from the community.[94]

The Christian influence on the *bamuchapi* is clear: the *bamuchapi* sang Christian hymns, destroyed shrines associated with "pagan" owners of the land and Ubutwa, and, initially at least, did not subject Christians to witchfinding ordeals.[95] However, interview evidence suggests that witchfinding sects and Watchtower became opposing forces. Watchtower members refused to admit that they could be involved in witchcraft and rejected the ordeals. Villagers, especially the chiefs who supported the *bamuchapi*, claimed that witches joined Watchtower precisely because they hoped to hide their witchcraft. Entrepreneurs who formed a core group of Watchtower members were accused of using nefarious means to gain wealth. Traders allegedly employed charms and even human body parts to sell their goods, and fishermen killed children and used them to chase fish into their nets.[96] Wealthy Watchtower members became targets of witchcraft accusations.

Conflict between witchfinders and church members revolved around the new meanings of wealth and patterns of inequality that accompanied the rise of the commercial fishery. Wealthy entrepreneurs and fishers, the *abakankâla* and *abanonshi*, used their money and new connections to reconstitute networks of allegiance. For such entrepreneurs, mutual aid within a church became more important than their social or kin obligations. Although witchfinders worked among different ethnic groups, accuser and accused were usually from the same family or linked through marriage. Accusations of witchcraft were related to family conflicts, or more precisely, the distribution of wealth within the family, between husbands, wives, and affinal kin. Accusers linked the unequal distribution of wealth to the vicissitudes of death, infertility, sickness, or general misfortune. Commerce and the unprecedented accumulation of things and money, which bought labor, goods, and followings, challenged leveling matrilineal ties and allowed a few big men to become capitalist entrepreneurs. Such changes were manifested in the hierarchies of church and given voice in the litigations of witchcraft trials.

The church transcended clan and kin and helped to reconstitute social and economic allegiances. By organizing its doctrine according to a universal faith rather than clan history, the church separated equality before God on the one hand and wealth of the individual on the other. However, a wealthy church member had both the blessing of God and the curse of potential dependents. Even if a church member gave generously to his congregation, he was not freed from the poorer members of his own clan, his immediate *ulupwa* family, and his affinal relatives. Indeed, big men became prime candidates for the ordeals of the witchfinders. Witchcraft trials allowed chiefs, witchfinders, and kin to engage and make demands on church members, their forms of wealth and their new ways. In the search for witches, believers grafted old stories of conquest onto colonial fables. Witches who dealt with the spirit world were agents of Satan. Europeans vested with evil power were representatives of "Rome." Villagers gathered at Watchtower assemblies instead of Ubutwa festivals to celebrate cross-kin and clan association. Ordeals and the purification of a community were combined with baptism. Preachers, *bamuchapi,* and *abashinganga* witchfinders replaced Ubutwa priests and owners of the land and lagoons.

Churches tended to challenge colonial forms of authority, especially chiefs; however, historians overemphasize their direct challenge to colonialism. Church congregations transcended kin and clan ties, challenged established patterns of allegiance at the level of family and polity, and defended the right of the individual to new forms of pious wealth. This, rather than the anticolonial content of these movements, was their most important feature and would be their most lasting legacy. If Christianity was a revolutionary force, then witch-purification movements can be seen as reactionary; they adopted an indigenous vocabulary of witchcraft, adapted it to biblical narratives, and embarked on their witch hunts. As Peter Geschiere has pointed out, witchcraft was not a "traditional" but a "modern" political force.[97] Nevertheless, in the colonial period, witchcraft accusations defended the obligations that the wealthy had toward their dependents, their clans, families, and affinal kin. They upheld older forms of wealth that valued camaraderie, equality, and ties between people.

Conclusions

The *abanonshi* and *abakankâla* entrepreneurs accumulated a new type of wealth measured not in people but in Congolese francs. The difference was that money was fungible; it could create new business ventures, it could buy urban goods, and it could even buy people, or at least their labor. Instead of charters over the land and lakes, the diffusion of

fungible wealth helped to form new hierarchies of power and fluid social identities. Business networks and churches challenged matrilineal
allegiances. Big men husbands claimed paternity over their children
while their poorer brothers-in-law lost their ties to their sisters and their
sisters' children. This strengthened the bilateral claims extending from
big men and weakened the bonds of poorer matrilinealages. As increased commercial wealth drove this revolution forward, witchfinders
were called on to make entrepreneurial upstarts remember obligations
toward kin, clan, and ruler.

Formally, authority over the fishery was vested in colonial chiefs; informally, an emergent civil society, based in Luapula's "marketable but
not bankable" economy, proved at least as important in converting access to the fishery into new forms of wealth and status. The *ulupwa* family and church congregation were the social groups most important for
investments in people and generating followings; for the most part, they
supplanted older corporate associations like the matrilineal clan and
Ubutwa. While control over the land and lakes supposedly fell to colonial states and their local representatives, resource rent was linked to
stories of the Bible and of witches, to the demands of families, to the
availability of reserves of capital and labor, and to strategies for conversion and investment. This chapter has attempted to identify historical
trends, including the emergence of numerous big men and their *ulupwa*
families; nevertheless, these changes were multidirectional and multi-
faceted. Some selfish fishers and traders, many of whom drew the wrath
of family, attempted to accumulate monetary wealth and only invested
in dependents to benefit from their labor. More generous and renowned
big men knew that their positions in families, churches, or in even more
extensive business networks were valuable assets that needed mainte-
nance and investment.

PART TWO

THE FISHERY

4

Mpumbu

Colonialism and Conservation

The result of the mpumbu was that people had very beautiful
houses. . . . Poverty came afterwards.
          Elliot Mwita Kankomba, Mambilima, 5 Jan. 1998

The spawning of the mpumbu fish was a much celebrated annual
event. For a few days after the first heavy rains and flooding, usually in
February, thousands of fish from Lake Mweru crowded near the rapids
of Mambilima and in the tributaries of the Luapula. The large females,
heavy with eggs, were set upon by numerous males until covered in a
milky liquid; they then released thousands of tiny eggs into the fast flowing water. During the release of the eggs, a gentle hiss could be heard, as
if the river had sighed. The water was so cloudy that it could not be
drunk. The fishing villagers called the spawning run *kapata*, an explo-
sion. It was said to have been led by a python-like nature spirit called
Winkonkelela and happened every year without fail.[1] But quite sud-
denly, in 1949, the mpumbu did not spawn in the Luapula and were
never to spawn in great numbers again. The massive increase in fish exports from Mweru-Luapula in the late 1940s had led to an unprecedented reduction in the mpumbu population and eventually brought
about their disappearance from the waters of Mweru-Luapula.

The people of Luapula tell many stories about the end of the
mpumbu spawning run. Often the owners of the lagoon are blamed for
having accepted bribes from colonial officials and traders, which led
them to ignore the correct rituals and allow overfishing: "The Greeks
prevented us from performing rituals; they said that they have the right
to kill fish at any time. They came with many goods and bribed the
chiefs; this is why the mpumbu disappeared."[2] Chief Nshinka Mulundu,

115

the *bamunyama* chief, was a frequent target of such allegations. Indeed, soon after his dismissal by the colonial government in 1946, the mpumbu spawning run ended. Mulundu's dismissal was so strongly associated with the mpumbu that some forty years later, when he reclaimed his throne in 1986, villagers hoped that the old chief would have the power to bring the mpumbu back to the Luapula.[3]

The favorite and most widely told story blames the Belgians for the disappearance of the mpumbu. White men, the story goes, caught a few mpumbu fish, placed rings on their gills, and returned them to the river. These frightened mpumbu then swam away, downstream into Lake Mweru, and then, not stopping, they swam into the Luvua, the Lualaba, then into the Congo River and eventually landed up in the Atlantic Ocean. Attracted by the glittering rings on these few fish, the rest of the mpumbu followed. They were never seen in the Luapula again. "It was the time of the Greeks from Kasenga," according to Musanda, a bitter Elephant Clan elder and Watchtower member. "They put rings on the fish. Why do you put rings on food? Who did this? The lord Jehovah was annoyed by what they did, and now the mpumbu have gone down in the waters. God has hidden them."[4]

Oral traditions are usually grounded in the interpretation of certain historical realities. Belgian ichthyologists did tag several thousand mpumbu in an effort to understand what Luapulan fishers were already intimately familiar with, the spawning patterns of the mpumbu. And in one sense at least, the fishers were correct in asserting that such scientific experiments and concomitant scientific conservation regulations were to blame. The disappearance of the mpumbu was the most blatant example of the subordination of colonial conservation ideals to economic and political interests.[5]

When there were signs that the mpumbu's spawning run was under threat, the colonial administrations, European *commerçants*, and African fishers and traders faced the crisis with different agendas dictated by their diverse political and economic needs. In essence, the resulting conflict came down to differences in the conception of common property. The Belgians opened the resource to the exploitation of all fishers and traders, especially capitalized Europeans; they wanted a fishing policy that would deliver the maximum amount of fish at the lowest cost to the mining economy and thought the best way to do this was to encourage experienced and capitalized European fishermen. The "scientific" conservation measures that they introduced were intended to facilitate their fishing activities by restricting African fishing during spawning, which they claimed was unsustainable. On the other hand, in Northern

Rhodesia, where the fishery was of marginal importance to the mining economy, the resource had been placed in Native Trust, ostensibly under the control of "tribal" chiefs. African fishermen in Northern Rhodesia blamed their declining catches on increased expatriate fishing on the lake; they wanted to continue their customary forms of fishing and protect their exclusionary rights to the resource. Northern Rhodesian officials, concerned with the efficacy and legitimacy of the Native Authorities, were sympathetic to claims by African fishermen that increased fishing by Europeans had led to a decline in stocks.

The Northern Rhodesian administration set about containing the political consequences of conservation measures by ensuring their implementation through the newly established Native Authorities, who they insisted were the custodians of "tribal" property. The end of the spawning run came at an especially sensitive time for the colonial government. Rural villagers, embittered against the colonial authorities for the attempted introduction of the conservation measures, joined their newly organized nationalist allies, who were mobilizing against the advent of the settler-dominated Central African Federation, and accused the British and Belgian colonial authorities of promoting European traders and fishermen above Africans.[6] They defied the new conservation regulations, leading to the first open rebellion against the colonial authorities in Mweru-Luapula since Mwata Kazembe X Kanyembo Ntemena surrendered his Lunda kingdom in 1899. Angry villagers on the banks of the Luapula River blamed colonial conservation measures and Greek fishermen for the disappearance of the mpumbu.

The end of the mpumbu spawning and the subsequent rebellion was the outcome of the rapidly increased exploitation of a targeted species by foreign and autochthonous fishers who hoped to maximize their economic gains. Recent changes in fishing tenure arrangements had facilitated new types of exploitation. In Northern Rhodesia, colonial chiefs managed "tribal" resources instead of owners of the lagoon; in the Belgian Congo, colonial officials declared the resource open to all. Henceforth, the colonial states, their officials and collaborators, would attempt to enforce an array of regulations to limit the exploitation of a resource that they considered to be some form of common property.

The Disappearance

In 1937, Chief Mulundu warned the governor of Northern Rhodesia of impending "trouble" in his country instigated by Congolese fishing in the Luapula.[7] Over the next few years, fishing effort increased further as the Belgian administration, attempting to ensure a stable supply of fish to the copper mines during the war years, encouraged exploitation by Greek fishermen and fish traders. An increased tonnage of fresh fish found its way to the Elisabethville markets and UMHK workers in the 1940s. It reached a high point of 1,935 tons of fresh fish and 558 tons of smoked in 1947 compared to 1,199 tons of fresh and 530 tons of smoked in 1945. Moreover, mpumbu formed an increasing proportion of the total fresh fish transported to Elisabethville. In 1947, mpumbu comprised 43 percent (833 tons) of all fresh fish in UMHK's refrigerators, compared to only half that proportion in 1945. The amount of mpumbu bought by UMHK in 1947 was around three times that of the second most-caught fish, ndomo-domo, and more than five times that of pale, which was to become the most important fish in the 1950s.[8]

Mpumbu are of the widespread *Labeo* genus (often commonly referred to as mudfish), which has over eighty different species spread throughout Africa and Asia. *Labeo altivelis* are generally strong swimmers and migrate upstream after heavy rains to spawn, sometimes even climbing rocks by using their mouths and pectoral fins. They graze on algae and detritus from the rocky bottoms of the rivers and lakes. In Mweru-Luapula, the mpumbu would swim upstream into the Luapula River from Lake Mweru after the first heavy rains until they reached Mambilima rapids or turned up one of the Luapula River's tributaries. Here, in the fast-flowing flood waters, usually at the base of a waterfall or a series of rapids, they would spawn. Successful spawning was linked to rainfall; without suitable flooding the fish could not migrate upstream and reach the spawning grounds. *Labeo altivelis* are still found in the Zambezi River where they live up to nine years and grow to eight pounds.[9]

When the rains were good and spawning successful, the mpumbu formed an important part of Luapula's subsistence and commercial catch. They were the most renowned and celebrated of Luapula's fish — in the following praise, the fish are compared to the eastern Lunda heroine, Nakafwaya, who desired many men and thus could not be possessed by any single man:

> Ulupumbu, stacked together
> Majesty, too great for one person
> Bream are their royal quills
> Ulupumbu are like Nakafwaya
> The one who desires many men
> Mwansa, carry in a basket
> And be cared for in the seasonal grass.[10]

The praise suggests how plentiful the mpumbu were and how regular their spawning patterns—they are cared for in the *ndao* grass that grows as the flood waters swell. To the fishers of Luapula, the spawning mpumbu were like Luapula's promiscuous heroine, who attracted more than one man and needed to be shared by many.

While many men could benefit from the mpumbu, water tenure arrangements were of particular importance to their capture, since they spawned in known locations, often at the base of rapids or waterfalls. Certain owners of the lagoon, often the heads of clans, like Mulundu of the Rat Clan, exerted resource rights over the collection of mpumbu and were responsible for opening the fishery after spawning began *(uku-fungule sabi)*. Mpumbu were easy to catch using a combination of weirs *(amâmba,* sing. *ubwâmba)* and traps *(imyôno,* sing. *umôno)* or floating gill nets *(ukusenswa);* at the height of spawning, fishers could simply drag baskets *(intende)* through the water.[11] In general, catch levels were related to strategic place and the amount of collective labor mobilized over a short period rather than fishing technology (although extensive and complicated weirs and traps were constructed, as illustrated in photos 1 and 2). The relative importance of water tenure vis-à-vis technology decreased in the open waters of Lake Mweru, where mpumbu increasingly came to be caught before they spawned by bottom-set gill nets. On the open lake, there were few customary controls over fishing and no owners of the lagoon.

In Mweru-Luapula prior to 1946, Greek and African fishers had their largest catches over a two- to three-week period during and just after spawning, when the river flooded in February and early March. A local district official reported that for fifteen to twenty days during this time more than twenty tons of mpumbu left Kasenga every day. Traders purchased a small male mpumbu for one franc, or a large gravid female, full of precious eggs, for two francs. Mpumbu roe was a delicacy for both Africans and expatriate Europeans (when prepared, the roe resembled caviar in taste and became an increasingly popular item in the expatriate market of Elisabethville). Traders extracted around one hundred kilograms of mpumbu roe for every ton of fish and thereby collected around two tons each day of the spawning season. Once transported on ice to Elisabethville, the roe could be sold at several times the lakeside price.[12]

In the year 1946–47, however, catching techniques changed. European fishermen, mostly Greek, began to lay long bottom-set gill nets on Lake Mweru from July to December, when the mpumbu gathered at

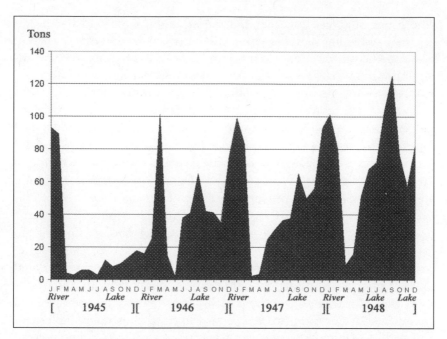

Figure 4. Purchases of mpumbu by UMHK from Kasenga, 1945–1948. From *Rapport annuel,* mission piscicole, 1947–1948, AA, IPAC AGRI 51.

the inlet of Luapula River before they spawned. The change is best illustrated by the amount of mpumbu purchased monthly by the UMHK.

   The high catches between late January and March of 1945–46 represent fish caught by African fishers in the Luapula River during the spawning season. The peaks between July and December represent fish caught by Europeans on the lake. Over three years, the timing of peak mpumbu yields shifted from the spawning season to the prespawning period. This shift represented the influx of predominantly European fishers with motorized boats and gill nets. Indeed, in 1948 catches during this period far exceeded catches during the previous spawning seasons. At the beginning of 1949, these huge lake catches were followed by a severe drought and the mpumbu ceased to aggregate in their previous massive spawning events. River catches during the conventional spawning season collapsed. The mpumbu remained in the lake in low numbers for several more years, but fishers no longer targeted them for significant commercial or subsistence fishing.

Colonial Conservation

Colonial efforts to conserve the fishery predate the disappearance of the mpumbu. In 1938 the Belgian administration introduced a closed season, a restriction on the mesh diameter of nets, and a tax on nets. Yet both fishers and *commerçants* ignored these measures during World War II, when the Belgians desperately tried to supply as many fish as possible to their mine workers. Under the influence of UMHK and the local *commerçants,* the Belgian administration had little interest in the implementation of conservation measures. On the other side of the river, the Northern Rhodesian administration gazetted legislative machinery for intervention in the fisheries in 1929, but did not embark on any comprehensive measures until 1943, when they introduced a minimum mesh diameter and a licensing system.

The Northern Rhodesian administration assigned responsibility for the enforcement of the regulations to the newly established Native Authorities. As long as the Native Treasury benefited from the licensing system, chiefs were eager to implement such measures and colonial officials reported the regulations were "acceptable to the more thoughtful element of the African communities concerned."[13] However, if the

Photo 1. Weirs and traps on the Luapula. Photograph by M. Halain, approx. 1940. Source: Mission piscicole: photos, Fonds du Gouverneur Général de Léopoldville. 14.216, AA.

Photo 2. Removing a trap from a weir on the Luapula. The typical way to catch mpumbu after they spawned. This type of fishing was long established on the Luapula and recorded by David Livingstone on the Kalungwishi River in 1867. Photograph by M. Halain, approx. 1940. Source: Mission piscicole: photos, Fonds du Gouverneur Général de Léopoldville. 14.216, AA.

Photo 3. An Ichombo on the Luapula. From the 1920s, predominantly Greek-owned boats traveled between fishing camps to purchase fish for export to the mining towns. In the 1940s, these boats began fishing with bottom-set gill nets. Photograph by M. Halain, approx. 1940. Source: Mission piscicole: photos, Fonds du Gouverneur Général de Léopoldville. 14.216, AA.

Photo 4. UMHK fish buyers at Kasenga. Representatives of the mining companies gathered at Kasenga to purchase fish, mostly mpumbu, for workers' rations. Photograph by M. Halain, approx. 1940. Source: Mission piscicole: photos, Fonds du Gouverneur Général de Léopoldville. 14.216, AA.

measures interfered with traditional fishing practices, the ability and will of the chiefs to enforce them was severely tested. In 1940, the district commissioner persuaded the Lunda Native Authority to issue orders to restrict the catching of fish at Mambilima during the spawning season. He was nevertheless sure that such regulations would remain a dead letter, since they interfered with the catching spree at the beginning of the mpumbu run, which, he wrote, "cannot be stopped without very serious consequences and breaches of the peace."[14]

After the war, both colonial administrations approached conservation issues with a greater seriousness. This commitment came to the fore in the late 1940s when the mpumbu's spawning run was threatened. The administrations agreed on the urgent need for measures to protect the fishing resources of Mweru-Luapula; yet they could not divorce conservation measures from the underlying economic and social issues that characterized their colonies. As in many other parts of colonial Africa, conservation measures and their implementation reflected the different approaches of the administrations, the wavering strengths of the colonial administrations on the ground, and the impact of different pressure groups on the administrations.[15]

A Northern Rhodesian colonial official, proud of what he thought to be the success of British indirect rule, summed up how he viewed the differences in policy of the administrations as they affected the fishery: "They [the Belgians] look over the heads of the Africans; we must try to look through the Native Authorities. They draw no distinction between European and African fishing; we regard the fishing as in trust for the Africans."[16] Indeed, the Belgian administrative apparatus attempted to function independently from the messy details of village politics and society. Colonial officials took responsibility for all the tasks of government and believed that their foremost duty was the *mise en valeur* of the colony. They encouraged expatriate merchants and fishermen to become capitalized entrepreneurs who would drive this process forward. Colonial ideologues argued that even if Africans were excluded in the short term, the development of the colony by Europeans was in their long-term interest. "The native," the vicar of Katanga argued, "will be awakened by our example . . . shaken out of his torpor. He will be freed from his state of stagnation."[17] Such was the spirit of colonial "paternalism" and *dominer pour servir*.[18]

The Northern Rhodesian administration was not very different. They shared the "civilizing mission" of the Belgians; they also believed that colonialism was a progressive force that would thrust Africa and Africans willy-nilly into the modern world. From the 1930s, however, indirect rule policies were taken seriously. The colonial administration placed some land and certain resources under the control of "tribal" chiefs and their councils. This became further formalized after 1947, when, as part of a colonywide reform of land tenure rules, the Mweru-Luapula fishery officially became part of "Native Trust" reserved for African use. A national directive, paraphrasing Lugard's doctrines and applying them to resource management, instructed colonial officers in Mweru-Luapula: "Enforcement of territorial laws and regulations governing natural resources must be carried out *by* Native Authorities *for* Central Government, and not *through* Native Authorities *by* Central Government."[19] Given the "traditional" role of chiefs as resource managers who conducted rituals such as opening the fishery *(ukufungule sabi)*, colonial administrators thought that the cooperation of chiefs in conservation measures was logical and might be effective. However, as pointed out in previous chapters, colonial chiefs were not the owners of the land and lagoons but Lunda rulers like Kazembe and the royal family. They had conquered the land and lakes but had never owned them or conducted rituals to open the fishery. Indirect rulers drawn from Lunda royals would find it difficult to enforce the unpopular colonial conservation regulations.

By contrast, the Belgians relied on chiefs as local authorities, but never intended them as independent organs of local government. Even while some chiefs in the Congo were the historic owners of the lagoons, they were firmly contained and constrained within the colonial administrative framework.[20] Colonial officials instructed chiefs to monitor and implement the fishing regulations, but their cooperation was less necessary than in Northern Rhodesia. Moreover, the fishery was not treated as "tribal" property controlled by chiefs but as common property regulated by the state and open to all for exploitation. The combined forces of the *mission piscicole* and the administration would ensure the enforcement of the regulations that applied to all, settlers and Africans. The Belgian administration had fostered a far more authoritarian and paternalistic system than in Northern Rhodesia.

Besides administrative framework and policy, economic considerations influenced how colonial regimes viewed local resources. In the 1940s the fishery was of greater strategic economic importance to the Belgian Congo than to Northern Rhodesia. While the mines of Northern Rhodesia's Copperbelt received a stable supply of beef from the south, the Katangan copper mines relied on fish from Mweru-Luapula as a source of animal protein for their workers. Thus, conservation had to remain consistent with the continued need for fish by UMHK (or "Union Rivière" as one Northern Rhodesian official quipped). Along with UMHK's needs, the newly arrived Greek fishermen and expatriate *commerçants* ensured the accommodation of their interests. The *mission piscicole* conducted scientific research and advised on policy; yet in the end, legislation had to meet the needs of the colonial economy and expatriate entrepreneurs.

The political realities in Northern Rhodesia required the administration to take a different tack. The administration was in a far more precarious position than that of the Belgian Congo; they did not want to antagonize the fishing and trading networks that had begun to forge connections to a burgeoning nationalist movement. Fewer capitalized expatriate fishermen and fish traders did business on the Northern Rhodesian side of the Luapula. The fishing industry was thus less organized and state oriented than in the Belgian Congo. Conservation measures could not rely on the persuasion and cooperation of a class of trader-fishermen; instead, the colonial administration had to deal with an antagonistic population that increasingly distrusted and successfully opposed administrative-led measures. If the colonial authorities used force to implement conservation measures, as they did in the Belgian Congo, an intensive and long-term investment in the use of force would have to be made. This became even more evident as an African national-ist opposition consolidated against settler political and economic power in the buildup to the much-opposed advent of the Central African Feder-ation in 1953.[21]

Despite the political, economic, and social differences in their colo-nies, the administrations had to agree on conservation measures and the logistics of their implementation. Much strategic bargaining ensued over the next years as the respective administrations attempted to en-sure that the conservation measures took into account their political limitations, economic needs, and administrative ideologies. Negotia-tions began in 1947 when the Belgians indicated that they intended to implement a closed season on the Luapula River for two months be-tween January and March. The mpumbu's spawning runs, which oc-curred for one to two weeks during this period, would thereby be pro-tected. The Northern Rhodesian administration objected. They argued that African fishers on the river would not accept a closed season for these two months, since commercial fishing on the river was only pos-sible during this period. If prohibited, commercial fishing would be lim-ited to the lake, where few African fishers owned big enough boats and long enough nets to prosper. For the Belgians, the prospect of the end of commercial fishing on the river was not a serious concern; by 1948 most expatriate fishermen and traders had relocated their enterprises from the river to Kilwa fishing camp on the shores of Lake Mweru, or Kilwa Island, where they fished from large boats using long gill nets. Protection of the river spawning run would not affect their fishing activities; a group of *commerçants* even appealed for a complete closure of the river to ensure the continued profitable exploitation of the lake fishery.[22]

After much persuasion, the Northern Rhodesian administration concurred with the Belgians, and at a joint meeting in the beginning of 1948 agreed to close the river from January to March. The closure ap-plied to most types of commercial fishing, with limited subsistence fish-ing allowed.[23] Nevertheless, even with these provisions, the Northern Rhodesian administration doubted that they could persuade African fishers to comply with the measures: "They are sure to point out that this situation would never have arisen but for the greed of the Greeks, and the short-sightedness of the Belgians, and in fact they are now being asked to share equally in the righting of a situation which in my opinion they did little to create."[24]

If the regulations were implemented at all in 1948, they were certainly unsuccessful. Fish, especially mpumbu, continued to flood the Kasenga markets and find their way to Elisabethville. A record 5,000 tons of fish passed through Kasenga that year (compared to a total of about 4,000 tons in 1947). In addition, the proportion of mpumbu in this catch increased from 43 percent to 56 percent.[25] As shown in figure 4, most of these fish were caught on the lake before they spawned. Experts blamed the absence of spawning in 1949 on the drought. Yet in 1950, in spite of the increased severity of the 1948 regulations, there was again a very poor spawning season. The ratio of mature to immature fish was three to two compared to the previously recorded one to one, which in this case probably reflected a lack of successful spawning and a decrease in the population of younger fish.[26] After 1950 the situation rapidly deteriorated: the catch of mpumbu in proportion to other fish declined from 56 percent in 1949 to 41 percent in 1950, 21 percent in 1951, and only 2.8 percent in 1952.[27]

The Belgian administration ignored the massive increase in lake fishing and insisted on the necessity of even more severe regulations against fishing in the river. Supported by researchers from the *mission piscicole*, the Belgians proposed a complete closure of the entire Luapula River to both commercial and subsistence fishing. They contended that the previous partial closure had proven ineffective. The director of fisheries argued that "it is in the *direct interest* of the Africans to whom we are tutors that we must prohibit fishing with nets and traps from the Katabulwe Lagoon to Johnston Falls [Mabilima]. . . . [W]hether the people of Luapula want it or not we must force them to follow their best interest.[28] The more vulnerable Northern Rhodesian administration countered that it was impossible for them to expect compliance with such a measure, especially since a food shortage had followed the 1949 drought. Instead, they recommended a prohibition of fish purchases in the valley by the Kasenga merchants. The Belgians refused: such a measure, they argued, did little to protect the mpumbu and only interfered with the supply of fish to UMHK.[29] In December 1951, after several months of negotiations, the Northern Rhodesian administration agreed reluctantly to prohibit subsistence and commercial fishing on the Luapula River from Mambilima to Katabulwe from January to March, at least until 1956.[30]

The Rebellion

Northern Rhodesian officials expected opposition, and indeed, it quickly emerged. At a heated meeting between the Lunda Native Authority and the district commissioner, Mwata Kazembe XV Brown Ngombe complained of the new law. He argued that the closed season was too long, far longer than the spawning season of the mpumbu, and would cause much suffering in fishing villages that relied on small-scale fishing for sustenance and commerce. Greek fishermen lined the river mouth with nets just beyond the closed area, and thus prevented the mpumbu from spawning in the river. The desperate district commissioner, who could not refute these allegations, forced Brown Ngombe to sign a declaration of loyalty to the government.[31]

Brown Ngombe's anger at the administration reflected the even greater indignation of the villagers and fishers who defied the new regulations. In Kashiba's village, north of Mulundu, villagers threatened four fish guards with death should they try to enforce the new legislation. Later, in the same village, a Belgian patrol boat, the *Marie Louise,* confiscated the nets of several fishers, destroyed fishing baskets, and arrested two fishermen. In retaliation, fishermen in twenty canoes attacked the *Marie Louise.* Policemen on board fired shots to repel them. One of the two arrested fishermen escaped and the other was taken to Kasenga. A few hours later almost two hundred fishermen from Kashiba crossed the border into the Belgian Congo and stormed Kasenga, demanding the release of their colleague. They stabbed a Belgian fish guard and knocked down the *commissaire de district,* only to be finally held back by Congolese soldiers, but not before they managed to secure the release of their friend from the nervous administrator. Afterward, fishermen held mass meetings in Kashiba and the fish guards fled the area. There seemed little chance of successfully enforcing the new regulations, but the *Marie Louise* stubbornly continued its patrols, always accompanied by several armed soldiers.[32] Even then, brave fishermen fought to recover their nets and basket fish traps. The physical assault of a Belgian fisheries officer by a Northern Rhodesian fisherman while the officer attempted to make an arrest prompted the governor-general of the Belgian Congo to complain to the governor of Northern Rhodesia: "The attitude of the Rhodesian natives appears arrogant and threatening."[33]

For Belgian officials, the rebellion in Northern Rhodesia proved the superiority of the Congolese colonial administration above what the governor-general of the Belgian Congo termed the "weak and reticent" approach of the British government toward their colonial subjects. Though the governor-general recognized that this was partly due to the Northern Rhodesian administration's reluctance to alienate African opinion against the Central African Federation, he thought it also reflected a "general tendency within the Colonial Office's policy." In the case of the defiance of the fishing regulations in Mweru-Luapula, the governor-general wrote, it was up to the Belgian administration to restore order and ensure that the rebellion did not succeed in weakening the administrations' resolve to enforce the fishing regulations.[34]

The Belgian accusations held some truth. The Northern Rhodesian administration and, in particular, officials in the Department of Game and Tsetse were sympathetic to the plight of the fishing villages. Among themselves they quietly admitted that Kazembe's condemnation of the Greek fishermen was just and accurate. The director of the Department of Game and Tsetse agreed that "the Africans were bearing the brunt of restrictions which would not be necessary at all if it were not for the European (Greek) fishermen catching such large quantities of fish in the Luapula and in particular in Lake Mweru."[35] In 1953 expatriate Congolese catches on the lake, often less than three miles from the closed area, continued to be huge and unsustainable. Near Kilwa, on the southern portion of the lake, there were about seventy mostly Greek-owned boats. The *Stanley* was sixty feet long and carried up to eighty nets, each eighty yards long, a total of about three and a half miles of netting. It had a storage capacity of six tons and caught up to six hundred kilograms in a single morning.[36] Besides their sympathy for African fishers, Northern Rhodesian officials feared that the regulations threatened to act as a catalyst to a provincewide rebellion. For this reason, the director of Game and Tsetse and the Kawambwa district administrator decided to amend the original regulations and permit subsistence fishing from noon on Monday to noon on Wednesday, despite Belgian protests. This was enough time, the administration reckoned, to allow for basic subsistence needs. "There is no excuse for further incidents," the director of Game and Tsetse asserted, and should they occur "a greater show of government authority is needed."[37]

Occasions often arose when "a greater show of government authority" proved necessary. A new police post at Kashiba and a mobile platoon joined regular police and river patrols to enforce the regulations and ensure compliance. Pressure also came to bear down on the chiefs. The situation in Chief Mulundu's village was as bad as Chief Kashiba's village, if not worse. The villagers of Mulundu suffered, for when there was no mpumbu, the entire commercial fishery upon which it was based collapsed. Moreover, the absence of the traditional catching spree further undermined the authority of the newly appointed Chimambi Mulundu, who had replaced the *bamunyama* Nshinka Mulundu. Teachers based at the nearby Johnston Falls mission (Mambilima) linked opposition to the fishing regulations to opposition to colonial rule in general and especially to the advent of the Central African Federation. Local teachers and activists Bunda Chisenga and Ration John Mwansa argued that the closed season only conserved fish for Europeans and that the aim of the federation was to hand over the fishery to Europeans.[38] This rang true given the continued prosperity of the *commerçant* fishermen. The complete prohibition of fishing during the previously profitable season was bitter medicine for the fishers of Mambilima who watched the Congolese *commerçants* get rich on the mpumbu, previously too bountiful for any one man to monopolize.

Defiance of the regulations continued. Angry fishermen threatened the fish ranger and fish guards after they tried to destroy fishing baskets.[39] In February 1953 Chief Chimambi Mulundu told the district commissioner that he refused to implement the fishing regulations against the will of his people.[40] In response to this defiance the provincial commissioner set up an "interview" with the chief. The provincial commissioner instructed him not to listen to "wicked politicians . . . such as Bunda Chisenga . . . [who] only want power for themselves." In the presence of the district commissioner, Mulundu agreed to support all government laws.[41] The authorities sent new fish guards to Mulundu's area to see to the continued enforcement of net mesh regulations toward the end of the closed season.[42] When Chimambi Mulundu announced the arrival of the new fish guard to his people, one young man told the guard that he was unwelcome in the area. The people of the village then told him to pack his bags and leave for they did not want any fish guards in the area. The villagers then turned to the chief and asked him if he wanted the fish guard to stay. "He must go today," Chimambi Mulundu replied. "I refuse him because you refuse him and you are the people of this place."[43] What seems to have been life preserving and politically astute behavior on the part of Chimambi Mulundu was not appreciated by the colonial authorities. He was suspended for three months and the district commissioner initially wanted him replaced. By siding with his people, however, Chimambi Mulundu had secured a certain leverage against the administration that his predecessor Chief Nshinka Mulundu did not possess. The provincial commissioner feared that his expulsion "may cause this part of the valley to come more directly under Congress [African National Congress] influence than it is at present."[44] The district commissioner agreed and reinstated Chimambi Mulundu as chief but required him to sign a declaration of loyalty to the government and to the Lunda Native Authority.[45]

This incident is important and representative of the situation of many chiefs across Luapula and Northern Rhodesia who were made responsible for the enforcement of unpopular legislations concerning land and other resources. Chiefs were not dull puppets of the colonial administration. Their success depended on their ability to mediate between their communities and the administration. If, as the administration sometimes demanded, they denied their people access to resources, their position was substantially weakened. If a chief was not respected by the traders and fishers, his removal from office would not threaten the administration with popular rebellion; if a chief had no local support or political contacts, his removal would go unnoticed in the only representative organs for Africans, the African Provincial Council and the African Representative Council. When the colonial authorities dismissed a series of chiefs following the 1953 protests, the administration was met with massive local and national resistance—complaints even reached London.[46] During late colonialism, resource management became the most controversial and contested aspect of colonial rule; if chiefs were to maintain their offices they had to find ways of placating their colonial rulers while at the same time ensuring that their subjects maintained access to resources.

On the Congolese side of the Luapula, too, African fishers complained of the levels of expatriate exploitation of the fishery. "Increasingly," the *commissaire de district* of Kasenga wrote in his 1953 annual report, "they [the fishermen] declare, like their Rhodesian brothers, that the Europeans are the cause of the disappearance of certain species of fish, due to their use of better equipment and numerous nets."[47] Nevertheless, there was little open resistance or rebellion in the Belgian Congo. At this time, the Congolese lacked a nationalist movement that could channel the fishermen's anger into visible protest and confrontation.[48] Another significant reason for the lack of protest was the fact that chiefs did not hold the same responsibility for the enforcement of such regulations. It was easier for villagers to confront an unpopular chief than to mobilize against the armed agents of a colonial state.

Colonial paternalism, including handouts from the state to local fishers, also stifled opposition from fishers in the Congo. The *fonds poisson* made nets, nylon fibers, and motor tires (out of which thread for nets were extracted) available for African fishing cooperatives. The *Fonds du Bien-Être Indigène* (FBEI) focused on Mweru-Luapula and built several schools and hospitals.[49] In spite of opposition from expatriate fishermen and *commerçants*, the governor of Katanga supported the creation of African fishing cooperatives that worked with the state.[50] Belgian carpenters trained Africans to manufacture large *ifyombo* boats for fishing and the administration established a school at Kilwa on Lake Mweru where experts instructed African fishers in more advanced fishing techniques and provided them with a background in fish conservation.[51] After inspecting the school, a Northern Rhodesian administrator commented that it was an example of "Belgian initiative on Lake Mweru which leaves us far behind."[52]

After the end of the much-resisted 1953 closed season, the Northern Rhodesian and Belgian administrations began to negotiate the regulations anew. The mpumbu had not returned to their regular spawning patterns. This time the Northern Rhodesians insisted that the Native Authorities be represented and the Belgians agreed, as long as they could also bring their chiefs. Thus, besides the regular administrators and fisheries officers, Chief Kanyembo, a member of the Kazembe royal family, and the Lunda Native Authority fish councilors represented the African fishers on the Northern Rhodesian side. Chief Kampombwe, a chief who was an owner of the lagoon who had given tribute to Mwata Kazembe, and Kapimbili, a Lunda aristocrat identified by the Belgians as the *Secrétaire de la Chefferie du Luapula*, represented the Congolese fishermen. The Congolese chiefs were conspicuously silent, only muttering a few words of support for the Belgian administration. Chief Kanyembo, by contrast, put forward the case of the African fishers in the most direct and stately manner possible for a colonial chief:

> When we were told not to catch any fish from the Luapula we discovered that there were many Europeans coming with many boats and there were no restrictions placed on them. . . . These bwanas are there nearly every day with their nets which they put into the water and no fish can escape from Lake Mweru to the Luapula. At that particular place where the Europeans are keeping their nets no African boat can approach because the water is deep and also that is the only place where fish can escape to spawn into the Luapula. . . . An African may own two nets but a European can have about 200 nets; therefore why should an African be restricted from fishing.[53]

Kanyembo also pointed out that African fishing of mpumbu only commenced after spawning, when the owner of the lagoon opened the fishing season and the adult fish returned to the lake. The blanket prohibition on fishing in the Luapula from the middle of January to the middle of March, demanded by the Belgians, prevented this type of fishing without any valid justification.

The most prominent Belgian administrator present, M. Schöller, the *commissaire provincial du Katanga*, disagreed. In a typical espousal of *dominer pour servir,* he insisted on the implementation of the regulations and that European fishing continue: "We are certainly not prepared to give favor to a proposal which intends to expel Europeans from Lake Mweru, because we think it is against the interests of the Natives. If one day the Natives will be able to fish in the lake, the Europeans will have shown the way to fish. There is not the slightest reason for expelling the Europeans from the lake."[54] Ultimately, after much bickering, the administrations reached a compromise solution. There was to be a complete ban from the middle of January to the middle of March, inclusive of both the river and the lake, thereby preventing European fishing on the lake. Certain types of subsistence fishing, like small-scale *ukutumpula* fishing (beating the water to chase fish into nets) were allowed on the river. The meeting viewed the limited prohibition of fishing on the lake and the approval of certain types of subsistence fishing as a concession to African fishers in exchange for their observance of the prohibition of commercial fishing on the river. The Belgians also agreed to discourage further investment by Europeans in the fishing industry and instead encourage expatriate purchases of fish from African fishermen. In fact this agreement was still to the obvious disadvantage of African river fishing. It ignored the fact that most European fishing took place on the lake between August and December and would thus remain unaffected.[55]

The Northern Rhodesian administration struggled to convince the Native Authorities of the necessity and impartiality of the new measures. The district commissioner called a special meeting to inform the Lunda Native Authority of the fish regulations. At the meeting, Kazembe told the district commissioner that his subjects would only obey the law if the Greeks were "taken out of the water." "Why should the Europeans stop the Africans from fishing," argued another Lunda Native Authority councilor, "when the African does not catch as much fish as the Greeks." The district commissioner replied that the law applied to both the Africans and the Greeks, on both the river and the lake. Finally, the district commissioner persuaded Kazembe and the Lunda Native

Authority to agree to the regulations, although they were never content with them.[56]

During these discussions the district commissioner promised to introduce several developmental measures to benefit the Lunda Native Authority and the fishers, just as the Belgians did on the other side of the river with the *fonds poisson* and FBEI. The Northern Rhodesian measures, however, were to fit along with a political-administrative framework that rested on the principles of indirect rule. First, the authorities introduced a fish levy of 1/4 d. per pound, to be paid by traders to the Lunda Native Treasury. The funds from the fish levy were to be directed toward the development of the fishery in much the same way as the *fonds poisson,* although the Native Authority and not the administration controlled the collection and disbursement of the funds.[57] The first major project, jointly financed by the administration and the Lunda Native Authority, was the purchase of a large fishing launch expected to compete with the Greek *ifyombo.* The district commissioner's report on the launch reveals the prevailing political tensions that drove the project:

> Politically the establishment of such a concern on our side of the water was essential . . . [due to] the extent of turmoil and resentment which existed in the minds of our fishermen during the last six months of 1953. In addition to this we were faced with a carefully concealed but definite desire on the part of the Belgian authorities to "grab" the whole of the economic potential of Lake Mweru and the Luapula River. . . . The greatest bone of contention was the fact that the Belgian nationals were getting a very large portion of the economic value of the fish which the Africans considered to be their right. Our government was prevented from taking positive action in turning the Belgian (Greek) fishermen off our waters so the only alternative was to try to get the African fishermen operating on a very much larger and more advanced scale. . . . The first launch was a Native Authority launch, also for political reasons. Senior Chief Kazembe had said either a Native Authority launch or no launch. . . . He had gone on to say "chase the Greek launches off" if you expect proper cooperation from us over fishing regulations. Hence there were only two alternatives. Either we failed to "chase off the Greek launches" and sat on the local fishermen with a squad of mobile police or we established an African-owned fishing launch on our side to be owned in the first place by the Lunda Native Authority with others to follow later. I chose the latter option.[58]

The launch was called the *Mwata Ngombe,* after the then Mwata Kazembe, Brown Ngombe. The Rural Development Fund and the Provincial Native Treasury Fund provided the capital outlay of £2,000 to purchase a large hull with a diesel engine, three plank boats, and thirty-four nets.[59] Kazembe appointed the crew of fourteen. On the 25th of March 1954, at the start of the season, Kazembe launched the *Mwata Ngombe* with much pomp and ceremony. He was dressed in ceremonial attire and virgins performed *chinkwasa* and *chilumwalumwa* dances for a crowd of over three thousand, including several of the surrounding chiefs and all of the local colonial officials. The *Mwata Ngombe* went out on its first fishing trip. Unfortunately, when it returned the next day the catch was disappointing. The crew had mounted the nets incorrectly, and a storm combined with bad navigation had destroyed the rudder. The Mwata distributed the few fish caught among his people.[60]

Over the next three months, for a variety of reasons, the *Mwata Ngombe* fishing launch failed to compete with the Greek fishing launches. Instead of employing the few African fishers skilled in fishing from an *ichombo* boat, Kazembe appointed his relatives who were accustomed to fishing with fish traps and nets launched from canoes.[61] Eventually, Kazembe hired out the *Mwata Ngombe* to another locally based fisherman, Katontoka, the headman of the largest fish trading town on Lake Mweru, Kashikishi. Up until that point Katontoka was a highly successful fisherman, with a plank boat, around twenty-four gill nets, and twenty laborers. After initial success, Katontoka also failed due to insufficient nets and repair facilities.[62] In short, the inadequate infrastructure on the Northern Rhodesian side of the Luapula and lack of capital resources dampened the takeoff of larger-scale African fishing ventures. The Mwenso brothers eventually bought the boat and managed to make a modest success of it by transporting fishers and traders along the lake and river.[63]

The Northern Rhodesian administration concentrated on several other projects, including the improvement of infrastructure and the establishment of an ice plant and jetty at Kashikishi. Development was the reward for the support of the conservation regulations. The administration hoped to compensate the loss of the river fishing resource by developing a viable and profitable African fishery based on the remaining lake fishing resources. Setting a standard for future African politicians and international donors, colonial officials used development as a political carrot. When African subjects were compliant, the colonial

administrations rewarded them with development; when they were con-
frontational, they threatened its withdrawal. In the face of ecological
disaster and its dire consequences for poor rural communities, colonial
states bolstered their authority by handing out gifts to select elites.

The Mpumbu's Guardian

The irony is that by 1954 these contested fishing regulations were
an anachronism. There were few reasons for the fishers of the valley to
object to them since the mpumbu no longer spawned in the Luapula
River. The mpumbu lasted in Lake Mweru for several more years and
continued to spawn on a smaller scale in the Kalungwishi River on the
eastern shore of Lake Mweru until the early 1970s, when they disappeared completely.[64]

Does our story of conflict and contestation over the resource tell
us why, in the end, the mpumbu disappeared? In fact, it seems that the
disappearance of the mpumbu cannot only be blamed on increased
African or Greek fishing. To be sure, as figure 4 indicates, the mpumbu
declined after massive catches by predominantly Greek fishermen on the
lake. But there were other factors that allowed for the massive increase in
production in the 1940s: after all, many of the Greek fishermen arrived
ten years prior and there existed no legal, financial, or technological constraints preventing them from achieving these high catch levels.

In the early 1940s, the Belgian administration had set about to identify obstacles to more intensive exploitation of the fishery. The administration, through the *agents* and *moniteurs-pêche*, instructed fishers in new
techniques of catching and preserving fish. They also supplied used
motor tires, out of which a stronger net fiber could be produced. Most
significantly, they identified crocodiles as an unnecessary and dangerous
vermin that prevented the intensive exploitation of the fishery. Crocodiles were, in the words of one colonial official, "*the biggest menace* to the
fishing industry in Luapula [his emphasis]." He suggested the *Force Publique* use them for target practice.[65] According to a colonial-era biologist,
"the crocodile is looked upon as something to be clubbed, netted,
snared, hooked, harpooned or shot."[66] Not only did crocodiles endan-
ger fishers and eat many fish (although subsequent research has shown
that crocodiles eat fewer fish than previously thought), they destroyed
nets, especially bottom-set gill nets. To avoid the destruction of nets,
fishers near the mouth of the lake had to use drifting gill nets or simply
rely on smaller traps and long lines and hooks.[67]

Although the suggestion that crocodiles be used for target practice was never acted on, in 1944 the Belgian administration and UMHK introduced measures to exterminate the prolific crocodile population. The administration and UMHK offered a bounty of 525 francs per head for a large crocodile, between 50 and 350 francs for smaller crocodiles, and 1.5 francs for an egg. Fishers immediately responded to this lucrative offer and a killing spree ensued. From 1945 to 1946 fishermen in Katanga killed 9,570 crocodiles and collected 81,319 eggs.[68] In fact, after a year it became necessary to decrease the bounty by about half since fishermen no longer caught fish and had instead become professional crocodile hunters.[69] One fisherman claimed to have accumulated as many as sixty crocodile skulls, loaded them onto his canoe, and sold them to the Belgians for tens of thousands of francs.[70] By the end of 1946 the administrator of Kasenga noticed that the number of crocodiles had diminished significantly.[71] The killing subsided after 1947 and continued on a smaller scale until the bounty was abolished in 1956.[72]

The last healthy spawning run of the mpumbu was in 1947. After decreasing the prolific crocodile population, expatriate fishermen could lay immense bottom-set gill nets that extended for several miles without fear that the crocodiles would create havoc with the nets during the night. Carefully positioned nets on the lake where mpumbu gathered before spawning caught several tons of fish in a single evening.[73] Moreover, despite being prohibited, long trawling seine nets were now used on the river and lake without fear of crocodiles.[74] The restrictions on the Luapula River, even if enforced, did little to prevent these harmful fishing techniques. Near the mouth of the Luapula, Lake Mweru is only ten to twenty feet deep and bottom-set gill nets easily blocked the mpumbu run. When the regulations finally prohibited fishing on the lake in 1953 as a "concession" to African fishermen, it was too late. In any event, the lake prohibition did not apply to the prespawning July to December period, when most mpumbu were caught on the lake.[75]

Inadvertently, the Belgian administration's crocodile-killing program undermined their conservation efforts. By disrupting bottom-set gill nets, crocodiles protected the fishery from environmentally harmful types of fishing. Colonial legislation could not prevent the extensive exploitation of mpumbu by African and expatriate fishermen, but tens of thousands of roaming crocodiles could. By 1947, the crocodile population was more than decimated, and the mpumbu's annual spawning came to an end. There would never again be a comparable protector of the mpumbu.

The measures intended to preserve the mpumbu only lasted for a few years. In 1959 the Kawambwa fisheries officer recognized that the restrictions were of little use and recommended that they be lifted; in 1960 the last meeting of the Anglo-Belgian Fisheries Board negotiated their end.[76] It was a remarkable meeting because it demonstrated how the rapid political changes of the late 1950s changed the influence and interests of the players and their different demands. In a complete reversal of colonial times, the Congolese Chief Nkuba Kawama, Nachituti's perpetual "brother" and Mwata Kazembe's "wife," made the most vocal demands. He insisted on the complete eradication of the prohibited fishing areas along with the expulsion of the Greek fishermen. Mwata Kazembe XVI Kanyembo Kapema was his most vocal opponent. The Mwata defended both the Greek fishermen and the retention of the prohibition in certain areas that were known to be spawning grounds for pale fish. The previous arrogance of the Belgian administrators was replaced by what one Northern Rhodesian official reported as a "fatalistic apathy. . . . They appeared a beaten force, dominated by the uncertainty of the future." The meeting agreed to the lifting of the closed season, although breeding grounds were to remain off-limits.[77] On the first day of Congolese independence, however, the Northern Rhodesian Secretary for Native Affairs instructed Luapula's provincial commissioner that Northern Rhodesia did not want any confrontation with the new Congolese authorities over this issue and that the prohibition should be lifted if the Congolese insisted.[78] In fact there was no effective state-led conservation on the lake for the next fifteen years.

Conclusions

The fishing regulations were tied to the politics of colonial states that conceived of and regulated "common resources" in very different ways. Although shrouded in a scientific and technocratic discourse, fishing regulations were never neutral or beyond these political influences. In the Belgian Congo, colonial administrators were obsessed with a sense of obligation toward the development of the colony. They coerced their colonial subjects and convinced the Northern Rhodesian administration into accepting their "scientific" regulations. At the same time, they protected the rights of capitalized expatriates to exploit the fishing resource, which they considered to be the best way to develop the local economy. In this sense, Luapula's folk wisdom was insightful: the men who put rings on the fish had been responsible for the mpumbu's disappearance.

In Northern Rhodesia, colonial political networks that controlled Native Trust resources limited the enforcement of unpopular legislation. The administration attempted to work with the Native Authorities who had managed to negotiate limited control over the implementation of the regulations. In the end, the Northern Rhodesian administration was forced to undertake more concrete development projects to placate and secure the support of the Native Authorities for conservation measures. While a few projects bore fruit, including the improvement of infrastructure and the construction of an ice plant, many others were bribes paid to Native Authorities to assure their political acquiescence. In both Northern Rhodesia and the Belgian Congo, new systems of common property replaced clan-based tenure systems: the Belgian administration opened access to capitalized foreigners while Northern Rhodesian colonial officials placed the fishery under the control of "tribal" chiefs.

Conservation in the colonies was all about the institutions, ideologies, and political struggles of the day. In the end, the fish regulations made little contribution to the actual conservation of fish. The disappearance of the mpumbu had less to do with the disregard for conservation regulations than with technological innovations in nets and types of fishing made possible by the extermination of crocodiles. The intense fishing effort that ended the mpumbu spawning run was facilitated by the Belgian crocodile extermination campaign, which allowed fishers to place more extensive gill nets overnight and block the mpumbu's spawning run. Since the 1950s, few mpumbu have been caught in either the river or lake; on the plus side, fishers and their nets are rarely disturbed by crocodiles.

For the fishers of Mweru-Luapula, decolonization brought hope for more just and equitable forms of management over their fishing resources. This chapter has explored the delicate political ecology of rural industries exploiting growing urban markets during colonialism. It has pointed to the dire environmental consequences of these industries. But, more importantly, it demonstrates the difficulties in developing command-style strategies to manage resources declared "public" or "communal," especially when exploitation is promoted by powerful networks of traders, protected by illegitimate states, and located along vast borders. Colonial regimes placed control of resources in the hands of administrators and appointed chiefs who had little legitimacy in the villages and found it difficult to enforce controls over lake fishing in the face of wealthy entrepreneurs, their *ifyombo* boats, and long, bottom-set gill nets. Even where command-and-control regulations seemed successful, they only lasted as long as the colonial state was backed by a suitable degree of force: they could hardly survive through decolonization, when emergent organs of civil society asserted themselves and state capacity collapsed.

5

Pale

States and Patrons

In the late 1970s and 1980s, Katebe Katoto, son of the entrepreneur Nissim Soriano and Mwata Kazembe XIV Chinyanta Nankula's sister, owned and managed the largest fishing venture on the lake. Katebe Katoto's fishing camp at Mulonde on the northwestern shore of Lake Mweru produced five to seven tons of fish per day during the high season of August to December. He had three large *ifyombo* boats, seventy-two smaller boats, several trucks, and his own refrigeration plant. At its height, his business employed around five hundred workers who fished, bought fish from networks of private fishers, and prepared fish to be transported and sold in Lubumbashi. In addition to a contract to supply fish to the Zairian copper mining corporation, Gécamines, Katebe Katoto owned a fishing gear shop and a retail fish outlet in Lubumbashi.[1]

In the valley, fishers reflected on Katebe Katoto's wealth, power, and success in stories that emphasized his local roots and placed him among the upper echelons of the Zairian elite. In one story, they claimed that Katebe Katoto had sought an audience with Mobutu Sese Seko. When he arrived at the presidential palace, Katebe Katoto offered to buy Lake Mweru from Mobutu. The big man of Zaire was said to have considered the matter, weighing potential profit against loss of legitimacy. In the end, Mobutu told Katebe Katoto that he had no right to sell the lake for it belonged to God. This is yet another "story of conquest," or rather a story of failed conquest, related to the negotiation over rights in Mweru-Luapula's fishery. Like the story of Nachituti's gift, it deals with the relationship between foreign conquerors and autochthonous leaders. Since Katebe Katoto was Mwata Kazembe XIV Chinyanta Nankula's sister's son, fishers recognized his ties to those who had ruled the Luapula Valley. In the postcolonial period, however, Katebe Katoto had

141

to negotiate with the new conqueror, Mobutu Sese Seko, and engage with the predatory postcolonial state. The story of Katebe Katoto's attempted purchase of the lake refers to the alliance of urban-based entrepreneurs and state officials who now ruled the valley and took the lion's share of its resources. But it warns that the lake ultimately belongs to God and could not be sold by Mobutu or controlled by his state. Like the stories of conquest that acted as ambiguous charters of rule in the precolonial period, such rumors and stories, as Luise White puts it in her study of rumors of vampires during colonialism, "address the workings of power and knowledge and how regimes use them."[2] The story of Katebe Katoto's attempted purchase informs us of the struggle between the predatory officials of the postcolonial state, wealthy businessmen, and the traders and fishers of Mweru-Luapula.

The fortunes of fishers and traders in the postcolonial period depended on the buoyant optimism of early independence as copper prices soared and, subsequently, the sudden collapse of copper prices, increased debt, and the erosion of state bureaucracies and urban economies. Rural industries like fisheries were initially subsidized by the mining economy; however, with its collapse, private initiatives took over from ambitious state-funded ventures. Moreover, with no secure income from the mines, urbanites looked to rural resources to gain some income. Migrants of different generations lived in new fishing camps and competed with autochthonous fishers. The fishers and farmers of Mweru-Luapula responded by protecting their wealth, sabotaging urban ventures, or in some cases building strategic alliances with them. Patronage networks surrounded traders like Katebe Katoto who supplied numerous fishers with nets on credit in exchange for promising their catch. Patrons who combined a system of dependency through trust and credit with access to external capital were best able to translate access to the fishery into resource rent, wealth, and power.

After the disappearance of the mpumbu, the more intensive zone of exploitation shifted from the river to the lagoons and open waters of Lake Mweru. Long nylon gill nets caught pale *(Oreochromis mweruensis)* and, to a lesser extent, a combination of chituku *(Tilapia rendalli)*, ntembwa *(Tylochromis mylodon)*, and makobo *(Serranochromis macrocephalus)*. In 1956 the construction of an ice plant on the southern shores of Lake Mweru at Kashikishi had encouraged the fresh fish trade in Zambia and particularly the trade in pale, which have an especially palatable flavor when eaten fresh (although juvenile pale were dried). While a number of species were exploited, the commercial basis of the fishery came to rest on pale, traded fresh with the urban centers from the lakeshore towns of Kashikishi in Zambia and Kilwa in Congo.

Pale spent much of their adult lives in the open waters of the lake, coming to the shallow floodplains and beaches for breeding. This life history, together with wider economic variables, structured tenure arrangements and the broader political economy of the fishery. In the shallow swamps, where stricter and older tenure rules applied, local villagers used traps, weirs, and beach seine nets to catch juvenile pale *(akacenje,* pl. *utucenje)*. They smoked, dried, or salted the juvenile pale and traded them with the urban areas. On the lake, by contrast, which was more open access but relied on capital-intensive equipment, private traders supplied fishers who lacked adequate gear with costly nylon gill nets best suited for the capture of adult pale. The traders would be paid back by a predetermined quantity of fish. This arrangement benefited the capitalized traders. They secured a faithful following of fishers and were sheltered from poor fishing seasons. Fishers who had acquired the nets on credit bore the brunt of the economic costs of poor fishing seasons since they remained with their debt. Moreover, by linking the price of a net to a quantity of fish, traders protected themselves from inflation, which would otherwise have eroded the value of their credit.

A distinctive rural-urban civil society emerged in both Zambia and Zaire. Trading associations in Zaire, dominated by wealthy businessmen, campaigned against abuses of state authority in the fishery. In Zambia, local associations of fishers laid down codes for employment and trading practices and attempted to prevent net theft. Imposed upon this local civil society were political parties—the United Independence Party (UNIP) in Zambia and the Mouvement Populaire de la Révolution (MPR) in Zaire. The respective parties consolidated power through the 1960s and 1970s in Zambia and Zaire, then slowly lost their hold over the countryside in the 1980s, until they finally surrendered to new regimes in the 1990s. The vicissitudes of state enforcement of fishing regulations were entwined with attempts by political parties to shore up their support by pandering to the interests of fishers. Finally, a series of international nongovernmental organizations (NGOs) identified Zambia's fishery as a potential growth point and encouraged regulations that would maximize production. At the same time they espoused a doctrine of "comanagement," which was occasionally at odds with their technical recommendations.

The Elusive Resilience of Pale

Demographic patterns in Mweru-Luapula changed in response to broader economic trends from the 1950s. Following a rapid period of urbanization around the time of independence, the urban and mining economy slowed down, which resulted in a decreasing rate of rural to urban migrancy and increased population densities in productive rural areas like Mweru-Luapula. Not only did fewer people leave for urban areas, but many urbanites also returned or established rural homes.[3] By the 1980s the river and lakeshore of Mweru-Luapula had become a densely populated home to around 400,000 people with 40,000 to 50,000 of them involved in the fishery as gear owners or workers (this excludes traders). [4] Along the valley road in Zambia, one village blended into the next, with no empty land or farms in between. The walk from a village to its cassava farms toward the plateau could be miles long; during times of cultivation and harvest, farmers, especially women, were forced to spend days away from their homes.

The nature and extent of changes in the lake and river cannot be simply linked to increased population density on the land. Instead, economic and environmental conditions as well as the rise of particular types of fishing need to be considered. The fish worst affected by increased fishing effort were those that went on yearly, long, and arduous spawning runs, either into the Luapula or Kalungwishi rivers, where intensive fishing activities interrupted spawning patterns. We have already seen how bottom-set gill nets across the mouth of the Luapula River led to the end of the mpumbu's spawning events in the 1950s. By the early 1970s the mpumbu did not even spawn in the Kalungwishi River and were no longer found in the fishery. Other large fish like manda (tiger fish: *Hydrocynus vittatus*) and sampa *(Heterobranchus longifilis)* had also diminished in population and size or disappeared completely.

Instead, the fishery came to rest on pale, or "green-headed bream" as they are known in English, after the distinctive coloration that flushes across their entire body. Pale had long been a favorite eating fish for the people of Luapula, second only to the mpumbu. Large-sized adult pale were the most prized of all. The following praise complains that pale are wasted on those who do not know how to eat them—they should be kept for the fishers of Luapula, who can appreciate the head of a pale.

> You, my pale, you have been wasted
> You have been given to an ignorant person

Dip polenta into the eye of the pale
This fish should be killed by a spear
Tasty and good to eat
Even without salt it is good
The maggot found in its tail is as good as beef.[5]

Pale's resilience despite intense exploitation was probably linked to its extended spawning periods that last for a number of months and to their protection of eggs and fry, which minimizes the disruption of fish reproduction and allows for the replenishment of stocks. The male fish construct several saucer-and-mound-type breeding nests in shallow sandy areas into which a female lays around thirteen hundred eggs six times at five-week intervals. Once fertilized, females mouthbrood the eggs, larvae, and small fry, leading to a relatively high juvenile survival rate.[6] After having reached the juvenile stage, so many fish have survived that the young pale can sustain a high mortality rate without it having a significant impact on their overall adult population numbers. The breeding patterns are thus relatively resilient to intense human exploitation unless nets are dragged along the sandy bottom, which destroys the nests. Instead, rainfall wields a more significant influence on pale stocks. When ample rainfall floods the riverine plains and creates shallow lagoons, adult pale have the opportunity to construct breeding nests. However, when the extent of shallows is limited, there is less space in which nests can be built; fishers using beach seine and bottom-set nets easily destroy the few nests that adult pale manage to build.

In a fashion similar to the owners of the lagoons who managed the mpumbu fishery, those who controlled the sandy shores where pale nesting activities took place benefited from the fishery. In these areas, adult and juvenile pale were caught in carefully constructed weirs and traps (see photo 6) and, more recently, a combination of different seine nets, often dragged from the beaches. Thus, at certain times and in certain places, strict tenure rules that favored local fishers applied. However, in the open lake where fishers used floating and bottom-set gill nets, a different form of tenure was established. The more significant relationship on the lake proved to be proximity to a trader, who acted as patron by guarding the nets from theft and distributing goods and fishing gear on credit in exchange for a promise of the catch. Thus, the pale fishery included, on the one hand, a precise locally defined tenure system based in breeding grounds exploited by small-scale or village-based fishers and, on the other hand, a more open-access lake fishery that relied on access to wealthy trading patrons. These different dimensions to the pale fishery would generate conflicts over attempted economic and environmental measures.

The most important breeding ground for pale was where the Luapula entered Lake Mweru, known as Chimbofuma Bay and Lagoon, which consisted of a number of sandbars, ideal for pale nests. In precolonial times, Chimbofuma was a highly controlled lagoon subject to the ritualized restrictions of the owners of the lagoons. It rested between Chisenga Island, owned by Nkuba and Kalandala, and Kanakashi and Isokwe Islands, toward the lake, all sought-after fishing grounds. During colonialism, ichthyologists, recognizing its importance as a breeding ground, declared part of this area, which they termed "Mifimbo" (presumably a corruption of Chimbofuma), closed to all fishing and tried to ensure that no one lived on the islands. The prohibition of fishing in Mifimbo did not last into independence; several villages were established on Isokwe and Kanakashi Islands and fishers steadily began to exploit the surrounding lagoons. In 1974, the Zambian government embarked on its first attempts at conservation measures by once again prohibiting fishing in this area. Other restrictions attempted by both Zambian and Zairian authorities from the early 1980s included a three-month closed period from December to March and prohibition of certain net mesh sizes and types of fishing, such as *ukutumpula* (driving fish into stationary gill nets by beating the water) and beach seining. Fishers who concentrated their activities on the lake supported these measures; however, those who relied on the lagoon fishery around Mifimbo challenged the regulations and prohibitions. The capacity of the state to enforce these regulations was weak—in general, especially during times of political upheavals, the regulations became a dead letter.

Despite a growing number of fishers, intense exploitation, and the failure to implement conservation measures, total pale catches over several decades remained somewhat constant. During the 1960s, the total catch of pale dropped for several years, and fishery officials thought this was due to the lapsing of the colonial closed period on the lake and river. Yet stocks recovered in the 1970s, fluctuated in the 1980s, and increased dramatically in the late 1990s, despite a constant increase in fishing effort.[7] The determining factor seems to have been rainfall; a good rainy season allowed for stock replenishment. When rainfall was low, there were few shallows for breeding, fishers easily destroyed breeding nests, and fish were generally exposed to more intensive human predation (since fish in less water are easier to catch). Thus, when there was not enough rainfall to ensure proper flooding, conservation regulations

Photo 5. Weirs on floodplains near Kanakashi Island to catch juvenile pale. These weirs are usually built by village labor and controlled by village leaders. The fish are smoked and sold in urban areas or to urban traders. Photograph by author, DRC, July 1998.

Photo 6. Loading an ichombo with goods to trade for fish, Kasenga. This Kasenga-based boat travels to remote and inaccessible fishing camps where traders purchased smoked fish. Photograph by author, Kasenga, DRC, July 1998.

Photo 7. Fish trader with smoked juvenile pale on an ichombo. Baskets of smoked fish from fishing camps and villages are loaded on to ifyombo boats. Photograph by author, DRC, July 1998.

had the greatest potential to benefit stock reproduction and replenishment. However, even without the enforcement of regulations and with poor rainfall, which was the case during most of the 1980s, there was little sign of "overfishing" to the level of stock collapse. While a decrease in effort might have increased the total productivity of the fishery, even this is uncertain; since the mid-1990s, with a few seasons of plentiful rainfall, total pale catches have increased along with a substantial increase in fishing effort.

Photo 8. Fresh fish trader at Mukwakwa fishing camp. Fresh fish traders wait at fishing camps until their iceboxes are full. Photograph by author, Mukwakwa, Zambia, August 1998.

Zambian Fisheries and Marketing Agencies

Between 1965 and 1974, when copper prices and government revenues soared, Zambians and Zairians, including the fishers of Mweru-Luapula, hoped that the new prosperity would reach the rural hinterlands.[8] Bulging government finances laid the basis for new systems of wealth based on state patronage that dispensed rewards from the urban centers to the rural hinterlands, either through centrally coordinated development plans or political favors that allowed certain individuals opportunities to profit from the circumvention of formal economic policies. In Zambia, the First National Development Plan (1966–70) established agencies to oversee the distribution of funds generated by the copper industry. The Credit Organization of Zambia (COZ), established in 1964 and then revamped to suit the development plan in 1966, financed small-scale farmers and businessmen to the order of 18 million kwacha, almost double what they had received in the colonial period.[9] State organs supplied rural inputs, including seed and fertilizer, to farmers.[10] While mostly oriented toward farmers, COZ also furnished fishers with 43,000 kwacha in loans and supplied subsidized nets from outlets of the state-run Nkwazi net manufacturer.[11]

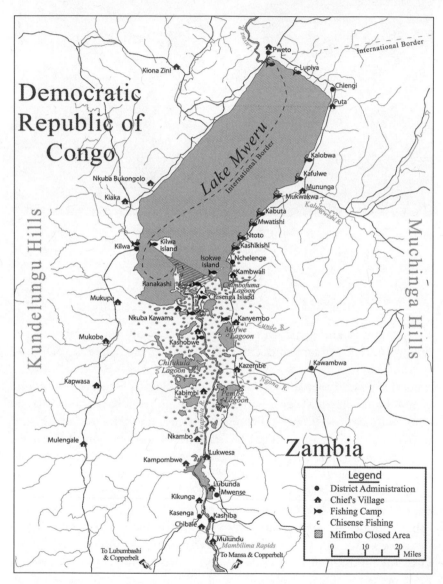

Map 4. Select villages and fishing camps, 1970s–1990s.

To better organize the logistics of dispensing loans, the government encouraged the formation of rural co-operatives.[12] Rural inhabitants responded enthusiastically and set up local organizations to receive the revenue dispensed from the center. In Kasumpa village, on the Luapula plateau, UNIP members established two farming co-operatives and a building co-operative. All received state loans and support for inputs, but failed as viable productive units.[13] This trend was not limited to isolated villages: rural co-operatives, self-help schemes, and village development committees sprang up across the province. Community development officers allocated state funds to these organizations. In 1969 the Luapula Development Committee reported 72 village committees and 57 women's clubs in Kawambwa District, 73 and 41 in Nchelenge District, and 86 and 60 in Mwense District.[14]

The state did not support all organizations. Like their colonial predecessors, they accused traders who took advantage of produce markets of exploiting both rural producers and urban consumers. Due to the difficulty of transporting farm produce, especially maize, and the relative predictability of the harvest, the state easily controlled marketing. In 1964 the Grain Marketing Board was established to service producers on the line of rail; the Agricultural Rural Marketing Board serviced more remote areas. They were amalgamated to form the National Agricultural Marketing Board (Namboard) in 1969.[15] A combination of marketing agencies and co-operative movements sponsored by the copper industry launched postcolonial development in an agrarian sector intended to become the food basket for the burgeoning urban areas. As in the colonial period, rural development was conceptualized as a platform from which to launch and support development programs that emphasized urban-based modernization. The constraints and conflicts engendered by this approach were soon apparent in the farming sector. Fair produce prices were difficult to predict, and due to uneven price incentives, rural producers farmed in an inefficient fashion with crops that were ill suited to local environmental conditions as well as regional markets.[16] The system would come crashing down with the decline of copper revenues in the 1970s.

In the fishing industry, officials sought to establish a similar combination of marketing agencies and rural co-operatives. They argued that traders exploited rural producers and overcharged for the fish that they brought to urban areas; they hoped to support producers while replacing traders, or at least their "exploitative" practices, with a single marketing board. Fishers were encouraged to form co-operative societies to look after operating needs like nets and boats. These co-operative societies would then work with a state marketing board that would eliminate the need for private traders.[17]

With the promise of state funds, fishers formed co-operative organizations. However, since the industry had grown on the basis of cooperation between fishers and traders, it was difficult to separate out these branches. The fishers' co-operatives quickly decided that their interests and profits were not best served by collaborating with the state marketing agency and, instead, that they wanted to work with local traders or trade fish themselves. Many allied themselves or amalgamated with the African Fisheries and Marketers Union (AFMU), an offshoot of the association first established in 1960 by Bunda Chisenga and other fish traders in opposition to the colonial-sponsored Co-operative Union. In January 1964, AFMU incorporated several fishing and trading associations into one association that covered "fishermen, fish traders, charcoal burners and general market vendors across the country."[18] Initially, AFMU hoped to work with the government and secure loans to improve their members' trading and fishing businesses.[19] The administration was suspicious and not as forthcoming with AFMU as they were with the farming co-operatives. Officials complained that "it is extremely difficult to identify the interests of the fishermen with those of the marketers," that there was "jealousy between the office bearers," and that the association was "not well enough organized to deserve financial aid."[20] Nevertheless, AFMU continued in its efforts and opened several branches of the organization around Lake Mweru. They met with fishery officials, held meetings with hundreds of fishers and with chiefs, including Mwata Kazembe XVII Paul Kanyembo, who apparently gave his support to the association.[21] The administration was, however, adamant: they argued that AFMU did not serve the interests of the industry in general but only "those of their individual office bearers." State aid was denied.[22]

Arguments against traders, even if well intended, were ill conceived and harmful to the fishery. Fishers were irrevocably tied to traders through networks of kin, dependents, and the flow of *nkongole* credit. Moreover, by subsidizing the *least* profitable aspect of the industry, the state encouraged a subversion of its development program. Borrowed capital was transferred to more profitable endeavors like trading. In fact, only by combining these distinct branches of production and marketing, and thereby taking advantage of private markets, could the co-operative societies enter into profitable ventures.[23] As James Pritchett

has noted for northwestern Zambia, such ill-conceived policies led development initiatives to be assessed in terms of cash delivered, which
could then be invested in more profitable endeavors, rather than declared aims.[24] Since there was no official record of the use and trans-
feral of funds dispensed to fishers, loan recovery was dismal, and in 1970
the rural credit program collapsed.[25]

. The fishers' co-operatives were meant to work with a single fish marketing agency. In 1967 the Ministry of Lands and Natural Resources
negotiated the establishment of a fish marketing agency with a Norwe-
gian entrepreneur who owned a fish purchasing and processing plant on
Lake Tanganyika. The following year, as part of the Mulungushi Reforms that sought to acquire majority shares in most major corporations,
the government purchased the majority share of the Zambian subsidiary
of the South African fish distributor Irwin and Johnson and set up Lake
Fisheries of Zambia (LFZ) as the agency responsible for the purchase and
distribution of fish within Zambia.[26] LFZ became one company within
the vast Industrial Development Corporation (INDECO) conglomera-
tion of parastatal industries that guided the Zambian economy into the
1970s. On the shores of Lake Mweru, in the trading town of Kashikishi,
LFZ set up a buying depot from where it hoped to monopolize fish purchases across the lake. Trade was oriented toward the fresh fish industry,
and refrigeration and cold storage facilities were established.

The initial and enduring problem faced by LFZ was the control of
fish prices. Before its creation in 1968, the purchase price for fish was
supposedly set; however, these prices were rarely respected. Private initiative was more important than pricing policy and the price of fish at
the lakeshore was generally higher than that decreed by the state.[27] With
the establishment of LFZ, the government renewed attempts to enforce
a maximum fixed price and gazetted a new fish price ordinance in 1967,
increasing prices slightly.[28] Still, state prices did not vary for different
types of fish and the price of dried fish was simply three times the price
of fresh (based on the assumption that since fresh fish reduced to a third
of its weight through the drying process, dried fish were worth three
times more). Such fish prices took no account of the costs of fishing,
processing, consumer preferences for different types of fish and types of
processing, and the rising prices of other foodstuffs and inputs.[29]

In addition to pricing policy, the real income of fishers was further
reduced by the decline in the catch per unit effort through the 1960s, as
pale stocks decreased or fishing effort increased beyond the maximum
sustainable yield. In 1972 fish prices were adjusted again, but were of a

similarly arbitrary nature—the Luapula fisheries officer still thought the prices "far too low to support any viable economic proposition."[30] In addition to the low prices, fishers complained that LFZ refused to purchase dried fish and did not provide fishers with goods and services like transport, nets, and twine to repair their nets. Subsidized nets were supposed to be made available by the state-run co-operative called Nkwazi, but Nkwazi often ran out of supplies.[31] LFZ retaliated by claiming that fishers sold their best catches to private traders, including Greeks from Zaire, and sold LFZ rotting fish. Fishers countered that given the low prices and the bad services of LFZ, they had little option but to sell to private traders, for, as any Zambian knew, "a fast ngwee [cent] is better than a slow kwacha [dollar]."[32] Conflict continued until the final collapse of LFZ in 1979. The Zairian traders proved to be more able to meet the demands of the fishing communities by maintaining networks of dependent fishers on the one hand and contracts with mining concerns on the other.

Zairian Patrons

Instead of state agencies, fishers on the lake returned to credit-based relationships with private traders. The preference of gill-net fishers for predominantly Zairian traders was linked to the supply of nets. The success of a fishing endeavor depended on the investment in a good quality net with a mesh size appropriate to the target species. Cooperation with traders who could supply nets was the best means of ensuring access to appropriate gear. For example, in the late 1970s fishermen had to switch mesh sizes to catch ntembwa and makobo as pale had declined in numbers. This required a shift in marketing and processing practices. Urban consumers did not enjoy fresh makobo and ntembwa enough to justify the cost of ice and the business of the fresh fish traders. In a popular song, makobo stays in the boat and is not eaten, like an unwanted spouse.[33] Instead, villagers smoked and salted makobo and ntembwa before selling them to traders or taking them to the urban markets themselves. Thus traders had to be willing to supply different nets and deal in different types of fish—fresh, smoked, or salted—depending on environmental conditions and market preference.[34] Fishers also had to ensure that their nets were not stolen; net theft was the single worst problem faced by fishers.[35] Traders with large *ifyombo* boats helped by allowing fishers to lay their nets near their boats, where guards looked after the nets (called *leleke*, meaning to let the nets sleep). In Zaire, most nets came from Katebe Katoto's Lubumbashi fishing wholesale store. When a fisher could not afford the net, Katebe Katoto gave it to him on credit, also in exchange for a future supply of fish. Thereby Katebe Katoto created a network of dependent fishers and ensured that his fishing camp at Mulonde received a steady supply of fish.[36]

Most fishers (these included a few women) owned one or two boats, one to ten gill nets, and might employ a few laborers. Many fishers were migrants from nearby Luapula villages or from the urban areas with limited capital.[37] To stay afloat with their nets in the water, these fishers thought it best to cooperate with a Zairian patron. So from the 1970s, the structure of the pale fishery began to rest on a few powerful Zairian patrons, who supplied independent but indebted fishers with nets, security against net theft, and a variety of other urban goods. In turn, the independent but indebted fishers employed a few workers who were paid by receiving a share of the catch or some of the goods supplied by Zairian patrons.

Trade in Zaire was also entwined with postcolonial political and economic developments. The Zairian state never achieved a similar legitimacy and capacity to direct development at the grassroots level as did the Zambian state. Instead, there was the facade of a developmentalist state, or what Crawford Young has termed the "shattered illusion of the integral state."[38] Mobutu consolidated power after his 1965 takeover and culled the array of political parties that characterized the First Republic. By 1967 a new constitution vastly reduced the autonomy of elected civilian government and centralized power into the personage of Mobutu. Branches of the MPR and its youth movement, the *Jeunesse du Mouvement Populaire de la Révolution* (JMPR), penetrated the countryside. In the towns of Mweru-Luapula, Kasenga, Kilwa, and Pweto, MPR and JMPR branches became the most important sites of formal political power.[39] National co-operative movements and marketing agencies proliferated, but proved even less able to intervene in the dynamics of small-scale agrarian production and trade than they had been in Zambia.[40]

The vital political and economic question in Zaire was how to deal with the vast expatriate-run concessionaire companies that dominated the entire economy. For many, "development" meant wrenching control of the Zairian economy from expatriates and placing it in the hands of Africans. Extensive nationalization, which was far more aggressive than the Zambian Mulungushi Reforms, became the vehicle for this task. In Katanga, the nationalization of UMHK and the creation of Géca- mines in 1967 was intended to address such economic inequities.[41] The fishery prospered until the Zairianization decree of 30 November 1973. Zairians were to take over all local industries and businesses; yet, the beneficiaries were not from the local communities. Lingala speakers and party officials from Kinshasa and Lubumbashi, allied to Mobutu, took over the expatriate-owned businesses and few locals from Mweru-Luapula benefited. A Hemba man from eastern Zaire grabbed the Kashobwe-based business of Nissim Soriano.[42] The *administrateur de zone*, Chibwe Pampala, who claimed to be a relative of Mobutu, took over the last functioning ice plant at Kasenga from its Belgian owner, Edmond Winkel, and in 1975 Winkel became an employee of Pampala.[43] The wealthy Kasenga-based Greek traders Antonio Macris and Sotorios, lost their business and also became employees of the new Zairian state capitalists.[44]

Expatriate traders who had married or had African children could preempt confiscation by handing over their businesses to their wives or children. Thus Nissim Soriano minimized damage to his business by handing over most of his assets before they were confiscated to his son, Katebe Katoto. At the time, Katebe Katoto was a schoolteacher who supplemented his income by trading fish. With the help of a contract to supply fish to Gécamines, Katebe Katoto rebuilt and even expanded his father's business.[45] Others followed the pattern: Benson Leon gave his business to his sons, David and Asland Kashiba, and Hadzi Phillip, one of the largest remaining Greek fishermen, also left his business to his five sons.[46] Nevertheless many expatriates left during this time. Their businesses collapsed, their houses eroded to dilapidated shells, and those who did not leave behind children have largely disappeared from popular memory.

The immediate impact of Zairianization was disastrous. Inexperienced northerners misused equipment, created tensions with local employees, and fomented widespread resentment. "With Zairianization," claimed one University of Lubumbashi researcher with reference to Kasenga, "a period of 'hellish' exploitation began for the rural proletariat."[47] There is some evidence that locals sabotaged the northern-run ventures; in 1975 a fire destroyed many of the boats and facilities in Kasenga's harbor.[48] An old businessman, David Lupandula, lamented that "everything fell apart. . . . The suffering began."[49] Indeed, the old expatriate patrons of Luapula's fishing industry collapsed and were replaced by unreliable and for the most part resented state beneficiaries.

After a few years, it was evident that the "Zairianization" of Luapula's fishery had failed. The businesses taken over by state elites collapsed or were repurchased by the sons of the original owners. Through the late 1970s and 1980s, large-scale Zairian producers and transporters regained their hold over the fishery. Besides Katebe Katoto, Zairians like Nicholas Paraskevas, son of a Greek fisherman and Congolese mother, distributed nets to hundreds of fishers on credit in exchange for their catch.[50] David Kashiba and his brother, sons of Benson Leon and his Luapulan wife, transported between thirty-five and forty tons of fish per month, which they sold to the diamond-mining parastatal, Miba.[51] Zairian *ifyombo* vessels with up to thirty plank boats in tow were often seen fishing out on the lake.[52] In language reminiscent of the Northern Rhodesian condemnation of Greek fishermen based in the Belgian Congo, Zambian fisheries officers in the 1980s complained that catches by the Zairian vessels were "enormous and if the fishing pressure continues at the present rate, the standard stocks are likely to be badly affected."[53]

The new entrepreneurs, who had learned from their previous experiences, formed trade organizations to defend themselves against the predatory Zairian state. In 1982 a group of Lubumbashi-based commercial fishers and traders joined in the *Association des Pêcheurs du Zaire* (APEZA) to campaign for the enforcement of uniform fishing regulations and to secure loans for fishers.[54] While the MPR did not trust independent associations, failed hegemony in the "shattered" state meant that the party could do little to prevent the rise of such civic organs.[55]

In the late 1980s the collapse of the Zairian economy and infrastructure combined with continued state harassment led some of the large fishing companies to relocate. A new, surfaced road on the Zambian side of the valley financed by donors and built by Italian contractors made Zambia's faraway urban areas more accessible than nearby Lubumbashi (the 135-mile road between Kasenga and Lubumbashi had deteriorated so much that it took more than twenty-four hours to negotiate and was often closed during the rainy season). Moreover, contracts with the large state-owned Zairian mining companies were no longer as lucrative. Katebe Katoto closed his operation in Mulonde since Gécamines no longer paid for the delivery of fish and the Lubumbashi road made the fresh fish trade risky. He collected his small fortune, relocated to Belgium, and left his fishing operations to his younger brother, Moses Katumbi. In 1993, Katumbi requested permission from the Zambian government to transfer the Mulonde fishing business to Zambia. A resident of Kitwe, Zambia, Katumbi had influential Zambian connections. He was a perpetual nephew of Mwata Kazembe and the blood cousin of the reigning Mwata Kazembe XVIII Munona Chinyanta (through the marriage of Munona's father's sister to Nissim Soriano). He was also a friend of the new Zambian president, Frederick Chiluba, who proved more forthcoming than Mobutu had toward his brother, Katebe Katoto (Chiluba has been accused of entering into a fraudulent U.S.$20.5 million arms deal with Katebe Katoto while he was president).[56] With the support of the Zambian government, Katumbi established a new fish-buying operation, Chani Fisheries (later renamed Tamba Bashila), next to the Nchelenge government offices. Given the long experience of the Soriano family with the fishers of Mweru, their operation was trusted and secured widespread support. Mwata Kazembe XVIII Chinyanta Munona became a shareholder in the business. Above all, Chani provided the gold of the retail fish business: credit in form of nets in exchange for future catches.[57] Chani, and later Tamba Bashila, embarked on several other ventures, including allegedly smuggling weapons from Kazembe's capital, Mwansabombwe, to Angola.[58]

A combination of Zambian businessmen, aid agencies, and state elites attempted to compete with the Congolese fish traders. The Dutch aid organization, Stichting Nederlandse Vrijwilligers (SNV), identified the fishery as a potential economic growth point. Like their expatriate colonial and postcolonial predecessors, they thought the fish marketing arrangement inefficient. To remedy this, in a joint program with Finn aid (Finnida), they relaunched a fish-buying and freezing corporation called Isabi Fisheries along the lines of LFZ (in fact it occupied the old LFZ premises). Local businessmen like Paul Chisakula purchased shares in the new venture and SNV brought in technical assistants to help with the managerial and production operations. In 1993, after a three-year launching period, Isabi Fisheries finally opened. Isabi fish buyers traveled with ice-filled fish boxes to the fishing camps on the southeastern shore and to Kilwa Island. When they returned, the fish were frozen in blast freezers and sold to Copperbelt traders.[59] But their success was limited for the same reasons that LFZ failed: they could not secure the clientage of fishers who preferred to exchange their fish with Chani Fisheries. Instead of cash, Chani Fisheries supplied trade goods and fishing gear in exchange for fish, and thereby secured a large clientele of indebted fishers. At the time of my research, in the late 1990s, Isabi Fisheries was on the verge of collapse.

Several state interventions that had attempted to catalyze economic activity and expand the Luapula's fishery had failed. The international aid organizations that tried to resurrect such failed schemes in the 1990s had learnt little from the history of such ventures. The credit-based patronage networks between Copperbelt-based traders and local fishers remained the dominant form of economic organization on the lake. Most important were the vast patronage networks headed by the sons of expatriate traders. Fine-tuned state development schemes that relied on an interventionist state failed due to limited state capacity and ill-conceived policies. We can see further evidence of this in the attempted reimplementation of conservation regulations in response to renewed fears of overfishing in the pale's breeding and nesting areas.

Weak States and Conservation

Stocks of pale in the lake were maintained by successful breeding in the shallow sandy lagoons. Thus the lake fishers and their patrons were always concerned that fishing in these areas be restricted. As in the colonial period, the entire fishery had legal status of common property governed by regulations developed by state and fisheries officials, even while informal forms of tenure, especially in the lagoons, were still significant. The colonial conservation measures first introduced in the late 1940s to protect the mpumbu's spawning run were eradicated or ignored by the early 1960s. African fishers associated these conservation regulations with the Belgian and British colonial governments and detested them; after independence, the new administrations abolished most fishing regulations or overlooked their existence. The first postcolonial restrictions concerned Mifimbo, where the Luapula River enters Lake Mweru, which was a significant breeding ground for pale. In or near Mifimbo, owners of the lagoons had long supervised and demanded tribute from fishers who used traps and weirs to catch mostly juvenile pale. In colonial times, fishing regulations prohibited exploitation in the area altogether. By the end of the colonial period, however, the regulations were not enforced and many of the restrictions promoted by the owners of the lagoon were not respected. Exploitation increased in the postcolonial period as new small-scale migrant entrepreneurs and fishers arrived. With declining stocks of pale through the 1960s, LFZ and capitalized gill-net fishers became concerned with small-scale fishing of juvenile pale in Mifimbo.[60]

In 1974, the Zambian fishing authorities decided to reintroduce strict regulations on fishing in Mifimbo to curtail the catching of juvenile pale. LFZ and the large-scale fishers applauded these measures, but small-scale fishers who earned their livelihood from fishing in the area resented the new regulations. They could not afford the larger nets and boats necessary for fishing on the open lake and instead relied on traps or smaller nets that caught juvenile pale. They refused to respect the new conservation regulations. The Zambian Department of Fisheries (DoF) found it difficult and expensive, due to fuel costs, to monitor the large expanse of river and marsh area that was only accessible by boat. When they did manage to conduct boat patrols, they regularly caught violators. Immediately after the implementation of the regulations, the DoF with police aid arrested six fishermen, confiscated one hundred nets and imprisoned the fishermen for three months.[61] In 1977, fishermen (probably those imprisoned the previous year) stole back the nets previously confiscated by the DoF.[62] Over the next decade, as the DoF's facilities and equipment deteriorated, they became less able to enforce restrictions on fishing in Mifimbo: a small, understaffed, and ill-equipped government bureaucracy could not guard a vast area from an increasing number of small-scale, poor fishers.[63] The capacity of local enforcers was at a low point.

In Zaire, departments of government concerned with fisheries were complicated bureaucracies without clear demarcations of duties. The Zairian Division of Fisheries *(Divisions des pêches et piscicultures)* had about 20 Kinshasa-based employees subordinated to the Department of Water and Forestry *(Département des eaux et forêts),* which had about 150 untrained monitors concerned with fisheries. The National Office of Fisheries *(l'Office national des pêches),* established in 1974 after Zairianization to aid indigenous fishers, had a personnel of over 120, a budget of $220,000, and no clear program of action. There were also several semi-autonomous research agencies often sponsored by international or Belgian aid organizations.[64] On the ground there were a number of officers at each fishery. At both Kasenga and Pweto there was a fisheries agent *(agent de pêche)* with several subordinates located in fishing villages and camps along the river. After 1964, however, patrols were impossible since their boat was broken and never repaired. In 1974 the Kasenga *agent de pêche* recommended scrapping all regulations since they could not be enforced.[65]

Throughout the 1980s the catch per fisher in the pale fishery continued to decline, probably due to an increasing number of fishers, or increasing fishing effort in general, rather than an absolute decline or collapse in stocks. Yet fishers and fisheries experts, who perceived the problem in terms of declining stocks, began to call for the reintroduction and strict enforcement of a closed season. They argued that pale would follow other species like mpumbu and disappear from the fishery.

The Zairian authorities agreed and implemented a closed season of three months between December and March. The closed season was modeled on the old colonial restrictions intended to protect the mpumbu; there was no clear ecological reason for closure during that season for the pale—at best, the closure would only lower general fishing effort. In the face of continued opposition by small-scale fishers, the fishery department appeared to abandon attempts to protect breeding grounds and instead arrived at the political compromise of closing the entire fishery for a few months (similar to the political compromise reached with the mpumbu closure). In addition to closure, nets were restricted to a mesh size of larger than fifty millimeters, a length of less than one hundred meters, and a maximum depth of two meters.

Due to the cooperation of the wealthier fishers, the regulations were enforced with some success. Coincidentally, there were also good rains that season, and after the closed season was lifted, pale proliferated.[66] In 1986, following the Zairian success, the Zambian authorities also agreed to a closed season of three months from December to March. The wealthy fishermen applauded this decision, but again the village fishers who worked independently of the large patrons complained that they were not able to support themselves during the closed period. Since there were more small-scale fishers and their influence was greater in the Zambian fishery compared to the Zairian fishery, there was greater resistance to the measures. Daud Samuel Kulaba, a moderately wealthy gill-net fisherman from Kashikishi, remembered: "The fisheries came and asked us if we could close the lake, because the Zairians were closing the lake. . . . The big fishermen said that it is better if we close the lake to allow the fish to breed. The small fishermen didn't support the closing of the lake, because during the closed season we can catch a lot of fish. . . . There were fights but because the big fishermen had lots of money they won. The small fishermen could not do anything."[67]

The DoF, with police support, went on aggressive patrols during the closed season and in 1986 confiscated some 145 nets, which were auctioned to the public. In 1987, the DoF reported continued resistance by fishers who thought the closed season was "too rigid." In response to widespread discontent, the DoF called a meeting with the ward chairmen, fishers, and chiefs to secure their support in enforcing the regulations and convincing the fishers of their necessity. Zambian officials argued that the conservation regulations were fair and made provision for poorer fishing households. Still, during that season they arrested fourteen fishermen (all later acquitted) and confiscated 341 nets.[68]

Unlike the colonial period, when chiefs played a major role in the enforcement of fishing regulations, fisheries officials and police enforced the first postcolonial regulations in both Zambia and Zaire. The state bureaucracy joined with an emergent civil society to negotiate and enforce conservation measures. In Zaire, regulations had to attain the support and cooperation of the large-scale commercial fishers like Katebe Katoto and the APEZA association. Conservation came to represent a new arena where state and social movements negotiated access to the fishery. In the colonial period, conservation was enforced through chiefs alongside a repressive state apparatus; in the postcolonial period, conservation was negotiated between peripheral structures of weak states and incipient organs of civil society.

Regulations enforced by underpaid (frequently unpaid) state officials alongside autonomous economic agents were not able to withstand political and economic pressures. Closure and conservation regulations became an opportunity for state officials to collect additional revenue by conducting what amounted to raids on fishers and traders. Instead of implementing the regulations, local officials were content to turn a blind eye in exchange for payment from the fishers. So-called "special consignments" of fish traveled on trucks between Kasenga and Lubumbashi. By bribing officials, the wealthy traders actually circumvented the regulations that they had supported and helped to develop. The regulations only helped to prevent competition from small-scale traders who could not afford to bribe the agents of the state. Toward the end of the 1980s, fish traders only needed a military patron to allow for the transport of fish during the closed season.[69] In Zambia, the post-1989 era of structural adjustments, when rural local government was meant to become financially independent, accentuated the problem. The 1991 Local Government Act encouraged rural district councils to raise their own finances and in 1995 the Nchelenge District Council increased the fish levy fivefold. Although the council promised to use the funds to improve infrastructure and conservation measures, many felt that the revenue remained with district officials.[70]

Fishers and many of their patrons began to resent demands by the local state or soldiers in the name of legislation that supposedly protected their resources. In Zaire they formed fishing committees and associations like the *Union Syndical des pêcheurs indépendents* (USPI) and the *Association culturelle des Shila du lac Moero* (ASHILAC). They argued that closure and the conservation regulations were acceptable as long as they were enforced fairly. USPI was created in 1990 to act against the numerous exactions and aggravations suffered by the fishers due to "certain over-zealous and unscrupulous functionaries and agents."[71] Similarly, in 1992, ASHILAC wrote to the Katangan governor to complain that while fishers accepted the closed season, it was not observed, as "certain agents with the complicity of military authorities neglect its strict enforcement and instead encourage fraud to their profit."[72]

Net theft increased due to a collapse in policing. The theft of nets had long been a problem, especially near the border where a fisher from Zambia might steal a Zairian's nets with few consequences (Zambians blamed Zairians and Zairians blamed Zambians for net thefts). But with the near collapse of the police forces, there was little chance of net recovery and thefts soared.[73] Many Zambian fishers simply packed up and relocated to Lake Mweru Wantipa, away from the border; others hired laborers to guard their nets in the evening or resorted to *ukutumpula* fishing methods that did not involve leaving nets overnight.[74] The Zambian authorities introduced net and boat licenses to combat thefts, but the DoF did not have enough personnel or sufficient authority to collect license fees.[75] Moreover, fishers did not trust state officials suspected of graft or even net theft. Instead, some Zambian fishers formed associations to combat net theft. When nets were stolen, the association investigated the matter and if the culprits were caught they were taken to the police after a severe beating.[76] Besides concerning themselves with the theft of nets, the associations drafted employment codes to govern the relationships between gear owners and laborers.[77] In Zambia, these fishing associations filled in gaps left by the absent or collapsed state and created a civic sphere utilized to negotiate resource allocation in the fishery.

In the late 1980s, as official state structures failed to implement laws, chiefs reconsolidated their power and influence in matters pertaining to the fishery. In lagoon areas, many Lunda chiefs, like Kambwali, tried to reinvent their control over the river and lakes by appointing new owners of the lagoons who were not the historic owners of the lagoons. These appointed owners were more directly linked to modern chiefs even while they invented forms of traditional authority through new tales of conquest and sorcery.[78] Yet an increasing number of fishers settled in the area and refused to obey unpopular decrees by hereditary rulers, especially when chiefs and owners lacked local legitimacy.[79]

On the lake, chiefs engaged with private patrons and the state bureaucracy to establish a stake in the fishery. While there were few "traditional" controls over the lake fishery since there were never any owners of the lagoons on the lake, chiefs still carved out an important role.

Those from the south of the valley demanded a portion of the fish levy collected by the district council or secured tribute payments from Isabi and Chani Fisheries. If not forthcoming, the chiefs prevented fish buyers from operating in their areas. On one occasion, Chief Mununga expelled representatives of Chani Fisheries for alleged "non-compliance with his rulings and disrespectful behavior."[80] However, chiefs generally found that greater profit lay in cooperating with the companies and the Zairian patrons. Mwata Kazembe XVIII Munona Chinyanta became a shareholder of Chani Fisheries, accepted a managerial position in the Lake Mweru Water Transport Company, and with his old rival, Chief Mununga, attended district council meetings concerning the fishery.[81]

The Promises of Democracy

Fishing regulations that relied on this precarious mélange of state and civic organs were easily toppled by winds of political change that blew through the valley. In Zambia, as disenchantment with UNIP spread, local politicians vied for support among the poorer villagers and fishers opposed to conservation regulations. By the early 1990s, UNIP was desperate to generate support in the rural villages, especially given the high levels of urban contestation and upheaval, and thus promised poorer fishers an end to unpopular regulations. Before the 1991 elections, politicians linked to the leading Zambian opposition party, the Movement for Multi-Party Democracy (MMD), also promised an end to the closed season and conservation regulations. But UNIP was not to be outdone, and their branches supported the settlement of a permanent fishing village on Kanakashi Island in the middle of the prohibited breeding grounds. They even secured funding for the building of a school on Kanakashi Island.[82] Mwata Kazembe XVIII Munona Chinyanta complained that the conservation regulations were disregarded because "we were always looking for votes." Previously, he claimed, there were owners of the lagoon to prevent people settling in these areas, but "because of political inclinations this system eroded."[83] During the 1991 elections there was no closed season in Zambia and villagers and migrants established a number of permanent fishing settlements in or near the Mifimbo breeding grounds.[84] With democracy, as the MMD slogan put it, "the hour has come"; goods would flow into the shops and there was little need for conservation.

After the MMD won the elections, an alliance of NGOs and large investors renewed a call for conservation measures. SNV and their fisheries advisors viewed closure as essential to the sustainability and future well-being of the fishery. But there were also more practical interests at work. The DoF easily ensured that Chani and Isabi halted operations during the closed season since the companies were based at or near the Nchelenge government offices; it was more difficult to actually prevent smaller-scale fishers from fishing. If there was a closure, the larger operations thought, it must be respected so that they benefited during the open season from increased catches. With the help of SNV, the DoF held fish conservation seminars that involved the new big ventures, Isabi and Chani, fishing associations, and chiefs. In 1993 all agreed to respect a closed season of three months from the beginning of December to the end of February, and a more thorough fish licensing system was also introduced.[85] To better facilitate consultation over the new measures, SNV and the DoF created the Nchelenge Fisheries Coordinating Committee (NFCC) in 1995. In the NFCC meetings, Isabi, Chani, SNV, the DoF, fishing associations, and an array of chiefs including Mwata Kazembe XVIII Chinyanta Munona negotiated issues pertaining to the conservation of the fishing resources. Isabi and Chani both agreed to provide contributions of fuel for the DoF's patrol boat.[86]

While the NFCC seemed a more viable and consultative arrangement for the enforcement of closure, problems remained. Fishing continued unhindered in areas inaccessible to the Nchelenge-based DoF, like the floodplains and lagoons. Officials believed that the only way to enforce the measures was through the chiefs. In a fashion similar to the colonial period, the "traditional" roles of conservation by the chiefs were resurrected into a justification for their involvement in the enforcement of regulations.[87] A few chiefs gladly took on the guise of new protectors of the fishery[88]; most, like Mwata Kazembe XVIII Munona Chinyanta, were more astute. He argued that when the chiefs are called on to enforce the regulations "we become [the fishermen's] . . . enemies while the government remains on good terms with them. . . . If we charge someone a goat, he goes to the ward councilor. Then the ward councilor will tell him that the chief has no power to charge him."[89] Chiefs in the 1990s had little authority to enforce conservation measures, especially when politicians in Zambia and soldiers in Zaire compromised these measures. Migrants to Mweru-Luapula, many of whom were urbanites, had little respect for the authority of chiefs to whom they had never given tribute. Above all, a chief had few means to punish offenders. As one fisherman put it, "What can chiefs' closure mean if the government closure does not mean that much to us?"[90] Chiefs had neither the authority nor the will to enforce unpopular legislation. Nevertheless, they put on the guise of concern that justified their meager stipends and augmented their much diminished local political status. They did not, however, enforce closure in the remoter parts of the lake. The vice president of the Nchelenge fishing association estimated that only one-twelfth of the lake actually remained closed.[91]

For fishers in Zaire, the violation of closure and fishing regulations became associated with Mobutu's corrupt soldiers. In the 1990s fishers and traders viewed the replacement of Mobutu's regime by a southern-led administration as an opportunity to get rid of parasitic state and military officials. In Luapula, issues surrounding conservation were central to this attempt. On the Zairian side of the river, fishing associations had made repeated appeals to the Lubumbashi authorities to prevent Mobutu's soldiers from confiscating nets and from demanding fish in exchange for permitting fishing during the closed season. In 1992, despite an attempt at closure, fisheries officers at Pweto reported that fishing camps were still open. Moreover, soldiers seized nets and demanded payment from fishers without the permission of the fisheries department or the government official, the *commissaire de zone*.[92]

After growing discontent in Shaba (now Katanga), which culminated in student protests and the "Lubumbashi massacre" of 1990, Mobutu appointed a "Native Katangese" as head of the province to deflect criticism. "Katangans" managed to fill the provincial administration with their own; they achieved a degree of autonomy from Kinshasa and kept Mobutu's notorious soldiers at bay.[93] They also expelled the "Kasaian" ethnic minority from Katanga. This urban-centered, politically inspired ethnic cleansing then spread to Mweru-Luapula. Luapulans rallied behind a "Katangan" identity that excluded "Kasaians," many of whom had long established themselves as fishers or traders. In 1992–93 "Katangans" chased "Kasaians" from the fishery.[94] Fishers enforced their own rules of access through the mobilization of ethnic identities linked to the political contestations of the postcolonial state.

By the mid-1990s, in both Zambia and Zaire, only coercive measures could ensure the continued enforcement of the regulations. Once again, the state had to be set apart from civil society, in a fashion similar to the functioning of the Belgian local administration. Authoritarianism, not democracy and consultation, buttressed the efforts of the state to restrict access to the fishery. "The government has made a big mistake," the old Kashikishi businessman Paul Chisakula argued in 1996, "When a fisherman is arrested for *kutumpula* during closure, he is taken to court and

charged K300 or K250. How many makobo is K250? Is it not two makobo? It is only one makobo. In the past the law used to be very strong.
When a person was caught during the closure he was charged a lot of
money or imprisoned for many days or two years. This made a fisherman think twice before he would leave for the lake."[95] In 1997, Paul
Chisakula's advice was followed and jail sentences introduced for offenders, as in the harsh colonial days. Closure was not perfect, but better than in the past.

In Zaire the strengthening of the state was even more crucial. In
1997, the rebel leader, soon to be president, Laurent Kabila and his soldiers took power. Kabila's anticorruption drive sought to distinguish his
administration from that of Mobutu. The soldiers refused to allow fishing during closure and fishers were too afraid to try their luck. Such "solutions" were ad hoc and unsustainable in the long term—two years
later Kabila's soldiers took on the same role as Mobutu's. As long as desperate migrants, dropouts from the collapsing urban economies, continued to flood the fishery and a growing rural population found no alternative employment, pale were called on to feed more mouths. There
was little that bankrupt states could do to control or even direct patterns
of economic development and fishing effort. Fisheries experts could
suggest optimum levels of exploitation; however, the fortunes of the
fishery would depend on the ongoing struggles between underpaid and
predatory state agents, trading patrons, and fishers.

Conclusions

This chapter has straddled three interrelated themes in the making of
the postcolonial fishery: environment, economy, and state capacity. The
productivity of the pale fishery was primarily linked to rainfall; despite
increased levels of exploitation, the pale fishery remained viable and
after good rains came bouncing back. Small-scale village fishers caught
juvenile pale during and after breeding in shallow lagoon areas using a
combination of traps, weirs, and nets. To catch pale on the lake, by
contrast, good-quality nylon nets were essential, and these were best
supplied through informal business networks linked to Lubumbashi-
based traders. Traders distributed nets to undercapitalized fishers;
thereby, capital could shelter itself from unreliable fishing seasons and
fishers could secure access to changing types of fishing gear. Although
all were reliant on pale stocks, the economic and environmental interests of the fishers, trading patrons, and state agents often diverged.

Traders and fishers dependent on the lake fishery supported efforts to prohibit fishing in the breeding areas where small-scale fishers sought to continue their customary forms of fishing. Underpaid state officials mediated between these groups even as they attempted to manipulate regulations to secure extra income for themselves.

In the face of state collapse and political contestation, fishers and traders in both Zambia and Zaire rallied behind local identities and formed organizations to regulate business. Where state collapse was greatest, in Zaire, the need to create and enforce some framework to conduct business and to defend fishers and traders from the state was most urgent. Katebe Katoto joined with other wealthy entrepreneurs to form associations that protected them from predation by strategic collaboration with certain state officials. Less formal social groups, from business associations between trusted fishers and traders to a regional "Katangan" ethnicity, further facilitated protection against state predation. In Zambia, too, fishers and traders formed associations to determine codes for employment and trade and to prevent theft of fishing gear. Nascent civic institutions and social formations emerged hand-in-glove with fragile state bureaucracies.

Luapula's fishing industry is a remarkable example of the success and tenacity of African business ventures despite continuing constraints. Businessmen like Katebe Katoto, Moses Katumbi, and David Kashiba were able to overcome successive economic crises and limited capital by creating networks of dependents rather than paying regular salaries. They worked through credit systems based on the distribution of nets and other urban goods desired by fishers and their families. The number of political and economic elites in Zambia and Congo who herald from Luapula underscores the importance of these business networks. Former Zambian president, Frederick Chiluba, for example, made his career by rising through the ranks of the Copperbelt trade unions; but the contacts provided by his Luapula connections were crucial in his political and economic ventures. And Katebe Katoto, who now refers to himself as Raphael Katoto, has indicated his interest in pursuing a senior position in the Congolese government, and according to the latest reports, is the vice president of the Rwandan-backed Congolese opposition party, Rassemblement congolais pour la démocratie.[96]

State attempts to intervene in the economy and environment in the form of marketing boards, nationalizations, closed fishing seasons, and restricted areas failed due to a lack of state capacity alongside the resilience of trader-fisher networks. This is not to argue that the invisible hand has worked to best effect: fine-tuned technocratic regulations could have perhaps resulted in higher catch levels by ensuring that fishing effort did not rise beyond levels that reduced stock productivity; yet, realistically, the capacity to introduce these measures was low. Even while "experts" proclaimed the necessity for "co-management," there was a widening gap between the economic and environmental regulations suggested by them and the expectations and demands of local fishers and entrepreneurs. As Inge Tvedten has observed for Namibia's Caprivi fishery, broader social, political, and economic contexts severely compromised solutions based on abstract ideas of "co-management."[97] The irony in the discourse of those international experts who declared the need for such bottom-up management regimes was that, in effect, organs of civil society, ranging from extensive trader-fisher patronage networks to local fishing associations, had taken over the functions of fishery management from collapsing states and ill-equipped fisheries departments.

6

Chisense

Wealth and Family

Grace Chama was eager to talk of her duties as a single mother, household head, and fish trader. The thirty-nine-year-old mother of four divided her time between her sister's home in Lusaka and Kabuta fish camp on the southeastern shores of Lake Mweru where her children stayed. She traveled hundreds of miles from Kariba and Kafue in the south of Zambia to the Luangwa Valley in the east and Lake Mweru and Tanganyika in the north in search of cheap fish. She would always return to sell the fish in the markets of Lusaka. Her meager profits would be reinvested in the fish trade, with a portion saved for the upbringing and education of her children. She claimed to be only one of an entire class of women who pursued this arduous work and lifestyle: "There are many women trading fish. Most of them are widows or are single, and it is the only way to make a living. A woman must do the work, maybe she has children without being married, or her husband does not work or lost his job; it is her only way for her to support the children."[1]

What accounts for the increasing importance of women in southern central Africa's rural-urban fish trade? In the 1950s, after all, fish trading in the urban markets was for the most part the terrain of entrepreneurial men. Women became fish traders through new commercial exchanges that grew out of predominantly female productive spheres previously considered to be part of the "subsistence" or "household" economy. In the urban areas, women began to trade in household supplies to earn extra cash as other more stable forms of financial support like salaried work became scarce or paid too poorly for subsistence. Rural women branched out from cassava farming and beer brewing into the fish business. Chisense fish, which could be traded in small quantities and were cheap to process, offered a point of entry to these small-scale entrepreneurs.

170

In the 1970s while washing dishes in the lake, women noticed a proliferation of small fish that they called chisense. Women had long dragged cloth through the shallows to catch these fish, which they used to prepare extra relish to accompany the cassava polenta eaten by their families. Although not new to the lake, the chisense fishery had never before developed into a commercially exploited resource. But in the 1970s, due to the abundance of the fish and the ease of capture, women began to use them for barter and trade. As profitability increased, men who had acquired financial capital from salaried employment, urban ventures, or other rural businesses returned to Mweru-Luapula and became involved in their capture. Soon a new chisense fishery emerged and offered those fishers and traders willing to invest in it far greater returns than the gill-net fishery.

In the gill-net fishery, men had monopolized and controlled profits; the chisense fishery opened up trading opportunities for those without significant amounts of capital, especially women. While only a few women like Anna Chilombo Kapapula became important traders in the colonial period, many more did so with the rise of the chisense fishery. There were economic and political reasons for both the lack of female participation in the early fishery and their integral involvement in the postcolonial period. The weight of catches per fisher in the gill-net fishery were far lower than the chisense fishery and processing was more capital intensive. Fishermen preferred to sell large fish like pale, which could easily rot, to a single, reliable purchaser, usually a man with money and a vehicle. Women, who generally lacked capital, found it difficult to participate in this rural-urban trade. In the chisense fishery, by contrast, catches were ample, easy to process, and once dried they could be stored for a long period. The fish could be distributed among a number of buyers, many of them local women, who did not need to invest a great deal of capital in processing and trade.

Access to urban markets was more open than in the colonial period, when the administration had encouraged men to go to the Copperbelt while restricting, or at least discouraging, the urbanization of women. There were a substantial number of women involved in diverse economic activities in the Copperbelt urban areas during colonialism[2]—yet the barrage of obstacles set up by the colonial state prevented the emergence of a viable class of female rural-urban traders. Thus, in general, during the colonial period men were able to monopolize access to urban markets for the sale of more profitable produce. From the 1960s, as state controls over the movement of women declined, men could no longer control access to dispersed fish resources and urban markets; women became autonomous producers and traders.

So far this study has tackled the problem of ownership and wealth by considering those who have tenure claims or, through their control of people, goods, or currencies, have managed to accumulate forms of wealth. However, this focus loses perspective on the majority of re-source users in the late twentieth century, especially women, who had few claims to rich fishing grounds or access to forms of capital and wealth, except for their control over their children. To correct this bias, this chapter is devoted to the chisense fishery, where a few fishers and traders have managed to achieve modest degrees of commercial suc-cess, but most are characterized by the shortage of capital resources. In-stead of extensive patronage networks, like those of Katebe Katoto, the rise of the chisense fishery allowed women the opportunity to consoli-date and accumulate wealth in the form of human and social capital. They managed to exert greater control over their children, often at the expense of absent or poor husbands, and re-affirm certain aspects of Luapula's matrilineal family ties. By doing so, women ensured that wealth held in people, especially in *ulupwa* families, remained a salient feature of Mweru-Luapula's political economy.

Greater economic autonomy for women allowed for the rise of a class of female rural-urban traders with weak ties to their husbands and stronger ties to their children, siblings, and parents. The decision to in-vest in social or family ties, rather than financial capital, was both cul-tural and economic—it is very difficult to separate these spheres in the realm of human agency. A woman's status was linked to her children, and thus children remained of significant value. More mundane and quotidian economic reasons were also important: children and family represented a more stable arena for investment than the accumulation of rapidly devaluing currencies; moreover, a child's labor as fisher or processor could be a boon to a household business. With the rise of the chisense fishery, the cultural legacy of a system of wealth in people com-bined with occasional labor shortages to encourage women to once again seek wealth through children.

The ability of chisense to withstand intense levels of exploitation, relatively open access to the resource, and an urban market hungry for cheap fish all combined to give economic form to the chisense fishery. Capitalized men who owned chisense fishing gear worked alongside rural women; these two groups formed the basis of chisense industry. Rural women achieved economic autonomy and accumulated human capital through investment in their chosen family network. When burdened with costly husbands, big women asserted independence over their households and their children. On the other hand, some women who had wealthy husbands invested in families oriented around their big men husbands and attempted to protect themselves from affective and economic claims by their own matrikin. As in the colonial period, conflict linked to inequalities within and between families was expressed through witchcraft allegations.

Chisense: The Fly of the Lakes

The decline of certain species like mpumbu and the limited profits of fishers dependent on pale seem to be a good example of the economic and environmental problems with common property resources identified by H. Scott Gordon and Garret Hardin. Yet common property resources are often evolving, dynamic, and complex environmental systems. This was especially the case in fisheries that have long been exposed to intense levels of human exploitation and have multiple exploitable species. Fishery economists have explored the complicated interactions found in such multispecies fisheries, where certain species "adjust" to fishing pressures and take advantage of available ecological niches—some fish might even proliferate due to the absence of their predators or competitors. Moreover, the exploitation of one type of fish might act to the benefit of certain types of entrepreneurs and to the detriment of others.[3] Most heavily exploited fisheries tend to be "fished down" in size; in other words, smaller species with a more rapid biological turnover tend to prosper in place of larger fishes.[4] Small fish and the fishers and traders who exploit them may become the beneficiaries of the tragedy of intensive exploitation of larger fish. So the tragedy of the commons is in the eye of the beholder; there are winners and losers.

　　Chisense *(Poecilothrissa moeruensis)* are small, silvery members of the Clupeidae family that reach a maximum size of about forty millimeters.[5] These pelagic fish, living in the upper layers of open waters, aggregate in large shoals and feed on plankton. Chisense have a number of natural predators, primarily manda (tigerfish: *Hydrocynus vittatus*) and lupata *(Schilbe mystus)* but also makobo *(Serranochromis macrocephalus)* and misibele *(Alestes macrophthalmus).*[6] It is unlikely that the increased exploitation of these larger fish led to a greater chisense population. Luapula's most exploited fish, mpumbu and pale, did not feed on chisense at all. And although stocks of predators like manda and lupata have declined, there is no evidence that this caused a rise in the number of chisense. Instead, the population of chisense seems most closely linked to levels of nutrients in the lake. Increased nutrient inputs to the lake support a larger planktonic community, upon which the chisense feeds. After periods of high rainfall in December and January, when nutrients flow from the flooded valleys and lagoons, chisense feed and breed, and their numbers increase. There is a slight possibility that the disappearance of fish like mpumbu, or perhaps of another small species that did not generate the same economic and political disruptions as mpumbu, had some effect on general nutrient levels in the lake, which in turn affected the chisense population; however, ichthyologists familiar with Mweru-Luapula think this is very unlikely.[7] It is more likely that increased nutrient levels linked to the growing lakeshore population and the use of artificial fertilizers contributed to an increase in chisense stocks.

Whatever the case, it seems that chisense were almost impervious to overfishing by any predator, fish or human. Chisense have an extremely high turnover rate. They live for a maximum of fifteen months and quickly replenish stock that perish due to natural causes or by predation. This remarkable feature of chisense can be expressed in biological terms by considering the ratio of production (total catch per year) to biomass (total weight at any one point in a year). For larger and longer-living fish, like mpumbu, the ratio would be less than one, which seems logical since in a single year fishers would not expect to be able to catch more than the total weight of the species. Remarkably, ichthyologists estimate that for chisense the ratio is between five and six! In other words, the weight of chisense caught in a single year can be up to six times greater than the total weight of all the fish present at any moment during that year. This ratio reflects the incredible ability of chisense to rapidly replenish their numbers. When a few bucketfuls of a species called kapenta *(Limnothrissa miodon)*, similar in biological qualities and with a productivity to biomass ratio of four, were introduced to the Kariba Dam, in a few years they supported an industry that harvested up to twenty-five thousand tons of fish every year. It is very difficult, nearly impossible, to provoke a biological tragedy of the commons. Chisense, in the words of one ichthyologist familiar with Mweru-Luapula, are like lakeflies, impossible to eradicate no matter how furiously they are swatted.[8]

This also means that the proliferation of chisense observed in 1970s was probably unrelated to the overexploitation of species like mpumbu or pale. However, even if there are no straightforward environmental explanations for the rise of the chisense fishery, there are definite economic ones linked to the biological qualities of chisense; those fish with the highest turnover rate were best suited to increases in human predation. Throughout the 1970s and 1980s the amount of fish from the gill-net fishery remained at around eight thousand tons. This meant that despite a growing number of fishers attempting to exploit the resource, the amount of fish at best remained constant, probably exploited well beyond the maximum sustainable yield, leading to a decline in profits per net and the precarious existence of the resource.[9] Chisense, as a fish with a higher biological turnover rate, offered higher catches—the maximum sustainable yield for such fish was much higher than for fish caught in the gill-net fishery. By the 1990s, from thirty to forty thousand tons of chisense were hauled out of the lake per year, almost five times the tonnage of the Zambian gill-net fishery! As the value of the chisense trade in Zambia approached 7 billion Zambian kwacha (approximately U.S. $7 million) per annum, chisense became the fishery's most lucrative resource.[10]

Instead of a few wealthy patrons emerging, as in the pale fishery, the chisense fishery was dominated by small- to medium-scale producers and traders. Capitalized men and poor rural women took advantage of continued urban demand for a cheap, nonperishable source of protein. Why were they able to dominate the industry instead of large-scale producers and traders? The biological features of the fish offer only a partial answer. When we consider the similar kapenta fishery of Lake Kariba, very different forms of economic organization emerged, with capitalized expatriate, mostly Zimbabwean, fishers dominating the industry instead of small- to medium-scale producers and traders.[11] The history of the chisense fishery and its spread over the last thirty years suggest some reasons for the different trajectories of these similar fisheries.

Chisense were found in greatest numbers near the nutrient-rich beaches of the eastern shore, from the northern tip near the Congolese town of Pweto to the Zambian town of Chiengi and parts of the southern lagoon areas from Kashikishi to Mukwakwa fishing camps (see map 4). In these areas human predation of chisense was not new. For as long as the villagers can remember, off the beaches of the northern stretches of Lake Mweru between Chiengi and Pweto, women walked in the shallows behind seine nets with woven baskets to catch small amounts of chisense for subsistence needs.[12] In the early 1970s more intensive fishing of chisense using small-mesh seine nets occurred on the northern beaches. By the mid-1970s chisense fishing spread southward and was taken up in the central eastern fishing camp of Mukwakwa. And by the late 1970s it covered most of the exploitable areas on the eastern lake-shore, from the northern town of Pweto to Kashikishi in the south-west.[13] When veteran kapenta fishermen from Lake Tanganyika brought new fishing techniques to Mweru-Luapula and catches increased, the modern chisense fishery emerged.

Chisense fishing was an entirely different undertaking compared to the gill-net fishing, where the success of a commercial fisherman de-pended on his specialized equipment, including expensive gill nets. At first women caught chisense by dragging cloth or small-mesh netting like mosquito nets near the shoreline. This technique required little cap-ital and few skills, but catches were small and could not sustain commer-cial activity. The new chisense fishing techniques adopted from Lake Tanganyika involved the use of several paraffin tilley lanterns mounted on floats and left overnight out on the lake some two hundred meters or more from the shore. The chisense fish were attracted to the light and gathered around the floating lantern. Before dawn, the fishers extin-guished the light and captured the chisense either through a scooplike net attached to long bamboo poles *(mutobi)*, a net mounted on an outrig-ger made from bamboo poles *(japan)*, or a seine net dragged between two plank boats. Methods changed; the more effective *japan* outrigger nets slowly replaced the simple *mutobi*, lift nets, and boat seines.[14]

There was no defined or established tenure system for the chisense fishery. The fish are pelagic, meaning that they are found in open wa-ters, and were thus a relatively open-acccess resource. There were no chiefs or owners of lagoons who had vested control over fishing rights over such areas; the colonial and postcolonial states also had little influ-ence. The lack of formal or informal tenure systems allowed new entre-preneurs to take advantage of the fishery. This held substantial benefits for migrants from the urban areas or from other rural areas and for rural women, all of whom held only tenuous claims over the fishery in the past. Relatively open access to the chisense fishery enabled opportu-nities for previously marginalized groups.[15]

The villagers and fishers of the lake are unsure who first brought the new methods from Lake Tanganyika. In Pweto, the center of the Con-golese chisense fishery, the fishers claim it was a Mr. Kiapi (or Chiapi in Zambian Bemba). Originally from Pweto, Kiapi went to Moba on Lake Tanganyika, some sixty miles northeast of his hometown, where he learnt how to catch chisense with lanterns. When he returned, he taught other fishers the new method.[16] In the Zambian town of Mu-nunga inhabitants recall that a Mr. Kasote learnt the techniques from Lake Tanganyika and brought them to the eastern shores of Lake Mweru.[17] Some attribute the new techniques to an expatriate fisheries officer called Scullion—a type of net was even named after him.[18] Most likely, a number of individual fishers, noticing the abundance of chisense in Mweru, went to Tanganyika to learn the new fishing techniques.[19] Whatever the precise history, it seems that new migrants with little or no attachment to local clans, owners of the lagoons, or established corporations, were the first to exploit the chisense fishery.

The new fishing entrepreneurs were a type of *abanonshi*, known for their commercial activities—whether engaged in fishing, trading, or a combination of both—and for their urban lifestyles. Where *abanonshi* migrants in the colonial period received remuneration through travel *to* the urban areas, the new *abanonshi* traveled *from* the urban areas to find their fortune in the production and trade of rural produce. Urban waged work, for men and women, had been lucrative in the years of the copper boom; from the late 1970s, however, the real value of salaries declined and rural farming, fishing, and trade became more attractive. As they had during the time of the mpumbu boom in the 1940s, many urbanites returned to take advantage of Mweru-Luapula's new fishery.

These pioneering chisense fishers cashed in on a lucrative industry. The first fishers who used lanterns caught more than three hundred kilograms of fish, several small boats full, in a single evening. Compared to the three to four kilogram average catch per one hundred-meter gill net in an evening during the same period, chisense were extremely profitable. Soon Mr. Kiapi had enough money to buy a vehicle and settle in Lubumbashi. Mr. Kasote opened shops and a gas filling station.[20] Like the rush to invest in a booming stock, the chisense fishery promised the first investors healthy profits. Unfortunately, also in a similar fashion to overtraded stocks, its real value and growth potential declined as the number of fishers multiplied. Nevertheless, one study conducted in the 1980s estimated that gill-net fishers earned a monthly average of one hundred to three hundred Zambian kwacha compared to four thousand Zambian kwacha earned by chisense fishers.[21] Another study of a town on the northern shores of Mweru estimated that chisense fishing brought in over 6 times more income than gill-net fishing and 170 times more income than farming! The researchers concluded that although little of the chisense catch covered subsistence needs, as a business it was "unbeatable if the capital is available from the start."[22] Indeed, throughout the 1970s and early 1980s pioneering chisense fishers became the new entrepreneurs of the lakeshore.

The lucrative chisense fishery attracted the attention of expatriate fisheries' research advisors and aid organizations who were hopeful of the wealth and benefits to rural households that the new fishery might bring. One U.S.-based NGO, the State of Jersey Overseas Aid Committee, provided loans to potential chisense fishers for the purchase of fishing equipment, including nets and lanterns, and reported a good loan recovery rate. The Zambian Department of Fisheries held training courses for new chisense fishers. While the loans were limited to a few fishers, they helped to act as a further catalyst to the rapid spread of new fishing techniques.[23]

The profitability of the chisense fishery for small- to medium-scale fishers also rested on their ability to avoid state pricing regulations and conduct business without the collaboration of larger rural-urban corporations. As mentioned in the previous chapter, in the 1970s there was a concerted effort by both Zairian fish buyers and the Zambian state monopoly, Lake Fisheries of Zambia, to set and stabilize fish prices. The chisense fishery, on the other hand, circumvented most state regulations and was conducted independently of the larger Zairian-run businesses. Neither LFZ nor Zairian traders bought chisense. Since the state did not consider the chisense fishery to be commercial, chisense fishers did not have to go through the harassment and the general costs of avoiding state regulation that other fishers encountered on a daily basis. They were less indebted to Zairian patrons for their gear and not concerned about net theft since they did not leave their nets for long periods; they had little reason to collaborate with wealthy patrons or state agencies.

Established net fishers had extensive investment in their nets and knowledge of traditional fishing techniques; they could not simply drop all these activities in favor of chisense. They would need to purchase new equipment like paraffin lamps and meshless material. Gill-net fishers remained indebted to and dependent on patrons who had loaned them nets. Insufficient access to credit facilities, except through pale-trading networks, prevented diversification into chisense fishery. Older migrants to the lake and autochthonous male fishers had a stake in their traditional businesses and many continued with their fishing practices.[24] Instead, it was the new *abanonshi* men who migrated to make money out of the chisense fishery. They had usually acquired a small amount of capital in salaried employment or trade and were willing to invest in new money-making ventures in the rural areas. They were cutting-edge entrepreneurs willing to take advantage of new technologies and environmental conditions.[25]

Women processed fish that they bought or bartered from men. At the point of purchase, chisense were measured in large metal basins called *bafu* (from the English "bath") that hold from twenty to twenty-five kilograms of fish. After purchase, they laid the fish out to dry on a smooth clean surface, preferably a drying platform of a hard clay made out of a combination of cassava porridge and mud or, in the northern stretches of the fishery, on the beach. They spread out the fish early in the morning; then around mid-morning they were turned over, and by midday the process was complete and the fish ready for sale or storage (in wet weather fire had to be used). They were the ideal export for the urban Copperbelt: kapenta, which resembles chisense in size, taste, and preparation, also means "prostitute" or "loose women," since they are so easy to prepare and quick to eat.

Urban Traders

In Luapula, women sold processed chisense fish to both rural dwellers and rural-urban traders. In the chisense fishing camps, people distinguish between those involved in the local fish trade and those who transport and sell produce in urban areas. Both local and rural-urban trading is described by the same verb *ukukungula,* to sweep up or scrape away, except trading with urban areas is known as *ukukungula* while the intensive form of the verb, *ukukungwisha,* describes local trading. To trade in the fish markets of the lake is to pursue the last drop of profit, to scrape the bottom of the barrel, compared to the rural-urban traders who sweep away most of the chisense and most of the profit. The vast majority of rural traders were women (a 1994 survey put it at 93 percent); by contrast, rural-urban traders were evenly spread between men and women. While most of the local traders listed their residence as the fishery, the rural-urban traders, who earned the lion's share of the profit, were predominantly from the Copperbelt, the destination of most of the chisense.[26] Yet there is also evidence that rural women were not victims of rural-urban traders. They managed to acquire enough capital to become rural-urban traders, to expand their initial capital and go to the urban areas, changing from *ukukungwisha* to *ukukungula* trade.[27] The chisense industry paved the way for the rise of an autonomous class of female rural-urban fish traders.

Women who had grown up or married in the urban areas also formed a significant proportion of rural-urban fish traders. The 1960s had been a time of rapid urbanization for Zambia and southern Zaire.

Rural villagers had migrated to the urban areas, and the number of
urban inhabitants reached 40 percent of the entire population. When
Robert Bates wrote his Luapula case study, *Rural Responses to Industrialization*, Zambia seemed well on the way to becoming an industrialized and
urbanized society. "Fewer people seem to be returning to the villages,"
Bates wrote, "and urban dwellers remit proportionately less to their
rural kin."[28] At least since the 1960s, if not earlier, a class of financially-
independent women had emerged in the urban areas of Zambia, described by one anthropologist as the "new women of Lusaka."[29] But in
the late 1970s the copper mining economy, which was at the base of
the newfound opportunities in the urban areas, began to slow down.
James Ferguson writes of how the contraction of the copper mining
economy reversed the expected path of Zambian urban development
and disrupted so-called permanent urbanization. Mine workers no
longer expected to remain in the Copperbelt's towns and looked to re-
tire to long-forgotten rural "homes."[30] If this was the case on the Zambian Copperbelt, the situation was even direr in southern Katanga's
towns, where the copper mines experienced even greater levels of economic mismanagement and disintegration: This was the unmaking of
Katanga's working class.[31] City-dwellers in Zambia and Zaire looked to
the rural areas, not only as safety nets for unemployment and retirement,
but for potential economic opportunities as their jobs disappeared and
salaries no longer sustained their families. Those who left the towns for
the rural areas farmed, fished, or collected goods for trade in the urban
markets—many of them became involved in chisense fishing and trade.

There are no systematic data on the rural-urban trading class
that emerged in the 1970s and early 1980s on the central African Copperbelt. It seems that men smuggled maize to Zaire, exported urban goods
to rural areas, or invested in new fishing enterprises. Urban women
desperate to supplement their husbands' declining incomes and rural
women in need of a cash income combined to form the backbone of
the traders who brought rural produce to the towns, especially fish and
vegetables. This trading class was no longer limited to a particular region like the male Luapula traders of the 1950s and 1960s but was national or even international. Traders kept informed of where the cheap-
est fish were available and in which urban market they might find the
best price. They spent weeks collecting fish in one fishery, say Tanganyika, then a week selling fish in an urban market, followed by another
trip to an entirely different fishery. In the fishing camps women slept in

temporary grass shelters or simply under mosquito nets. In the urban markets they slept in depots with their fish if they were fortunate or, if not, simply below their fish stalls. It was a tough existence, but moderately profitable. At the end of a few months, a woman might be able to return home, pay for the children's school fees and clothing, and perhaps even invest in some other money-making venture where the work was not as arduous.

Lista Kanokelya Chasekwa, or Bana Kasali (the mother of Kasali), had a relatively successful and fortunate life as a fish trader. Her father was a fisherman near Lukwesa in the 1930s and 1940s, where he had sold fish to the Greek traders. She was educated at a nearby mission and married a government employee who worked in several different Zambian towns. Since her husband's salary was not sufficient for the upkeep of her household, she began to trade in fish. At first, in 1971, she went to either Mpulungu on Lake Tanganyika to buy kapenta or Lake Mweru Wantipa to buy pale. She took the fish to Ndola on the Copperbelt to trade. In the late 1970s she heard of the chisense boom in Luapula and returned to her home region to buy fish. In those days, she claimed, traders took large quantities of chisense to Ndola. Profits were good: a ninety-kilogram bag of dried chisense cost forty kwacha at the lake and sold for fifty-five to sixty kwacha in the urban markets. There was no tax and state-sponsored transport was cheap. She returned from the Copperbelt with goods, like paraffin, which could be sold to the chisense fishermen. By the early 1980s her profits increased enough to open a bank account. Then in the early 1990s she bought her own fishing nets and boats and employed fishermen. Indeed she became such a prominent member of her village near Kashikishi that Chief Kambwali appointed her as headwoman.[32]

Bana Kasali had been lucky enough to exploit the early chisense boom by carefully monitoring where comparative advantage lay in the fish trade. But if too many traders went to a single fishery or an urban market, profits diminished. Knowledge about conditions of supply at the fishery and demand in the urban markets was the crucial advantage. If there were cheap chisense to purchase from Kashikishi, a trader rushed over there; but she had to beware of seasonal and monthly variations. For example, few chisense were caught in the cold months of June and July, and, if the moon was full, chisense could not be caught by paraffin tilley lanterns; under such conditions, scarcities could double the lakeshore price. She needed to be aware of urban market conditions: It was no good to arrive in the middle of the month since nobody had money; the best time to sell was on pay day. If school fees needed to be paid or school uniforms bought, the fish did not sell, for some things were more important than good relish.[33]

The female fishmongers of Lubumbashi, Zaire, were similar. In the 1980s there was still a significant fresh fish trade run by Katebe Katoto. Dried and salted fish were, nevertheless, in demand. Most of this fish came from Mweru-Luapula, since infrastructure in Zaire had increased the cost of transport from other fisheries and more profitable markets in Kasai limited exports from other fisheries to Lubumbashi. Traders from Mweru-Luapula, a significant proportion of them Zambians, gathered in a single neighborhood and sold their fish on a street next to Lubumbashi's railway, called *ndjandja*, where fifty years previously the Greek traders had first established their businesses. Traders generally bought chisense in Zambia, since chisense stocks were more prevalent on the eastern shore of the lake and chisense fishing was prohibited in Zaire between 1981 and 1986. Bana Kalenga, for example, was born in the Zairian town of Kasenga on the Luapula River in 1950. She married in the 1960s and by 1979, when she started fish trading, was on her way to having her eighth child. At first she traded dried pale that she bought in the lagoons where the Luapula enters Lake Mweru. Through trade she managed to buy nets and employ fishermen. When her fishing nets were stolen, she began to buy chisense in Kashikishi, Zambia.[34]

The more capitalized the trader, the more fish she purchased and the farther she traveled. Profit depended on relative accessibility, and the more remote market vis-à-vis the fishery (and competing fisheries) promised better returns. Traders bought chisense in twenty-five-, fifty- or ninety-kilogram bags. Those who bought twenty-five-kilogram bags were likely to remain within Luapula, traveling to a nearby town like Mansa to retail the fish themselves. By contrast, those who bought ninety-kilogram bags were probably destined for the Copperbelt towns or Lusaka, where they would sell the fish to retailers.[35]

Frequently urban fishmongers in Zambian and Zairian markets did not buy the fish from the rural areas themselves but relied on wholesalers. The center for the wholesale chisense trade was the Zambian town Kitwe. Chisense retailers from across the Copperbelt bought their supplies here.[36] In Lubumbashi wholesalers also catered to the Kasaian markets and sold to merchants who transported the fish to Mbuji-Mayi, the diamond capital of Kasai, where food was often in short supply and profits easy to make. The urban fishmongers who bought from the wholesalers were almost exclusively women who sought either to supplement their husbands' salaries or to eke out a meager existence for themselves. They did not earn as much as the rural-urban traders, yet their work was not as difficult and dangerous. Many chose this existence above the hardships of rural-urban trade.[37]

The fish markets in town and countryside were well-ordered, with relations between sellers and buyers mediated by set rules and elected officials. Women paid a fee to the council for a market stall or worked with a depot owner to whom she paid a standard fee for the storage of her fish until it was all sold. While retail prices for larger dried fish were officially dictated by the state, or at least remained relatively constant, prices for chisense fluctuated according to conditions of supply and demand.[38] Within a single market, women would agree to a price, but through a variety of means they bargained with their buyers or gave a little extra fish *(basela)* to secure their clientage. There were often conflicts in the market place that needed forums for resolution. A buyer complained that he had not received the correct quantity; sometimes a dishonest seller placed wax at the bottom of her measuring container or shrunk the plastic container with boiling water. The vendors elected market leaders or chairs to adjudicate over these disputes. Occasionally these were women, but female marketers preferred men, for, as one marketer put it, "there is jealousy [between the women]. . . . [T]hey fear that person [the leader] can kill them . . . so they select men because men are stronger than women."[39] The traders considered a man to be less self-interested and a somewhat impartial mediator who ensured a judgment would be respected.

Men based in the urban areas also played a role in fish-trading activities. Generally, they had more capital available than women and thus participated in different activities. It was rare to find a man actually selling fish in the market. More common were those who transported large quantities of fish to sell wholesale to urban fishmongers or to wholesale traders from other areas. Alternatively, urban-based men owned depots in the city markets where women deposited their fish and slept in exchange for a set fee. If these urban-based men made enough extra capital they might invest in rural ventures with high returns. The chisense industry in the 1970s and 1980s presented such profitable opportunities, and some men returned from the cities with capital and fishing gear to the chisense camps of Lake Mweru.

Photo 9. Chisense fishing boat. The fishing boats arrive ashore in the early morning after a night on the lake. Note the tilley lanterns and scoop nets mounted on bamboo poles. Photograph by author, Kashikishi Fishing Camp, January 1998.

Photo 10. Distributing the chisense catch. Women wait in the early morning with their *bafu* to collect a portion of the catch. Photograph by author, Kashikishi Fishing Camp, January 1998.

Photo 11. Drying and processing chisense. The chisense is dried and processed on a platform of cassava and mud in about one day. Photograph by author, Kashikishi Fishing Camp, January 1998.

Photo 12. Rural traders in Kashikishi fishing camp. Traders with *bafu* of dried chisense sell the fish in different denominations to local residents and to rural-urban traders. Photograph by author, Kashikishi Fishing Camp, January 1998.

Photo 13. Bus with chisense. Buses and trucks loaded with fish head to the urban areas. Photograph by author, Kashikishi, January 1998.

Photo 14. Urban fish depot. The fish traders and their children live in urban depots generally run by men until their fish are sold. Soweto Market, Lusaka. Photograph by author, June 1998.

The Ulupwa Family: Big Women on a Small Scale

New types of rural-urban exchanges affected the economic and social lives of rural women and their families. In Mweru-Luapula, women have long been known for their independence from husbands—the "Black Suffragettes" of Dan Crawford were mentioned in chapter 1. Yet when the cash economy spread across the valley in the early twentieth century, men secured activities in the commercial realm and circumscribed women's entrepreneurial activities. Although there were exceptions, such as the case of Anna Chilombo Kapapula detailed in chapter 2, women in Luapula were made responsible for productive tasks that did not earn large amounts of cash, like cassava planting, harvesting, and preparation of the tuber. This was not uniform across Zambia or Zaire. In the villages and fishing camps near the lake, the association between women and agricultural work became especially accentuated compared to the villages far away from the fishery, where husband and wife shared tasks associated with farming more evenly. Close to the fishery, men engaged in money-making fishing while women worked in the cassava fields. The cassava they produced was either consumed by their households or exchanged for fish.[40]

Anthropologist Lisa Cligget has argued that weakened controls by older matrilineages in the Gwembe Valley of southern Zambia, combined with the increased importance of a cattle and cash economy, led to women's increasing economic dependence on men and, in an effort to counter this dependence, greater investment by women in "motherhood."[41] The chisense fishery is a similar example of the weakening— or nonexistence—of older clan and lineage holds over resource rights and economic activity; yet the results for women were somewhat different. Many rural women were able to invest directly in the chisense industry as traders and a few as gear owners. For some, these new economic opportunities reduced dependence on men, while also allowing for investment in "motherhood" and stronger ties with their children. These big women on a small scale redefined matrilineal affiliations as they established their own *ulupwa* families without husbands. On the other hand, women married to big men husbands often reacted by strengthening ties with their husbands and making the husband-wife pair the basis of their *ulupwa* family.

By the 1970s the villages and fishing camps along the lake consisted of a combination of older autochthonous and more recent migrant fishing and farming families. In Mweru-Luapula, while the *ulupwa* family unit was bilateral, autochthonous villagers were members of extended matrilineages, the old clans of Luapula; for Luapulans, matrilineal ideology remained a "traditional" discourse and was even articulated as a type of moral economy. When a man married and had children, his mother's family remained his close kin, and his own children were often of less or at least of equal importance to the children of his sisters. A husband ensured that his wife had access to certain productive resources like land; however, his wealth did not belong to his wife and children alone. A man might have children from different wives and contribute little to their collective well-being, saving his wealth for his mother's family instead (although his wives' families would make constant demands on him). A woman in such a marriage maintained a degree of autonomy over her particular household. She was, in effect, often the provider for a household that had weak ties to a husband and received only occasional aid from him. Instead, she was far closer to her own children, siblings, and parents.

Among migrant men and women whose kin were far away, by contrast, different support networks, inheritance patterns, and divisions of labor emerged. Even those who had once lived in Mweru-Luapula had spent years in salaried urban employment and were long accustomed to living apart from their wider family networks. Occasionally men migrated to the fishing camps with an already constituted nuclear unit of wife and children and thereby escaped demands of their old kin. Alternatively, they adapted to an older pattern of Luapulan assimilation by marrying women in nearby villages and becoming part of their wives' families (this is, after all, how the Lunda were said to have "conquered" Luapula). Migrating women, usually traders, also married fishermen to gain reliable fish supplies. In all cases the new male and female *abanonshi* engaged with Luapula's clans and families to establish their own distinctive corporate groups. The emergence of rural social formations with a bilateral and strong matrilineal influence was not as much due to the force of Luapula's "traditions" as to the particular nature of the encounter between urban traders and rural families. In other words, rather than remaining an ossified tradition, Luapula's corporate groups were re-created as they engaged with, and adapted to, new economic and social conditions.[42]

The demand for money was a crucial element in giving form to new gendered social and familial arrangements. Villagers did not exist on cassava and fish alone. Money had long been essential, especially for women: children went to school and, although fees during the 1970s to

1980s were still minimal, there were a number of expenses like clothes and books; parishioners needed donations for the church and special occasions; women prized fashionable clothes; houses constructed out of sun-dried brick required materials; and locally produced clay pots and containers were increasingly rare as women preferred items made from plastic and aluminum. The hut and poll taxes of colonialism are usually described as the force that drove the African peasantry into a monetized economy. Although women were spared the payment of tax, like men had been during colonialism, the spreading market economy made many demands on them and their financial resources.

Before the rise of the chisense industry, rural women had a number of alternatives for earning cash. Many sold home-brewed beer *(kachasu)*, liquor *(lutuku)*, or soft drink *(munkoyo)* to local villagers. Or they sold cassava, dried or pounded into flour. The trade was mostly with the fishermen since trade in cassava with the urban areas was not profitable; cheap state-sponsored maize flour was abundant in urban areas and near the most important infrastructural arteries until the middle of the 1980s. Alternatively, women bartered cassava for fish, and then traded the fish. After processing the fish, either by drying, smoking, or salting it—the choice depended on the cost of salt or firewood, the size of the fish, and where the fish were to be marketed—women sold the fish to rural-urban traders. When these activities became extremely profitable, as in the early development of the chisense industry, women were able to invest earnings in other activities. If they made enough money as fishmongers they could expand into rural-urban trade or invest in fishing gear and employ men to fish for them (although this was rare—in 1994 only 4 percent of chisense gear owners were women).[43] These were the dynamics behind the formation of an autonomous class of female household entrepreneurs in the early 1970s. They undertook small-scale commercial activities due to the failure of men to fully provide for their households. As earnings increased these small-scale ventures became fully fledged businesses.[44]

The profits of a woman's business were directed toward her immediate *ulupwa* family, generally meaning her children. "Nowadays there are many more women in this trade [fish]," claimed one interviewee who compared the nature of rural women's economic activities to men. "The reason is that men do not know how to keep money. If they trade, they start drinking beer, misusing money. But women know about money, we think about our children, how to keep money and to progress."[45] Men were bound to social networks requiring reciprocation, often brought about by numerous lovers. The "misuse" of money was not entirely irrational: Why invest in your children if they do not belong to you? Women, by contrast, looked after their own households. They invested in their children, a worthwhile investment, for children would then belong to the mother. They represented wealth.

Such arrangements were matters of strategic investment choices rather than tradition. For example, wealthy big men were more likely to exert stronger control over household finances, their wives, and children. In such households, although there was a gendered division of labor, both husband and wife contributed to the same household and considered themselves part of a single *ulupwa*. A woman's trading ventures occurred on behalf of her husband, not independent from him. Often she sold the fish that he caught or tended the farmlands, planting cassava and other crops. Some of this produce might be traded or bartered; much was destined for the family pot. For example, Bana Chisakula married the wealthy businessman, by then an *umukankâla*, Paul Chisakula, in 1969 and worked in his shops. Bana Mulenga, the wife of the *umukankâla* Joshua Mulenga, also remained married for more than forty years, traveling between the Copperbelt and Luapula with him. In both cases, the sons and daughters of these marriages were involved in their fathers' business activities. Wealthy men could have lovers and occasionally had second wives, but a woman and her children would only remain with a husband if they were sufficiently rewarded. In effect, these wealthy husband and wife pairs constituted self-contained *ulupwa* families. A wife's maternal family struggled to make and justify affective or economic claims on these families.[46]

On the other hand, many women involved in the fishery were either autonomous heads of households or wives in marriages where men provided only partially for the household. In poorer households, husbands were reluctant to allow their wives to partake in urban trade. Small-scale local processing and trading was often difficult enough for a husband to accept; urban trade went beyond the confines of marriage. In fact, if a man married a woman involved in the fish trade, he often insisted that she desist. Men did not place much faith in weak marriage ties when there was money to be made and their wives' families were nearby. And their suspicions were often justified; women deserted poor husbands to participate in new urban opportunities or to start business ventures with their own families. Rural women had the potential to become urban traders, but their position largely depended on their marital status and their willingness to disobey or divorce their husbands.

This, in turn, was related to the economic status of husbands and the extent to which they provided for their wives' families.[47] The ability to make money independently from their husbands enabled women to challenge Luapulan patriarchy, especially poor patriarchs, and to reassert their roles as mothers and control over their own children. Women gained extra income from extramarital affairs or divorced poor husbands. They also invested in their children, from whom they could expect income or at least labor in the future.[48]

Challenges, conflicts, and subsequent negotiations between husbands and wives and, in turn, between extended bilateral and nuclear families were mediated in different institutions. The evangelical church movement continued to provide opportunity for the consolidation of a rural-urban civil society.[49] Based on research conducted in the period 1974–75, anthropologist Karla Poewe argued that the evangelical church movement, especially the Jehovah's Witnesses and Seventh-day Adventists, which together formed 60 percent of the church-attending population at the time of her research, provided a framework for the renegotiation of marital practices. The Jehovah's Witnesses preached a radical message that undermined matriliny by providing a strong framework for the development of nuclear households and constraining polygyny. Under these conditions, women were more willing to invest greater trust in their husbands and were less prone to seek or accept divorce. Seventh-day Adventists, by contrast, were more reformist in outlook; members still had significant matrilineal ties and did not make a thorough investment in their spouses and husband-wife families. However, the church still protected men from redistributionist claims by wives' families.[50]

Poewe's correlation between stable marriages and church membership is convincing, although her causal link might be flawed: attitudes that she ascribes to different theories of salvation might have had more to do with economic conditions of the household. Those households with access to capital resources had more stable marriages and were in turn attracted to the Jehovah's Witnesses and Seventh-day Adventist churches.[51] Moreover, the question that needs explication is whether what Poewe terms a "structural contradiction inherent in matriliny," that is between a husband-wife pair and matrikin, was not in fact accentuated in certain economic contexts.[52] Was the high rate of divorce, ascribed by Poewe in the ethnographic present to this inherent structural contradiction, always a feature of Luapulan society or was it tied to new types of opportunities and inequalities? Interviews suggest that divorce became more of a possibility with the widening of commercial opportunities due

to the profitable trade in dried fish and chisense. As wives became less reliant on their husbands' economic provisions in the form of fish, land, or
cash, they were increasingly able to dispose of useless husbands who contributed little to their households and consumed resources that wives
produced or earned. Women with poor or polygynous husbands chose
divorce, relied on their matrikin and children, and were less interested in
church membership. Women who managed to become rich, like Bana
Kasali did not bother with marriage, especially if she already had children or other kin (brothers, nephews, and nieces) with whom her wealth
could be shared and in whom she could invest. The cost of a husband
was too great a burden for these small-scale big women.[53]

Women married to wealthy men, on the other hand, chose to form
a different type of family. By joining the Jehovah's Witnesses or the
Seventh-day Adventists, which both have important restrictions on divorce and on extravagant expenditure by husbands on social networks,
these women appealed to an outside authority to restrict the flow of
wealth from her husband's business away from the husband-wife pair.
This would be the best choice should a husband be involved in capital-
intensive farming or fishing. Indeed, according to Poewe's own data,
women with "productive" husbands did not place their trust in their
matrikin and concentrated their investments on an *ulupwa* surrounding
their husbands.[54]

In a qualitative study conducted by the DoF of eight women involved
in the fish business, four had been divorced (two of those divorced had
been divorced twice). All of the divorced women supported their children and relied on their labor or fishing activities. Bana Kasakula, for
example, was the head of a typically poor family unit *sans* husband. She
purchased gill nets with profits from selling charcoal. Her sons fished
for her with these nets on a boat rented from another fisher or worked
for other fishers. They gave the fish earned or caught to Bana Kasakula,
who smoked and traded them. Her ultimate aim was to earn enough
money to buy a boat for her sons so that they did not have to work for
other fishermen. Only two women out of the eight were married for
more than fifteen years, both of them to husbands who controlled significant capital resources. Bana Ntoshi's husband owned an *ichombo* boat,
two chisense nets, and many gill nets; he was described as a "super rich
fisher." While not as wealthy, Bana Kasanshi's husband was previously
a store owner in Lusaka, then moved to Mweru-Luapula where he
purchased a boat, a chisense net, and four tilley lanterns. He employed
four fishers to catch chisense for him while he ran a bicycle repair shop.

In such wealthy households, families were organized around stable husband-wife pairs.[55]

Karla Poewe argues, following the structuralist arguments of Emmanuel Terray, that matrilineal descent practices acted like a type of false consciousness by obscuring the development of the relations of production in Luapula. "Matrilineal redistributionists" looked to gain from their lineage positions rather than realizing their common class interests.[56] Indeed, matrilineal descent practices could tie labor within a matrikin to fishing or trading enterprise. Labor was surrendered in exchange for the possibility of future remuneration. But matriliny was not an all-encompassing *Weltanschauung* that manifested itself in the same way in all cases. Different groups appealed to alternative ideologies and used them in different ways. Moreover, matrilineages, like the older clans of the valley, were not significant economic corporate groups in the chisense fishery. Wealthy husband and wife pairs consolidated families that attempted to contain the redistributionist demands of matrikin. One way to achieve moral purchase while restricting such demands was through the membership of Seventh-day Adventist or Jehovah's Witness churches.[57] Poor relatives, on the other hand, could appeal to a "traditional" ideology of matrilineal redistribution to make demands on such families. Such instrumental use of matrilineal ideology was not always necessary. Women hardly needed matrilineal beliefs to explain investment in their children and legitimate their struggle to survive without husbands. For them, the only alternative was a household that had to feed successive poor and useless husbands and boyfriends.

Recriminations between selfish families and hungry kin, between those who held things as wealth and those who held people (or labor) as wealth, took the form of witchcraft accusations. When asked about the use of witchcraft, the older traditionalists of the valley pointed to the chisense fishers and to the young rural-urban traders or *abanonshi* who enriched themselves through "greed" and the rejection of their "traditional" obligations. All the chiefs of Mweru-Luapula agreed that witchcraft had increased with the chisense industry and its new business opportunities. "It [witchcraft] has increased. . . . We have these businessmen—abanonshi—young men who want more money and become rich. And fishermen also want more money," according to the young Chief Mununga.[58] "It has increased because of the business," claimed an elder at Chief Kambwali's palace who emphasized how the poor demand money from wealthy relatives. "They accuse their relatives or other people so that they can get money. . . . [I]t's also common with some nets. People can use medicines or the blood of people to catch fish."[59] Perhaps an elder at Chief Puta's court put it best when he related witchcraft to a "difference between people" and to competition between and within families: "What has made it like this is that there is a difference between people. One is poor and one has a good life. The poor will bewitch the rich. Why? I am poor and he is rich. It also works the other way round. Big men [abakankâla] have charms to increase their riches. A big man can kill someone's daughter to place her in his business. Business has made it worse because everyone kills one another."[60]

Witchcraft was the moral economy of the fishery. In a fashion similar to the purifying movements and *bamunyama* accusations during colonialism, those left out by the new opportunities in the fishery brought the wrath of witchcraft to bear on the more fortunate. From the late 1970s, however, divisions were more disparate and a few colonial collaborators could not be singled out. Wealthy *abanonshi* could be found in all the villages and towns of Mweru-Luapula. Villagers turned to trusted village-level elites, preachers or chiefs, to mediate and adjudicate over the many disputes linked to the new economy. In another context Peter Geschiere and Francis Nyamnjoh noticed that urban-rural relations have become "a hotbed for rumors about potent occult forces. . . . Villagers tend to suspect urbanites of using occult forces to enrich themselves, while urbanites profess to be afraid of the leveling impact of the villagers."[61] In Zambia, as James Ferguson has pointed out, "witchcraft" was a form of violent confrontation between rural dwellers and urban arrivals. (The violence of witchcraft was real; after all, it could include poisoning.)[62] Witchcraft accusations were part of the struggle over the meanings and forms of wealth—a struggle between fishers and traders, between rural and urban traders, and between men and women and their respective arenas of investment. Through "witchcraft," families discussed fortune and misfortune, in other words, the problems of wealth, poverty, and social obligation.

The rise of the chisense fishery allowed women greater economic autonomy and held the potential to transform the workings of their households. Women were able to loosen the bonds of patriarchy and some managed to invest in forms of wealth more appropriate to their lives and experiences. Although Nachituti freed herself from Mwata Kazembe, the benefits of this freedom were not always clear. Women remained attached to men who managed to accumulate capital resources through the fishery. Women with poor husbands, on the other hand, did not invest in long-term marriages. Many became itinerant traders, big women on a small scale, renowned for their independent existence and their sexual infidelities.[63]

Tragedy in the Chisense Fishery?

In the 1990s fishers reported decreased chisense catches. They complained that in the 1980s they were able to fill a boat with one lantern while in the mid-1990s it took more than ten lanterns to catch the same amount.[64] The labor and capital costs of chisense fishing alongside small catches made it less lucrative.[65] Thousands of fishers, however, continued to search for profit through exploitation of chisense. Despite decreased individual catches, total chisense production did not decline. On the contrary, judging by reports conducted by the Zambian DoF, the total production of chisense in 1994 was well below its potential maximum. The decreased chisense catch per fisher indicated instead a rise in the number of chisense fishers. By 1997, in Zambia alone there were 1,422 chisense gear owners, each of whom employed a crew of about five. Nearly half of the gear owners claimed to have only begun fishing in the last five years.[66] Indeed, the districts where chisense fishing was most common, Chiengi and Nchelenge, experienced the highest growth in population in all of Zambia between 1990 and 2000.[67] As formal employment in the urban areas declined, retrenched workers moved to the villages of Luapula and invested leftover earnings in fishing equipment. When I conducted my research in the late 1990s, there were so many tilley lanterns floating on the lake that at night it appeared as if a city of lights danced on the horizon.

Trade has become more difficult and less profitable. With the increased number of fishers and declining catches per fisher, traders no longer rely on a single fisherman for daily supplies and fish are more difficult to purchase. Women rush from one boat to the next to fill their containers with fish, struggling and fighting among themselves to secure their *bafu* of chisense. The urban traders have to travel to more remote areas to ensure that they receive adequate supplies at a low price. In the aftermath of the collapse of the mining economies of Zambia and Zaire, privatization, and the introduction of structural adjustment programs in Zambia, formal employment has declined and more autonomous or single women rely on the trade to support their households. Men who can no longer sustain fishing activities because of declining profits alongside high costs, or who have lost their urban jobs, also turned to trade (in the late 1990s women reported an increase in the number of men trading fish). Many more fishers and traders are chasing Mweru-Luapula's most resilient resource.

Profits from the chisense fishery have fallen in line with H. Scott Gordon and Garret Hardin's views. Although it would require a far more efficient means of exploitation than lamps and mosquito nets to provoke a biological tragedy, profit margins have declined. Has the chisense industry, Mweru-Luapula's most open-access and resilient resource, fallen victim to inexorable logic of the tragedy of the commons? From the perspective of creating a viable capitalist class, it has; on the other hand, from the perspective of those without capital resources, the chisense industry is as valuable and as important as ever. As urban pensions decline to under one dollar a month, the "flies of the lakes," with their remarkably high biological rate of turnover, are still more successful generators of forms of wealth and food security than the copper mines and the promised benefits of privatization in an age of structural adjustments.

Conclusions

In the early 1980s, the urban economies of the Zambian and Congolese Copperbelts began a period of prolonged recession from which they have yet to emerge. Urban dwellers looked to informal activities like smuggling or the trade in rural produce to survive and a few returned to the villages of their parents to farm or fish. Some carried newly acquired tilley lanterns, mosquito nets, and boats to try their luck as chisense fishermen. Women in urban areas also turned to trading activities with low barriers to entry; the trade in dried fish and chisense was the perfect business for these desperate entrepreneurs. A class of itinerant urban traders filled the scattered fish markets of Lusaka, Lubumbashi, and the Copperbelt towns. Marginalized groups in the rural areas, especially women, engaged with these new entrepreneurs and also managed to secure some cash and livelihood expenses from processing and trading chisense.

From its origins as a resource lightly exploited for local subsistence, the chisense fishing industry became Mweru-Luapula's most important commercial resource. The exploitation of chisense encouraged a new wave of capitalized fishers to settle in burgeoning fishing camps and towns. Newcomers benefited from almost open access to the pelagic fishery, the relatively low costs in acquiring chisense fishing equipment, and easily learned skills. This prevented a few producers and traders from monopolizing the fishery. In rural areas, the most significant impact of the chisense fishery was the creation of new spheres of commerce controlled by women. Female processors took charge of the drying and local sale of the fish. If they earned enough cash, they diversified their economic activities and became directly involved in rural-urban trade. Such big women on a small scale could leave poor husbands and boyfriends and invest in their children and their families.

The chisense fishery of today supports tens of thousands of Zambians and Congolese traders and fishers whose existence would otherwise be far more precarious. In the face of political, ecological, and economic instability, the fishery remains crucial in providing food and opportunities for the accumulation of appropriate forms of wealth by small-scale producers and traders. The fishery allows for investment in families; while costly at times, they are still considered the best safety net against an uncertain future.

Conclusion

Tragic Assumptions

The history of a rather peripheral venture in the economic landscape of the twentieth century forces us to reflect on some of the central and still fashionable assumptions and formulas underlying that most imperial of social sciences, "development studies." One of its leading proponents and much-quoted scholars, Hernando de Soto, has recently argued that only legally integrated property systems can convert the earnings and savings of the poor into capital.[1] Only through an accepted and recognized system of property registration can capitalism extend beyond a narrow elite and benefit those at the bottom. This is not a new idea. "An established idea of property is the source of all industry among individuals, and, of course, the foundation of public prosperity," Alexander Dow wrote with reference to India in the late eighteenth century.[2] In a fishery, property rights are always difficult to define. Even where legal rights to the resource have supported fishers in creating larger-scale businesses and provided models for business organization in general, the long-term economic and environmental sustainability of fishing has been threatened by the difficulty of providing incentives to limit the size of the fishers' catch. This feature of a fishery has long been understood by economists and has been popularized by environmentalists as "the tragedy of the commons."

Yet a fishery is more than a theoretical economic model; it is a site of settlement, production, and exchange permeated with history, memory, and culture. Rules of access and ownership exist even when not codified in law. In fact, in Mweru-Luapula, an imposed colonial system defined the fishery as a legal "commons" subject to an array of regulations rather than "owned" according to indigenous forms of title. This turns the conventional historical narrative on its head. Instead of capitalism enclosing the commons, it was colonial capitalism that liberated the

land and lakes from autochthonous forms of ownership. This relationship between tenure, economic development, and political authority has
contributed to some of the "underdeveloped" features of capitalism in
Africa, where producers are constantly indebted and tied to widening
arrays of corporate groups in their efforts to secure claims to resources.

This book began by exploring how the people of Mweru-Luapula
embedded the lake, river, and lands in narratives that divided control
over resources and people between clans and kings. The most important
narrative was that of Nachituti's gift of the land and lakes to Mwata
Kazembe, which provided a charter for Lunda rule over the people
while recognizing the heads of autochthonous clans as owners of the
land and lagoons. While such narratives were not forgotten in the colonial period, colonial states imposed new legal regimes that defined the
fishery as a "tribal" commons and thereby transformed, or at least divided, control over resources into formal and informal realms. Formally,
colonial chiefs and officials regulated the fishery and ignored former
charters to resource ownership; informally, old and new corporate
groups challenged colonial regulations. Selected indirect and direct rulers ostensibly controlled valuable resources, but they maintained only a
tenuous grasp upon them.[3]

This work has presented the most difficult scenario for problems of
tenure: a resource with complicated precolonial rules of ownership
that was located on a border where two colonial and postcolonial states
with little local legitimacy imposed similar but distinct—and at times
competing—regulations governing resource access. When tenure rules
are so imprecise and regulations governing property rights are rarely
enforced, informal rules of access and ownership tend to prosper. And
such informal rules have to rely on informal enforcers—in particular,
the social networks that surround the resource users. So fishers have
sought to counteract unstable tenure rights with investments in social
networks. Such networks, whether extensive patronage systems headed
by wealthy traders or, more modestly, extended families, have proved to
be a more stable arena for investment and accumulation than money or
property. Wealth in Luapula has remained tied to social relationships.

Hernando de Soto argues that only when informal forms of title are
formalized into an integrated property system can property rights lead
to the formation of capital and the rise of capitalist business ventures.[4]
Even if desirable, this goal is not easy to achieve. Informal forms of title
invoke historically layered claims to resources and are mobilized by
multiple claimants. In Africa, colonialism distanced precolonial forms

of title from the emergent formal legal realm and promoted colonial chiefs as resource managers. Postcolonial states, having only a tenuous grip on the countryside, have let such chiefs continue to mediate access. Yet rural producers still mobilize memories of original "owners" and tell stories of new economic elites that weaken the control of chiefs.

Informal rights in resources have had limited success in overcoming the "fisherman's problem," that is, preventing the exploitation of a resource beyond the point at which catches and average profits decline. A few large businesses arose as certain resource users invested in new equipment and gained advantage over others or as traders extended lines of credit in exchange for catches and thereby increased the scale of their businesses. Overall, however, the fishery has been characterized by the resilience and proliferation of small-scale businesses. Newly arrived migrants have not respected old communal restrictions, and older inhabitants have not respected the rules of imposed political agents, whether chiefs or state officials. More nets have meant less fish per net. However, to call this a "tragedy" is to opt for a narrowly defined trajectory of economic growth. In the case of the chisense fishery, the lack of economic consolidation and the absence of both historical and contemporary access rights provided valuable opportunities for those unable to participate in other economic activities. In the hinterland of central Africa's collapsing copper mines, forms of wealth that emerged out of the chisense fishery rested on, and were invested in, social relationships best suited to the needs of households and their small-scale enterprises. From the perspective of Luapula's chisense fishers, the narrative of economic "tragedy" misses some of the more significant realms of success.

From the perspective of biological diversity, it is not difficult to defend the idea of a "tragedy." In Mweru-Luapula, at least, there is little doubt that aggregate fishing effort increased dramatically over the last century and that the lake and river witnessed spurts of environmental change, adjustment, and decline in fish diversity. Yet the emphasis should be on species change—the rise of ecosystems that supported smaller species better suited to intense levels of human predation. Several historians of Africa's environment have challenged claims of an early period of natural harmony destroyed by the arrival of colonialism and capitalism.[5] The history of Mweru-Luapula's commercial fishery illustrates a similar process of change and resilience despite the constant cries of "overfishing" and "unsustainability" by state officials since the 1940s. Environmental change was evident, but conservation measures were highly politicized and represented the interests of various resource users. Regulations that claimed to conserve fish stocks were often used by colonial and postcolonial states to control, and in some cases tax, Luapula's fiercely independent networks of fishers and traders.

The social, political, and economic foundations of tenure rights are not easy to establish and protect; nor is it easy to convert such rights into appropriate forms of wealth. In Mweru-Luapula, entrepreneurs have chosen to invest in a combination of human networks and capital resources appropriate to their social, economic, and environmental worlds. There is no reason to expect that political economies based on investments in social relationships will disappear with economic development and the spread of commercial, exchange-based economies, nor will forms of title become more clearly delineated. The history of Mweru-Luapula's fishery demonstrates that both of these commonplace assumptions need to be reconsidered. The rise of more secure rights in resources, accompanied by investments in forms of wealth that generate capital divorced from society, is neither a necessary condition for economic development nor its inevitable outcome.

APPENDIX

ABBREVIATIONS

NOTES

GLOSSARY

BIBLIOGRAPHY

INDEX

APPENDIX

Select Commercial Fish of Mweru-Luapula

This table includes the fish most important to this study. It is not a comprehensive list, which can be found in Zambia, DoF, *A Scientific Classification with English and Zambian Language Classification of Zambian Fish Species* (Lusaka: Government Printers, 1977).

BEMBA NAME	ENGLISH NAME	SCIENTIFIC NAME	PREFERRED PROCESSING
Bongwe	Blunt-Toothed Catfish	*Clarias ngamensis*	Smoked
Chisense		*Poecilothrissa moeruensis*	Sun-dried
Chituku	Redbreast Tilapia	*Tilapia rendalli*	Fresh/Smoked
Kachenje	Juvenile Green Bream	*Oreochromis mweruensis*	Sun-dried/Smoked
Lupata	African butterfish	*Schilbe mystus*	Smoked
Lusa		*Mormyrops longirostris*	Smoked/Fresh
Makobo	Purple Bream	*Serranochromis macrocephalus*	Smoked/Salted
Manda	Tiger Fish	*Hydrocynus vittatus*	Smoked
Mbowa	Shovel-Nose Cat Fish	*Auchenoglanis occidentalis*	Smoked
Milonge	Sharptooth Catfish	*Clarias theodorae*	Smoked
Misibele	Torpedo Robber	*Alestes macrophthalmus*	Sun-dried/Fresh
Mpumbu	Luapula Salmon	*Labeo altivelis*	Fresh/Smoked
Ndomondomo/			
Umukape	Bull dog	*Marcusenius macrolepidotus*	Smoked
Ntembwa	Humped-Back Bream	*Tylochromis mylodon*	Smoked/Salted
Pale	Green-Headed Bream	*Oreochromis mweruensis*	Fresh/Smoked
Sampa	Vundu	*Heterobranchus longifilis*	Smoked/Fresh

ABBREVIATIONS

AA	Archives Africaines
AE	Affaires Etrangères
AFMU	African Fishers and Marketers Union
ANC	African National Congress
APEZA	Association des Pécheurs du Zaire
ASHILAC	Association culturelle des Shila du lac Moëro
BA	Bibliothèque Africaine
BSAC	British South Africa Company
CdD	Commissaire de district
CO	Colonial Office
DC	District Commissioner
DoF	Department of Fisheries
DRC	Democratic Republic of the Congo
FAO	Food and Agricultural Organization of the United Nations
FBEI	Fonds du Bien-Être Indigène
JMPR	Jeunesse du Mouvement Populaire de la Révolution
LNA	Lunda Native Authority
LFZ	Lake Fisheries of Zambia
LP	Luapula Province
MMD	Movement for Multi-Party Democracy
MPR	Mouvement Populaire de la Révolution
NAZ	National Archives of Zambia
NGO	Nongovernmental Organization
NP	Northern Province
NR	Northern Rhodesia
NFCC	Nchelenge Fisheries Coordinating Committee
PC	Provincial Commissioner
PRO	Public Record Office
SDA	Seventh-day Adventist Church
SNV	Stichting Nederlandse Vrijwilligers
UMHK	Union Minière du Haut Katanga
UNILU	Université de Lubumbashi
UNIP	United Independence Party

UNZA	University of Zambia
USPI	Union Syndical des pêcheurs indépendants
WFA	White Fathers' Archive
ZCCM	Zambia Consolidated Copper Mines
ZNBC	Zambia National Broadcasting Corporation

NOTES

Introduction

1. Jane Guyer, "Wealth in People, Wealth in Things—Introduction," *Journal of African History* 36.1 (1995): 90.

2. African environmental history most relevant to this work are Emmanuel Akyeampong, *Between the Sea and the Lagoon: An Eco-Social History of the Anlo of Southeastern Ghana* (Athens: Ohio University Press, 2001); Robert Harms, *Games Against Nature: An Eco-Cultural History of the Nunu of Equatorial Africa* (Cambridge: Cambridge University Press, 1987); Helge Kjekshus, *Ecology Control and Economic Development in East African History: The Case of Tanganyika, 1850–1950* (Berkeley: University of California Press, 1977); James Giblin, *The Politics of Environmental Control in Northeastern Tanzania, 1840–1940* (Philadelphia: University of Pennsylvania Press, 1992); James Fairhead and Melissa Leach, *Misreading the African Landscape: Society and Ecology in a Forest-Savanna Mosaic* (Cambridge: Cambridge University Press, 1996).

3. In general, historians have been slow to add social and economic complexity to the "ecosystemic" approach of human-nature encounters pioneered by anthropologists in the 1970s. A clear exception is Robert Harms; for his discussion of approaches to human-nature encounter and the ecosystem approach, see Harms, *Games Against Nature*, 246–53.

4. H. Scott Gordon, "The Economic Theory of a Common Property Resource: The Fishery," *Journal of Political Economy* 62.2 (1954): 124–42.

5. Garret Hardin, "The Tragedy of the Commons," *Science* 162 (1968): 1243–47.

6. See, for example, R. B. Rettig and J. C. Ginter, *Limited Entry as a Fishery Management Tool* (Seattle: University of Washington Press, 1978). For the argument applied to property regimes in general, see Hernando de Soto, *The Mystery of Capital: Why Capitalism Triumphs in the West and Fails Everywhere Else* (New York: Basic Books, 2000).

7. Bonnie McCay and James Acheson, *The Question of the Commons: The Culture and Ecology of Communal Resources* (Tucson: University of Arizona Press, 1987). For a qualified defense of common property theory against such critiques, see

Ottar Brox, "Common Property Theory: Epistemological Status and Analytical Utility," *Human Organization* 49.3 (1990): 227–35, 229.

8. This discussion is not yet resolved and depends on geographic area. For East Africa the seminal work is Kjekshus, *Ecology Control and Economic Development.* For southern Africa, Scoones and Beinert criticize authoritarian and misguided state interventions; however, Beinert contends that commercial settler agriculture has not necessarily led to environmental degradation. Ian Scoones, "Range Management Science and Policy: Politics, Polemics, and Pasture in Southern Africa," in *The Lie of the Land: Challenging Received Wisdom on the African Environment,* ed. Melissa Leach and Robin Mearns (Oxford: James Currey, 1996), 34–53; William Beinert, "Soil Erosion, Animals, and Pasture over the Longer Term: Environmental Destruction in Southern Africa," in *The Lie of the Land,* ed. Leach and Mearns, 54–72. For a nuanced view of struggles over common resources and the implications of privatization on Tswana land and water resources, see Pauline Peters, *Dividing the Commons: Politics, Policy, and Culture in Botswana* (Charlottesville: University Press of Virginia, 1994).

9. For a defense of the commons against privatization in the U.S. context, see Theodore Steinberg, *Slide Mountain or the Folly of Owning Nature* (Berkeley: University of California Press, 1995). A critique of developmental perspectives based on privatizing the commons is Michael Goldman, ed., *Privatizing Nature: Political Struggles and the Global Commons* (London: Pluto Press, 1998), 1–53.

10. Randy T. Simmons and Peregrine Schwartz-Shea, "Method, Metaphor, and Understanding: When Is the Commons Not a Tragedy," in *The Political Economy of Customs and Culture: Informal Solutions to the Commons Problem,* ed. Terry L. Anderson and Randy T. Simmons (Lanham, Md.: Rowman and Littlefield, 1993), 1–11.

11. Sara Berry, *Chiefs Know Their Boundaries: Essays on Property, Power, and the Past in Asante* (Portsmouth N.H.: Heinemann, 2001), 198. Also see Sara Berry, "Social Institutions and Access to Resources," *Africa* 59.1 (1989): 41–55.

12. Steinberg, *Slide Mountain or the Folly of Owning Nature,* 10.

13. Daniel Bromley and Michael Cernea, "The Management of Common Property Natural Resources: Some Operational Fallacies," World Bank Discussion Papers, no 57 (World Bank, October 1989).

14. For medieval forests in England, see Jean Birelle, "Common Rights in the Medieval Forest: Disputes and Conflicts in the Thirteenth Century," *Past and Present* 117 (1987): 22–49. R. W. Hoyle points to the negotiated nature of customary tenant rights and copyhold in sixteenth-century England in "An Ancient and Laudable Custom: The Definition and Development of Tenant Right in North-Western England in the Sixteenth Century," *Past and Present* 116 (1987): 24–55. A detailed study of the erosion of "common rights" in the early modern period is J. M. Neeson, *Commoners: Common Right, Enclosure, and Social Change in England, 1700–1820* (Cambridge: Cambridge University Press, 1993).

15. Richard Hoffman, "Economic Development and Aquatic Ecosystems in Medieval Europe," *The American Historical Review* 101.3 (June 1996): 654.

16. E. P. Thompson, *Customs in Common* (New York: New Press, 1991), 151.

17. Ibid., 159.

18. Quoted and discussed in Peter Coates, *Nature: Western Attitudes Since Ancient Times* (Cambridge: Polity Press, 1998), 92.

19. The rights-in-persons argument has been most effectively applied when trying to understand and clarify slavery in Africa; for an introduction, see Suzanne Miers and Ivan Kopytoff, "African 'Slavery' as an Institution of Marginality," in *Slavery in Africa* (Madison: University of Wisconsin Press, 1977), 3–78. These arguments rest in part on the influential work of Jack Goody. See *Tradition, Technology, and the State in Africa* (London: Oxford University Press, 1971).

20. Elizabeth Colson, "The Impact of the Colonial Period on the Definition of Land Rights," in *Colonialism in Africa, 1870–1960,* ed. Victor Turner (Cambridge: Cambridge University Press, 1971), 3:193–215, 199.

21. John Thornton, *Africa and Africans in the Making of the Atlantic World* (Cambridge: Cambridge University Press, 1992), 76.

22. Bronislaw Malinowski, *Crime and Custom in Savage Society* (London: Routledge, Kegan and Paul, 1926; reprint, Paterson, N. J.: Littlefield, Adams and Co., 1962), 19.

23. Jane I. Guyer and Samuel M. Eno Belinga, "Wealth in People as Wealth in Knowledge: Accumulation and Composition in Equatorial Africa," *Journal of African History* 36.1 (1995): 91–120.

24. For an introduction to the extensive work of the relationship between memory and identity, see John Gillis, "Memory and Identity: The History of a Relationship," in *Commemorations: The Politics of National Identity* (Princeton: Princeton University Press, 1994), 3–24. For recent scholarship from Africa, see Richard Werbner, ed., *Memory and the Postcolony: African Anthropology and the Critique of Power* (New York: Zed Books, 1998).

25. C. G. Trapnell, *The Soils, Vegetation, and Agriculture of North-Eastern Rhodesia: Report of the Ecological Survey* (Lusaka: Government Printer, 1953), 70–71.

26. For a history of the Shila state, see Mwelwa C. Musambachime, "Changing Roles: The History of the Development and Disintegration of the Shila State to 1740," M.A. thesis, University of Wisconsin, 1976.

27. Eastern Lunda praise poems were recited in a form of Luba and not the Ruund language of Mwaant Yaav's court, indicating that Lunda titles were probably bestowed on a Luba-related lineage. The oral traditions of the eastern Lunda are recorded in Mwata Kazembe XIV Chinyanta, *Ifikolwe Fyandi na Bantu Bandi,* translated by Ian Cunnison as *Historical Traditions of the Eastern Lunda* (Lusaka: Rhodes-Livingstone Institute, 1961). For praise poems in archaic Luba, see Jacques Chileya Chiwale, trans. and ann., *Royal Praises and Praise Names of the Lunda of Northern Rhodesia: Their Meaning and Historical Background*

(Lusaka: Rhodes Livingstone Institute, 1961). Also see Giacomo Macola, *Kingdom of Kazembe: History and Politics in North-Eastern Zambia and Kataga to 1950* (Hamburg: LIT Verlag, 2002), 40–42. Macola, based on evidence of Portuguese traders, reckons that even while they were of Luba descent, the nineteenth-century eastern Lunda court spoke a type of Ruund. *Kingdom of Kazembe*, 42.

28. The best known is Hamed bin Muhammed el-Murjebi, nicknamed "Tippu Tip." See Heinrich Brode, *Tippoo Tib: The Story of His Career in Central Africa*, trans. H. Havelock (1911; reprint, Chicago: Afro-Am Press, 1969), 59–70; François Bontinck, ed., *L'Autobiographie de Hamed ben Mohammed el-Murjebi Tippo Tip (ca. 1840–1905)* (Brussels: Académie royale des sciences d'outre-mer, 1974); Ian Cunnison, "Kazembe and the Arabs to 1870," in *The Zambesian Past: Studies in Central African History*, ed. E. Stokes and R. Brown (Manchester: Manchester University Press, 1966), 226–37.

29. Hugues Legros, *Chasseurs d'ivoire: Une histoire du royaume Yéke du Shaba (Zaire)* (Brussels: Editions de l'Université de Bruxelles, 1996); Auguste Verbeken, *Msiri: Roi du Garanganze* (Bruxelles: Louis Cypers, 1956), 23–128. For an account of the state and trading activities during the 1880s, see Frederick Stanley Arnot, *Garanganze or, Seven Years' Pioneer Mission Work in Central Africa* (London: James E. Hawkins, 1890), 172–243.

30. Ian Cunnison, *History on the Luapula: An Essay in the Historical Notions of a Central African Tribe* (Cape Town: Oxford University Press, 1951; reprint, Manchester: Manchester University Press, 1969).

31. For an overview, see individual chapters in J. M. Schoffeleers, ed., *Guardians of the Land: Essays on Central African Territorial Cults* (Gwelo: Mambo Press for the University of Salisbury, 1979), 47–207. For the Luba see Thomas Reefe, *The Rainbow and the Kings: A History of the Luba Empire to 1891* (Berkeley: University of California Press, 1981); for the Mbona cult, see J. M. Schoffeleers, *Rivers of Blood: The Genesis of a Martyr Cult in Southern Malawi* (Madison: University of Wisconsin Press, 1992); for shrines in Motopos see Terence Ranger, *Voices from the Rocks: Nature, Culture, and History in the Motopos Hills of Zimbabwe* (Oxford: James Currey, 1999), 19–26; for the Lozi, see Gwyn Prins, *The Hidden Hippopotomus: Reapraisal in African History: The Early Colonial Experience in Western Zambia* (Cambridge: Cambridge University Press, 1980), 139–50.

32. Thomas Reefe, "The Societies of the Eastern Savanna," in *History of Central Africa*, eds. David Birmingham and Phyllis M. Martin (London and New York: Longman, 1983), 1: 160–204, esp. 168.

33. For precolonial environmental management in East Africa, see Steven Feierman, *Peasant Intellectuals: Anthropology and History in Tanzania* (Madison: University of Wisconsin Press, 1990), 69–93. Also see essays by James L. Giblin and Michelle Wagner in *Custodians of the Land: Ecology and Culture in the History of Tanzania*, ed. Gregory Maddox, James Giblin, and Isaria N. Kimambo (London: James Currey, 1996), 127–52, 175–99.

34. Jean-Loup Amselle, *Mestizo Logics: Anthropology of Identity in Africa and Elsewhere* (Stanford: Stanford University Press, 1998), 95. For relationships between owners and rulers in West Africa, see Edna Bay, *Wives of the Leopard: Gender, Politics, and Culture in the Kingdom of Dohomey* (Charlottesville: University Press of Virginia, 1998), 40–80; Sandra Greene, *Sacred Sites and the Colonial Encounter: A History of Meaning and Memory in Ghana* (Bloomington: Indiana University Press, 2002), 15–18.

35. Ranger, *Voices from the Rocks,* 19–26.

36. Mutumba Mainga, *Bulozi under the Luyana Kings: Political Evolution and State Formation in Pre-Colonial Zambia* (London: Longman, 1973); Andrew Roberts, *A History of Zambia* (New York: Africana Publishing Co., 1976), 96–99.

37. Schoffeleers, *Rivers of Blood,* 160–72.

38. Audrey Richards, *Land, Labour, and Diet: An Economic Study of the Bemba Tribe* (London: Oxford University Press, 1939), 351–80.

39. Schoffeleers, *Guardians,* 8.

40. Allen Roberts notes the importance of snakes to the nearby Tabwa ecological cults. *Animals in African Art: From the Familiar to the Marvelous* (New York: Museum for African Art, 1995), 63. Also see chapter 2.

41. The best attempt to do so is in Musambachime, "Changing Roles," 27–60. My interviews were not as revealing of these Shila traditions.

42. Colson, "Colonial Period and Land Rights," 197.

43. E. P. Thompson noticed that with respect to tenure law during colonialism in Africa, there was a "remarkable series of reversals of Whig ideology, the settlement of extensive lands in the superordinate ownership of the State, combined with measures to inhibit the growth of private property in land." *Customs in Common,* 174. Also see, Colson, "Colonial Period and Land Rights," 198.

44. For Asante chiefs, see Berry, *Chiefs Know Their Boundaries,* 1–34.

45. Samuel N. Chipungu, "Accumulation from Within: The Boma class and the Native Treasury in Colonial Zambia," in *Guardians in Their Time: Experiences of Zambians under Colonial Rule, 1890–1964* (London: Macmillan, 1992), 74–96.

46. Sara Berry, *No Condition Is Permanent: The Social Dynamics of Agrarian Change in Sub-Saharan Africa* (Madison: University of Wisconsin Press, 1993), 22–42.

47. Mahmood Mamdani, *Citizen and Subject: Contemporary Africa and the Legacy of Late Colonialism* (Princeton: Princeton University Press, 1996).

48. For specific reference to chiefs of Mweru-Luapula, see David Gordon, "Owners of the Land and Lunda Lords: Colonial Chiefs in the Borderlands of Northern Rhodesia and the Belgian Congo," *International Journal of African Historical Studies* 34.3 (2001): 315–37.

49. Joseph Miller, *Way of Death: Merchant Capital and the Angolan Slave Trade* (Madison: University of Wisconsin Press, 1988).

50. Matrilineal relationships in Africa were especially thought to be destined for disappearance. For a summary of such arguments, see Mary Douglas, "Is Matriliny Doomed in Africa?" in *Man in Africa*, ed. Mary Douglas and Phyllis M. Kaberry (London: Tavistock, 1969), 121–35. For the Luapula Valley, see Karla A. Poewe, *Matrilineal Ideology: Male-Female Dynamics in Luapula, Zambia* (London: Academic Press, 1981).

51. Thomas Spear, *Mountain Farmers: Moral Economics of Land and Agricultural Development in Arusha and Meru* (Berkeley: University of California Press, 1997), 12.

52. Jean Philipe Platteau, "Small-Scale Fisheries and Evolutionist Theory," in *Fishing for Development: Small-Scale Fisheries in Africa*, ed. Inge Tvedten and Björn Hersoug (Stockholm: Nordiska Afrikainstutet, 1992), 90–104.

53. For Californian fisheries see Arthur F. McEvoy, *The Fisherman's Problem: Ecology and Law in the California Fisheries, 1850–1980* (Cambridge: Cambridge University Press, 1986). For Japan see David Howell, *Capitalism from Within: Economy, Society, and the State in a Japanese Fishery* (Berkeley: University of California Press, 1995). For the North Atlantic cod fishery see Mark Kurlansky, *Cod: A Biography of the Fish That Changed the World* (New York: Penguin, 1998), 62–173.

54. James M. Acheson, *The Lobster Gangs of Maine* (Hanover, N.H.: University Press of New England, 1988).

55. James Ferguson, *Expectations of Modernity: Myths and Meanings of Urban Life on the Copperbelt* (Berkeley: University of California Press, 1999).

1. Nachituti's Gift

1. Dan Crawford, *Thinking Black* (London: George H. Doran Co., 1913), 234; Cunnison, *History on the Luapula;* Mwata Kazembe XIV Chinyanta Nankula, *Ifikolwe Fyandi na Bantu Bandi,* trans. Ian Cunnison as *Historical Traditions of the Eastern Lunda* (Lusaka: Rhodes-Livingstone Institute, 1961), 53–58.

2. Ian Cunnison, *The Luapula Peoples of Northern Rhodesia: Custom and History in Tribal Politics* (Manchester: Manchester University Press, 1959). There is some dispute over the exact dating of the Kazembes' reigns, especially in the nineteenth century. I have not entered the debate and simply indicate uncertainty in my diagram. See Ian Cunnison, "The Reigns of the Kazembes," *Northern Rhodesia Journal* 3.2 (1956): 131–38. Andrew Roberts, "Tippu Tip, Livingstone, and the Chronology of Kazembe," *Azania* 2 (1967): 115–31.

3. Jan Vansina, "Traditions of Genesis," *Journal of African History* 15.2 (1974): 317–22, 321. Discussion on the historical validity of oral traditions has been prolific. The most influential discussion of Luba and Lunda traditions include structuralist Luc de Heusch, *Le Roi ivre ou l'origine de l'Etat* (Paris: Gallimard, 1972). For a defense of the historical value of Ruund oral traditions, see Jeffrey J. Hoover, "The Seduction of Ruwej: Reconstructuing Ruund History (The Nuclear Lunda: Zaire, Angola, Zambia), Ph.D. dissertation, Yale

University, 1978, 125–56. For Luba traditions, see Thomas Reefe, *The Rainbow and the Kings*, 23–48.

4. Vansina, "Traditions," 320. Unfortunately, in the case of the story of Nachituti and Kazembe's conquests, Vansina treated the oral evidence as faithful renditions of the past. See Jan Vansina, *Kingdoms of the Savanna: A History of Central African States until European Occupation* (Madison: University of Wisconsin Press, 1968), 165–74.

5. Jean and John Comaroff, *Of Revelation and Revolution: Vol. 1 Christianity, colonialism, and consciousness in South Africa* (Chicago: University of Chicago Press, 1991); J. D. Y. Peel, "For Who Hath Despised the Day of Small Things? Missionary Narratives and Historical Anthropology," *Comparative Studies in Society and History* 37.3 (1995): 581–607. For a critique of the Comaroffs' contention of the lack of Tswana narrative, see Paul Landau, "Hegemony and History in Jean and John L. Comaroff's *Revelation and Revolution*," *Africa* 70.3 (2000): 501–19, esp. 515–16.

6. Robert Cancel, *Allegorical Speculation in an Oral Society: The Tabwa Narrative* (Berkeley: University of California Press, 1989).

7. Schoffeleers, *Rivers of Blood*, 60–72.

8. Macola, *Kingdom of Kazembe*, 79–80.

9. Perpetual kinship has been explored in Ian Cunnison, "Perpetual Kinship: A Political Institution of the Luapula Peoples," *Rhodes-Livingstone Journal* 20 (1955): 28–48. On the use of history in Luapula in the 1940s, see Cunnison, *History on the Luapula*. Jeffrey J. Hoover describes "perpetual kinship" as "the constitutional idiom of Lunda political thought." "The Seduction of Ruwej," 114.

10. David M. Gordon, "Orality, Memory, and Historical Time on the Luapula (Zambia)," paper presented to the Orality and Literacy 3: Memory Conference, Rice University, 10–12 October 2003.

11. Marcel Mauss, *The Gift: The Form and Reason for Exchange in Archaic Societies*, trans. W. D. Hall (London: Routledge, 1990); originally published as *Essai sur le don* (Press Universitaires de France, 1950).

12. The early story of Lunda conquest is based on Mwata Kazembe XIV, *Ifikolwe Fyandi*, 1–52. Cunnison, *The Luapula Peoples*, 147–56; Edouard Labrecque, "Histoire des Mwata Kazembe," *Lovania* 16 (1949): 9–33. Written sources from the journals of Almeida de Lacerda (1798), the Angolan *pombeiros* (1806–10), and Gamitto (1831–32) contain limited references to these traditions. The journals of Lacerda and the Angolan *pombeiros* have been edited and translated in R. F. Burton, *The Lands of Cazembe* (London: Royal Geographic Society, 1873), and A. C. P. Gamitto, trans. Ian Cunnison, *King Kazembe and the Marave, Cheva, Bisa, Bemba, Lunda, and Other Peoples of Southern Africa* (2 vols.) (Lisbon, Portugal: Junta de investigações do ultramar, 1960). A better translation of the *pombeiros* is P. J. Baptista, trans. and ann. A. Verbeken and M. Walraet, *La Première Traversée du Katanga en 1806. Voyage des "Pombeiros" d'Angola aux Rios de Sena* (Brussels: Mem. Inst. Colonial Belge, 1953). These sources have been used by

Jan Vansina in *Kingdoms of the Savanna,* 165–74. The most recent and thorough evaluation of the oral traditions and written sources in the early history of Kazembe's kingdom can be found in Macola, *Kingdom of Kazembe,* 67–103.

13. Based on the testimony of Lacerda's expedition, which on its visit to the Kazembe Kingdom in 1798 reported that Kazembe crossed the Luapula and settled in the Luapula Valley some sixty years earlier. Burton, *Lands of Cazembe,* 126; Macola, *Kingdom of Kazembe,* 72.

14. Ian Cunnison argues that certain historical clichés transcended particular lineage histories and became part of the general "universal" history of the valley. Cunnison, *History on the Luapula,* 10.

15. Godwin Mwewa (Dyulu Kabeya). Mwansabombwe, 30 Dec. 2000.

16. de Heusch, *Le Roi ivre ou l'origine de l'Etat;* Hoover, "The Seduction of Ruwej"; Leon Verbeek, *Mythe et culte de Kipimpi* (Bandundu, Zaire: CEEBA, 1982).

17. Karen Sacks, *Sisters and Wives: The Past and Future of Sexual Equality* (Westport, Conn.: Greenwood, 1979).

18. For example, for the Kanongesha see Robert E. Schecter, "History and Historiography on a Frontier of Lunda Expansion: The Origins and Early Development of the Kanongesha," Ph.D. dissertation, University of Wisconsin, 1976, 166–83.

19. Jan Vansina, personal communication. Also see, White Fathers, *The White Father's Bemba-English Dictionary* (Ndola: The Society of the Missionary for Africa, 1954; reprint, 1991). Nkuba apparently derived his name after being cursed by his father, who claimed "let lightning fall on you" *(Nkuba ikuponene);* Nkuba then decided that, like lightning, he will fall on a country far away, the Luapula Valley. Edouard Labrecque, "Abashila ne misango yabo ya kwipaila isabi," manuscript written with Shila Elders, 1947–49, White Fathers' Archive (henceforth WFA), Lusaka,1-M-OT-34 Shila.

20. Mwata Kazembe XIV, *Ifikolwe Fyandi,* 53–58. Giacomo Macola has demonstrated how the writing of *Ifikolwe Fyandi* was entwined with missionary concerns, ethnic competition, and rivalry between contenders for the throne. "Literate Ethnohistory in Colonial Zambia: The Case of *Ifikolwe Fyandi na Bantu Bandi,*" *History in Africa* 28 (2001): 187–201.

21. David P. Henige, "'The Disease of Writing': Ganda and Nyoro Loyalists in a Newly Literate World," in *The African Past Speaks: Essays on Oral Tradition and History,* ed. Joseph C. Miller (Hamden, Conn.: Archon Books, 1980), 240–61; Jan Vansina, *Oral Tradition; a study in historical methodology,* trans. H.M. Wright (London: Routledge and Kegan Paul, 1965), 42–45. For the impact of literacy on Bemba narratives more generally, see Kevin B. Maxwell, *Bemba Myth and Ritual: The Impact of Literacy on an Oral Culture* (New York: Peter Lang, 1983).

22. Luise White, *Speaking with the Vampires: Rumor and History in Colonial Africa* (Berkeley: University of California Press, 2000), 263.

23. Mwata Kazembe XIV, *Ifikolwe Fyandi,* 54.

24. The word and dance seem related to the Luba royal investiture dance, the *kutomboka*. Thomas Q. Reefe, *The Rainbow and the Kings*, 44.

25. "Newatemwa ukupoke fyalo mukucimfya; Neupelwa ifyalo na bantu; Abanandi bapelwa imbushi ne mikoko." Quoted in Chiwale, trans. and ann., *Royal Praises*, 16. Also see Mwata Kazembe XIV, *Ifikolwe Fyandi*, 37.

26. "Nine Kalandala nebo . . . Newaipaye Nkuba nabamwana Nkuba bonse pamo pene; Ulya Nkuba umwine wa Chisenga; Namunyine wakwe pamo pene." Chiwale, *Royal Praises*, 14.

27. For example, see the version recorded in Cunnison, *History on the Luapula*, 17–19.

28. I use the term "aristocrats" to describe the variety of officials and title-holders who surrounded Mwata Kazembe's court. They would include *abakalunda* or *abakalulwa* (known in colonial and postcolonial contexts as the Lunda Electoral College), the territorial governors, *abachilolo* (sing, *chilolo*), and other individuals who held special duties *(imyanso)* within the court. Macola, and to a lesser extent Cunnison, treats these as distinct types of representatives or offices in the Kazembe Kingdom. In my view, the offices frequently overlapped and were not distinctly defined.

29. Macola, *Kingdom of Kazembe*, 115–22.

30. Ibid., 67–103.

31. Macola argues this was primarily over local resources, while Reefe emphasizes access to Bisa long-distance trade routes. Macola, *Kingdom of Kazembe*, 107–12; Reefe, *The Rainbow and the Kings*, 132–39.

32. Baptista, *La première traversée du Katanga*, 92–94; Macola, *Kingdom of Kazembe*, 101–3.

33. Macola, *Kingdom of Kazembe*, 136–54; Hugues Legros, *Chasseurs d'ivoire*; Brode, *Tippoo Tib*, 59–70; Cunnison, "Kazembe and the Arabs to 1870."

34. Gamitto, *King Kazembe*, 2:125, 128–29, 111–14; Baptista, *La première traversée du Katanga*, 55–60, 92–94; Burton, *Cazembe*, 125, 148–49.

35. Gamitto, *King Kazembe*, 2:111.

36. Macola, *Kingdom of Kazembe*, 90. For a similar process among the Kanongesha, Ndembu, and Mwela lineages to the west of the central Lunda, see Robert E. Schecter, "History and Historiography on a Frontier of Lunda Expansion," 227–304. For the influence of wife givers in lineage societies through the exchange of "wealth-in-knowledge," also see the work of Rosalind Shaw, *Memories of the Slave Trade: Ritual and the Historical Imagination in Sierra Leone* (Chicago: University of Chicago, 2002), 167.

37. Henceforth, I will not distinguish between the subclan lineage *(ichikota)* and the clan *(umukowa)*. While there may have been several lineages in any one clan, I will identify the clan name rather than the specific lineage.

38. Andrew Roberts, *A History of the Bemba: Political Growth and Change in North-East Zambia before 1900* (London: Longman, 1973), xxix, 18. Roberts and Reefe have emphasized, however, the importance of matrilineal clans across

south central Africa before colonialism. Roberts, *A History of Zambia*, 72–73; Reefe, "The Societies of the Eastern Savanna," 160–204, esp. 166.

39. Joseph M. Doucette, *The Clans of the Bemba and Some Neighbouring Tribes* (Ndola, Zambia: Mission Press, n.d.).

40. My observations of the workings of Luapula's clans among the older residents of the valley generally conform to those found in Cunnison, *The Luapula Peoples*, 62–82.

41. Within this so-called matrilineal belt lay a variety of succession and descent practices that depended on prevailing economic practices rather than ossified traditions. For an indication of the variety of forms of social organization, see Vansina, *Kingdoms of the Savanna*, 24–28.

42. This level of kin organization was described but underestimated in Cunnison, *The Luapula Peoples*, 83–84.

43. Cunnison, *The Luapula People*, 75.

44. Cunnison distinguishes between clans east and west of the Lualaba system, with Lunda clans originating west of the Lualaba. He recorded the *Kosa* (Tortoise) Clan as common to Kazembe and *abakalunda*. My research did not find the *Kosa* of much importance; the Elephant Clan had replaced it. The transformation of the *Kosa* Clan into the Elephant Clan needs further investigation. It is possible that after 1940 the last remnants of the western clan system were incorporated into the eastern. Clans that existed in both eastern and western systems, such as the Goat Clan, managed to continue. Cunnison, *The Luapula Peoples*, 156–64. However, Cunnison's classification of clans west of the Lualaba as "Lunda" is problematic, given that Jeff Hoover claims that the clan system was not significant among the Ruund. "Kosa" also might have been a generic term for Lunda aristocrats rather than a "Tortoise Clan." Hoover, "The Seduction of Ruwej," 257–65.

45. Cunnison, *The Luapula Peoples*, 232.

46. Guyer and Belinga, "Wealth in People as Wealth in Knowledge," 91–120.

47. This history has been reconstructed from the sometimes-contradictory accounts of several different Goat Clan elders. Moses Mwelwa Kasau, Kasau, 30 Dec. 2000; Cosmos Ngoi Kaniembo Chinkonkole (Chisami), Mbereshi, 2 Jan. 2001; Gosam Mwelwa (Koni), Koni, 3 Jan. 2001; Achim Kabaso (Kanyemba), Kanyemba, 6 Jan. 2001; Chibwidi, Chibwidi, 10 Jan. 2001; Dalas Mpanga (Bana Kamweka), Mwansabombwe, 13 Jan. 2001; John Ilunga (Chilalo), Chilalo , 15 Jan. 2001; Amon Mukobe (Shanyemba) , Shanyemba, 16 Jan. 2001.

48. The belt is commonly known as *inshipo;* however, in many of the praises it is referred to as *chiseba* or *lukanga*. For a description from 1831, see Gamitto, *King Kazembe*, 2:18.

49. Another variation on this praise begins, "You can succeed a slave or a cow" (Mwababimbile akasha namungombe) since the belt can be taken from the skin of a slave or cow.

50. "Nifwebo baKaindu akamutamba ngombe; Beneba batamba chibundi; Ilunga wamusanga ulupele imikonso; Mwata Kazembe wamusanga; Ninebo tulo ulalika abacenjela." This praise was recited by the present Chilalo, Gersham Mulonda Chema (Chilalo), Chilalo , 15 Jan. 2001.

51. David Livingstone, *The Last Journals of David Livingstone*, 2 Vols., London: John Murray, 1874, 1:252. Also see Cunnison, *The Luapula Peoples*, 214.

52. Livingstone, *Last Journals*, 1:304–5.

53. Cunnison, *The Luapula Peoples*, 212.

54. Jan Vansina, personal communication; White Fathers, *Bemba-English Dictionary*.

55. Labrecque, "Abashila," WFA; Musambachime's less detailed account claims it was Nkuba's daughter and does not give her a name. "Changing Roles," 32–33.

56. Nachituti means "mother of Chituti," but in the eastern Lunda accounts the name of her son is unknown, even when questioned explicitly. The Lunda are simply not interested in the son, Chituti; his name is irrelevant.

57. Musambachime, "Changing Roles," 103–7; Labrecque, "Abashila," WFA. I have also heard the story from Mununga and Councilors, Mununga's Palace, 26 June 1998.

58. Labrecque, "Abashila," WFA

59. Cunnison, *The Luapula Peoples*, 34–35.

60. Leon Verbeek, *Filiation et usurpation: Histoire socio-politique de la region entre Luapula et Copperbelt* (Tervuren, Belgium: Musée royal de l'afrique centrale, 1987), 166.

61. For a more complete account and analysis see Verbeek, *Filiation et usurpation*, 9–16; Verbeek, *Mythe et culte de Kipimpi*.

62. Macola, *Kingdom of Kazembe*, 92.

63. There is a second "Pacalala Nkuba," on Lake Mweru, about forty miles from Chisenga Island. Musambachime, "Changing Roles," 44. This again demonstrates the generic nature of the praises or proverbs but the particular places to which they refer.

64. According to Thomas Reefe, the practice of a political chief symbolically marrying an earth priest (or owner of the land) was common to the region. Reefe, "Societies of the Eastern Savanna," 169.

65. Cunnison, *The Luapula Peoples*, 212–13; Godwin Mwewa (Dyulu Kabeya), Mwansabombwe, 30 Dec. 2000.

66. Gamitto, *King Kazembe*, 2:116.

67. Cunnison, *The Luapula Peoples*, 232.

68. Macola, *Kingdom of Kazembe*, 92; Dan Crawford, *Thinking Black: Twenty-Two Years without a Break in the Long Grass of Central Africa* (New York: George H. Doran Co., 1913), 232–34.

69. Mwata Kazembe XIV, *Ifikolwe Fyandi*, 58. Cunnison also noticed different versions of the story told to him by Shila and Lunda informants, *History on the Luapula*, 18–19.

70. See, for example, Musambachime, "Interview with Chisenga Island Elders," 14 May 1975. These include Kalandala and the heir apparent to the Nkubaship. This account informs Musambachime, "Changing Roles," 103–7.

71. For a reevaluation of Frazer's "scapegoat king" and sacred kingship see Luc de Heusch, "The Symbolic Mechanisms of Sacred Kingship: Rediscovering Frazer." *The Journal of the Royal Anthropological Institute* 3.2 (1997): 213–232.

72. For this suggestion, see Crawford, *Thinking Black*, 428.

73. *Shingulu* and *Nangulu: Shi-* is father, *Na-* mother, and *ingulu* can best be translated as a nature spirit.

74. Mwelwa C. Musambachime, "The Ubutwa Society in Eastern Shaba and Northeast Zambia to 1920," *International Journal of African Historical Studies* 27.1 (1994): 77–99. Some details not in this article can be found in Mwelwa C. Musambachime, "Ubutwa: A Study of the Role and Function of a Secret Society in Eastern Zaire and North-East Zambia to the 1920s," n.d., ca. 1991–93; Dugald Campbell, "A Few Notes on Butwa: An African Secret Society," *Man* 14.38 (1914): 76–81; Dugald Campbell, *In the Heart of Bantuland: A Record of Twenty-Nine Years' Pioneering in Central Africa* (1922; reprint, New York: Negro University Press, 1969), 96–106. Also drawn from author interviews: Godwin Mwewa (Dyulu Kabeya), Mwansabombwe, 12 Dec. 2000; John Ilunga, Chilalo, 15 Jan. 2001; Alam Lukwesa, Musanda , 16 Jan. 2001. Verbeek suggests that Ubutwa might have been an adaptation of Christian doctrines learned from the Portuguese in the Tete region of east Africa during the eighteenth and nineteenth century. The best evidence for this is the spread by Ubutwa of the term "Lesa" for God—the term adopted by missionaries—and Lukele Nganga for Lesa's son, presumably Jesus. Leon Verbeek, *Le monde des esprits au sud-est du Shaba et au nord de la Zambie* (Rome: Libreria Ateneo Salesiano, 1990), 13.

75. Reefe, *The Rainbow and the Kings*, 46. Insofar as the notion existed among the central Lunda, it was found in the *kabung,* pl. *tubung,* which also probably had Luba origins. Hoover, "The Seduction of Ruwej," 527; Vansina, personal communication. A similar title existed in the Kanongesha polity. See Robert E. Schecter, "History and Historiography on a Frontier of Lunda Expansion," 166.

76. Mary Nooter Roberts and Allen F. Roberts, *Memory: Luba Art and the Making of History* (New York: Museum for African Art, 1996), 28.

77. Mununga and Councilors, Mununga, 27 Aug. 1998; Mwata Kazembe XIV, *Ifikolwe Fyandi*, 64. Livingstone, *Last Journals*, 1:252.

78. For conquest of the Chishinga/Rat Clan, see Musambachime, "Changing Roles," 54; Mwata Kazembe XIV, *Ifikolwe Fyandi*, 65–66. Nowadays, both of the Lubunda and Mulundu titleholders deny having paid tribute to Kazembe and declare that Kazembe was not allowed to enter their palaces. Mulundu acknowledges giving Kazembe ivory as a peace offering. Joseph Muyape (Lubunda), Lubunda's Palace, 8 Oct. 1997; Nashinka Mulundu and Councilors, Mulundu's Palace, 9 Jan. 1998. But Giraud's eyewitness testimony from 1883 records Mulundu switching allegiances from Kazembe to Msiri.

Victor Giraud, *Les lacs de l'Afrique équatoriale, voyage d'expédition exécuté de 1883 à 1885* (Paris: Libraire Hachette, 1890), 362–63; Quoted in Macola, *Kingdom of Kazembe,* 149–50. By the second half of the nineteenth century the Lunda aristocrats Mulanda, Chiyombo, and Kawala were also found in the south of the valley. Macola, *Kingdom of Kazembe,* 86.

79. Cunnison, *The Luapula Peoples,* 218–20.

80. These rites would form part of *ulutambi* custom. Ian Cunnison, "A Note on the Lunda Concept of Custom," *Rhodes-Livingstone Journal* 14 (1954): 20–29.

81. Edward Mukamba, Kabalenge, 5 Jan. 2001. *Iminkono* is the name of the papyrus *uluko* when it becomes sweet.

82. William Katwe Chishala, Makandwe River, 30 Dec. 2000.

83. The full name of Mweru is *Mwelu mukata mukandanshe,* which means "the wide expanse of water which the locusts cannot cross." Few of my informants, and no Lunda, remembered this name; they did not know the origin of the name "Mweru." Mwelwa C. Musambachime, "Development and Growth of the Fishing Industry in Mweru-Luapula, 1920–1964," Ph.D. dissertation, 2 Vols., Unversity of Wisconsin, 1976, 1:28.

84. The story of Kaponto settling the land and creating Lake Mweru by burning the plains is not remembered in the Lunda heartland. Mununga and his councilors knew the story. It is best recorded in Cunnison, *The Luapula Peoples,* 34–35. Mununga and Councilors, Mununga's Palace, 26 July 1998. For eastern Lunda and Bwile, see Macola, *Kingdom of Kazembe,* 108.

85. The Bwile should not be confused with Kaponto's people, Bwilile, called Abena Bwilile by the Lunda and Shila because they ate themselves, meaning they did not pay tribute to any chief. For an account of Bwile migration, see Musambachime, "Changing Roles," 97–101; Puta and Councilors, Puta's Palace, 27 July 1998.

86. Campbell, *In the Heart of Bantuland,* 196.

87. For an overview of all the different fishing techniques, see Musambachime, "Development and Growth," 1:48–73.

88. Livingstone was presented with nshipo, which he compared to whitebait. Livingstone, *Last Journals,* 1:300.

89. Livingstone, *Last Journals,* 1:244.

90. Mununga and Councilors, Mununga's Palace, 26 July 1998; Puta and Councilors, Puta's Palace, 27 July 1998.

91. Moses Mwelwa Kasau, Kasau, 30 Dec. 2000; Achim Kabaso (Kanyemba), Kanyemba, 6 Jan. 2001. For Nunu water lords, see Robert Harms, *Games Against Nature,* 64–65.

92. For Akankubunkubu, see the song, "Kankubu-nkubu kalefumya mita" in Labrecque, "Abashila," WFA; Mulundu and Councilor, Mulundu's Palace, 9 Jan. 1998. For a series of rites recorded in the late nineteenth century, see Crawford, *Thinking Black,* 420–28.

93. Moses Mwelwa Kasau, Kasau, 30 Dec. 2000; Achim Kabaso

(Kanyemba), Kanyemba, 6 Jan. 2001; Musambachime, "Development and Growth," "Interview with Kashiba elders," 2:13, "Interview with Fisto Mulongo, 18 April 1974," and "Interview with Mwilwa Calwe Kashimoto," 2:2; Verbeek, *Le monde des esprits*, 177–98; Cunnison, *The Luapula Peoples*, 218–19.

94. "Twaliitalile twaatusha; Nomba twalaafungwila abantu ukwipaya isabi. Tupeni umunani memipashi." Mulundu and Councilor, Mulundu's Palace, 9 Jan. 1998.

95. Mulundu and Councilor, Mulundu's Palace, 9 Jan. 1998; Report on the Native Fishing Industry 3 Dec. 1929, SEC 2/252, National Archives of Zambia (henceforth NAZ); Cunnison, *History on the Luapula*, 21.

96. Cunnison, *The Luapula Peoples*, 219.

97. For detailed rites, see Verbeek, *Le monde des esprits*, 179–89. Audrey Richards recorded similar rites on the Bemba Plateau in the 1930s. *Land, Labour, and Diet*, 351–80.

98. "Niwe nankoko kapala mashala; Cibule ku cabaku; Niwe tola tola mulomo wa nkoko; Utasha kalembe." Quoted and trans. in Musambachime, "Development and Growth," 1:53.

99. Livingstone, *Last Journals*, 1:244; Labrecque, "Abashila," WFA.

100. Compare to the big men and big women of chapters 3 and 6; or to the river big men of Robert Harms, *Games Against Nature*, 113–15.

101. Livingstone, *Last Journals*, 1:244; Crawford, *In the Heart of Bantuland*, 194–95.

102. The story of Nakafwaya was told by the most recent of Nakafwaya's "sisters," Lafwe Kashobwe, Mwansabombwe, 2 Jan. 2001; Prince Dyulu Kabeya, Mwansabombwe, 30 Dec. 2000. A fragmented version can be reconstructed from Mwata Kazembe XIV, *Ifikolwe Fyandi*, 72, 83, 90, 113, 117. Macola recites the story of Nakafwaya captured by Msiri. I suspect that this would be an inheritor to the Nakafwaya title. Cf. Macola, *Kingdom of Kazembe*, 159 n.84.

103. Achim Kabaso (Kanyemba), Kanyemba, 6 Jan. 2001. Kabaso was born in 1929, and his testimony is probably a more accurate view than many of the other Lunda representatives. He is illiterate and thus less subject to the distortions emanating from written versions of the Lunda oral tradition like the *Ifikolwe Fyandi* text.

104. Campbell, *In the Heart of Bantuland*, 109.

105. Godwin Mwewa (Dyulu Kabeya), Mwansabombwe, 30 Dec. 2000.

106. The more common Bemba word for cassava is *kalundwe*. I am unable to find the origin of the word *tute*. The White Fathers dictionary lists them as synonyms. White Fathers, *Bemba-English Dictionary*.

107. *Last Journals*, 1:251, 302. Some thirty years later, Dan Crawford reported meeting the same Nakafwaya. G. E. Tilsley, *Dan Crawford: Missionary and Pioneer in Central Africa* (London: Oliphants, 1929), 401.

108. This was revealed in numerous interviews. Also see, Cunnison, *The Luapula Peoples*, 6; Mwata Kazembe XIV, *Ifikolwe Fyandi*, 34.

109. In the history of the spread of cassava across central Africa, Jan Vansina distinguishes between its limited spread for trading elites and its later and limited acceptance as a food staple. "Histoire du Manioc en Afrique Centrale avant 1850," *Paideuma* 43 (1997): 255–79.

110. Burton, *Lands of Cazembe,* 100–101, 129; Baptista, *La Première Traversée du Katanga,* 71, 101. In 1831, Gamitto also mentions being offered cassava by Kazembe. *King Kazembe,* 2:10.

111. Livingstone, *Last Journals,* 1:248.

112. By the end of the nineteenth century the Bemba had adopted limited cassava production from the Bisa, who had probably learnt it from Kazembe's Lunda. Roberts, *A History of the Bemba,* 211.

113. The best account of *chitemene* cultivation of finger millet is the classic Audrey Richards, *Land, Labor, and Diet.* A re-study that historicizes Audrey Richard's analysis of *chitemene* is Henrietta L. Moore and Megan Vaughan, *Cutting Down Trees: Gender, Nutrition, and Agricultural Change in the Northern Province of Zambia, 1890–1990* (Portsmouth, NH: Heinemann, 1994).

114. Trapnell, *The Soils, Vegetation, and Agriculture,* 70–71.

115. Richards, *Land, Labor, and Diet,* 289–328. Moore and Vaughan argue that Richards exaggerated the impact of differentiated labor migration on agricultural production and underestimated the variety of agricultural strategies that could be adopted. *Cutting Down Trees,* 85–101.

116. Fani Luwenga (Bana Kalifungwe), Kashiba, 19 July 1998; Beauty Chola, Diwell Kapya, and Lilya Kabwita, Nkomba, 30 July 1998.

117. Crawford reports that the Shila were able to summon the hippos by calling to them. Crawford, *Thinking Black,* 463–66.

118. Livingstone, *Last Journals,* 1:248.

119. Achim van Oppen, *Terms of Trade and Terms of Trust: The History and Context of Pre-colonial Market Production around the Upper Zambezi and Kasai* (Münster: LIT Verlag, 1993), 87–98. Anita Spring and Art Hansen, "The Underside of Development: Agricultural Development and Women in Zambia," *Agriculture and Human Values* 2.1 (1985): 60–67. Also see James Pritchett, *Lunda-Ndembu: Style, Change, and Social Transformation in South Central Africa* (Madison: University of Wisconsin Press, 2001), 52, 182–83. Vansina also recognizes the transformation of gendered labor relations and the intensification of women's work linked to cassava cultivation. Vansina, "Histoire du Manioc," 276.

120. While the Luapula Valley was undoubtedly a source for slaves for trade, especially trade directed toward Mozambique and the Swahili coast in the nineteenth century, no historian has examined the use of slave labor in the precolonial Luapula Valley in detail. Macola contends that "tribute" was a more important form of labor than slaves, but the distinction between these forms of labor is unclear, and he does not explore the use of female slave labor. *The Kingdom of Kazembe,* 132–33. Oral testimony of the late nineteenth century indicates that a system of female slavery was common and even widespread

and dominant. See Marcia Wright, "Bwanikwa: Consciousness and Protest," in *Strategies of Slaves and Women: Lifestories from East / Central Africa* (London: James Currey, 1993), 151–78.

121. Crawford makes special reference to the *Budindu* society of women, which might have also developed charters of ownership. *Thinking Black*, 229–53, esp. 234–35. Cunnison also refers to it as a women's secret society that had died out by the time he did his field work. *The Luapula Peoples*, 204. I was not able to gather any testimony about *Ubulindu*.

122. When Lacerda arrived in the valley in 1798 he found it clear of trees. Burton, *Lands of Cazembe*, 100. In the 1850s Livingstone reported that the valley was "thickly studded" with villages only one hundred to two hundred yards apart. *Last Journals*, 1:247.

123. The waterfall *ichitutawile* became known as *Ntumba Chushi* in the colonial period.

124. Gosam Mwelwa (Koni), Koni, 2 Feb. 2001.

125. Verbeek suggests that the veneration of the ancestor *Shakapanga* should be associated with the word for bush, *mpanga*, rather than the Luba word *kapanga*, meaning creator. Although *Shakapanga* was not a spirit ancestor among my informants, the ceremonies of the bush were similar. Verbeek, *Le monde des esprits*, 16, 37–50.

126. Paul Chisakula, Kashikishi, 27 Oct. 1997.

127. "Ba Luunda pa kupoke calo ca Bashila elyo ninshi batendeke ukuupa banakashi Bashila. Kabili Bashila balefulisha, BaLuunda balicepele." Labrecque, "Abashila," WFA.

128. Crawford, *Thinking Black*, 234.

129. "Mwata Kazembe ali no lulumbi lukalamba sana, pantu bonse kale balicimbile ku fita fikali fya kwa Mwata Kazembe, imfumu ikalamba ya ba Luunda." Labrecque, "Abashila," WFA.

130. Crawford, *Thinking Black*, 234.

131. Cunnison, *History on the Luapula*, v. Gamitto also commented on the importance of history for the Lunda in 1831–32. *King Kazembe*, 130.

2 The Colonial Net

1. Quoted in Jean Stengers, "Leopold II and the Association Internationale du Congo," in *Bismarck, Europe, and Africa: The Berlin Conference 1884–5 and the Onset of Partition*, ed. S. Förster, W. J. Mommsen and R. Robinson (London: Oxford University Press, 1988), 229–246, 237.

2. The renowned expeditions were those of Lacerda in 1798–99, the Angolan *pombeiros* of 1806–10, and Monteiro and Gamitto in 1831–32. Sir Richard Burton promoted Victorian interest in Kazembe by translating the journals of Lacerda into English and publishing them with a translation of the *pombeiros* and a résumé of Monteiro and Gamitto, *Lands of Cazembe*.

3. King Leopold's International Association of the Congo had secured the Congo-Zambezi watershed in 1885, which included the mineral-rich Katanga. A more precise border would only be established in the Anglo-Belgian agreement of 1894. Conflict over the border led to two commissions. For the Anglo-Belgian border commission of 1911–13, see Commission Délimitation 1911–13, Affaires Étrangères/I (henceforth AE/I) 272/334, Archives Africaines (henceforth AA); Mission de délimitation Moëro-Tanganyika, 1911–13, Cartographie (henceforth CART) 2071/343–51, AA. Further conflict led to a second commission in 1921–25. Commission Délimitation Katanga-Rhodésie 1921–25, AE/II 2962/852, AA. For the British perspective on the creation of the border see documents in Public Record Office (henceforth PRO), Colonial Office (henceforth CO) 795/136/4501611.

4. This is according to the edited diaries of Dan Crawford in Tilsley, *Dan Crawford*, 158. Also see Verbeken, *Msiri: Roi du Garanganze*, 23–128; Arnot, *Garanganze*, 172–243. Crawford accepted slaves from local rulers or war refugees to form the basis of his Christian community. For this, the people of Luapula named him *Konga Vantu*, or Gatherer (or Enticer) of the People. Tilsley, *Dan Crawford*, 244.

5. There are a variety of stories about Kazembe's battles with the British. The colonial documentation denies defeat in 1897, yet this is contradicted by both oral testimony and Dan Crawford's diary. The Lunda version can be found in Mwata Kazembe XIV, *Ifikolwe Fyandi*, 109–11. For the colonial viewpoint, see Kawambwa District Notebook, 237–38, KSG 3/1, National Archives of Zambia (henceforth NAZ). The BSAC administrator H. T. Harrington has a slightly different version. See "The Taming of Northern Rhodesia," *Northern Rhodesia Journal* 3.2 (1954): 3–20, 12; Tilsley, *Dan Crawford*, 397–98. Macola has attempted to reconcile these and other versions in *Kingdom of Kazembe*, 161–89.

6. Moore and Vaughan, *Cutting Down Trees*, 3–15.

7. Cunnison, *The Luapula Peoples*, 44–45, 120.

8. Harms makes a similar observation regarding the Nunu fishery on the lower Zaire River. *Games Against Nature*, 219.

9. Barrington Moore, *Social Origins of Dictatorship and Democracy: Lord and Peasant in the Making of a Modern World* (Boston: Beacon Press, 1967), 438; Stanley Trapido, "South Africa in a Comparative Study of Industrialization," *Journal of Development Studies* 7 (1970–71): 309–20. For Katanga see Bogumil Jewsiewicki, "Unequal Development: Capitalism and the Katanga Economy, 1919–1940," in *The Roots of Rural Poverty in Central and Southern Africa*, ed. Robin Palmer and Neil Parsons (Berkeley: University of California Press, 1977), 317–44.

10. Pierre Ryckmans, *Dominer pour servir* (Brussels: Editions Universelle, 1948). For a discussion of paternalism see Crawford Young, *Politics in the Congo: Decolonization and Independence* (Princeton: Princeton University Press, 1965), 59–72.

11. Edouard Bustin discusses this in his study of the relations between the Lunda paramount Mwaant Yaav and the subordinate Cokwe. Despite colonial policy favoring "minority" groups, the Lunda were able to maintain their authority over certain subordinate groups. *Lunda under Belgian Rule: The Politics of Ethnicity* (Cambridge, Mass.: Harvard University Press), 65–98. Also see Young, *Politics in the Congo*, 128–29.

12. Verbeek, *Filiation et usurpation*, 318, 338–39.

13. An 1891 decree permitted the governor general to recognize chieftaincies but did not insist on them as homogeneous administrative units. Bustin, *Lunda Under Belgian Rule*, 49. The process of selection of these chiefs in Mweru-Luapula can be found in Dossiers Kasenga and Pweto, IPAC 14.160, AA.

14. For maps of the changing administrative divisions in Katanga, see Bustin, *Lunda under Belgian Rule*, 99.

15. Chefferies Luapula-Moëro, Dossiers: Kasenga, Pweto, IPAC 14.160, AA.

16. It was again renamed Katanga Province in 1947, although it did not return to its previous size.

17. It remained part of this district. In 1952 a separate *territoire de Pweto* was created to administer the area around Lake Mweru.

18. Higginson, *A Working Class in the Making: Belgian Colonial Labour Policy, Private Enterprise, and the Africa Mineworker, 1907–1951* (Madison: University of Wisconsin Press, 1989), 130–31.

19. "Twali ne mfumu shikengele pa kulanda pali Bwana." Leon Verbeek, *L'histoire dans les chants et danses populaires: La zone culturelle Bemba du Haut-Shaba (Zaire)* (Louvain-la-Neuve: Centre d'histoire de l'Afrique, 1992), 24–25.

20. Verbeek, *L'histoire dans les chants*, 23.

21. "Il rend grands services, il est soumis, respectueux; loyal et dévoué. Mais il est encore un peu sauvage malgré ses essais d'imiter l'européen dans son habillement et son mobilier. Il est donc parfois brutal, toujours despote." Rapport, Chefferie de Kambo, 25 June 1938, Dossier Kasenga, IPAC 14.160, AA.

22. Decision No. 18, 6 Feb. 1935, Dossier Kasenga, IPAC 14.160, AA.

23. "Les populations ont surtout échappé à l'emprise du Service Territorial en Territoires d'Elisabethville et de Kasenga et il faut bien le reconnaître si la situation est restée bonne, c'est l'effet du hasard et non à l'administration." Rapport, district du Haut-Katanga, 1949, RA/AIMO 86, AA.

24. Young, *Politics in the Congo*, 69.

25. Documentation of the *mission piscicole* is in the Archives Africaines. Its creation is detailed in Mission Piscicole: divers, IPAC AGRI 14.228, 75, AA.

26. Rapports Annuels, 1946–49, IPAC AGRI 75, AA.

27. "Malgré les nombreuses réunions ténues avec les indigènes, et dans lesquelles ceux-ci reconnaissaient que les restrictions sur la pêche conformaient leur anciennes restrictions coutumières, il a existé un léger manque de compréhension." Rapport d'activité, 4ème Trimestre, 1948, IPAC 13.047, AA.

Legislation was not designed to conform to customary restrictions, although colonial officials liked to emphasize the similarities. A note comparing the new legislation with customary restrictions is in étude—évolution législation pêche, IPAC AGRI 14.222, AA.

28. Elizabeth Colson and others have given much attention to the formal and legal proclamations in favor of the rights of colonial chiefs in the Belgian Congo, while ignoring their actual limitations in the face of the Belgian colonial state. Colson, "Colonial Period and Land Rights," 206–7.

29. Harrington, "The Taming of Northern Rhodesia," 12–13.

30. Mwelwa C. Musambachime, "The Social and Economic Effects of Sleeping Sickness in Mweru-Luapula, 1906–1922," *African Economic History* 10 (1981): 151–73; Macola, *Kingdom of Kazembe*, 203–4.

31. Cunnison, *The Luapula Peoples*, 120.

32. Report on Native Fishing Industry, 3 Dec.1929, SEC 2/252, NAZ.

33. For more details about the loss of aristocratic control in general, see Macola, *Kingdom of Kazembe*, 229–38; Kawambwa District Notebook, Chiefs, KSG 3/1, NAZ.

34. Godwin Mwewa (Dyulu Kabeya), Mwansabombwe, 30 Dec. 2000.

35. Note on the Bena Mbeba and their pretensions, June 1937, Kawambwa District Notebook, KSG 3/1, NAZ.

36. Kawambwa Tour Report 5, 1938, SEC 2/872, NAZ.

37. Kawambwa Tour Report 8, 1936, SEC 2/872, NAZ. Although there are no reliable figures for the 1930s, by the 1950s the population density of the valley ranged from 30 to 70 people per square mile, mostly concentrated next to roads or along the river. This was from three to six times the density of plateau areas. The total population of Kawambwa District of Zambia based on the 1956 sample census was 125,620. George Kay, *A Population Map of the Luapula-Bangweulu Region of Northern Rhodesia with Notes on the Population* (Lusaka: Rhodes-Livingstone Institute, 1962).

38. Mulundu and Councilors, Mulundu's Palace, 9 Jan. 1998; Lubunda, Lubunda's Palace, 8 Oct. 1997; Kawambwa District Notebooks, Note on the Mbeba and Their Pretensions, June 1937, KSG 3/1, NAZ.

39. Kawambwa District Notebooks, Note on the Mbeba and Their Pretensions, June 1937, KSG 3/1, NAZ; Annual Report, Kawambwa District, 1935, SEC 2/1299, NAZ.

40. Kawambwa Tour Report, Sept. 1939, SEC 2/873, NAZ.

41. Karen Fields, *Revival and Rebellion in Colonial Central Africa* (Princeton: Princeton University Press, 1985), 192.

42. Mulundu and Councilors, Mulundu's palace, 9 Jan. 1998; Elliot Mwitwa Kankomba, Charles Muyembe, and Joshua Chama Mambilima, 5 Jan. 1998.

43. Jackson Bwangu and Joshua Lumbule, Mambilima, 31 Dec. 1997; Elliot Kankomba, Charles Muyembe, and Joshua Chama, Mambilima, 5 Jan.

1998; District Commissioner (DC). Kawambwa to Provincial Commissionaer (PC) Northern Province (NP), Kasama, 3 Sept. 1945, SEC 2/1002, NAZ. First quoted in Mwelwa C. Musambachime, "The Impact of Rumour: The Case of the Banyama Scare in Northern Rhodesia, 1930–1964." *The International Journal of African Historical Studies* 21 (1998): 201–215, esp. 210.

44. Elliot Kankomba,Charles Muyembe, and Joshua Chama, Mambilima, 5 Jan. 1998.

45. DC Kawambwa to PC NP Kasama, 2 July 1944, SEC 2/1263, NAZ.

46. The killing of adulterous men is described in much detail by Campbell, *In the Heart of Bantuland*, 51.

47. Administrative Enquiry at Kawambwa over Chief Mulundu, 28 Dec. 1945 and 31 Jan. 1946, SEC 2/1202, NAZ. Musambachime argues that the expulsion of Mulundu by the colonial authorities was closely tied to the bamunyama accusations. The colonial administration was certainly aware of the rumors, but the evidence indicates that the reasons for his dismissal were the adultery accusations. The most decisive evidence is a letter that Nshinka Mulundu submitted to the Zambian administration requesting reinstatement in 1986 in which he carefully explains the reasons for his dismissal. Mwense District Council files, CONF 1/9/5; cf. Musambachime "The Impact of Rumor," 210.

48. Macola, *Kingdom of Kazembe*, 209–12.

49. Musambachime, "Development and Growth," 1:236–37; Kawambwa District Notebooks, KSG 3/1, NAZ.

50. Lukwesa and Kanyembo, sons of Kazembes, replaced Chiboshi and Mukwampa in 1933 and 1940 respectively. The aristocrat, Mwinempanda, lost his area to Chishinga Chief Munkanta in 1934. Kawambwa District Notebook, Chiefs, KSG 3/1, NAZ; Macola, *Kingdom of Kazembe*, 237–38.

51. Annexure to Kawambwa Tour Report 9, 1936, SEC 2/871, NAZ.

52. Kawambwa Tour Report 6, 1937, SEC 2/872, NAZ.

53. Ibid.

54. H. H. Thomson, "Memorandum on the Policy and Structure of Local Government in the Rural Areas of Northern Rhodesia," Box 95 (A), NAZ.

55. Minutes of Lunda Native Authority meeting, 26 Oct. 1954, NP 2/1/7, NAZ.

56. Pritchett, *Lunda-Ndembu*, 52–77.

57. Across Zambia, political entrepreneurs attached themselves to colonial rulers. Samuel Chipungu has referred to the rise of a "Boma" class in Samuel N. Chipungu, "Accumulation from Within: The Boma Class and the Native Treasury in Colonial Zambia," in *Guardians in Their Time*, 74–96.

58. Kawambwa Tour Report 7, 1937, SEC 2/872, NAZ.

59. Kawambwa Tour Report 5, 1938, SEC 2/872, NAZ.

60. For the alliance of educated and traditional aristocrats that led to the writing of *Ifikolwe Fyandi*, see Macola, "Literate Ethnohistory in Colonial Zambia."

61. Mwata Kazembe XVIII Munona Chinyanta, Mwansabombwe, 29 Oct. 1997; Daniel Mutobola, Lunde, 27 Oct. 1997; Lunda Native Authority Minutes, Meetings and Agendas, NP 2/1/7, NAZ.

62. Lunda Native Authority Tour Report, 5/1948, NP 2/2/4, NAZ.

63. Mwata Kazembe XVIII Munona Chinyanta, Mwansabombwe, 29 Oct. 1997.

64. Lunda Native Authority Tour Reports, 1953–58, NP 2/2/20, NAZ; Mulundu Tour Reports, 1950–55, NP 2/6/12, NAZ.

65. Elijah S. M. Chibwalwe, Kashiba, 3 Jan 1998.

66. Macola, *Kingdom of Kazembe*, 246.

67. Ian Cunnison, "The Installation of Chief Kazembe XV," *Northern Rhodesia Journal* 5 (1952): 7; quoted in Macola, *Kingdom of Kazembe*, 247.

68. "Fwebo mulilu chibongo; Mwata wafwile bakazembe; Ine nshalika nebo; Lelo naumfa lulumbi; Naumfwa Kazembe nafwa kwaMwata; Natie wakwe nasuit wakwe. Afwile one day ukwabula kubola; Elyo bakabumbu baumfwile; Bapangile naleave; Ukwababula kubola nokushikwa; Kabumbu nokufika kwena; Kanshi aitwala mumfwa. Mwebolowa mfumu muluunda; Kapyeneni; Mwata Kabumbu nafwa; Kwena nga ninganda mulundu; Niupstayi we nganda amalata. Bamulundu nabamushyota; Ebalelwila kapyana Mwata; Twali mukenye bamulundu mwandi wepyana; Twakakokole; Pantu tabwaishibe ifya lile baMwata. Nomba tukwete baKanyembo; BaKanyembo Mfumu yesu muluunda; Nabobene twaliumfwile kwamusangu, brother; Ukuti baKanyembo nimfwa; Kabili nasuti yashe kabumbu; Tendamo ena kumulandu ukulwalilila. Kwena nanagu mwapyana baKanyembo; Tamwakokole; Pantu tamwaishibe ifya lile baMwata; Mwebantu kwena kanobakapanyike umusungu;Tabakamulowe; Pantu ni govementi." This version of the song is from Isaac Mapiki, recorded in 1961*Kazembe*, Tape ZHS 618, Zambia National Broadcasting Corporation (henceforth ZNBC), trans. by Walima Kalusa. The author recorded a similar version sung by a musician in Luapula in 1998. Mwansa Lampson, Kashikishi, 17 Jan. 1998.

69. For the colonial perspective on this conflict, see Note on the Bena Mbeba and their Pretensions, Kawambwa District Notebook, KSG 3/1, NAZ.

70. For another example from the closely related Tabwa peoples, see Allen Roberts, *Animals in African Art*, 63.

71. Moses Mwelwa Kasau, Kasau, 30 Dec. 2000. For Cunnison's description of the shrine, see *The Luapula Peoples*, 225.

72. Harms, *Games Against Nature*, 219.

73. Literally "owner of the village." The Bemba term is not gendered and it is not uncommon to find women in this position.

74. William Katwe Chishala, Makandwe River, 30 Dec. 2000.

75. Edward Mukamba, Kabalenge, 5 Jan. 2001.

76. Chibwidi, Chibwidi, 10 Jan. 2001.

77. "Neupelwa ifyalo na Bantu, Abanandi bapelwa imbushi ne mikoko."

Quoted in Jacques Chileya Chiwale, trans. and ann., *Royal Praises*, 16. Also see Mwata Kazembe XIV, *Ifikolwe Fyandi*, 37.

78. Schoffeleers, *Guardians of the Land*, 1.

79. For tribalism across southern Africa and northwestern Zambia, see Leroy Vail, "Introduction: Ethnicity in Southern African History," in *The Creation of Tribalism in Southern Africa* (Berkeley: University of California Press, 1989); and R. J. Papstein, "From Ethnic Identity to Tribalism: The Upper Zambezi Region of Zambia, 1830–1981," in *The Creation of Tribalism in Southern Africa*, ed. Vail, 1–19, 372–94.

3. The Meanings of Wealth

1. Mike Kolala, Kashiba, 4 Nov. 1997.

2. A precise translation of "big man" would be *umukalamba* (pl. *abakalamba*). However, *umukalamba* generally refers to importance in terms of kin relations and gerontocratic status rather than wealth. A wealthy elite of big men, by contrast, would be *abakankâla*.

3. An interesting use of some of these terms is a Kalela song by Abel Mulenga from the 1960s, *Mwaliba nobunoshi bwa chuma ne filyo ifingi*. Matongo translates this as "There is plenty of wealth in the form of money and food," but perhaps it would be more accurate as "There is business from plenty of treasures and food." Albert B. K. Matongo, "Popular Culture in a Colonial Society: Another Look at the *Mbeni* and *Kalela* Dances," in *Guardians in Their Time: Experiences of Zambians Under Colonial Rule, 1860–1964*, ed. Samuel N. Chipungu (London: Macmillan, 1992), 180–217, esp. 211.

4. "Marketable but not bankable" economies have long been a feature of Africa's "informal economy," which is often a large or majority proportion of all economic activity. The literature on the informal economy is too extensive to cite in full here. The works most influential to this study include: Janet MacGaffey, ed., *The Real Economy of Zaire: The Contribution of Smuggling and Other Unofficial Activities* (Philadelphia: University of Pennsylvania Press, 1991); Jane Guyer, *Marginal Gains: Monetary Transactions in Atlantic Africa* (Chicago: University of Chicago Press, 2004). By the 1940s, many of Luapula's leading entrepreneurs had bank accounts and mobilized capital; they still engaged with the predominantly "informal" economy.

5. I use the term *commerçant* to refer exclusively to expatriate traders and fishermen mostly based in the Congo.

6. Other terms include *bachinondo* (sing. *muchinondo*) and *basulwishi* (sing. *musulwishi*). Mwelwa C. Musambachime offered advice on the finer distinctions. Personal communication.

7. Especially copper crosses, for which we have sufficient archaeological evidence. Pierre de Maret, "L'évolution monétaire du Shaba entre le 7è et le 18è siècles," *African Economic History* 10 (1981):117–49; Eugenia Herbert, *Red Gold of*

Africa: Copper in Pre-Colonial History and Culture (Madison: University of Wisconsin Press, 1984), 103–12, 154–60.

8. Richards, *Land, Labour, and Diet,* 116.

9. Kawambwa Tour Report 8/1950, SEC 2/877, NAZ.

10. Guyer, *Marginal Gains,* 68–82. "Conversion" refers to Paul Bohannan's classic arguments about conversion in Tiv spheres of exchange. "Some Principles of Exchange and Investment among the Tiv," *American Anthropologist* 57.1 (1955): 60–70.

11. In 1925 Comité Spécial du Katanga/UMHK created the *Compagnie d'élevage et alimentation du Katanga* (ELEKAT) to oversee the supply of urban areas with food. ELEKAT in turn signed contracts with suppliers like the *Société de transport et commerce du Luapula-Moëro,* which began to monopolize the purchase of fish from the lake. By 1927 there were seventeen expatriates—five Greeks, four Belgians, three Italians, three Englishmen, a "Jew," and an "Arab"—based at Kasenga. Cembe, "La production et la commercialisation du poisson au Luapula-Moëro, 1920–59." Mémoire, Université de Lubumbashi (UNILU henceforth), 1986, 40, UNILU.

12. Mwelwa Musambachime emphasizes the African origins of the fish trade and details some of the earliest trader-entrepreneurs in "Development and Growth," 1:79–160. Also see Ilunga Saloum-Ya Mutombo, "Politique coloniale et commerce au Katanga (1940–1959)," Mémoire, UNILU, 1980, 61, UNILU.

13. In 1935 a Belgian entrepreneur installed the first ice factory at Kasenga, followed by another in 1939 and a third in 1941. Kadiebwe Kapambu-Kabaswa-Kutuswa, "Monographie socio-économique du Territoire de Kasenga, 1933–1958," Mémoire, UNILU, 1976, 50, Université de Lubumbashi. For similar constraints faced by African businessmen in colonial Zambia (although note the growth of Luapula's African businesses from the late 1930s), see Yona Ngalaba Seleti, "Entrepreneurship in Colonial Zambia," in *Guardians in Their Time,* ed. Chipungu, 147–79.

14. For colonial policy regarding commerce, see A. Delcommune, *L'avenir du Congo belge menacé* (Brussels: J. Lebègue, 1919), 222–77. For an example from eastern Congo, see Janet MacGaffey, *Entrepreneurs and Parasites: The Struggle for Indigenous Capitalism in Zaire* (Cambridge: Cambridge University Press, 1987), 39.

15. Rapport d'inspection économique, Kasenga, Dec. 1939, IPAC 9.590, AA. European businessmen, who had representation in the advisory provincial council *(Conseil de Province)* protested against these traders on the grounds that they drove up prices and took business from them. Researchers attached to the fishing department *(Mission piscicole du Katanga)* who studied the marketing arrangements of the fishing economy informed colonial administrators that African traders wasted 17.6 percent of fish transported compared to only 3.3 percent for European traders. M. C. Montagne, Mission Piscicole du Congo belge, Fisheries Conference, Elisabethville, June 1949, SEC 1/390, NAZ.

16. "Non seulement ils constituent eux-mêmes un main d'œuvre perdue pour des chefferies . . . mais encore ils enlèvent de la main d'œuvre aux entreprises européennes. Ils se dérobent à toute prestation personnellement et soutirent dans certains territoires une grande partie de ce que j'appellerai le 'potentielle indigène' à leur profit." Commissaire de district (henceforth CdD), Rapport Trimestriel, 2ème semestre, 1924, AIMO 1697, AA.

17. By 1934, eight of these *centres* existed along the river and the lake between Kasenga and Pweto. Kapambu-Kabaswa-Kutuswa, "Monographie socio-économique," 50, UNILU. The administration never had the capacity to enforce this system and informal trade flourished. Kadiebwe Kapambu "Monographie Socio-économique," 80. Economic reports that detail problems of informal trade can be found in IPAC 9.590, AA.

18. Higginson, *A Working Class in the Making*, 113–52.

19. Report of the Fisheries Advisory Committee, 1951, SEC 1/1034, NAZ.

20. This was approximately £350. Rapport Aron Ngwashi, 21 Apr. 1953, IPAC 13.030, AA.

21. Kapambu-Kabaswa-Kutuswa "Monographie Socio-économique," 87, UNILU.

22. Abraham Soriano, Lubumbashi, 16 June 1998.

23. David Kashiba, Lubumbashi, 15 June 1998.

24. Nicholas Paraskevas, Lubumbashi, 16 June 1998.

25. D. U. Peters, "A Visit to Kilwa Island and the Africa Oil Palm," *Northern Rhodesia Journal* 2.1 (1954): 9.

26. Muteba Mwaba, Kasenga, 15 July 1998.

27. Cunnison's remarks are quoted and discussed in Lyn Schumaker, *Africanizing Anthropology: Fieldwork, Networks, and the Making of Cultural Knowledge in Central Africa* (Durham: Duke University Press, 2001), 141. The label "degenerate" or "marginal" would differ from Northern Rhodesia to the Belgian Congo; in the Belgian Congo many senior officials complained that colonial district officers had "degenerated" and taken on African mistresses; even if this occurred in Northern Rhodesia, it would not be referred to in the official correspondence. See, for example, Inspection du poste détaché de Kilwa, 8 Aug. 1950, Dossier Pweto, IPAC 10.751, AA.

28. "Le Congo est riche; pour nous ce fut une vraie chance d'y venir, et nous ne désirons ni rentrer en Grèce ni quitter votre Colonie. . . . Il est rare de rencontrer dans le monde entier un pays où l'on puisse vivre aussi tranquille qu'au Congo." Rapport d'inspection économique, Kasenga, Dec. 1939, IPAC 9.590, AA.

29. Rapport 1933, RA/AIMO 106, AA.

30. In the early development of the fishery the administration considered allowing European fishermen in the deeper waters where fishing from African canoes was limited; later they decided that such fishing would undermine the

political authority of the chiefs. Report on Native Fishing Industry, 3 Dec. 1927, SEC 2/252, NAZ.

31. DC Mporokoso to PC, NP, 3 June 1952, SEC 6/14, NAZ.

32. From the 1930s to 1950s several conflicts erupted between Northern Rhodesian and Congolese fishermen and chiefs, as well as with the growing number of Greek fishermen. DC W. F. Stubbs to PC, Kasama, 24 Apr. 1936; Chief Secretary G. C. Fallows to Provincial Commissioner, NP, 16 June 1936, SEC 1/1022, NAZ; Kawambwa District Notebooks vol. 3, 20, KSG 3/1, NAZ. In Northern Rhodesia regulations required fishermen to purchase licenses from the Native Authorities, and migrants were charged an increased fee. Kawambwa Tour Report 6/1937, SEC 2/872, NAZ.

33. Dauti L. Yamba, the renowned nationalist, worked for Zlotnik in Mwansabombwe. See Dauti L. Yamba, "Genesis of the Struggle for Independence in Zambia," contribution to the Symposium on Zambian Independence, Mulungushi Hall, 1971; Daniel Lukwesa, Chimba, 19 Jan., 1998. Howard Kamanga, a prosperous Kazembe-based businessman, took over the position of Zlotnik's shop manager from Dauti L. Yamba. Howard Kamanga, Mwansamombwe, 15 Oct. 1997.

34. Local consumers were reported as having "an overwhelming desire . . . for a plenitude of consumer goods." They often appealed to the authorities for European-owned shops, especially Zlotnik's *macipisha* stores. Kawambwa Tour Report 5/1947, SEC 2/874, NAZ; Harry Kazembe Mwenso, Mwense, 26 Dec. 1997.

35. Booker C. Kapapula, Mansa, 2 Oct. 1997.

36. "Sole, Sole; Weuli ne sabi; Ala umucele uno; Ala ulupiya luno; Ala insalu shino." Translated and quoted in Musambachime, "Development and Growth," 1:87.

37. Cunnison, *The Luapula Peoples*, 25.

38. Secondhand clothes, now known as *salaula*, were named *kombo* during the colonial period after the Congolese town Mokambo where they were thought to originate. Karen Transberg Hansen, *Salaula: The World of Secondhand Clothing in Zambia* (Chicago: Chicago University Press, 2000), 70–76.

39. Joshua C. Katongola, Mulundu, 17 July 1998.

40. Harry Kazembe Mwenso, Mwense, 26 Dec. 1997.

41. Booker C. Kapapula, Mansa, 2 Oct. 1997; also see Musambachime, "Development and Growth," vol. 2, "Interview with Anna Chilombo," 1–3; Robert Cancel, "Interview with Anna Chilombo, Kabwe, 1994."

42. Chola Kasonga, William Mukate, Barnabas Kanyenda. Nkomba, 4 Nov. 1997. Nkomba Village, 4 Nov. . 1997; Beauty Chola, Diwell Kapya, and Lilya Kabwita, Nkomba Village, 30 July 1998; Fani Luwenga Kalifungwe, Kashiba, 19 July 1998.

43. During the author's fieldwork, most residential sections were virilocal. Historical records show, however, that residence sections were sometimes

uxorilocal, especially for a short period after marriage when a man would labor in his in-laws' fields. Cunnison, *The Luapula Peoples*, 123; Congo belge, "La Famille chez les Bashila," *Bulletin des juridictions indigènes et droit coutumier congolais* 4 (1935), 102, Bibliothèque Africaine (henceforth BA).

44. During my interviews with the Nkomba family, several unmarried, divorced, or widowed sisters resided at their brother's residence. Chola Kasonga, William Mukate, Barnabas Kanyenda. Nkomba , 4 Nov. 1997 ; Beauty Chola, Diwell Kapya, and Lilya Kabwita, Nkomba Village, 30 July 1998; Fani Luwenga Kalifungwe, Kashiba, 19 July 1998.

45. My observations agree with Mary Douglas's contention that matriliny is compatible with economic growth as long as labor continues to be valued. In times of stagnation, or labor surplus, the system would come under increasing pressure. Mary Douglas, "Is Matriliny Doomed in Africa," in *Man in Africa*, 121–35. See chapter 6 below and the work of Karla Poewe for a further discussion of these issues.

46. Ian Cunnison to Symon, Re: Fishing, 22 Mar. 1949, SEC 5/176, NAZ.

47. Chola Kasonga, William Mukate, Barnabas Kanyenda. Nkomba, 4 Nov. 1997.

48. For an account of the rise of the fresh fish trade located around Kashikishi in the 1950s, see Musambachime, "Development and Growth," 1:249–58. For the postcolonial period, see chapter 5.

49. Marvis Miracle, "African Markets and Trade on the Copperbelt" in *Markets in Africa*, ed. Paul Bohannan and George Dalton (Evanston: Northwestern University Press, 1962), 724–28; Musambachime, "Development and Growth," 1:249–58.

50. The percentages indicate weight of total fish traded. Calculated from Monthly Percentage of Fresh Fish Traded, 1954–56, SEC 6/129, NAZ.

51. Export of Fish through Kawambwa District, June 1956, SEC 2/129, NAZ.

52. Although rural to urban migration was still dominant, there was a significant rate of return to the rural areas and continued links to villages of origin. James Ferguson criticizes the "progressive modernization" narrative that stresses the emergence of a stable, working class independent of rural ties. Instead he argues that workers continued to have significant rural ties after migration. *Expectations of Modernity*, 38–81. For a contrary view, see Hugh Macmillan, "The Historiography of the Transition on the Zambian Copperbelt—Another View," *Journal of Southern African Studies* 19.4 (1993): 681–712.

53. Notes of Meeting, 17 Dec. 1942 and 19 July 1943, 10.7.10B, Zambia Consolidated Copper Mines (henceforth ZCCM); Circular re: African voluntary savings scheme, 17 July 1960, 13.4.8A, ZCCM. For a general account of the 1935 and 1940 strikes, see Henry S. Meebelo, *African Proletarians and Colonial Capitalism: The Origins, Growth, and Struggles of the Zambian Labour Movement to 1964* (Lusaka: Kenneth Kaunda Foundation, 1986), 59–130.

54. Paul Kapasa Chisakula, Kashikishi, 21 Oct. 1997; Robert Bates, "Interview with Chisakula," 12 May 1971, Robert Bates Collection, UNZA Special Collections; Kawambwa Tour Report 13/1956, NP 2/2/34, NAZ.

55. Luka Mumba stopped trading fish, but expanded into several other businesses, including shops and a rest house in Mansa. Bright Mumba, Mansa, 6 Oct. 1997. For Mwamfuli's village see G. Fryer "Mwamfuli's Village: The New Fulcrum of the Bangweulu Fish Trade," *The Northern Rhodesia Journal* 3.6 (1953): 483–88.

56. Fish Export Return, 1956, SEC 6/129, NAZ.

57. Beauty Chola, Diwell Kapya, and Lilya Kabwita, Nkomba Village, 30 July 1998; Fani Luwenga Kalifungwe, Kashiba, 19 July 1998.

58. Mwata Kazembe's Report on Visit to Lake Mweru, 26 July 1950, NP 2/2/20, NAZ.

59. Anna Chilombo Kapapula died in March 1998. My information relies on the interviews conducted by Robert Bates in 1971, Mwelwa Musambachime in 1979, and Robert Cancel in 1994, combined with secondary accounts and my interviews with other family members. Booker C. Kapapula, Mansa, 2 Oct. 1997; Brian Kapapula, Mansa, 7 Nov. 1997; Musambachime, "Development and Growth," "Interview with Anna Chilombo," 2:1–6; Robert Cancel, "Interview with Anna Chilombo, Kabwe 1994"; Robert Bates, "Interview with Mrs. Chilombo," 25 July 1971, Robert Bates Collection, UNZA Special Collections. For Mabel Shaw see Letter no. 6, 1 Aug. 1959, MSS.AFR.S.1502, Shaw Papers, Rhodes House Library, Oxford University. According to Jane Parpart, Mabel Shaw had a talent for identifying "respectable" standards for African women, see Jane L. Parpart "'Wicked Women' and 'Respectable Ladies': Reconfiguring Gender on the Zambian Copperbelt, 1936–1964," in *"Wicked" Women and the Reconfiguration of Gender in Africa*, ed. Dorothy L. Hodgson and Sheryl A. McCurdy (Portsmouth N.H.: Heinemann, 2001), 274–92, 274–75.

60. Richards, *Land, Labour, and Diet,* 116.

61. Lunda Native Authority Minutes, 7 Nov. 1948, NP 2/1/7, NAZ. Native Authorities became responsible for divorce cases in the 1930s. A. L. Epstein, "Divorce Law and Stability Among the Lunda of Kazembe," *Rhodes-Livingstone Journal* 14 (1954): 1–19; Congo belge, "La Famille chez les Bashila," *Bulletin des juridictions indigènes et droit coutumier congolais* 4 (1935): 105–6, BA.

62. Lunda Native Authority Minutes, 8 Sept. 1949, NP 2/1/7, NAZ. Since the 1940s chiefs had complained of the number of village women traveling to and residing in Elisabethville. Kawambwa Tour Report 6/1939, SEC 2/873, NAZ. The British vice consul in Elisabethville complained of the number of unattached Northern Rhodesian women from Luapula. Report on Northern Rhodesian Natives in Katanga, 31 Dec. 1936, SEC 2/165, NAZ. For Northern Rhodesian restrictions on women in the urban Copperbelt and defiance of them, see Jane L. Parpart, "'Where Is Your Mother?': Gender, Urban

Marriage, and Colonial Discourse on the Zambian Copperbelt, 1924–1945," *International Journal of African Historical Studies* 27 (1994): 241–71.

63. Rapport Annuel, Kasenga, 1948, RA/AIMO 106, AA.

64. "Les juges se trouvent en général désemparés devant ces situations nouvelles; ignorant de la fonction sociale qu'ils ont a remplir, ils prononcent des sanctions insuffisants ou maladroits, incapable de freiner un libertinage qui n'a que trop tendance à se généraliser." Rapport Annuel, Pweto, 1953, RA/AIMO 162, AA.

65. "Abanakashi ni nkaka; Edakabolala, abashaishibikwa; Balitemwa indalama sana; Cilumendo cinjela kuli ba mwansakabinga; cine bakapenta." James and Caleb Siame, *Abanakashi ni Nkaka*. Lusaka, 1955, ZHS 1790, trans. by Walima Kalusa, ZNBC.

66. Terence Ranger, "The Invention of Tradition in Colonial Africa," in *The Invention of Tradition*, ed. Terence Ranger and Eric Hobsbawm (Cambridge: Cambridge University Press, 1983), 211–62. For marriage and customary law, see Martin Chanock, *Law, Custom, and Social Order: The Colonial Experience in Zambia and Malawi* (Cambridge: Cambridge University Press, 1985). For sisters and wives in general, see Karen Sacks, *Sisters and Wives*.

67. "Abantu teepakufwa, mayo; Pantu icalo teepabubi; Ala, ifimanya fyaliseeka; Ala, kwena nalewalesa bakayapya." *Kiwa Mununga*, Bartolomeo Bwalya, *Kiwa Mununga*, 1963, Tape ZHS 618, trans. Walima Kalusa, ZNBC. Another song complains of witchcraft in the Lake Mweru town of Nchelenge, *Ubuloshi mu Nchelenge*, Mwelu radio band, n.d., Tape ZHS 165, trans. Christopher Mwambazi, ZNBC.

68. Crawford translates *Konga Vantu* as Gatherer of People. However, the Bemba verb—*Konga* has a more precise meaning: to lure or entice under false pretences. White Fathers, *Bemba-English Dictionary*, 269; G. E. Tilsley, *Dan Crawford*, 244.

69. For Northern Rhodesian missions see Robert I. Rotberg, *Christian Missions and the Creation of Northern Rhodesia* (Princeton: Princeton University Press, 1965); Robert I. Rotberg, "Plymouth Brethren and the Occupation of Katanga, 1886–1907," *Journal of African History* 2 (1964): 285–97; Frederick Stanley Arnot, *Garanganze*, 172–243. For Johnston Falls mission, see Willie Lammond, "Outline History of Johnston Falls Mission Mostly from Memory," Mambilima Mission manuscript; Willie Lammond, "The Luapula Valley," *Northern Rhodesia Journal* 2.5 (1955): 52; Tilsley, *Dan Crawford*, 325–32. Crawford, *Thinking Black*, 467–68; Macola, *Kingdom of Kazembe*, 183–84. The White Fathers would establish a mission at Lufubu in the 1930s from where Edouard Labrecque conducted his investigations into the history of the valley; however, their religious influence was limited.

70. Jackson Bwangu and Joshua Lumbule, Mambilima, 31 Dec. 1997.

71. Crawford, *Thinking Black*, 476–77.

72. Crawford, *Thinking Black*, 484.

73. Henry S. Meebelo, *Reactions to Colonialism: A Prelude to the Politics of Independence in Northern Zambia, 1893–1939* (Manchester: Manchester University Press, 1971), 135–36.

74. John Higginson, "Liberating the Captives: Independent Watchtower as an Avatar of Colonial Revolt in Southern Africa and Katanga, 1908–1941," *Journal of Social History* 26.1 (1992): 55–80; Fields, *Revival and Rebellion in Colonial Central Africa*. For the protonationalist role of Watchtower on the Bemba plateau see Meebelo, *Reaction to Colonialism*, 133–85.

75. Harrington, "The Taming of North-Eastern Rhodesia," 16.

76. Sholto Cross, "Jehovah's Witness and Socio-Economic Change in Luapula Province," Political Science Workshop, University of Zambia, n.d., 8–11, UNZA; Higginson, "Liberating the Captives," 63–65.

77. Cunnison's estimations are based on a survey of five villages. Unfortunately there are no data on religious affiliation for the entire valley for this period. Ian Cunnison, "A Watchtower Assembly in Central Africa," *International Review of Missions*, 40.160 (1951): 456–69; Cunnison, *The Luapula Peoples*, 205–8.

78. Cunnison, "A Watchtower Assembly in Central Africa."

79. Cross, "Jehovah's Witness and Socio-Economic Change," 11–13.

80. Daniel Kamuchoma, Kashikishi, 16 Oct. 1997; Goodson Mulewambola, Kashiba, 19 July 1998; Moses Mwembya, Kaseketi, 20 July 1998.

81. For an account of an assembly near Mwansabombwe, see Cunnison, "A Watchtower Assembly in Central Africa," 456–67.

82. Goodson Mulewambola, Kashiba, 19 July 1998; Moses Mwembya, Kaseketi, 20 July 1998.

83. "Une certaine effervescence d'origine mystique ou superstitieuse aggravé . . . par des tendances xénophobes." AIMO Rapport 1931, AIMO 1737, AA. For their view of Watchtower, see Congo belge, "Kitawala," in *Bulletin des juridictions indigènes et droit coutumier congolais*, 10 (1944): 231–36, BA.

84. AIMO, Katanga, *Rapport Annuel, 1950*, 24, Bibliothèque Africaine (henceforth BA).

85. AIMO, Katanga, *Rapport Annuel, 1953*, 33, BA.

86. Moses Mwembya, Kaseketi, 20 July 1998; Goodson Mulewambola, Kashiba, 19 July 1998; Gerald Chisenga, Kashiba, 2 Nov. 1997; Jonathan Kabaso, Mwense, 8 Oct. 1997; Joshua C. Katongola, Mulundu, 17 July 1998.

87. Sholto Cross notes a correlation between positions of rank in the Watchtower church and economic status. He argues that "aspiration [to wealth] rather than achievement is the significant factor of membership." "Jehovah's Witness and Socio-Economic Change," 16, UNZA.

88. Kawambwa Tour Report 1/1937, SEC 2/871, NAZ.

89. Joshua C. Katongola, Mulundu, 17 July 1998; Moses Mwembya, Kaseketi, 20 July 1998; Goodson Mulewambola, Kashiba, 19 July 1998; Cross, "Jehovah's Witness and Socio-Economic Change in Luapula Province," 17–18; Fields, *Revival and Rebellion*, 71.

90. Fields, *Revival and Rebellion,* 69.

91. Cunnison, "A Watchtower Assembly in Central Africa," 457; Cunnison, *The Luapula Peoples,* 206; Lunda Native Authority Minutes, 1950, NP 2/1/7, NAZ.

92. Older residents of the valley still talk of the 1934 purification. Goodson Mulewambola, Kashiba, 19 July 1998. A song was composed about the purification, *Mucaka ca 1934.* Lunzuwa School Choir, 1950, Tape ZHS 1730, ZNBC. Audrey Richards also wrote a short article about the 1934 purification. "Un mouvement modern pour déceler les sorciers: Les bamucapi," *Bulletin des juridictions indigène et droit coutumier congolais,* 3 (1937): 82–90, BA. See also Fields, *Revival and Rebellion,* 78–89. Belgian administrators outlawed the movement, arguing that it threatened public order and peace. Nevertheless, years later the *bamuchapi,* along with several other magical associations, still had a presence. Policiers chefferies, CdD Kasenga to Administrateur Territoriale Haut Katanga, 26 Sep. 1934, IPAC 13.447, AA; CdD's Note, 1940, RA/AIMO 86, AA.

93. Campbell, *In the Heart of Bantuland.*

94. Moses Mwembya, Kaseketi, 20 July 1998; Goodson Mulewambola, Kashiba, 19 July 1998; Shakalyata, Mwinempanda,and Kalandala, Mwansabombwe, 15 Jan. 1998; James Mulalami, Mulalami, 15 Jan. 2001. Also based on a number of informal discussions with chief's councilors and witchfinders.

95. Mwelwa C. Musambachime, "Ubutwa: A Study of the Role and Function of a Secret Society in Eastern Zaire and North-East Zambia to the 1920s," unpublished paper, [1991–93?], 31; Fields, *Revival and Rebellion,* 78–90.

96. Fields, *Revival and Rebellion,* 78–90; Goodson Mulewambola, Kashiba, 19 July 1998; James Kabwebwe (Kambwali) and Councilors, Kambwali's Palace, 13 Jan. 1998; Moses Mwembya, Kaseketi, 20 July 1998.

97. Peter Geschiere, *The Modernity of Witchcraft: Politics and the Occult in Postcolonial Africa* (Charlottesville: University Press of Virginia, 1997).

4. Mpumbu

1. The story of the mpumbu spawning run has been described to me in numerous interviews cited throughout this chapter. The best description of the spawning run by a colonial observer was a Belgian scientist who described the Mululushi tributary of the Luapula during spawning in 1950. La pêche au Katanga, IPAC 14.219, AA.

2. Moses Mwelwa, Kasau, 30 Dec. 2001.

3. Upon being reinstated, Mulundu assembled the villagers and cast his net into the river. Those who witnessed the event claim that when he pulled the net back to the bank there was a large, struggling mpumbu. Elliot Mwitwa Kankomba and Charles Muyembe, Mambilima, 5 Jan. 1998; Jackson Bwangu and Joshua Lumbule, Mambilima, 31 Dec. 1997; Nshinka Mulundu and Councilors, Mulundu's Palace, 9 Jan. 1998; Mwense District Council files, CONF 1/9/5.

4. Alam Lukwesa, Musanda, 16 Jan. 2001.

5. The Belgian study was conducted by F. Matagne. An initial study was published but the final conclusions remain unpublished in the Archives Africaines. F. Matagne, "Premières notes au sujet de la migration des Pumbu," *Bulletin Agricole* 41 (1950): 793–894; Service Piscicole Elisabethville, Contribution à l'étude de la migration préparatoire au frai du Labeo altivelis et son frai au Luapula Moëro, IPAC 14.205, AA.

6. Mwelwa C. Musambachime has demonstrated the nationalist links to the mpumbu rebellion in "Rural Political Protest: The 1953 Disturbances in Mweru-Luapula," *The International Journal of African Historical Studies* 20.3 (1987): 453–57. Other examples linking rural rebellion to wider nationalist uprisings in other contexts are: William Beinart and Colin Bundy, *Hidden Struggles in Rural South Africa* (Johannesburg: Ravan Press, 1987), and Feierman, *Peasant Intellectuals: Anthropology and History in Tanzania* (Madison: University of Wisconsin Press).

7. Extracts from informal discussions with chiefs at Kawambwa, 18 Sept. 1937, SEC 2/252, NAZ.

8. M. Halain, Note on fisheries problem on Mweru-Luapula, 15 Jan. 1948, NP 2/1/6, NAZ.

9. Dennis Paine, "Lake Mweru: Its Fish and Fishing Industry," *Northern Rhodesian Journal* 1.2 (1950): 7–13, esp. 11.; J. J. Soulsby, "Some Congo Basin Fishes of Northern Rhodesia: Part 1," *Northern Rhodesian Journal* 4.3 (1960): 231–46; Paul Skelton, *A Complete Guide to Freshwater Fishes of Southern Africa* (Halfway House: Southern Book Publishers, 1993), 176–81.

10. "Cibunge-bunge lupumbu; Cibundu-bundu wa ku bunduka; Bapale masango; Nakafwaya ulupumbu; Ciyafwaya balume milongo; Mwansa-museke; No kusungwa mu ndao." This archaic Shila praise was translated with the help of Andrew Billing Chalawila. The above English translation best conveys its original meaning. The praise can be found in Labrecque, "Abashila," WFA.

11. A more complete account of Bemba terms and diagrams for Luapula's fishing technology can be found in Mukaya Mukanga, *Ubupalu Bwe Sabi* (Ndola, Zambia: Mission Press, 1999), 27–93. This is also covered, but less extensively, in Musambachime, "Development and Growth," 1:48–63.

12. Kawambwa Tour Report, 26 Nov. to 18 Dec. 1946, SEC 6/236, NAZ. The mpumbu "caviar" industry began in 1939. La situation économique de la région Kasenga, Dec. 1939, IPAC 9.590, AA.

13. Northern Rhodesia, Dept. of Game and Tsetse, *Annual Report 1943*, Special Collections, UNZA. The Lunda Native Treasury earned £239.10 from net licenses in 1945, which was its largest source of income. DC Kawambwa to Director of Game and Tsetse, 22 Mar. 1945, SEC 6/191, NAZ.

14. DC Kawambwa to PC, NP, 28 Nov. 1940, SEC 6/191, NAZ.

15. The literature on colonial conservation measures has become quite extensive. An introduction to the literature and themes can be found in William Beinart, "Introduction: The Politics of Colonial Conservation," *Journal of Southern African Studies* 2 (1989): 143–62.

16. Director of Game and Tsetse to Member for Agriculture, 13 Mar. 1953, SEC 6/372, NAZ.

17. "L'indigène éveille par l'exemple de notre travail et par l'instruction que nous lui donnons, secoue sa torpeur. Il se dégage de son état de stagnation." Problèmes indigènes au Luapula-Moëro, 29 Oct. 1947, IPAC 14.210, AA.

18. Pierre Ryckmans, *Dominer pour servir*.

19. H. H. Thomson, DC, "Memorandum on Policy and Structure of Local Government in the Rural Areas of Northern Rhodesia," Box 95A, NAZ.

20. Kalombo Mwindi, "Histoire politico-administratif du Territoire de Sakania, 1940–1960," Mémoire, UNILU, 1979, UNILU.

21. Settlers in Northern Rhodesia formed a political federation with Southern Rhodesia (Zimbabwe) and Nyasaland (Malawi) in 1953. For early nationalist opposition to Federation, see David C. Mulford, *Zambia: The Politics of Independence, 1957–1964* (Oxford: Oxford University Press, 1967), 1–55.

22. N. Giorgas to Gouverneur Général du Congo Belge, 21 Jan. 1951; Kawambwa Tour Report 26 Nov. 1947, SEC 6/236, NAZ.

23. Report on Anglo-Belgian Meeting, 15 Jan. 1948, NP 2/1/6, NAZ.

24. Fisheries Officer to Director of Game and Tsetse, 26 Jan. 1948, NP 2/1/6, NAZ.

25. Northern Rhodesia, Dept. of Game and Tsetse, *Annual Report 1948*, Special Collections, UNZA.

26. Report of Anglo-Belgian Advisory Board, 15 Mar. 1950; Fisheries Officer to Director of Game and Tsetse, 15 Dec. 1951, NP 2/1/6, NAZ.

27. Director of Game and Tsetse to Member for Agriculture, 22 Feb. 1953, SEC 6/372, NAZ.

28. "Je suis convaincu que dans l'intérêt direct des populations dont nous sommes les tuteurs nous devons interdire la pêche aux filets et aux nasses sur le bief Katabulwe—Chutes Johnstons [Mambilima]. . . . Aussi, que les populations du Luapula le veuillent ou non, nous devons les forcer dans leur intérêt direct." Directeur du Service Piscicole to Director of Game and Tsetse, 2 Feb. 1951, SEC 6/236, NAZ.

29. Minutes of Anglo-Belgian Advisory Board, 18 Dec. 1951, NP 2/1/6, NAZ.

30. According to the Fish Control (Mweru-Luapula) Regulations of 1952, NP 2/1/6, NAZ.

31. Minutes of a meeting of the Lunda Native Authority and the DC, 12 Jan. 1951, SEC 6/372, NAZ.

32. Bonwell Chikwa, Kashiba, 30 Dec. 1997; Philip Chona Yatemwa Kafimbwa, Kashiba, 26 Dec. 1997; Fish Ranger to Director of Game and Tsetse, 8 Jan. 1953; Fisheries Officer to the Director of Game and Fisheries, 23 Feb. 1953, SEC 6/372, NAZ; Musambachime, "Development and Growth," 1:289.

33. Gouverneur Général du Congo Belge to Governor of Northern Rhodesia, 26 Feb. 1953, SEC 6/372, NAZ.

34. Dossier: Legislation, Correspondance et Instructions; Gouverneur Général du Congo Belge to Gouverneur de Katanga, 18 May 1953, IPAC 13.047, AA.

35. Director of Game and Tsetse to Member for Agriculture, 2 Feb. 1952, SEC 6/372, NAZ.

36. Fisheries Officer, Tour Report 2/1953, SEC 6/372, NAZ.

37. Director of Game and Tsetse to Member for Agriculture, 2 Feb. 1952, SEC 6/372, NAZ.

38. Elliot Mwitwa Kankomba and Charles Muyembe, Mambilima, 5 Jan. 1998.

39. Fisheries Officer to Director of Game and Tsetse, 23 Feb. 1953, SEC 6/372, NAZ.

40. Ibid.

41. Ibid. Minutes of an Interview between the PC and Mulundu, 2 Mar. 1953, SEC 6/372, NAZ.

42. Both the Northern Rhodesian and the Belgian administration rotated fish guards every few months to prevent abuse of their offices. Guards were known to confiscate nets, only to use them themselves, or demand fish for personal consumption. Similar abuses occurred in the Belgian Congo. Fish Ranger's Monthly Report, 31 Mar. 1948, SEC 6/178, NAZ; Dossier: Rapports avant 1954; Agent pêche to Administrateur Territoriale, 7 Feb. 1946, IPAC 13.047, AA; AIMO Rapport 1945, RA/AIMO 86, AA.

43. Administrative Enquiry into the conduct of Chief Mulundu, 4 July 1953, SEC 5/251, NAZ.

44. PC to DC Kawambwa, 17 July 1953, SEC 5/251, NAZ.

45. Despite the fact that Kazembe had supported Mulundu's defiance. DC to PC, 27 July 1953, SEC 5/251, NAZ; Mwata Kazembe to DC Kawambwa, 27 July 1953, NP 2/6/17, NAZ. Chief Kambwali, the perpetual "uncle" to Mwata Kazembe and ruler of the area where the Luapula enters Lake Mweru, suffered a similar fate after permitting fishing in the Chimbofuma lagoon. He was suspended and later reinstated. PC's note on recent events in Kawambwa and Ft. Rosebery Districts, [1953?], NP 2/7/14, NAZ.

46. In Luapula the dismissed chiefs were all from the Lake Bangweulu area and included Chiefs Kasoma, Mulukwa, and Milambo. This was also a fishing area, but not as prosperous as the Luapula Valley and thus did not have as powerful business and political networks. Political Intelligence Reports, 1951–53, CO 1015/463, PRO.

47. "Des plus en plus, ils déclarent comme leurs frères rhodésiens que ce sont les européens qui sont la cause de la disparition de certaines espèces de poissons, par l'emploi de matériel perfectionné et de nombreux filets." AIMO Rapport, 1953, RA/AIMO 86, AA.

48. Urban ethnic associations formed from the early 1950s would coalesce into a more radical protest movement in 1959. See Herbert Weiss, *Political*

Protest in the Congo: The Parti Solidaire Africain During the Independence Struggle (Princeton: Princeton University Press, 1967), 3–63.

49. Projet de création d'une zone d'action massive au Luapula-Moëro, 1953, FBEI 35/98, AA.

50. An effort to establish a fishing cooperative at Kilwa in 1949 was scuttled by the *commerçants* who feared the price of fish would be driven up. But in 1953 the governor of Katanga argued that political and economic considerations made the participation of Africans in larger-scale fishing necessary and argued for the creation of a cooperative. Kitoto Mulamba, "Histoire de la population du Territoire de Kasenga, 1939–1958," Mémoire, UNILU, 1984–85, UNILU; Gouverneur du Katanga to Gouverneur Général du Congo Belge, 12 Nov. 1953, FBEI 35/98, AA.

51. Kisabi Honoré Kiuma , Kasenga, 15 July 1998; Prosper Kabinda, Kashikishi, 12 Jan. 1998.

52. Memorandum of a Visit to Kilwa, 17 Oct. 1953, SEC 6/13, NAZ.

53. Minutes of the Anglo-Belgian Fisheries Conference at Ft. Rosebery, 29 June 1953, SEC 6/13, NAZ.

54. Ibid.

55. Dossier: Reunions Anglo-Belge—Pêche. Compte Rendu 22 Aug. 1953, IPAC 13.039, AA.

56. Minutes of the Lunda Native Authority meeting to Discuss the Fish Regulations, 22 Aug., 1953, NP 2/1/7, NAZ.

57. Minutes of LNA meeting, 26 Oct. 1954, NP 2/1/7, NAZ.

58. Kawambwa Tour Reports, 22–24 Oct. 1954, SEC 2/881, NAZ.

59. Kawambwa District Notebook vol. 3, KSG 3/1, NAZ.

60. Mweru-Luapula Reports, 1954, SEC 6/530, NAZ; Kawambwa District Notebook vol. 3, KSG 3/1, NAZ.

61. Furthermore it seems that they were not particularly keen on fishing for Kazembe. The DC reported that they were often drunk and did not bother to lift the nets out of the water for days, resulting in the fish rotting. When fish were caught, instead of selling the fish legally, the fishermen kept a portion of the catches, which they sold far above the controlled price and pocketed the profits. T. G. Murphy to Fish Officer Ft. Rosebery, 26 July 1954, SEC 6/470, NAZ.

62. Kawambwa District Notebook vol. 3, KSG 3/1, NAZ; Kawambwa Tour Reports, 6–10 Oct. 1954, SEC 2/881, NAZ.

63. Harry Kazembe Mwenso, Mwense, 26 Dec. 1997; Tour Report of Mweru Fishing Camps 3/1956, SEC 2/883, NAZ.

64. Holis Chilufya, Kafulwe, 26 July 1998; Chief Mununga and Councilors, Mununga's Palace, 26 July 1998.

65. "LA GRAND MENACE contre le commerce de poisson du Luapula." La situation commercial et économique de la région de Kasenga et du Moëro, 1939, IPAC 9.590, AA.

66. H. B. Cott, "The Status of the Nile Crocodile in Uganda," *The Uganda Journal* 18.1 (1954): 1–12. The treatment of crocodiles as vermin by colonial authorities throughout Africa is dealt with in Mwelwa C. Musambachime, "The Fate of the Nile Crocodile in African Waterways," *African Affairs* 86 (1987): 197–207.

67. E. C. Thomson to Secretary of Native Affairs, 1 Aug. 1961, ML 1/6/8, NAZ.

68. In Kasenga territory alone 3,838 crocodiles were killed and 50,787 eggs collected. Dossier: Lutte Crocs. Statistiques de destruction des crocodiles, IPAC 13.042, AA. "Crocodiles" in *Service des eaux et forêts, chasse et pêche* 4.14 (1954): 130–35.

69. After two years the bounty was further reduced and UMHK was replaced by the *fonds poisson* as the bounty supplier.

70. Oral evidence collected by Musambachime, "Development and Growth," 1:183–84.

71. AIMO Rapport, 1946, RA/AIMO 86, AA.

72. Dossier: Lutte Crocs. Correspondence and Statistics, IPAC 13.042, AA.

73. Muteba Mwaba, Kasenga, 15 July 1998.

74. Elliot Mwitwa Kankomba, Charles Muyembe, and Joshua Chama. Mambilima, 5 Jan. 1998. Seine nets were introduced from eastern Zambia by migrant fishermen who settled in Luapula. Musambachime, "Development and Growth," 1:55.

75. This explanation was first given by a Northern Rhodesian colonial official when the administration was discussing the effects of lifting the conservation regulations. E. C. Thomson to Secretary of Native Affairs, 1 Aug. 1961, ML 1/6/8, NAZ.

76. Fisheries Officer to Director of Game and Fisheries, 31 Oct. 1959, SEC 6/372, NAZ.

77. Minutes of the Anglo-Belgian Fisheries Advisory Board, 7 Apr. 1960, SEC 6/372, NAZ.

78. Secretary for Native Affairs to PC, Luapula Province, 1 July 1960, SEC 6/372, NAZ.

5. Pale

1. Abraham Soriano, Lubumbashi, 16 June, 1998. Information was also gathered from several confidential interviews and documentation in Kasenga and Nchelenge.

2. White, *Speaking with the Vampires,* 43.

3. For an account of these trends from a predominantly urban perspective, see Ferguson, *Expectations of Modernity;* also see chapter 6, below.

4. Numbers are difficult to estimate since the Luapula Valley does not form a single administrative district. According to the 1980 Zambian census, a total

of 209,089 people lived in the three districts of Kawambwa, Nchelenge, and Mwense, of which Mweru-Luapula forms about four-fifths of the total population. The 1990 census puts the population of the four districts (Chiengi became a separate district) at 290,684. The 1984 Zairian census puts the population of three districts, of which Mweru-Luapula forms part, at 316,704. Zambian survey data from the 1990s records that around 10,000 individuals owned their fishing gear. Assuming the same proportion of individuals involved in the fishery on the Zairian side would put the number at over 20,000. However, the Zairian population figures probably include a lesser proportion involved in the fishery, hence I would estimate the total number of fishers (owning gear) to be at least 15,000. A conservative estimate of the total number of crew and traders who also gain a significant portion of their revenue from the fishery would put the total at around 50,000. Population figures from Zaire, *Définitive totales* (Kinshasa: Institut National de la Statistique 1991); Zambia, *1980 Census of Population and Housing* (Lusaka: Central Statistic Office, 1981); Zambia, *1990 Census of Population and Housing* (Lusaka: Central Statistic Office, 1991). Fishing Survey figures from P. A. M van Zwieten, B. H. M. Aarnink, and C. K. Kapasa, "How Diverse a Fishery Can Be! Structure of the Mweru-Luapula Fishery Based on the Frame Survey 1992 and a Characterization of the Present Management Strategies," ML/1996/Report no. 25, DoF. For the 2000 census, see chapter 6, below.

5. "We pale wandi, namonaula; Namupela muluba; Kutobela atobela pale mu linso; Ndiungu, mwine malela; Nsansabwe ndilwa kuwama; Nangu tamuli mucele cawama; Mititi ya kapepe mwali ngombe." Translated with the help of Andrew Billing Chalawila. The original can be found in Labrecque, "Abashila," WFA.

6. J. J. Soulsby, "Some Congo Basin Fishes of Northern Rhodesia: Part 1," 241–42; Paul Skelton, *A Complete Guide to Freshwater Fishes of Southern Africa*, 176–81. *Oreochromis mweruensis* was previously known as *Oreochromis macrochir* until re-classified as a species in E. Schwank, "Behaviour and colour differences between *Oreochromis macrochir* and *O. mweruensis* (Teleostei: Cichlidae)," *Ichthyological Exploration in Freshwaters* 5.3 (1994): 267–280.

7. It is unclear if recorded stock numbers include catches of juvenile pale; many of these and general pale exports to the Congo are unlikely to have been recorded. Still, the general patterns seem to stand and confirm anecdotal evidence provided by fishers. See, for example, numbers cited in B. H. M. Aarnink, C. K. Kapasa, and P. A. M. van Zwieten, "Our Children Will Suffer: Present Status and Problems of Mweru-Luapula Fisheries and the Need for a Conservation and Management Action Plan," prepared for United Nations Development Programme/Food and Agricultural Organization of the United Nations (henceforth FAO) Regional Project, 1993, DoF.

8. In the fiscal year following independence, Zambian government revenue almost doubled. Copper prices and their influence on government revenue

in Zambia is covered in Robert Bates, *Rural Responses to Industrialization: A Study of Village Zambia* (New Haven: Yale University Press, 1976), 104–10. For Zaire, see Crawford M. Young and Thomas Turner, *The Rise and Decline of the Zairian State* (Madison: University of Wisconsin Press, 1985), 306–9.

9. The U.S. Agency for International Development and FAO suggested COZ become the sole agency responsible for rural credit. Report of Working Party on Proposals for the Establishment of a State Credit Organization, 26 May 1965, ML 1/19/86, NAZ; Bates, *Rural Responses,* 116.

10. Bates, *Rural Responses,* 116.

11. Manager COZ to Minister of Lands and Natural Resources, 14 Aug. 1965, ML 1/19/86, NAZ.

12. C. Stephen Lombard, *The Growth of the Co-operative Movement in Zambia, 1914–1971* (Manchester: Manchester University Press, 1971); Stephen A. Quick, "Bureaucracy and Rural Socialism in Zambia," *Journal of Modern African Studies* 15.3 (1977): 379–400.

13. Robert Bates provides a detailed ethnography of these co-operatives. He shows that the farming co-operatives failed and became indebted to the state due to badly functioning rural support services. The building co-operative only succeeded insofar as it was able to take advantage of private markets, such as using the truck to transport fish and fish traders. *Rural Responses,* 130–56.

14. Report on Luapula Community Development, 29 Oct. 1969, Ministry of Rural Development 1/8/24, NAZ.

15. For an account of the history and functioning of the boards and their relationship to the co-operatives and pricing policy, see Doris Jansen Dodge, *Agricultural Policy and Performance in Zambia* (Berkeley: University of California Press, 1977), 79–139.

16. This was a problem characteristic of many rural African economies during the 1970s. See Robert Bates, *Markets and States in Tropical Africa: The Political Basis of Agricultural Policies* (Berkeley: University of California Press, 1981).

17. Memorandum on Fishing Co-operatives, 1965, ML 1/18/5, NAZ.

18. President of the AFMU to Minister of Land and Natural Resources, 14 Dec. 1963, ML 1/18/4, NAZ.

19. Their first request was for funds to establish a cold storage plant for fish in the Copperbelt town of Kitwe. President of the AFMU to Minister of Land and Natural Resources, 14 Dec. 1963, ML 1/18/4, NAZ.

20. Assistant Secretary to Ministry of Land and Natural Resources to Permanent Secretary, 7 Feb. 1964, ML 1/18/4, NAZ.

21. AFMU Tour Report of Mweru-Luapula, 24 Apr. 1964, ML 1/18/4, NAZ.

22. Record of a Meeting to Discuss Policy Toward Fishermen's Associations, 22 May 1964, ML 1/18/4, NAZ.

23. See the case study of the Katofyio building society. Bates, *Rural Responses,* 130–56.

24. Pritchett, *Lunda-Ndembu*, 67–68.

25. In 1970 COZ was purchased by the Agricultural Finance Company (AFC) and took over its outstanding debt. AFC did not furnish loans to the fishery because of the low recovery rate for COZ loans. Note by Director of Game and Fisheries, 20 Aug. 1968, ML 1/19/39, NAZ; Notes of Assistant Secretary, 14 Apr. 1972, ML 1/15/39, NAZ; Bates, *Rural Responses*, 152.

26. Projects Manager to Permanent Secretary, 18 Mar. 1967, ML 1/15/36, NAZ; Report and Recommendations of Inquiry into LFZ, 21–26 Jan. 1972, ML 1/15/34, NAZ.

27. Chief Fisheries Officer to Director of Game and Fisheries, 18 June 1965, ML 1/15/1, NAZ.

28. Fisheries Economist, Note on Fish Prices, 3 Aug. 1972, ML 1/15/39, NAZ.

29. If state prices were respected, which is unlikely, the real income of fishermen would have dropped by 16 percent between 1964 and 1969. Calculated in Bates, *Rural Responses*, 157.

30. Fisheries Economist, Note on Fish Prices, 3 Aug. 1972, ML 1/15/39, NAZ; Provincial Fisheries Officer to Director, Dept. of Wildlife, Fisheries, and National Parks, 9 Sept. 1972, ML 1/15/39, NAZ.

31. Luapula Annual Report, 1977, DoF, Chilanga.

32. Minutes of Meeting between LFZ and Fishermen, Nchelenge, 24 Jan. 1972, ML 1/15/39, NAZ; Tour Report on Fish Prices and Marketing in Northern and Luapula provinces, 1971, ML 1/15/39, NAZ. A fisheries commission recommended tighter state control over LFZ and an end to any profiteering by the company, but the conflict was not resolved. Report and Recommendations into LFZ, 26 Jan. 1972, ML 1/15/39, NAZ.

33. "You who were satisfied; you married the makobo that stays in the boat [is not eaten]: Mwashele kuyanganyanga; Mwaupilwe nacimakobo chashele mubwato." Augustine Mukoyo, *Waapilwe Nacimakobo*, ZHA 142 n.d., trans. Walima Kalusa, ZNBC.

34. Data about fishing techniques are derived from observation and a series of interviews in Kashikishi and in several eastern fishing camps and villages: Augustus Chiwale, Kashikishi, 13 Jan. 1998; Holis Chilufya, Kafulwe, 26 July 1998; Kabel Kaoma, Kashikishi, 11 Jan. 1998; Daud Samuel Kulaba, Kashikishi, 12 Jan. 1998; Gabriel Kunda, Kashikishi, 14 July 1998; Hello Mwaba, Kashikishi, 12 Jan. 1998; John Mwila and Mwand Mulenga, Mukwakwa, 25 July, 1998.

35. Luapula Annual Report, 1980, DoF, Chilanga.

36. Rapport annuel de Zone de Kasenga, 1986, Service de l'environnement et conservation, Kipushi; Abraham Soriano, Lubumbashi, 16 June 1998.

37. For statistics concerning Zambian fishers see Van Zwieten et al., "How Diverse a Fishery Can Be!," 27–36, DoF.

38. M. Crawford Young, "The Shattered Illusion of the Integral State," *Journal of Modern African Studies*, 32.2 (1994): 247–65.

39. Kabundi-Mpenga Ka'mpeng, "La problématique du développement rural au Zaire: Réflexion sur les conditions de vie des masses rurales dans la zone de Kasenga." Mémoire, UNILU, 1975–76, UNILU.

40. For a summary of state agricultural programs see David Shapiro and Eric Tollens, *The Agricultural Development of Zaire* (Aldershot: Avebury, 1992).

41. Young and Turner, *Rise and Decline*, 288–96.

42. Abraham Soriano, Lubumbashi, 16 June 1998.

43. Musambachime, "Development and Growth," vol. 1: 317; Musambachime, "Development and Growth," vol. 2, Interview with Edmond Winkel, Kasenga, 21 Apr. 1975.

44. Antonio Macris, Kasenga, 28 Dec. 1997.

45. Abraham Soriano, Lubumbashi, 16 June 1998.

46. David Kashiba, Lubumbashi, 15 June 1998; Muteba Mwaba, Kasenga, 15 July 1998.

47. Kabundi-Mpenga Ka'mpeng, "La problématique du développement rural au Zaire: Réflexion sur les conditions de vie des masses rurales dans la zone de Kasenga." Mémoire, UNILU, 1975–76, 79.

48. Musambachime, "Development and Growth," 1:317–18.

49. David Lupandula, Kasenga, 17 Dec. 1997.

50. Nicholas Paraskevas, Lubumbashi, 16 June, 1998.

51. David Kashiba, Lubumbashi, 15 June 1998.

52. Nicholas Paraskevas, Lubumbashi, 16 June, 1998; Abraham Soriano, Lubumbashi, 16 June, 1998.

53. Luapula monthly reports, July–Sept., 1982, DoF, Chilanga.

54. Dossier: Coopérative de Pêche, Kasenga, Constitution APEZA, Service de l'environnement et conservation, Kipushi.

55. Young, "The Shattered Illusion of the Integral State."

56. According to allegations made by President Mwanawasa in a special address to parliament on July 11, 2002. See articles in *Times of Zambia* and *Daily Mail*, 12 July 2002.

57. Abraham Soriano, Lubumbashi, 16 June 1998; NFCC 3/14/2, Application by Katebe Katoto Jr., 1992, Nchelenge District Council Files. Mwata Kazembe's involvement in Chani Fisheries is reported in Nettie Aarnink, "Socio-Political Struggles over Fish," in *Towards Negotiated Co-management of Natural Resources in Africa,* ed. Bernhard Venema and Hans van den Breemer (Piscataway, N.J.: Transaction Publishers, 1999), 275–301, esp. 281.

58. For smuggling allegations see "Ostend Airport/Arms Running," http://users.skynet.be/cleanostend/clos_en.htm. After the revelation of gun-running and corruption allegations, the assets of Tamba Bashila have been seized by the Zambian government. *The Post*, 11 Mar. 2003.

59. Patrick Daka, Kashikishi, 21 July, 1998.

60. Between 1965 and 1969 pale declined from 75 percent to 10 percent of the total catch. The amount per catch effort declining from 10 kilograms per 100 meters of gill net to 3.5 kilograms. Zambia, Dept. of Wildlife, Fisheries, and National Parks, *Annual Report,* 1970, UNZA.

61. Luapula Annual Reports, 1976, DoF, Chilanga.

62. Luapula Monthly Report, Feb. 1977, DoF, Chilanga.

63. Luapula Annual Reports, 1976–89, DoF, Chilanga.

64. R. Aubrey, "Les pêches du Zaire: Etude Technico-économique d'Ensemble," n.d, Service de l'environnement et conservation, section pêche, Lubumbashi. In the mid-1980s FAO attempted to centralize these functions into the *Service National de Promotion et Développement de Pêche.*

65. Chef de Zone Luapula-Moero to Directeur Provincial des Affaires Agricoles, 24 Jul. 1964; Agent de pêche to Chef Eaux et Forêts, 25 Feb. 1974, Service de l'environnement et conservation, section pêche, Lubumbashi.

66. Coordination Sous-Regionale de l'environnement et conservation, Rapport 1986, Service de l'environnement et conservation, Kipushi.

67. Daud Samuel Kulaba, Kashikishi, 12 Jan. 1998.

68. Annual Reports, 1985–87, DoF, Chilanga.

69. Dossier: Rapport d'activités, 1991–94, Rapport annuel Kasenga, Service de l'environnement et conservation, Kipushi; Confidential interviews.

70. Aarnink, "Socio-Political Struggles over Fish," 282–83.

71. "Les exactions, les brimades et tracasseries dont les pêcheurs ont toujours été victimes de la mesure de certains fonctionnaires et agents trop zélés et peu scrupuleux." Dossier: Coopératives de Pêche, Statuts de l'USPI, Service de l'environnement et conservation, Kipushi.

72. Certains agents de l'environnement de connivence avec quelques autorités militaires ont toujours semblé négliger l'application stricte de cette mesure par contre la fraude qui leur est bénéfice. Dossier: Coopératives de Pêche, Président (ASHILAC) to Gouverneur Katanga, 11 May 1992, Service de l'environnement et conservation, Kipushi.

73. Gabriel Kunda, Kashikishi, 14 Aug. 1998.

74. Annual Report, 1980; Monthly Report, Apr.–Sept. 1981, DoF, Chilanga.

75. Annual Report, 1987, DoF, Chilanga.

76. John Mwila and Mwanda Mulenga, Mukwakwa, 25 July 1998; Augustus Chiwale, Kashikishi, 13 Jan. 1998. In 1985 fishers launched the Lupiya Fishing Association to prevent net thefts and provide aid for members, and in 1990 several similar associations combined to form the Lake Mweru Fishing Association. Report on Fish Conservation Seminar for Fishers and Chiefs, 30 Oct. 1992; Lake Mweru Fishing Association, Constitution, 1990, DoF, Nchelenge.

77. Lake Mweru Fishing Association, Constitution, 1990, DoF, Nchelenge.

78. Interesting examples of the conflict over the appointment and duties of owners of the lagoons in the 1990s can be found in N. Oudwater, "Eating with

the Chiefs: A Study of the Present Management of the Mweru-Luapula Fishery," March 1997, Report no. 4, 1997, 57–60, DoF, Nchelenge.

79. Aarnink claims Mwata Kazembe and Kambwali allowed fishers to settle in Kanakashi in the Chimbofuma protected area in exchange for tribute. Aarnink, "Socio-Political Struggles over Fish," 287. This is possible but unlikely since in the 1980s villagers disliked Kambwali, who was considered a lackey of Mwata Kazembe XVIII. In all likelihood, he had little control over who settled where. For the conflict between Kambwali's villagers and Kazembe and Kambwali's lack of local legitimacy, see: Telegram: Provincial Secretary to District Secretary, 3 Sept. 1976; Telegram: Provincial Secretary to District Governor, 4 Oct. 1976; Telegram: Provincial Secretary to Mwata Kazembe, 7 Jan. 1977; Telegram: Provincial Secretary to District Governor, 28 Mar. 1977, CAB 52/3/5, Kawambwa District Council Files; Danford Kamuchoma, Kashikishi, 16 Oct. 1998; Chief Kambwali, Kambwali's Palace, 13 Jan. 1998; James Musenga Mulenga, Shishibeti, 14 Aug. 1997.

80. Aarnink, "Socio-Political Struggles over Fish," 282.

81. *The Daily Mail,* 16 May 1998.

82. Prosper Kabinda, Kashikishi, 12 Jan. 1998.

83. Minutes of the Third NFCC Meeting, 23 Feb. 1996, NFCC 3/14/2, Nchelenge District Council Files.

84. Ibid.

85. Report on Fish Conservation and Management Seminar, 11–12 Nov. 1993, NFCC 3/14/2, Nchelenge District Council Files.

86. Minutes of NFCC Meetings, 1995–96, NFCC 3/14/2, Nchelenge District Council Files.

87. Although not celebratory of traditional conservation, N. Oudwater attributes the "traditional" roles of owners of the lagoon much importance. However, as this work has pointed out, the historic roles of owners of the lagoon had been thoroughly undermined and transformed over the last century. Furthermore, the *Mutomboko* tribute, cited by Oudwater, only occurred after *Umutomboko* took its modern form in 1971. Oudwater, "Eating with the Chiefs," DoF, Nchelenge. For the Mutomboko ceremony and the reinvention of chieftaincies after colonialism, see David M. Gordon, "The Cultural Politics of a Traditional Ceremony: Mutomboko and the Performance of History on the Luapula," *Comparative Studies in Society and History* 46.1 (January 2004): 63–83.

88. Chief Puta, for example, argued that "Power has been taken away from the chiefs, so government must give people who control the lake back the power." His councilor, however, advised that "if people are arrested and imprisoned, the chief cannot do it alone. It is better to work with the government." Chief Puta and councilors, Puta's Palace, 27 July 1998.

89. Meeting with local leaders, fishermen's associations, and fisheries staff, 24 Nov. 1996, NFCC 3/14/2, Nchelenge District Council Files.

90. Quoted in Oudwater, "Eating with the Chiefs," 63.

91. Augustus Chiwale, Kashikishi, 13 Jan. 1998.

92. Dossier: Rapport d'activité Pweto, Rapport de la fermeture de la pêche, 1992–93, Service de l'environnement et conservation, Kipushi.

93. The decay and collapse of Mobutu's regime and the failed attempt to form a democratic state are best recorded in a series of edited collections: Jean-Claude Willame, ed., *Zaïre, années 90: Vers la Troisième République* (Brussels, CEDAF, 1991); Info-Zaire, *Zaire 1992–1996,* vols. 1 and 2 (Paris: Karthala, 1996–97). For a partial and contested account of the Lubumbashi massacre, see Fr. Victor Digekisa Piluka, *Le massacre de Lubumbashi* (Paris: Karthala, 1993).

94. This led to a rapid drop in fish production and sales. Dossier: Rapport d'activités, 1991–94, Rapport annuel Kasenga, Service de l'environnement et conservation, Kipushi; Confidential interviews.

95. Minutes of a meeting with local leaders, fishermen's associations, and fisheries staff, 24 Nov. 1996, NFCC 3/14/2, Nchelenge District Council Files.

96. United Nations Integrated Regional Information Networks, 16 June 2003. See http://allafrica.com/stories/200306170253.html.

97. Inge Tvedten, "'If You Don't Fish You Are Not a Caprivian': Freshwater Fisheries in Caprivi, Namibia," *Journal of Southern African Studies* 28.2 (2002): 421–39.

6. Chisense

1. Grace Chama, Kamwala Market, Lusaka, 30 June 1998.

2. See for example, A. L. Epstein, *Urbanization and Kinship: The Domestic Domain on the Copperbelt of Zambia, 1950–1956* (London: Academic Press, 1981); Karen Tranberg Hansen, *Keeping House in Lusaka* (New York: Columbia University Press, 1997); Jane Parpart, "'Where Is Your Mother?'" 241–71; and Parpart, "'Wicked Women' and 'Respectable Ladies,'" 274–92.

3. James A. Wilson, "The Economic Management of Multispecies Fisheries," *Land Economics* 58.4 (1982): 417–34.

4. The best example is the anchovy/sardine fishery, where anchovies tend to prosper when sardines are heavily exploited. See McEvoy, *The Fisherman's Problem,* 8–9.

5. Chisense is sometimes termed *Microthrissa moeruensis*. Fisheries biologist Paul van Zwieten has noticed two types of chisense with different breeding and feeding patterns, although their taxonomic status is as yet unknown. P. A. M. van Zwieten, B. H. M. Aarnink, C. K. Kapasa, and P. Ngalande, "The Biology, Fishery, and Trade of Chisense from Mweru-Luapula: Status of Present Knowledge," ML/1996/Report no. 31, 28–36, DoF, Nchelenge. For an overview of the *Clupediae* see Paul Skelton, *A Complete Guide to Freshwater Fishes of Southern Africa,* 109–11.

6. Van Zwieten et al., "The Biology, Fishery, and Trade," 74, DoF, Nchelenge. An experiment conducted in 1985 determined that the amount

of chisense in the stomachs of makobo, ntembwa, and misibele was 75 percent, 60 percent, and 50 percent respectively. Annual Report Mweru-Luapula, 1985, DoF, Chilanga.

7. Paul van Zwieten, personal communication, 18 Oct. 2000.

8. Paul van Zwieten, personal communication, 4 Dec. 2000.

9. "Supplement to Report on Joint Meeting on Mweru-Luapula held on 22 July 1996," DoF, Nchelenge.

10. Calculated at 1995–96 average exchange rate. Calculations of chisense for Zambia in 1994 estimate 39,940 tons, and 36,494 tons in 1995, with a potential production of between 67,000 to 95,000 tons. Van Zwieten et al., "The Biology, Fishery, and Trade," 4, 86, DoF, Nchelenge. Estimates based on the 1997 frame survey put chisense production between forty and fifty thousand tons. P. A. M. van Zwieten, P. C. Goudswaard and C. K. Kapasa, "Mweru Luapula is an open exit fishery where a highly dynamic population of fishermen makes use of a resilient resource base," in E. Jul-Larsen, J. Kolding, R. Overa, J. R. Nielsen (eds.), *Management, co-management or no management? Major dilemmas in southern African freshwater fisheries* (FAO: Rome, 2003), 1–33.

11. Ragnhild Overå, "Market Integration and Fishing Effort in Lake Kariba, Zambia," unpublished paper for Christian Michelsen Institute Seminar, 21–22 (1999); A. P. Cheater, "The Zimbabwe Kapenta Fishery," in *Studies of the Fishery on Lake Kariba*, ed. M. F. C. Bourdillon, A. P. Cheater, and M. W. Mulphree (Gweru: Mambo Press, 1985), 96–132.

12. This was recalled in a number of interviews. In 1948 the Kawamba fish ranger noted chisense fishing, as it was a contravention of the 1948 fishing regulations that specified large net mesh sizes. Chisense fishing was, however, permitted, for it was thought to be subsistence oriented. Fish ranger report, 3/1948, NP 2/1/19, NAZ.

13. Mweru-Luapula monthly reports, 1976–80, DoF, Chilanga. For detailed breakdown on changing locations of chisense fishers in 1994–95 that shows a concentration in the northeast, see van Zwieten et al., "The Biology, Fishery, and Trade," 15–19, DoF, Nchelenge.

14. Nets were made from meshless materials that ranged from mosquito nets to curtains and cloth. Systematic surveys of chisense fishing techniques were only conducted by the Zambian DoF in the 1980s. In 1985 they found that about 65 percent of chisense fishers used a scoop or dip net and about 30 percent used boat seines (the rest were traditional methods). More than 80 percent of nets were made of meshless material. Annual Report, 1985, DoF, Nchelenge. In 1994, 65 percent used *japan* nets, 31 percent seine nets, and 3 percent *mutobi*. Van Zwieten et al., "The Biology, Fishery, and Trade," 11–15, DoF, Nchelenge.

15. For a comparative case of a relatively open-access fishery, see Christophe Béné et al., "Inland Fisheries, Tenure Systems, and Livelihood Diversification in Africa: The Case of the Yaéré Floodplains in Lake Chad Basin," *African Studies* 62.2 (2003): 187–212, esp. 204.

16. Sande Kabwe, Bupe Manda, Hilbert Kavunda, and Claude Kisamba, Pweto, 12 July 1998.

17. Chief Mununga and Councilors, Mununga's Palace, 26 July 1998; Gabriel Kunda, Kashikishi, 14 July, 1998. A Zambian report names "Sikasote" as the man who brought the new techniques from Tanganyika in 1975/76. E. S. Ngula, "Problems of Fisheries Management in the Zambian Sector of Lake Mweru-Luapula," in *Report on the Technical Consultation of Luapula–Mweru by Zaire and Zambia (Lusaka 08–10 August, 1990)*, ed. M. Maes (Bujumbura, Burundi: Project For Inland Fisheries Planning, United Nations Development Program / FAO, 1990).

18. Van Zwieten et al., "The Biology, Fishery, and Trade," 27, DoF, Nchelenge.

19. Luapula Monthly Report, Jan.–Feb. 1980, DoF, Chilanga.

20. Sande Kabwe, Bupe Manda, Hilbert Kavunda, and Claude Kisamba, Pweto, 12 July 1998; Chief Mununga and Councilors, Mununga, 27 July 1998.

21. V. M. Kanondo, "Fisheries Statistical Systems in Zambia with Particular Reference to Lake Luapula-Mweru," in *Report on the Technical Consultation of Luapula-Mweru*, 30–31.

22. J. M. S. Allen and C. K. Chileya, "'The Unbaptised': Farming in a Fishing Econonmy. A Case from the Mweru Lakeshore," Paper Prepared for the European Congress of Sociology, 1–4 April, 1986, 13–14.

23. Annual Report, 1985, DoF, Nchelenge; Van Zwieten, "The Biology, Fishery, and Trade," 27, DoF, Nchelenge.

24. Jean Philippe Plateau has identified the lack of diversification due to limitations in access to credit as a widespread feature of Africa's fisheries. "Small-Scale Fisheries and Evolutionist Theory," in *Fishing for Development: Small-Scale Fisheries in Africa*, ed. Inge Tvedten and Björn Hersoug (Stockholm: Nordiska Afrikainstutet, 1992), 90–104, 101. Luapula data are based on my interviews with several older fishers, all of whom did not consider changing to chisense fishing. Gabriel Kunda, Kashikishi, 14 Aug. 1997; Daud Samual Kulaba, Kashikishi, 12 Jan. 1998; Kabel Kaoma, Kashikishi, 11 Jan. 1998.

25. Quantitive data to support this argument is difficult to come by largely because fishers will insist on their "residency" in the fishery to emphasize their rights to fish. Statistics collected by P. A. M. Van Zwieten et al. in 1992 have 97 percent of fishers claiming the fishery as their residence, but this does not indicate anything about the source of their capital or their past. "The Biology, Fishery, and Trade," 11, DoF, Nchelenge. From a 1997 survey, P. A. M. Van Zwieten P. A. M. van Zwieten, P. C. Goudswaard and C. K. Kapasa demonstrate high mobility into and out of the fishery, "Mweru Luapula is an open exit fishery." My arguments rest on numerous discussions and qualitative assessment, especially Sande Kabwe, Bupe Manda, Hilbert Kavunda, and Claude Kisamba, Pweto, 12 July 1998; Gabriel Kunda, Kashikishi, 14 July 1997; Daud Samual Kalaba, Kashikishi 12 Jan. 1998; Kabel Kaoma, Kashikishi, 11 Jan. 1998.

26. Van Zwieten et al., "The Biology, Fishery, and Trade," 97–103, DoF, Nchelenge.

27. Pauline Ngandu, Mansa, 7 July 1998; Helene Mwila, Cecile Ilunga, Musumbi Mukeki, Kilufya Nyombo, Lubumbashi, 9–10 June 1998; Roda Bwanga, Queen Chisunka, Chinyanta Kanyembo, and Josephine Miyambo, Soweto Market, Lusaka, 29 Jun. 1998; Allen and Chileya, "'The Unbaptised,'" 28.

28. Bates, *Rural Responses*, 187.

29. Ilsa M. Glazer Schuster, *New Women of Lusaka* (Palo Alto, Calif.: Mayfield Publishing Co., 1979).

30. Ferguson, *Expectations of Modernity*, 123–165. For general interventions that point to the problem of urban poor compared to rural poverty, see Vali Jamal and John Weeks, *Africa Misunderstood, or Whatever Happened to the Rural-Urban Gap?* (London: Macmillan Press, 1993); Deborah Potts, "Shall We Go Home? Increasing Urban Poverty in African Cities and the Migration Processes," *The Geographic Journal* 161.3 (1995): 245–64.

31. Cf. John Higginson, *A Working Class in the Making.*

32. Lista Kanokelya Chasekwa, Sindone, 23 July 1998.

33. Data about Zambian female urban fishmongers are derived from observation and a series of interviews in Lusaka's fish markets. Roda Bwanga, Queen Chisunka, Chinyanta Kanyembo, and Josephine Miyambo, Soweto Market, Lusaka, 29 June, 1998; Grace Chama, Kamwala Market, Lusaka, 30 June 1998.

34. Françoise Kalenga, Lubumbashi, 9 June, 1998. Other interviews with Lubumbashi marketeers included Helene Mwila, Celine Ilunga, Musumbi Mukeki, Kilufya Nyombo, Lubumbashi, 9–10 June 1998.

35. A survey conducted at Nchelenge fish barrier in 1995 shows that only 37 percent of 25-kilogram bags reached Lusaka or the Copperbelt whereas 95 percent of 90-kilogram bags reached Lusaka and the Copperbelt. B. H. M Aarnink, "The Fish Trade and Tax Base of Lake Mweru," Report no. 36, 1996, DoF, Nchelenge.

36. Chinyanta Kanyembo, Soweto Market, Lusaka, 29 June 1998.

37. Bana Kalenga, Helene Mwila, Cecile Ilunga, Musumbi Mukeki, Kilufya Nyombo, Lubumbashi, 9–10 June 1998.

38. By the late 1990s, fishers and traders did not adhere to price controls for most fish. In Zaire under Mobutu marketeers informed me that price controls were not respected. Stefani Matobo, Kasenga, 15 July 1998. The new Congolese regime (1997) demanded adherence to fixed prices. In Zambia price controls were abolished in 1991.

39. Sela Mwaba, Kashikishi, 22 July 1998. Markets were divided into sections, and it seems a section head could be a woman; for example, a woman would be in charge of the chisense section, but a man would be the market chairman. Benedict Mumba, Kashikishi, 22 July 1998.

40. The supply of fish to a household was by no means secure, for a man

might choose to sell all his fish or give them to another wife's household. Allen and Chileya, "'The Unbaptised,'" DoF, Nchelenge; B. H. M. Aarnink, "Fish and Cassava Are Equally Important in Livelihood Strategies of Women in Mweru-Luapula Fishery," Report no. 40, 1996, DoF, Nchelenge.

41. Lisa Cligget, "'Male Wealth' and 'Claims to Motherhood': Gendered Resource Access and Intergenerational Relations in the Gwembe Valley, Zambia," in *Gender at Work in Economic Life*, ed. Gracia Clark (Walnut Creek Calif.: AltaMira, 2003), 207–24.

42. As theorized in the classic article, Mary Douglas, "Is Matriliny Doomed in Africa?"

43. Although they employ more fishers than male gear owners—on average 5.7 compared to 4.8. Van Zwieten et al., "The Biology, Fishery, and Trade," 19, DoF, Nchelenge.

44. My information about rural female fishmongers is from observation and interviews conducted in the Zambian town of Kashikishi and the Congolese town of Kasenga. Alice Mboba, Osia Mufya, Albertina Shala, Mika Chansa, Elizabeth Chungu, Sela Mwaba, Benedict Mumba, Josephine Mwewa, and Judith Kalumbwa Mumba, Kashikishi, 23–24 July 1998; Bupe Cama and Mushibwe Kibwe, Kasenga, 16 July 1998. Good examples from smaller villages can be found in Aarnink , "Fish and Cassava," DoF, Nchelenge. The other prominent female industry was beer and liquor production and sale. Information comes from observation and Rosemary Chilapa and Kasama Kalumbi, Kashiba, 19 Aug. 1998.

45. Lista Kanokelya Chasekwa, Sindone, 24 July 1998.

46. Paul Chisakula's sister's son, Joseph, played an important role in the business. Nevertheless after Paul Chisakula's death, the business passed on to the daughter. Celestine Chisakula, Kashikishi, 24 July 1998; Rebecca Mulenga, Kashikishi, 23 July 1998.

47. Examples are found in the case studies in DoF, Nchelenge; Aarnink, "Fish and Cassava," DoF, Nchelenge. Also Alice Mboba, Osia Mufya, Albertina Shala, Mika Chansa, Elizabeth Chungu, Sela Mwaba, Benedict Mumba, Josephine Mwewa, Judith Kalumbwa Mumba, Kashikishi, 23–24 July 1998; Bupe Cama and Mushibwe Kibwe, Kasenga, 16 July 1998.

48. In Zambia, out of fifteen female fishmongers interviewed by the author, six were divorced, five were widowed, and four still married (two to employed husbands and two to polygynous husbands who provided only partially to the household). By contrast, in DRC all five female fishmongers interviewed were still married. This may reflect the dominance of the Catholic church in Zaire; alternatively, it might have been research bias, since I was not as familiar with the Congolese women interviewed.

49. For the importance of the church as civic organization in Zambia, see Isaac Phiri, "Why African Churches Preach Politics: The Case of Zambia," *Journal of Church and State* 41.2 (1999): 323–47.

50. Karla O. Poewe, "Religion, Matriliny and Change: Jehovah's Witness and Seventh-Day Adventist in Luapula, Zambia," *American Ethnologist* 5.2 (1978): 303–21, esp. 303–21.

51. Interviews and observation by the author also noted stable marriages among both Jehovah's Witnesses and Seventh-day Adventist (SDA) members. But the author also observed more stable patterns among regular church members of a variety of denominations. More definitive data would compare a greater variety of church congregations and economic conditions over time.

52. Karla O. Poewe, "Regional and Village Economic Activities: Prosperity and Stagnation in Luapula, Zambia," *African Studies Review* 22.2 (1979): 77–93, 77.

53. Alice Mboba, Osia Mufya, Albertina Shala, Mika Chansa, Elizabeth Chungu, Sela Mwaba, Benedict Mumba, Josephine Mwewa, Judith Kalumbwa Mumba, Kashikishi, 23–24 July 1998.

54. Poewe, "Religion, Matriliny, and Change," 312.

55. Aarnink, "Fish and Cassava," 22–29, DoF, Nchelenge.

56. Poewe, "Regional and Village Economic Activities," 77–93.

57. The highest number of wealthy Luapulan businessmen interviewed belonged to SDA, followed by Watchtower. Seven out of twelve Luapulan businessmen near the Zambian lakeshore interviewed belonged to SDA, three to Watchtower, one to United Church of Zambia, and one to Christian Mission in Many Lands. The ascendeny of SDA over Watchtower may be related to the greater work and commitment that the Watchtower church demands of members. There is no data about total membership figures, although I would estimate that there were equal numbers of SDA and Watchtower members. According to Poewe, these two denominations constituted 60 percent of Kashikishi's church-attending population (98 percent of the total population was Christian). "Religion, Matriliny, and Change," 319.

58. Chief Mununga and Councilors, Mununga's Palace, 27 Aug. 1998.

59. Chief Kambwali and Councilors, Kambwali' Palace, 13 Jan. 1998.

60. Chief Puta and Councilors, Puta's Palace, 27 July 1998.

61. Peter Geschiere and Francis Nyamnjoh, "Witchcraft as an Issue in the 'Politics of Belonging': Democratization and Urban Migrants' Involvement with the Home Village," *African Studies Review* 41.3 (1998): 69–91, 72.

62. James Ferguson, *Expectations of Modernity*, 118–21.

63. The fishmongers of Lusaka are often accused of "prostitution" by men. There are rumors that female fishmongers sleep with fishermen in exchange for fish. Predictably, no one fishmonger admitted to this, although several claimed that such things did in fact happen. Roda Bwanga, Queen Chisunka, and Chinyanta Kanyembo, Soweto Market, Lusaka, 29 June 1998. Grace Chama, Kamwala Market, Lusaka, 30 June 1998.

64. Sande Kabwe, Bupe Mande, Hilbert Kavunda, and Claude Kisaba, Pweto, 12 July 1998.

65. See, for example, reports in Aarnink , "Fish and Cassava," 24, DoF, Nchelenge.

66. P. A. M. van Zwieten, P. C. Goudswaard and C. K. Kapasa, "Mweru Luapula is an open exit fishery."

67. Comparisons are only possible between 1990 and 2000, since prior to that Chiengi was part of Nchelenge district. Chiengi's annual growth rate between 1990 and 2000 was 5.9 percent, the highest in all of Zambia's seventy-two districts, representing an absolute increase from 47,290 to 83,824 (36,534). Nchelenge's annual growth rate of 4.3 percent was sixth in terms of all Zambia's districts, but the increase in the total from 72,761 to 111,119 (38,358) exceeded even Chiengi. This does not include formal refugees from the DRC, but some of the increase might be accounted for by those who crossed the border and were able to pass as Zambians. Zambia, *2000 Census of Population and Housing* (Lusaka: Central Statistic Office, 2003).

Conclusion

1. De Soto, *The Mystery of Capital*.

2. Quoted in Thompson, *Customs in Common*, 168.

3. The tenuous hold of indirect rulers in Mweru-Luapula is further explored in Gordon, "Owners of the Land and Lunda Lords."

4. De Soto, *The Mystery of Capital*, 181–89.

5. Melissa Leach and James Fairhead, to name the most influential, suggest that the pristine forest environment of precolonial West Africa was a figment of colonial science's imagination. James Fairhead and Melissa Leach, *Misreading the African Landscape: Society and Ecology in a Forest-Savanna Mosaic* (Cambridge: Cambridge University Press, 1996).

GLOSSARY

The meanings and orthography of the following terms may differ across south central Africa. The glossary refers to usage in the Luapula Valley and, where appropriate, indicates the probable origin of the term. For nouns in different classes, I have indicated their most common usage, followed by their plural or singular.

Government, Politics, Religion, and Ethnicity

The glossary includes political titles and colonial chiefs most relevant to the history of the Luapula Valley. It should not be treated as a complete list.

abacanuma	Those who stand behind the king; members of the king's mother's clan.
abêna (sing. umwina)	The people of; precedes a clan or ethnic designation. Abêna Mbushi (the Goat Clan); Abêna Luapula (the people of Luapula).
akatongo (pl. ututongo)	Area "owned" by *umwine wa mpanga/kapanda.*
bamuchapi	Witch finding and purification movement (from Nyanja).
Bemba	The Bemba peoples (AbaBemba) or Bemba language (Chibemba).
boma	Administrative office in Northern Rhodesia and Zambia.
Bwilile	People without chiefs. Luapula autochthones.
Bwile	Ethnic designation of Luba settlers on northern Mweru. Perhaps related to Bwilile
Chitimukulu	Title for the paramount of the Bemba people and colonial chief.
chikolwe (pl. bachikolwe)	Lineage head.
chilolo (pl. bachilolo)	Hereditary eastern Lunda titleholder who governed an *iyanga* territory (Ruund, chilol).
ichikota (pl. ifikota)	Matrilineage.
ingulu	Nature spirit.

257

imfumu	Chief or ruler.
inshipo	Leather belt and Lunda insignia given by Goat Clan (Ruund, nshipw).
iyanga (pl. amayanga)	Portion of land given to aristocrat to rule as a colony.
Kalandala	Title for eastern Lunda aristocrat who ruled Chisenga Island.
Kambwali	Title for colonial chief drawn from royal family.
Kanyembo	Title for colonial chief drawn from royal family.
Kashiba	Title for eastern Lunda aristocrat and colonial chief.
Luba	Members of the Luba political confederation sharing institutions, narratives, and insignia of rule.
Lubunda	Title for Rat Clan owner of the land and colonial chief.
Lunda	Members of the Lunda political confederation sharing institutions, narratives, and insignia of rule.
Mulundu	Title for Rat Clan owner of the lagoon and colonial chief.
Mununga	Title for Shila owner of the land and colonial chief.
Mwaant Yaav	Title for paramount of central Lunda.
Mwadi	Principal wife of Mwata Kazembe.
Mwata Kazembe	Title for paramount of eastern Lunda and colonial chief.
Nachituti	Title for Nkuba's perpetual sister.
Nakafwaya	Title for eastern Lunda heroine.
Nkuba	Title for Shila ruler and owner of lagoon.
ntombo	Wife given to Mwata Kazembe by clan leaders or aristocrats (Ruund, ntombw).
Puta	Title for Bwile lord and colonial chief
Shila	Fisher. Became an ethnic designation with Lunda conquest.
ubutwa	Political association of the Shila.
ubuloshi	Witchcraft.
ukufungule sabi	Opening the fishery. Duty of the owner of the lagoon.
ulupwa	Bilateral family.
umukowa (pl. imikowa)	Matrilineal clan.
umupashi (pl. imipashi)	Ancestral spirit.
Umutomboko	Royal dance of conquest, celebrated yearly since 1961.

umwine (pl. abêne)	Owner; expresses identity with. Refers to natural resources like bush *(mpanga)*, lagoons *(kabanda)*, or titles and people, as in the owner of a chief *(imfumu)* or village *(mushi)*.

Fishing, Agriculture, and Entrepreneurship

abakalamba (sing. umukalamba)	Big men/women defined in terms of kin position and gerontocratic status.
abakankâla (sing. umukankâla)	Big men/women defined by wealth and generosity.
abanonshi (sing. umunonshi)	Individuals who seek wealth through commerce.
amalalika (sing. ilalika)	Nets left overnight.
amakonde (sing. ubukonde)	Gill nets.
amâmba (sing. ubwâmba)	Weirs.
amasumbu (sing. isumbu)	Gill nets.
chitemene	Slash and burn agriculture typical of plateau Bemba.
chipya	High grass and few trees typical of the Luapula Valley.
commerçant	European traders based in the Congo.
ifyombo (sing. ichombo)	Diesel-powered boats used to collect or catch fish.
imikwau (sing. umukwau)	Seine nets, set by canoe and dragged to shore.
imyôno (sing. umôno)	Traps, generally used with an *amâmba* weir.
intende	Basket used to catch fish by small-scale fishers.
japan	Net mounted on an outrigger.
Kombo	Secondhand clothing imported from the Congo.
leleke	Leaving nets overnight near large *ifyombo*.
miombo	Plateau vegetation. Savanna woodlands.
mputa	Mound agriculture.
mutobi	Scoop net often used for chisense.
nkongole	Credit.
Salaula	Secondhand clothing.
Scullion	Net used for chisense.
tute	Cassava.
ubwali	Thick polenta made out of maize or cassava.
ukutumpula	Driving fish into gill nets using sticks.
ukusenswa	Letting nets drift with the current.

BIBLIOGRAPHY

Books, Dissertations, and Articles

Aarnink, Nettie. "Socio-Political Struggles over Fish." In *Towards Negotiated Co-management of Natural Resources in Africa,* ed. Bernhard Venema and Hans van den Breemer, 275–304. Piscataway, N.J.: Transaction Publishers, 1999.

Acheson, James M. *The Lobster Gangs of Maine.* Hanover, N.H.: University Press of New England, 1988.

Akyeampong, Emmanuel. *Between the Sea and the Lagoon: An Eco-Social History of the Anlo of Southeastern Ghana.* Athens: Ohio University Press, 2001.

Allen, J. M. S., and C. K. Chileya. "'The Unbaptised': Farming in a Fishing Economy. A Case from the Mweru Lakeshore." Paper prepared for the European Congress of Sociology. 1–4 April, 1986.

Amselle, Jean-Loup. *Mestizo Logics: Anthropology of Identity in Africa and Elsewhere.* Palo Alto, Calif.: Stanford University Press, 1998.

Anderson, D., and R. Grove, eds. *Conservation in Africa: People, Policies, and Practices.* Cambridge: Cambridge University Press, 1987.

Arnot, Frederick Stanley. *Garanganze, or Seven Years' Pioneer Mission Work in Central Africa.* London: James E. Hawkins, 1890.

Baptista, P. J. *La Première Traversée du Katanga en 1806. Voyage des Pombeiros d'Angola aux Rios de Sena,* trans. and ann. A. Verbeken and M. Walraet, Brussels: Mem. Inst. Colonial Belge, 1953.

Bates, Robert. *Markets and States in Tropical Africa: The Political Basis of Agricultural Policies.* Berkeley: University of California Press, 1981.

———. *Rural Responses to Industrialization: A Study of Village Zambia.* New Haven, Conn.: Yale University Press, 1976.

Bay, Edna. *Wives of the Leopard: Gender, Politics, and Culture in the Kingdom of Dohomey.* Charlottesville: University Press of Virginia, 1998.

Bayart, Jean François. *The State in Africa: The Politics of the Belly.* London: Longman, 1993.

Beatty, D. M. F. "Cash Surpluses of Fishing Units on Lake Mweru, 1966." *Fisheries Research Bulletin* 5 (1971): 351–77.

———. *Results of a Fish Marketing Survey in Zambia, 1964–5.* Lusaka: Government Printers, 1969.

Becker, James M., Andrew M. Hamer, and Andrew R. Morrison. *Beyond Urban Bias in Africa: Urbanization in an Era of Structural Adjustment.* London: James Currey, 1994.

Beinart, William. "Introduction: The Politics of Colonial Conservation." *Journal of Southern African Studies* 2 (1989): 143–62.

———. "Soil Erosion, Animals, and Pasture over the Longer Term: Environmental Destruction in Southern Africa." In *The Lie of the Land: Challenging Received Wisdom on the African Environment,* ed. Melissa Leach and Robin Mearns, 74–72. Oxford: James Currey, 1996.

———. "Soil Erosion, Conservation and Ideas about Development: A South African Exploration." *Journal of Southern African Studies* 11 (1984): 52–83.

Beinart, William, and Colin Bundy. *Hidden Struggles in Rural South Africa.* Johannesburg: Ravan Press, 1987.

Béné, Christophe, Koané Midjimba, Emma Bilal, Thomas Jolley and Arthur Neiland. "Inland Fisheries, Tenure Systems, and Livelihood Diversification in Africa: The Case of the Yaéré Floodplains in Lake Chad Basin." *African Studies* 62.2 (2003): 187–212.

Berman, Bruce J., and John Lonsdale. *Unhappy Valley: Conflict in Kenya and Africa.* London: James Currey, 1992.

Berry, Sara. *Chiefs Know Their Boundaries: Essays on Property, Power, and the Past in Asante.* Portsmouth N.H.: Heinemann, 2001.

———. *No Condition Is Permanent: The Social Dynamics of Agrarian Change in Sub-Saharan Africa.* Madison: University of Wisconsin Press, 1993.

———. "Social Institutions and Access to Resources." *Africa* 59.1 (1989): 41–55.

Beveridge, Andrew A., and Anthony R. Oberschall. *African Businessmen and Development in Zambia.* Princeton, N.J.: Princeton University Press, 1970.

Birelle, Jean. "Common Rights in the Medieval Forest: Disputes and Conflicts in the Thirteenth Century." *Past and Present* 117 (1987): 22–49.

Bohannan, Paul. "Some Principles of Exchange and Investment among the Tiv." *American Anthropologist* 57.1 (1955): 60–70.

Bontinck, François, ed. *L'Autobiographie de Hamed ben Mohammed el-Murjebi Tippo Tip (ca. 1840–1905).* Brussels: Académie royale des sciences d'outre-mer, 1974.

Bozzoli, Belinda, ed., *Class, Community, and Conflict: South African Perspectives.* Johannesburg: Ravan Press, 1987.

Bratton, Michael. *The Local Politics of Rural Development: Peasant and Party-State in Zambia.* Hanover, N.H.: University Press of New England, 1980.

Brelsford, M. W. *Fishermen of the Bangweulu Swamps: A Study of the Fishing Activities of the Unga Tribe.* Lusaka: Rhodes-Livingstone Institute, 1946. Reprint, Manchester: Manchester University Press, 1972.

Brode, Heinrich. *Tippoo Tib: The Story of His Career in Central Africa.* Trans. H. Havelock. 1911. Reprint, Chicago: Afro-Am Press, 1969.

Bromley, Daniel and Michael Cernea, "The Management of Common Property Natural Resources: Some Operational Fallacies." World Bank Discussion Papers, no. 57 (Oct. 1989). World Bank.

Brox, Ottar. "Common Property Theory: Epistemological Status and Analytical Utility." *Human Organization* 49.3 (1990): 227–35.

Bundy, Colin. *The Rise and Fall of the South African Peasantry.* Berkeley: University of California Press, 1979.

Burton, R. F. *The Lands of Cazembe.* London: Royal Geographic Society, 1873.

Bustin, Edouard. *Lunda under Belgian Rule: The Politics of Ethnicity.* Cambridge, Mass.: Harvard University Press, 1975.

Callaghy, T. M. *The State-Society Struggle: Zaire in Comparative Perspective.* New York: Columbia University Press, 1984.

Campbell, Dugald. "A Few Notes on Butwa: An African Secret Society." *Man* 38 (1914): 76–81.

———. *In the Heart of Bantuland: A Record of Twenty-Nine Years' Pioneering in Central Africa.* 1922. Reprint, New York: Negro University Press, 1969.

Campbell, W. K. H. *Report on the Rural Economic Development.* Lusaka: Government Printers, 1961.

Cancel, Robert. *Allegorical Speculation in an Oral Society: The Tabwa Narrative.* Berkeley: University of California Press, 1989.

Chanock, Martin. *Law, Custom, and Social Order: The Colonial Experience in Zambia and Malawi.* Cambridge: Cambridge University Press, 1985.

Cheater, A. P. "The Zimbabwe Kapenta Fishery." In *Studies of the Fishery on Lake Kariba,* ed. M. F. C. Bourdillon, A. P. Cheater, and M. W. Mulphree, 96–132. Gweru: Mambo Press, 1985.

Chipungu, Samuel N., ed. *Guardians in Their Time: Experiences of Zambians under Colonial Rule, 1890–1964.* London: Macmillan, 1992.

Chiwale, Jacques Chileya. trans. and ann. *Royal Praises and Praise Names of the Lunda of Northern Rhodesia: Their Meaning and Historical Background.* Lusaka: Rhodes-Livingstone Institute, 1961.

Chiwele, Dennis K., Pumuo Muyatwa-Sipula, and Henrietta Kalinda. *Private Sector Responses to Agricultural Marketing Liberalisation in Zambia: A Case Study of Eastern Province Maize Markets.* Uppsala: Nordiska Afrikainstitutet, 1996.

Cligget, Lisa. "'Male Wealth' and 'Claims to Motherhood': Gendered Resource Access and Intergenerational Relations in the Gwembe Valley, Zambia." In *Gender at Work in Economic Life,* ed. Gracia Clark, 207–24. Walnut Creek, Calif.: AltaMira, 2003.

Coates, Peter. *Nature: Western Attitudes Since Ancient Times.* Cambridge: Polity Press, 1998.

Colson, Elizabeth. "The Impact of the Colonial Period on the Definition of Land Rights." In *Colonialism in Africa, 1870–1960,* vol. 3, ed. Victor Turner, 193–215. Cambridge: Cambridge University Press, 1971.

Comaroff, Jean and John Comaroff. *Of Revelation and Revolution: Vol. 1 Christianity, colonialism, and consciousness in South Africa.* Chicago: University of Chicago Press, 1991.

Cott, H. B. "The Status of the Nile Crocodile in Uganda." *The Uganda Journal* 18.1 (1954): 1–12.

Crawford, Dan. *Thinking Black: Twenty-Two Years without a Break in the Long Grass of Central Africa.* New York: George H. Doran Co., 1913.

Crehan, Kate. *The Fractured Community: Landscapes of Power and Order in Rural Zambia.* Berkeley: University of California, 1997.

Crehan, Kate and Achim Van Oppen, eds. *Planners and History: Negotiating Development in Rural Zambia.* Zambia: Multi-Media Publications, 1994.

Cronon, William. *Nature's Metropolis: Chicago and the Great West.* New York: W. W. Norton, 1991.

Cross, Sholto. "The Watch Tower Movement in South Central Africa, 1980–1945." D.Phil. thesis, Oxford University, 1973.

Cunnison, Ian. "The Death and Burial of Chief Kazembe XIV." *Northern Rhodesia Journal* 1 (1951): 46–51.

———. "History and Genealogies in a Conquest State." *American Anthropologist* 59 (1957): 20–31.

———. *History on the Luapula: An Essay in the Historical Notions of a Central African Tribe.* Rhodes-Livingstone Paper 21. Cape Town: Oxford University Press, 1951. Reprint, Manchester: Manchester University Press, 1969.

———. "The Installation of Chief Kazembe XV." *Northern Rhodesia Journal* 5 (1952): 3–10.

———. "Kazembe and the Arabs to 1870." In *The Zambesian Past: Studies in Central African History,* ed. E. Stokes and R. Brown, 226–37. Manchester: Manchester University Press, 1966.

———. "Kazembe and the Portuguese, 1798–1832." *Journal of African History* 2 (1961): 61–76.

———. *The Luapula Peoples of Northern Rhodesia: Custom and History in Tribal Politics.* Manchester: Manchester University Press, 1959.

———. "A Note on the Lunda Concept of Custom." *Rhodes-Livingstone Journal* 14 (1954): 20–29.

———. "Perpetual Kinship: A Political Institution of the Luapula Peoples." *Rhodes-Livingstone Journal* 20 (1955): 28–48.

———. "The Reigns of the Kazembes." *Northern Rhodesia Journal* 3 (1956): 131–38.

———. "A Watchtower Assembly in Central Africa." *International Review of Missions* 40.160 (1951): 456–69.

de Heusch, Luc. *Le Roi ivre ou l'origine de l'Etat.* Paris: Gallimard, 1972.

———. "The Symbolic Mechanisms of Sacred Kingship: Rediscovering Frazer." *The Journal of the Royal Anthropological Institute* 3.2 (1997): 213–32.

de Maret, Pierre. *Fouilles archéologiques dans la vallée du Haut-Lualaba.* Tevuren: Musée Royal, 1974.

———. "L'évolution monétaire du Shaba entre le 7è et le 18è siècles," *African Economic History* 10 (1981): 117–49.

de Soto, Hernando. *The Mystery of Capital: Why Capitalism Triumphs in the West and Fails Everywhere Else.* New York: Basic Books, 2000.

Delcommune, A. *L'avenir du Congo belge menacé.* Brussels: J. Lebègue, 1919.

Derricourt, Robin. *People of the Lakes: Archaeological Studies in Northern Zambia.* Zambian Papers no. 13. Manchester: Manchester University Press, 1980.

Dixon Fyle, M. "Agricultural Improvement and Political Protest on the Tonga Plateau, Northern Rhodesia." *Journal of African History* 18.4 (1977): 579–96.

Dodge, Doris Jansen. *Agricultural Policy and Performance in Zambia.* Berkeley: University of California Press, 1977.

Doucette, Joseph M. *The Clans of the Bemba and Some Neighbouring Tribes.* Ndola, Zambia: Mission Press, n.d.

Douglas, Mary. "Is Matriliny Doomed in Africa?" In *Man in Africa,* ed. Mary Douglas and Phyllis M. Kaberry, 121–35. London: Tavistock, 1969.

Epstein, A. L. "Divorce Law and Stability among the Lunda of Kazembe." *Rhodes-Livingstone Journal* 14 (1954): 1–19.

———. *Scenes from African Copperbelt Life: Collected Copperbelt Papers.* Edinburgh: Edinburgh University Press, 1992.

———. *Urbanization and Kinship: The Domestic Domain on the Copperbelt of Zambia, 1950–1956.* London: Academic Press, 1981.

Fairhead, James, and Melissa Leach. *Misreading the African Landscape: Society and Ecology in a Forest-Savanna Mosaic.* Cambridge: Cambridge University Press, 1996.

Feierman, Steven. *Peasant Intellectuals: Anthropology and History in Tanzania.* Madison: University of Wisconsin Press, 1990.

Ferguson, James. *Expectations of Modernity: Myths and Meanings of Urban Life on the Copperbelt.* Berkeley: University of California Press, 1999.

Fetter, Bruce. "African Associations in Elisabethville, 1910–1935: Origins and Development." *Études d'histoire Africaine* 6 (1974): 205–23.

———. *The Creation of Elisabethville.* Palo Alto, Calif.: Hoover Institution Press, 1976.

———. "The Union Minière and Its Hinterland: A Demographic Reconstruction." *African Economic History* 12 (1983): 67–77.

Fields, Karen. *Revival and Rebellion in Colonial Central Africa.* Princeton, N.J.: Princeton University Press, 1985.

Fryer, G. "Mwamfuli's Village: The New Fulcrum of the Bangweulu Fish Trade." *Northern Rhodesia Journal* 3.6 (1953): 483–88.

Gamitto, A. C. P. *King Kazembe and the Marave, Cheva, Bisa, Bemba, Lunda, and Other Peoples of Southern Africa, Being the Diary of the Portuguese Expedition to That Potentate in the Years 1831 and 1832.* 2 Vols. Trans. Ian Cunnison. Lisbon, Portugal: Junta de investigações do ultramar, 1960.

Gann, L. H. *A History of Northern Rhodesia: Early Days to 1953*. London: Chatto & Windus, 1964.

Geheb, Kim, and Marie Therese Sarch, eds. *Africa's Inland Fisheries: The Management Challenge*. Kampala-Uganda: Fountain Publishers, 2002.

Gérard-Libois, Jules. *Katanga Secession*. Madison: University of Wisconsin Press, 1966.

Gertzel, Cheryl, ed. *The Dynamics of the One-Party State in Zambia*. Manchester: Manchester University Press, 1984.

Geschiere, Peter. *The Modernity of Witchcraft: Politics and the Occult in Modern Africa*. Charlottesville: University Press of Virginia, 1997.

Geschiere, Peter and Francis Nyamnjoh."Witchcraft as an Issue in the 'Politics of Belonging': Democratization and Urban Migrants' Involvement with the Home Village."*African Studies Review* 41.3 (1998): 69–91.

Giblen, James. *The Politics of Environmental Control in Northeastern Tanzania, 1840–1940*. Philadelphia: University of Pennsylvania Press, 1992.

Gillis, John. "Memory and Identity: The History of a Relationship." In *Commemorations: The Politics of National Identity*, 3–24. Princeton: Princeton University Press, 1994.

Giraud, Victor. *Les lacs de l'afrique equatoriale, voyage d'expedition executé de 1883 à 1885*. Paris: Libraire Hachette, 1890.

Gluckman, Max. *Custom and Conflict in Africa*. Oxford: Oxford University Press, 1957.

———. *The Judicial Process among the Barotse of Northern Rhodesia*. Manchester: Manchester University Press, 1955.

Goldman, Michael. ed. *Privatizing Nature: Political Struggles and the Global Commons*. London: Pluto Press, 1998.

Goody, Jack. *Tradition, Technology, and the State in Africa*. London: Oxford University Press, 1971.

Gordon, David M. "The Cultural Politics of a Traditional Ceremony: Mutomboko and the Performance of History on the Luapula." *Comparative Studies in Society and History* 46.1 (January 2004): 63–83.

———. "Orality, Memory, and Historical Time on the Luapula (Zambia)." Paper presented at the Orality and Literacy 3: Memory Conference, Rice University, 10–12 October 2003.

———. "Owners of the Land and Lunda Lords: Colonial Chiefs in the Borderlands of Northern Rhodesia and the Belgian Congo." *International Journal of African Historical Studies* 34.2 (2001): 315–37.

Gordon, H. Scott. "The Economic Theory of a Common-Property Resource: The Fishery." *Journal of Political Economy* 62.2 (1954): 124–42.

Gould, David J. "Local Administration in Zaire and Underdevelopment." *Journal of Modern African Studies* 15 (1977): 370–90.

Gould, Jeremy. *Luapula: Dependence or Development?* Vammala, Finland: Finnish Society for Development Studies, Monograph 3, 1989.

Greene, Sandra. *Sacred Sites and the Colonial Encounter: A History of Meaning and Memory in Ghana*. Bloomington: Indiana University Press, 2002.

Grevisse, Fernand. *Le centre extra-coutumier d'Elisabethville*. Brussels: Institut Royal Colonie Belge, 1954.

Guyer, Jane. *Marginal Gains: Monetary Transactions in Atlantic Africa*. Chicago: University of Chicago Press, 2004.

———. "Wealth in People, Wealth in Things—Introduction." *Journal of African History* 36.1 (1995): 83–90.

Guyer, Jane, and Samuel M. Eno Belinga. "Wealth in People as Wealth in Knowledge: Accumulation and Composition in Equatorial Africa." *Journal of African History* 36.1 (1995): 91–120.

Haagerad, Angelique. *The Culture of Politics in Modern Kenya*. Cambridge: Cambridge University Press, 1995.

Hansen, Karen Tranberg. *Keeping House in Lusaka*. New York: Columbia University Press, 1997.

———. *Salaula: The World of Secondhand Clothing in Zambia*. Chicago: University of Chicago Press, 2000.

Hardin, Garret. "The Tragedy of the Commons." *Science* 162 (1968): 12433–38.

Harms, Robert. *Games Against Nature: An Eco-Cultural History of the Nunu of Equatorial Africa*. Cambridge: Cambridge University Press, 1987.

Harries, Patrick. *Work, Culture, and Identity: Migrant Laborers in Mozambique and South Africa, c. 1860–1910*. Portsmounth, N.H.: Heinemann, 1994.

Harries-Jones, Peter. *Freedom and Labour: Mobilization and Political Control on the Zambian Copperbelt*. Oxford: Backwell, 1975.

———. "'Home-Boy' Ties and Political Organization in a Copperbelt Township." In *Social Networks in Urban Situations*, ed. J. C. Mitchell, 297–347. Manchester: Manchester University Press, 1969.

Harrington, H. T. "The Taming of North-Eastern Rhodesia." *Northern Rhodesia Journal* 3.2 (1954): 3–20.

Henige, David P. "'The Disease of Writing': Ganda and Nyoro Loyalists in a Newly Literate World." In *The African Past Speaks: Essays on Oral Tradition and History*, ed. Joseph C. Miller, 240–61. Hamden, Conn.: Archon Books, 1980.

Herbert, Eugenia. *Red Gold of Africa: Copper in Pre-Colonial History and Culture*. Madison: University of Wisconsin Press, 1984.

Higginson, John. "Liberating the Captives: Independent Watchtower as an Avatar of Colonial Revolt in Southern Africa and Katanga, 1908–1941." *Journal of Social History* 26.1 (1992): 55–80.

———. *A Working Class in the Making: Belgian Colonial Labour Policy, Private Enterprise, and the Africa Mineworker, 1907–1951*. Madison: University of Wisconsin Press, 1989.

Hochschild, Adam. *King Leopold's Ghost: A Story of Greed, Terror, and Heroism in Colonial Africa*. New York: Mariner Books, 1999.

Hoffman, Richard. "Economic Development and Aquatic Ecosystems in Medieval Europe." *The American Historical Review* 101.3 (1996): 631–69.

Hoover, Jeffrey J. "The Seduction of Ruwej: Reconstructing Ruund History (The Nuclear Lunda: Zaire, Angola, Zambia)." Ph.D. dissertation, Yale University, 1978.

Howell, David. *Capitalism from Within: Economy, Society, and the State in a Japanese Fishery.* Berkeley: University of California Press, 1995.

Hoyle, R. W. "An Ancient and Laudable Custom: The Definition and Development of Tenant Right in North-Western England in the Sixteenth Century." *Past and Present* 116 (1987): 24–55.

Hyden, Goren. *Beyond Ujamaa in Tanzania.* Berkeley: University of California Press, 1980.

Iliffe, John. *The African Poor: A History.* Cambridge: Cambridge University Press, 1987.

———. *Africa: The History of a Continent.* Cambridge: Cambridge University Press, 1995.

Info-Zaire. *Zaire 1992–1996*, vols. 1 and 2. Paris: Karthala, 1996–97.

Jamal, Vali, and John Weeks. *Africa Misunderstood, or Whatever Happened to the Rural-Urban Gap?* London: Macmillan Press, 1993.

Jewsiewicki, Bogumil. *Modernisation ou destruction du village Africain: l'économie politique de la "modernisation agricole" au Congo belge.* Brussels: CEDAF, 1983.

———. "Unequal Development: Capitalism and the Katangan Economy, 1919–1940." In *The Roots of Rural Poverty in Central and Southern Africa*, ed. Robin Palmer and Neil Parsons, 317–42. Berkeley: University of California Press, 1977.

Johnstone, Frederick. *Class, Race and Gold: A Study of Class Relations and Racial Discrimination in South Africa.* Boston: Routledge and Kegan Paul, 1976.

Jul-Larsen, E., J. Kolding, R. Overå, J. R. Nielsen. eds. *Management, co-management or no management? Major dilemmas in southern African freshwater fisheries.* Rome: FAO Fisheries Technical Paper 426/1–2, 2003.

Jul-Larson, E., and P. van Zwieten. "African Freshwater Fisheries: What Needs to be Managed." *Naga, World Fish Quartely* 25.3–4 (2002): 35–40.

Kanondo, V. M. " Fisheries Statistical Systems in Zambia with Particular Reference to Lake Luapula-Mweru." In *Report on the Technical Consultation of Luapula-Mweru by Zaire and Zambia (Lusaka 08–10 August, 1990)*, ed. M. Maes. Bujumbura, Burundi: Project For Inland Fisheries Planning, United Nations Development Program / FAO, 1990.

Kaunda, Kenneth. *A Humanist in Africa.* London: Longman, 1966.

———. *Zambia Shall Be Free.* London: Heinemann, 1962.

Kay, George. *A Population Map of the Luapula-Bangweulu Region of Northern Rhodesia with Notes on the Population.* Lusaka: Rhodes-Livingstone Institute, 1962.

Kayumbe, Badye. "Capitalisme et destruction des sociétés lignagères dans l'ancien Territoire de Sakania au Zaire (1870–1940): Communautés rurales, main d'œuvre et 'accumulation primitive' du mode de production colonial." Thèse, UNILU, 1985–86.

Kitching, G. *Class and Economic Change in Kenya: The Making of an African Petite Bourgeoisie*. New Haven, Conn.: Yale University Press, 1980.

Kjekshus, Helge. *Ecology Control and Economic Development in East African History: The Case of Tanganyika, 1850–1950*. Berkeley: University of California Press, 1977.

Kurlansky, Mark. *Cod: A Biography of the Fish That Changed the World*. New York: Penguin, 1998.

Labrecque, Edouard. "Histoire des Mwata Kazembe." *Lovania* 16 (1949): 9–33

Lammond, Willie. "The Luapula Valley." *Northern Rhodesia Journal* 2.5 (1955): 50–55.

Landau, Paul "Hegemony and History in Jean and John L. Comaroff's *Revelation and Revolution*." *Africa* 70.3 (2000): 501–19.

Lawson, R. M., and E. Kwei, *African Entrepreneurship and Economic Growth: A Case Study of the Fishing Industry*. Accra: University of Ghana, 1974.

Legros, Hugues. "Aux racines de l'identité: memoire et espace chez les Yéke du Shaba, Zaire." *Journal des Africanistes* 65.2 (1995): 201–20.

———. *Chasseurs d'ivoire: Une histoire du royaume Yéke du Shaba (Zaire)*. Brussels: Editions de l'Université de Bruxelles, 1996.

Lemarchand, René. *Political Awakening in the Belgian Congo*. Berkeley: University of California Press, 1964.

Livingstone, David. *The Last Journals of David Livingstone*, ed. H. Waller, 2 Vols. London: John Murray, 1874.

Lombard, C. Stephen. *The Growth of the Co-operative Movement in Zambia, 1914–1971*. Manchester: Manchester University Press, 1971.

Lombard, C. Stephen, and A. H. C. Tweedie. *Agriculture in Zambia Since Independence*. Lusaka: Institute for African Studies, 1974.

MacGaffey, Janet. *Entrepreneurs and Parasites: The Struggle for Indigenous Capitalism in Zaire*. Cambridge: Cambridge University Press, 1987.

———, ed. *The Real Economy of Zaire: The Contribution of Smuggling and Other Unofficial Activities*. Philadelphia: University of Pennsylvania Press, 1991.

Macmillan, Hugh. "The Historiography of the Transition on the Zambian Copperbelt—Another View." *Journal of Southern African Studies*. 19.4 (1993): 681–712.

Macola, Giacomo. *The Kingdom of Kazembe: History and Politics in North-Eastern Zambia and Katanga to 1950*. Hamburg: LIT Verlag, 2002.

———. "Literate Ethnohistory in Colonial Zambia: The Case of *Ifikolwe Fyandi na Bantu Bandi*." *History in Africa* 28 (2001): 187–201.

Maddox, Gregory, James Giblin, and Isaria N. Kimambo. Ed. *Custodians of the Land: Ecology and Culture in the History of Tanzania*. London: James Currey, 1996.

Maes, M. ed. *Report on the Technical Consultation of Luapula-Mweru by Zaire and*

Zambia (Lusaka 08–10 August, 1990). Bujumbura, Burundi: Project For Inland Fisheries Planning, United Nations Development Program / FAO, 1990.

Maimbo, Fabian J. M., and James Fry. "An Investigation in the Terms of Trade between Rural and Urban Sectors of Zambia." *Africa Social Research* 12 (1971): 95–110.

Makasa, Kapasa. *Zambia's March to Political Freedom.* London: Heineman, 1985.

Malinowski, Bronislaw. *Crime and Custom in Savage Society.* London: Routledge, Kegan and Paul, 1926. Reprint, Paterson, N.J.: Littlefield, Adams and Co., 1962.

Maloka, Tshidiso, and David Gordon. "Chieftainship, Civil Society, and the Political Transitionin South Africa." *Critical Sociology* 22.3 (1996): 37–55.

Mamdani, Mahmood. *Citizen and Subject: Contemporary Africa and the Legacy of Late Colonialism.* Princeton, N.J.: Princeton University Press, 1996.

———. "Indirect Rule and the Struggle for Democracy: A Response to Bridget O'Laughlin." *African Affairs* 99 (2000): 43–46.

Matagne, F. "Premières notes au sujet de la migration des Pumbu." *Bulletin Agricole* 41 (1950): 793–894.

Mauss, Marcel. *The Gift: The Form and Reason for Exchange in Archaic Societies.* Trans. W. D. Hall. London: Routledge, 1990. Originally published as *Essai sur le don.* Press Universitaires de France, 1950.

Matongo, Albert B. K. "Popular Culture in a Colonial Society: Another Look at the *Mbeni* and *Kalela* Dances." In *Guardians in Their Time: Experiences of Zambians Under Colonial Rule, 1860–1964,* ed. Samuel N. Chipungu, 180–217. London: Macmillan, 1992.

Maxwell, Kevin B. *Bemba Myth and Ritual: The Impact of Literacy on an Oral Culture.* New York: Peter Lang, 1983.

McCay, Bonnie, and James Acheson. *The Question of the Commons: The Culture and Ecology of Communal Resources.* Tucson: University of Arizona Press, 1987.

McCracken, John. "Fishing and the Colonial Economy: The Case of Malawi." *Journal of African History* 28 (1987): 413–29.

McEvoy, Arthur F. *The Fisherman's Problem: Ecology and Law in the California Fisheries, 1850–1980.* Cambridge: Cambridge University Press, 1986.

Meebelo, Henry S. *African Proletarians and Colonial Capitalism: The Origins, Growth, and Struggles of the Zambian Labour Movement to 1964.* Lusaka: Kenneth Kaunda Foundation, 1986.

———. *Reactions to Colonialism: A Prelude to the Politics of Independence in Northern Zambia, 1893–1939.* Manchester: Manchester University Press, 1971.

Meillasoux, Claude. "From Production to Reproduction." *Economy and Society* 1 (1972): 93–105.

Miers, Suzanne and Ivan Kopytoff, eds. *Slavery in Africa.* Madison: University of Wisconsin Press, 1977.

Migdal, Joel. *Strong Societies and Weak States: State-Society Relations and State Capabilities in the Third World.* Princeton, N.J.: Princeton University Press, 1988.

Miller, Joseph. *Way of Death: Merchant Capital and the Angolan Slave Trade.* Madison: University of Wisconsin Press, 1988.

Miracle, Marvis. "African Markets and Trade on the Copperbelt." In *Markets in Africa,* ed. Paul Bohannan and George Dalton, 724–8. Evanston, Ill.: Northwestern University Press, 1962.

Mitchell, J. C. "The African Middle Class in British Central Africa." In *Development of a Middle Class in Tropical and Sub-Tropical Countries,* 222–33. Brussels: Incidi, 1956.

———. *African Urbanization in Ndola and Luanshya.* Lusaka: Rhodes-Livingstone Institute, 1954.

———. *The Kalela Dance.* Rhodes-Livingstone Paper no. 27. Manchester: Manchester University Press, 1956.

Moloney, James A. *With Captain Stairs to Katanga.* London: S. Low, Marston and Co., 1893.

Monga, Célestin. *The Anthropology of Anger: Civil Society and Democracy in Africa.* Boulder, Colo.: Lynne Reinner, 1996.

Moore, Barrington. *Social Origins of Dictatorship and Democracy: Lord and Peasant in the Making of a Modern World.* Boston: Beacon Press, 1967.

Moore, Henrietta L., and Megan Vaughan. *Cutting Down Trees: Gender, Nutrition, and Change in the Northern Province of Zambia, 1890–1990.* Portsmouth, N.H.: Heinemann, 1994.

Mottoulle, Léopold. *Politique sociale de l'UMHK pour sa main-d'œuvre indigène.* Brussels: Institut Royal Colonial Belge, 1946.

Mukanga, Makaya. *Ubupalu Bwe Sabi.* Ndola-Zambia: Mission Press, 1999.

Mukenge, Leonard. "Businessmen of Zaire: Limited Possibilities for Capital Accumulation." Ph.D. dissertation, McGill University, 1974.

Mukupo, Titus B., ed. *Kaunda's Guidelines.* Lusaka: TBM Enterprises, 1970.

Mulford, David C. *Zambia: The Politics of Independence, 1957–1964.* Oxford: Oxford University Press, 1967.

Munro, William. *The Moral Economy of the State: Conservation, Community Development, and State Making in Zimbabwe.* Athens: Ohio University Center for International Studies, 1998.

Musambachime, Mwelwa C. "The Agricultural History of the Mweru-Luapula Area to 1940." In *Zambian Land and Labour Studies,* vol. 3, ed. Robin Palmer, 1–27. Lusaka: National Archives, 1996.

———. "Changing Roles: The History of the Development and Disintegration of the Shila State to 1740." M.A. thesis, University of Wisconsin, 1976.

———. "Development and Growth of the Fishing Industry in Mweru-Luapula, 1920–1964." 2 Vols. Ph.D. dissertation, University of Wisconsin, 1981.

———. "The Fate of the Nile Crocodile in African Waterways." *African Affairs* 86 (1987): 197–207.

———. "The Impact of Rumour: The Case of the Banyama Scare in Northern

Rhodesia, 1930–1964." *The International Journal of African Historical Studies* 21 (1998): 201–15.

———. "Rural Political Protest: The 1953 Disturbances in Mweru-Luapula." *The International Journal of African Historical Studies* 20.3 (1987): 437–53.

———. "The Social and Economic Effects of Sleeping Sickness in Mweru-Luapula, 1906–1922." *African Economic History* 10 (1981): 151–73.

———. "The Ubutwa Society in Eastern Shaba and Northeast Zambia to 1920," *International Journal of African Historical Studies* 27.1 (1994): 77–99.

———. "Ubutwa: A Study of the Role and Function of a Secret Society in Eastern Zaire and North-East Zambia to the 1920s." Unpublished paper, [1991–93?].

Mutambwa, Mulumbwa, and Leon Verbeek. *Bulumbu: Un mouvement extatique au sud-est du Zaire à travers la chanson traditionelle.* Tervuren: Musée royal de l'afrique centrale, 1997.

Mwata Kazembe XIV Chinyanta Nankula. *Ifikolwe Fyandi na Bantu Bandi,* translated by Ian Cunnison as *Historical Traditions of the Eastern Lunda.* Lusaka: Rhodes-Livingstone Institute, 1961.

Neeson, J. M. *Commoners: Common Right, Enclosure, and Social Change in England, 1700–1820.* Cambridge: Cambridge University Press, 1993.

Ngula, E. S. "Problems of Fisheries Management in the Zambian Sector of Lake Mweru-Luapula." In *Report on the Technical Consultation of Luapula-Mweru by Zaire and Zambia (Lusaka 08–10 August, 1990),* ed. M. Maes. Bujumbura, Burundi: Project For Inland Fisheries Planning, United Nations Development Program / FAO, 1990.

Nyirenda A. A. "African Market Vendors." *Rhodes-Livingstone Journal* 22 (1957): 31–55.

Overå, Ragnhild. "Market Integration and Fishing Effort in Lake Kariba, Zambia." Unpublished seminar paper. Christian Michelsen Institute. Seminar, 21–22, 1999.

———. "Partners and Competitors: Gendered Entrepreneurship in Ghanaian Canoe Fisheries." Dissertation for Dr.Polit., University of Bergen, 1998.

Paine, Dennis. "Lake Mweru: Its Fish and Fishing Industry." *Northern Rhodesia Journal* 1.2 (1950): 7–13.

Palmer, Robin, and Neil Parsons, eds. *The Roots of Rural Poverty in Central and Southern Africa.* Berkeley: University of California Press, 1977.

Palmer, R. H., ed. *Zambian Land and Labour Studies,* vol. 3. Lusaka: National Archives Occasional Paper, no. 2, 1976.

Papstein, R. J. "From Ethnic Identity to Tribalism: The Upper Zambezi Region of Zambia, 1830–1981." In *The Creation of Tribalism in Southern Africa,* ed. Leroy Vail, 372–94. Berkeley: University of California Press, 1989.

Parpart, Jane L. *Labor and Capital on the African Copperbelt.* Philadelphia: Temple University Press, 1993.

———. "'Where Is Your Mother?': Gender, Urban Marriage, and Colonial

Discourse on the Zambian Copperbelt, 1924–1945." *International Journal of African Historical Studies* 27 (1994): 241–71.

———. "'Wicked Women' and 'Respectable Ladies': Reconfiguring Gender on the Zambian Copperbelt, 1936–1964." In *"Wicked" Women and the Reconfiguration of Gender in Africa*, ed. Dorothy L. Hodgson and Sheryl A. McCurdy, 274–92. Portsmouth, N.H.: Heinemann, 2001.

Peel, J. D. Y. "For Who Hath Despised the Day of Small Things? Missionary Narratives and Historical Anthropology." *Comparative Studies in Society and History* 37.3 (1995): 581–607

Perrings, Charles. *Black Mineworkers in Central Africa: Industrial Strategies and the Evolution of an African Proletariat in the Copperbelt, 1914–1941*. New York: Holmes and Meier, 1979.

Peters, D. U. "A Visit to Kilwa Island and the African Oil Palm." *Northern Rhodesia Journal* 2.1 (1954): 9–23.

Peters, Pauline. *Dividing the Commons: Politics, Policy, and Culture in Botswana*. Charlottesville: University Press of Virginia, 1994.

Phiri, Bizeck Jube. "Zambia: The Myth and Realities of 'One-Party' Participatory Democracy." *Genève-Afrique* 29.2 (1991): 10–24.

Phiri, Isaac. "Why African Churches Preach Politics: The Case of Zambia," *Journal of Church and State* 41.2 (1999): 323–47.

Piluka, Fr. Victor Digekisa. *Le massacre de Lubumbashi*. Paris: Karthala, 1993.

Platteau, Jean Philipe. "Small-Scale Fisheries and Evolutionist Theory." In *Fishing for Development: Small-Scale Fisheries in Africa*, ed. Inge Tvedten and Björn Hersoug, 90–104. Stockholm: Nordiska Afrikainstutet, 1992.

Poewe, Karla A. *Matrilineal Ideology: Male-Female Dynamics in Luapula, Zambia*. London: Academic Press, 1981.

———. "Regional and Village Economic Activities: Prosperity and Stagnation in Luapula, Zambia." *African Studies Review* 22.2 (1979): 77–93.

———. *Religion, Kinship, and Economy in Luapula, Zambia*. Lewinston, N.Y.: E. Mellen Press, 1989.

———. "Religion, Kinship, and Labor in Luapula: Prosperity and Economic Stagnation of Lake and River Fishing Communities." Ph.D. dissertation, University of New Mexico, 1976.

———. "Religion, Matriliny, and Change: Jehovah's Witness and Seventh-Day Adventist in Luapula, Zambia." *American Ethnologist* 5.2 (1978): 303–21.

Potts, Deborah. "Shall We Go Home? Increasing Urban Poverty in African Cities and the Migration Processes." *The Geographic Journal* 161.3 (1995): 245–64.

Prichett, James. *Lunda-Ndembu: Style, Change, and Social Transformation in South Central Africa*. Madison: University of Wisconsin Press, 2001.

Prins, Gwyn. *The Hidden Hippopotomus: Reapraisal in African History: The Early Colonial Experience in Western Zambia*. Cambridge: Cambridge University Press, 1980.

Quick, G. "Some Aspects of the African Watchtower Movement in Northern Rhodesia." *International Review of Missions* 24 (1940): 216–26.

Quick, Stephen A. "Bureaucracy and Rural Socialism in Zambia." *Journal of Modern African Studies* 15.3 (1977): 379–400.

Ranger, Terence. "The Invention of Tradition in Colonial Africa." In *The Invention of Tradition,* ed. Ranger and Hobsbawm, 211–62. Cambridge: Cambridge University Press, 1983.

———. *Voices from the Rocks: Nature, Culture, and History in the Motopos Hills of Zimbabwe.* Oxford: James Currey, 1999.

Reefe, Thomas Q. *The Rainbow and the Kings: A History of the Luba Empire to 1891.* Berkeley: University of California Press, 1981.

———. "The Societies of the Eastern Savanna." In *History of Central Africa,* vol. 1. ed. David Birmingham and Phyllis M. Martin, 160–204. London: Longman, 1983.

Reno, William. *State and Corruption in Sierra Leone.* Cambridge: Cambridge University Press, 1995.

Rettig, R. B., and J. C. Ginter, *Limited Entry as a Fishery Management Tool.* Seattle: University of Washington Press, 1978.

Richards, Audrey. *Land, Labour, and Diet in Northern Rhodesia: An Economic Study of the Bemba Tribe.* London: Oxford University Press, 1939.

———. "Un mouvement modern pour déceler les sorciers: les bamucapi." *Bulletin des Juridictions Indigène* 3 (1937): 82–90.

Roberts, Allen F. *Animals in African Art: From the Familiar to the Marvelous.* New York: Museum for African Art, 1995.

———. "Fishers of Men: Religion and Political Economy Among Colonised Tabwa." *Africa* 54.2 (1984): 49–70.

Roberts, Andrew. *A History of the Bemba: Political Growth and Change in North-East Zambia before 1900.* London: Longman, 1973.

———. *A History of Zambia.* New York: Africana Publishing Co., 1976.

———. "Migrations from the Congo." In *A Short History of Zambia,* ed. Brian Fagan, 101–120. Nairobi: Oxford University Press, 1966.

———. "Pre-Colonial Trade in Zambia." *African Social Research* 10 (1970): 715–46.

———. "Tippu Tip, Livingstone, and the Chronology of Kazembe." *Azania* 11 (1967): 115–31

Roberts, Mary Nooter, and Allen F. Roberts. *Memory: Luba Art and the Making of History.* New York: Museum for African Art, 1996.

Robinson, E. A. G. "The Economic Problem." In *Modern Industry and the African,* ed. Merle Davis, 136–74. London: Macmillan, 1967. First published 1933.

Rotberg, Robert I. *Christian Missions and the Creation of Northern Rhodesia.* Princeton: Princeton University Press, 1965.

———. "Plymouth Brethren and the Occupation of Katanga, 1886–1907." *Journal of African History* 2 (1964): 285–97.

———. *The Rise of Nationalism in Central Africa: The Making of Malawi and Zambia.* Cambridge, Mass.: Harvard University Press, 1972.

Ryckmans, Pierre. *Dominer pour servir.* Brussels: Editions Universelle, 1948.

Sacks, Karen. *Sisters and Wives: The Past and Future of Sexual Equality.* Westport, Conn.: Greenwood, 1979.

Scarrit, James R. "The Decline of Political Legitimacy in Zambia: An Explanation Based on Incomplete Data." *African Studies Review* 22.2 (1979): 13–38.

Schatzberg, Michael. *Politics and Class in Zaire.* New York: Africana Publishing Co., 1980.

Schecter, Robert E. "History and Historiography on a Frontier of Lunda Expansion: The Origins and Early Development of the Kanongesha." Ph.D. dissertation, University of Wisconsin, 1976.

Schoffeleers, J. M. *Rivers of Blood: The Genesis of a Martyr Cult in Southern Malawi.* Madison: University of Wisconsin Press, 1992.

Schoffeleers, J. M., ed. *Guardians of the Land: Essays on Central African Territorial Cults.* Gwelo: Mambo Press for the University of Salisbury, 1979.

Schumaker, Lyn. *Africanizing Anthropology: Fieldwork, Networks, and the Making of Cultural Knowledge in Central Africa.* Durham, N.C.: Duke University Press, 2001.

Schuster, Ilsa M. Glazer. *New Women of Lusaka.* Palo Alto, Calif.: Mayfield Publishing Co., 1979.

Schwank, E. "Behaviour and colour differences between *Oreochromis macrochir* and *O. mweruensis* (Teleostei: Cichlidae)." *Ichthyological Exploration in Freshwaters* 5.3 (1994): 267–80.

Scoones, Ian. "Range Management Science and Policy: Politics, Polemics, and Pasture in Southern Africa." In *The Lie of the Land: Challenging Received Wisdom on the African Environment,* ed. Melissa Leach and Robin Mearns, 34–53. Oxford: James Currey, 1996.

Scott, Ian. "Middle Class Politics in Zambia." *African Affairs* 77 (1978): 321–34.

Seleti, Yona Ngalaba. "Entrepreneurship in Colonial Zambia." In *Guardians in Their Time: Experiences of Zambians Under Colonial Rule, 1860–1964,* ed. Samuel N. Chipungu, 147–79. London: Macmillan, 1992.

Shapiro, David, and Eric Tollens. *The Agricultural Development of Zaire.* Aldershot, U.K.: Avebury, 1992.

Shaw, Rosalind. *Memories of the Slave Trade: Ritual and the Historical Imagination in Sierra Leone.* Chicago: University of Chicago Press, 2002.

Simmons, Randy T. and Peregrine Schwartz-Shea, "Method, Metaphor, and Understanding: When Is the Commons Not a Tragedy." In *The Political Economy of Customs and Culture: Informal Solutions to the Commons Problem,* ed. Terry L. Anderson and Randy T. Simmons, 1–11. Lanham, Md.: Rowman and Littlefield, 1993.

Skelton, Paul. *A Complete Guide to Freshwater Fishes of Southern Africa.* Halfway House: Southern Book Publishers, 1993.

Soulsby, J. J. "Some Congo Basin Fishes of Northern Rhodesia: Part 1." *Northern Rhodesia Journal* 4.3 (1960): 231–46.

———. "Some Congo Basin Fishes of Northern Rhodesia: Part 2." *Northern Rhodesia Journal* 4.4 (1960): 319–34.

Spear, Thomas. *Mountain Farmers: Moral Economics of Land and Agricultural Development in Arusha and Meru.* Berkeley: University of California Press, 1997.

Spring, Anita and Art Hansen. "The Underside of Development: Agricultural Development and Women in Zambia." *Agriculture and Human Values* 2.1 (1985): 60–67

Steinberg, Theodore. *Slide Mountain or the Folly of Owning Nature.* Berkeley: University of California Press, 1995.

Stengers, Jean. "Leopold II and the Association Internationale du Congo." In *Bismarck, Europe, and Africa: The Berlin Conference 1884–5 and the Onset of Partition,* ed. S. Förster, W. J. Mommsen, and R. Robinson, 229–46. London: Oxford University Press, 1988.

Terray, Emmanuel. "Classes and Class Consciousness in the Abron Kingdom of Gyaman." In *Marxist Analyses and Social Anthropology,* ed. Maurice Bloch, 85–136. London: Malaby Press, 1975.

Thompson, E. P. *Customs in Common.* New York: New Press, 1991.

Thornton, John. *Africa and Africans in the Making of the Atlantic World.* Cambridge: Cambridge University Press, 1992.

Tignor, Robert. *Capitalism and Nationalism at the End of Empire: State and Business in Decolonizing Egypt, Nigeria, and Kenya, 1945–1963.* Princeton, N.J.: Princeton University Press, 1998.

———. *The Colonial Transformation of Kenya.* Princeton, N.J.: Princeton University Press, 1976.

Tilsley, G. E. *Dan Crawford: Missionary and Pioneer in Central Africa.* London: Oliphants, 1929.

Tordoff, William, ed. *Politics in Zambia.* Manchester: Manchester University Press, 1974.

Trapido, Stanley. "South Africa in a Comparative Study of Industrialization." *Journal of Development Studies* 7 (1970–71): 309–20.

Trapnell, C. G. *The Soils, Vegetation, and Agriculture of North-Eastern Rhodesia: Report of the Ecological Survey.* Lusaka: Government Printer, 1953.

Tvedten, Inge. "'If You Don't Fish, You Are Not a Caprivian': Freshwater Fisheries in Caprivi, Namibia." *Journal of Southern African Studies* 28.2 (2002): 421–39.

Vail, Leroy. ed. *The Creation of Tribalism in Southern Africa.* Berkeley: University of California Press, 1989.

Van Bilsen, A. A. J. *Un plan de trente ans pour l'émancipation de l'Afrique belge.* Brussels: 1956.

Van Oppen, Achim. *Terms of Trade and Terms of Trust: The History and Context of*

Pre-colonial Market Production around the Upper Zambezi and Kasai. Münster : LIT Verlag, 1993.

Van Sittert, Lance. "'To Live This Poor Life': Remembering the Hottentots Huisie Squatter Fishery, Cape Town, c. 1934–1965." *Social History* 26.1 (2001): 1–21.

Van Zwieten, P. A. M., P. C. Goudswaard and C. K. Kapasa. "Mweru Luapula is an open exit fishery where a highly dynamic population of fishermen makes use of a resilient resource base." In *Management, co-management or no management? Major dilemmas in southern African freshwater fisheries*, eds. E. Jul Larsen, J. Kolding, R. Overa, J. R. Nielsen, 1–33. FAO: Rome, 2003.

Vansina, Jan. "Histoire du Manioc en Afrique Centrale avant 1850." *Paideuma* 43 (1997): 255–79.

———. *Kingdoms of the Savanna: A History of Central African States until European Occupation*. Madison: University of Wisconsin Press, 1968.

———. *Oral Tradition: A Study in Historical Methodology*. Trans. by H. M. Wright. London: Routledge and Kegan Paul, 1965.

———. "Traditions of Genesis." *Journal of African History* 15.2 (1974): 317–22.

Vellut, Jean-Luc. *Les bassins miniers de l'ancien Congo belge: essai d'histoire économique et sociale*. Brussels: CEDAF, 1981.

Verbeek, Leon. *Filiation et usurpation: histoire socio-politique de la region entre Luapula et Copperbelt*. Tervuren: Musée royal de l'afrique centrale, 1987.

———. *Initiation et mariage dans la chanson populaire des bemba du Zaire*. Tervuren: Musée royal de l'afrique centrale, 1993.

———. *Le monde des esprits au sud-est du Shaba et au nord de la Zambie*. Rome: Libreria Ateneo Salesiano, 1990.

———. *L'histoire dans les chants et les danses populaire: la zone culturelle Bemba du Haut-Shaba (Zaire)*. Louvain-la-Neuve: Centre d'histoire de l'Afrique, 1992.

———. *Mythe et culte de Kipimpi*. Bandundu, Zaire: CEEBA, 1982.

Verbeken, Auguste. *Msiri: Roi du Garanganze*. Brussels: Louis Cypers, 1956.

Vercruijsse, E. *The Penetration of Capitalism*. London: Zed Books, 1984.

Weiss, Herbert. *Political Protest in the Congo: The Parti Solidaire Africain During the Independence Struggle*. Princeton, N.J.: Princeton University Press, 1967.

Werbner, Richard, ed. *Memory and the Postcolony: African Anthropology and the Critique of Power*. New York: Zed Books, 1998.

White Fathers, Zambia. *The White Fathers' Bemba-English Dictionary*. Ndola: The Society of the Missionary for Africa, 1954. Reprint, 1991.

White, Luise. *Speaking with the Vampires: Rumor and History in Colonial Africa*. Berkeley: University of California Press, 2000.

Willame, Jean-Claude. *Patrimonialism and Political Change in the Congo*. Palo Alto, Calif.: Stanford University Press, 1972.

———. *L'automne d'un despotisme: Pouvoir, argent, et obéissance dans la Zaire des années quatre-vingt*. Paris: Karthala, 1992.

———, ed. *Zaïre, années 90: Vers la Troisième République*. Brussels: CEDAF, 1991.

Wilson, Godfrey. *An Essay on the Economics of Detribalization in Northern Rhodesia.* Parts 1 and 2. Livingstone: Rhodes-Livingstone Institute, 1941, 1942.

Wilson, James A. "The Economic Management of Multispecies Fisheries." *Land Economics* 58.4 (1982): 417–34.

Wolpe, Harold, ed. *The Articulation of Modes of Production*. London: Routledge and Kegan Paul, 1980.

Wright, Marcia, ed. *Strategies of Slaves and Women: Lifestories from East/Central Africa*. London: James Currey, 1993.

Yamba, Dauti L. "Genesis of the Struggle for Independence in Zambia." Contribution to the Symposium on Zambian Independence, Mulungushi Hall, 1971.

Young, Crawford M. *The Colonial State in Comparative Perspective*. New Haven, Conn.: Yale University Press, 1995.

———. *Politics in the Congo: Decolonization and Independence*. Princeton, N.J.: Princeton University Press, 1965.

———. "The Shattered Illusion of the Integral State." *Journal of Modern African Studies* 32.2 (1994): 247–65.

Young, Crawford M., and Thomas Turner. *The Rise and Decline of the Zairian State*. Madison: University of Wisconsin Press, 1985.

Young C. E. "Rural-Urban Terms of Trade." *Africa Social Research* 12 (1971): 91–94.

Zambia. *1980 Census of Population and Housing*. Lusaka: Central Statistics Office, 1981.

Zambia. *1990 Census of Population and Housing*. Lusaka: Central Statistics Office, 1993.

Zambia. *2000 Census of Population and Housing*. Lusaka: Central Statistics Office, 2003.

Zambia. DoF. *A Scientific Classification with English and Zambian Language Classification of Zambian Fish Species*. Lusaka: Government Printers, 1977.

Archival Documentation

Detailed archival citations are found in the endnotes. Below are abbreviated lists of the files.

I. ZAMBIA

National Archives of Zambia (NAZ), Lusaka
District Notebooks

KDF 3/1 Fort Rosebery District Notebooks.
KSG 3/1 Kawambwa District Notebooks.
KSW 2/1 Chiengi District Notebook.

Native Secretariat

SEC 1/ to SEC 6/ Northern Rhodesian Native Secretariat documents dealing
with Luapula and Northern Province.

Northern/Luapula Province

NP 2/1/ to NP 2/7/ Native Authority Tour Reports and Minutes.

Ministry of Lands and Natural Resources

ML 1/4/ to ML 1/19/ Ministry of Land and Natural Resources Reports on
Fisheries, 1964 to 1970.

Ministry of Foreign Affairs

FA 1/1/ Ministry of Foreign Affairs documentation about relations with the
Congo.

Ministry of Local Government and Housing

LGH 1/1 to LGH 9/3 Ministry of Local Government Reports, 1964 to
1970.

Ministry of Rural Development

MRD 1/8/24 Luapula Province Development Committees, 1968–69.

Ministry of Agriculture

MAG 1/2/6 Minutes of the Luapula Provincial Team, 1958–63.

MAG 1/2/31 Luapula Provincial Development Committee, 1964–65.

Native Affairs

NR 17/42 Marketing-Fish, 1948–1954.

NR 17/48 Pilot Fish Marketing Project, 1958.

Miscellaneous

Box 34A   Zambia Central Statistical Office, Census of Africans, Kawambwa
District. Lusaka: Government Printers, 1980.

Box 41   Central Statistical Office, Fisheries Statistics, 1965–70.

Box 65   Campbell, W. H., "Report on the Co-op Movements in Northern
Rhodesia," n.d. (1955–61?).

Box 76A   Northern Rhodesia *Report of Fisheries Advisory Committee on Fish of
Northern Rhodesia*. Lusaka, 1951.

Northern Rhodesia, Dept. of Game and Tsetse Control, Fisheries
Annual Reports, Lusaka, 1952–58.

Box 76C   Northern Rhodesia Ministry of Native Affairs: Game and
Fisheries, *Annual Reports*, Lusaka, 1959–63.

Box 95A   Zambia. Ministry of Local Government, *Annual Reports*, 1963–65.

Zambia. *Report of the Committee on Local Administration*, 1987.

Assorted documents on the local government of Northern
Rhodesia

Box 95D   Zambia. *Report on the Working Party Appointed to Review the System of
Decentralized Administration*. Lusaka, 1972.

Box 165   Ministry of Agriculture and Water Development: *Fisheries Annual
Reports*, 1980–81. Lusaka, 1980–82.

University of Zambia (UNZA), Special Collections, Lusaka

Cross, Sholto. "Jehovah's Witness and Socio-Economic Change in Luapula Province," Political Science Workshop, University of Zambia, n.d.

Hall, D. "Notes on the Positions of Chiefs in Northern Rhodesian Administration," [1958?].

Musambachime, Mwelwa C. Transcripts of Mweru-Luapula Interviews.

Mwandela, W. R. *An Outline of Local Government in Zambia.* Lusaka, 1966.

Northern Rhodesia. *Department of Community Development Conference.* Lusaka, 1963.

Northern Rhodesia. Department of Game and Tsestse, *Annual Reports.* Lusaka, 1943–50.

Northern Rhodesia. Joint Fisheries Research Organization, *Annual Reports.* Lusaka, 1950–55.

Northern Rhodesia. *Report on the Intensive Rural Development in the Northern and Luapula Provinces of Northern Rhodesia.* Lusaka, [1962?].

Thomson, H. H. "Memorandum on the Policy and Structure of Local Government in the Rural Areas of Northern Rhodesia." [1960?].

UNIP. *A UNIP Manual of Rules and Regulations Governing the 1973 Election.* Lusaka, 1973.

UNIP. *National Council Resolutions on Agricultural Policy.* Lusaka, 1990.

Zambia. *An Introduction to the Civil Service.* Lusaka, 1967.

Zambia. *Back to the Land through Rural Reconstruction Centres.* Lusaka, 1977.

Zambia. *Decentralization: A Guide to Integrated Local Administration.* Lusaka, 1981.

Zambia. *Decentralized Government: Proposals for Integrated Local Government Administration.* Lusaka, 1979.

Zambia. Dept. of Wildlife, Fisheries, and National Parks, *Annual Report, 1970.*

Zambia. *District Councils Revenue and Capital Estimates.* Lusaka, 1985.

Zambia. *Report on Functions of Rural Local Authorities and on Financial Relationship between Central Government and Rural Local Authorities.* Lusaka, 1966.

Zambia. *Village Productivity and Ward Development Committees.* Lusaka, 1971.

University of Zambia, Institute for Social and Economic Research, Lusaka

Ministry of Natural Resources and Tourism. *Fisheries Reports,* 1968–74.

Ministry of Lands, Natural Resources and Tourism. *Fisheries Annual Report,* 1975.

DoF. *Fisheries Statistics,* 1955–66.

DoF. *A Scientific Classification with English and Zambian Language Classification of Zambian Fish Species.* Extract from Annual Report, 1971. Lusaka, 1972.

Department of Fisheries (DoF), Chilanga

DoF. *Annual Reports,* 1964–71, 1990–97.

Luapula Monthly and Annual Reports, 1976–80.

Luapula Monthly and Annual Reports, 1981–94.
Mweru-Luapula Fishery Statistics Correspondence File, 1968–98.

Department of Fisheries (DoF), Nchelenge: Assorted Documents and Reports

Aarnink, B.H.M. "Fish and Cassava Are Equally Important in Livelihood Strategies of Women of Mweru-Luapula Fishery." Report no. 40, 1996.

Aarnink, B. H. M. "The Fish Trade and Tax Base of Lake Mweru." Report no. 36, 1996.

Aarnink B. H. M., C. K. Kapasa, and P. A. M. van Zwieten. "'Our Children Will Suffer': Present Status and Problems of Mweru-Luapula Fisheries and the Need for a Conservation and Management Action Plan." Prepared for UNDP/FAO Regional Project, 1993.

Kanema, R. H. "'Farming in a Fishing Economy': Literature Review of Agriculture in Nchelenge District, Luapula Province." SNV-Netherlands, 1995.

Lake Mweru Fishing Association: Chipungu Ward Constitution, 1990.

Machisa, E. G. Frame Survey at Luapula-Mweru, 1971–72.

Oudwater, N. "Eating with the Chiefs: A Study of the Present Management of the Mweru-Luapula Fishery." Report no. 4, 1997.

Report on Discussions between DoF and Fishing Community on Draft Fisheries Act, n.d.

Report on Seminar with Chiefs and Fishing Associations on Draft Fisheries Act, 26 Nov. 1997.

Report on the Fish Conservation Seminar for Mweru-Luapula Fishers and Traditional Chiefs, 30 Dec. 1992.

Report on the Technical Consultation on Mweru-Luapula shared by Zaire and Zambia, Lusaka, 8–10 Sept. 1990.

Report on Zambia/Zaire Joint Meeting on Mweru-Luapula Fisheries held on 22 July 1996 in Nchelenge.

Research Division. *Annual Reports,* 1983, 1985.

Van der Aalst. "Knowledge, Attitudes, and Practices of Fishermen and Other Community Members on Conservation and Management of the Fish Resource." Report no. 44, 1997.

Van Zwieten, P. A. M., B. H. M. Aarnink, C. K. Kapasa, and P. Ngalande. "The Biology, Fishery, and Trade of Chisense from Mweru-Luapula: Status of Present Knowledge." Report no. 31, 1996.

Van Zwieten, P. A. M and C. K. Kapasa . "Lake Mweru-Luapula: Analysis of the Gillnet Surveys of 1982 to 1985 and 1994 to 1996." Report no. 37, 1996.

Van Zwieten, P. A. M, B. H. M. Aarnink, and C. K. Kapasa. "How Diverse a Fishery Can Be! Structure of the Mweru-Luapula Fishery Based on the Frame Survey 1992 and a Characterization of the Present Management Strategies." Report no. 25, 1996.

District Council Files
Nchelenge
LP 101/1/4. Chiefs and Headmen.
NDC 101/1/11. Chiefs and Retainers.
NDC 101/3/15. Market Advisory Committee.
NFCC 3/14/2. Nchelenge Fisheries Coordinating Committee.
Mwense
CONF/1/9/1–5. Records of Chief Kashiba, Lubunda, Lukwesa, and Mulundu.
Kawambwa
AFN/6/1. African Administration: Chiefs and Headmen.
AFN/66A-1. Chiefs-General.
CAB/52/3/5. Snr. Chief Mwata Kazembe.
FISH/4/1. Fish Industry: Lake Mweru.
TNG/4/1. Fisheries.

Zambia Consolidated Copper Mines (ZCCM) Archives, Ndola
10. to 18. Files from Mufulira.

Zambia National Broadcasting Corporation (ZNBC), Lusaka: Songs
Augustine Mukoyo. *Waapilwe Nacimakobo*. ZHS 142, n.d.
Bartolomeo Bwalya. *BaKanyembo Balifwa*. ZHS 180, n.d.
Bartolomeo Bwalya. *Kwa Mununga*. ZHS 618, n.d.
Bartolomeo Bwalya. *Nshakasendama mwa Lukwesa*. ZHS 52, Mufulira, 1952.
Frank Shitima. *Ku Mwansambombwe*. ZHS 976, Kazembe, 1956.
Isaac Mapiki. *Kazembe*. ZHS 618, 1961.
Ituna School Choir. *Kwa Mpweto*. ZHS 931, 1956.
James and Caleb Siame. *Abanakashi ni Nkaka*. ZHS 1790, Lusaka, 1955.
Kalembeleka's Choir. *We Cinjelengwe*. ZHS 1631, Lusaka, 1952.
Kantachenga's Choir. *Lekeni Nkafwe*. ZHS 1629, 1957.
Kazembe Native Authority Choir. *Pale*. ZHS 1616, Mbereshi, 1952.
Lunzuwa School Choir. *Mucaka ca 1934*. ZHS 1730, 1952.
Luwingu Girls' Choir. *Mwelu, Mwelu*. ZHS 974, 1956.
Mambilima Choir. *Kampombwe Nacila*. ZHS 1533, 1957.
Mpunga Mwela Radio Band, *Ubuloshi mu Nchelenge*. n.d.
Mulenga's Choir. *We Cinjelengwe*. ZHS 976, Kazembe. 1956.
Mulundu Brothers. *Imfumu Shesu Shonse*. ZHS 8, n.d.
Musonda. *Mwelu*. ZHS 40, 1970.
Mwansabombwe Choir. *Belenga*. ZHS 1432, 1967.
Mwansabombwe Choir. *Ifwe Ku Mwesu*. ZHS 1431, Lusaka, 1967.
Mwelu Radio Band. *Ubuloshi mu Nchelenge*, n.d., Tape ZHS 165, n.d.
Nshanyembu Primary School. *Bakazembe*. ZHS 175, n.d.

Thomas Maluma. *Bwela ku Mwansabombwe.* ZHS1706, Lusaka, 1950.
Thomas Muloma's Trio. *Mwebeloshe* Mfumu. ZHS 1678, Lusaka, 1961.
William Yakutumana. *Maggie Tuleya.* ZHS 1372, Lusaka, 1968.

White Fathers' Archives (WFA), Lusaka

Edouard Labrecque. "Abashila ne misango yabo ya kwipaila isabi," manuscript
written with Shila Elders, 1947–49, 1-M-OT-34 Shila.

Chibwalwe Papers, Kashiba, Zambia.

Documents relating to Mutomboko Ceremony and Kashiba's Chieftaincy.

Robert Cancel, University of San Diego, Calif.

Interview with Anna Chilombo, Kabwe, 1994.

Mambilima Mission, Zambia

Lammond, Willie. "Outline History of Johnston Falls Mission Mostly from
Memory."

Newspapers

African Eagle, 1953–62.
Enterprise: Indeco Journal, 1969–91.
The Post.
The Times of Zambia.
The Daily Mail.

2. UNITED KINGDOM

Public Record Office (PRO)

Colonial Office: CO 670 to CO 1015 Northern Rhodesian Documentation to
1960.

Rhodes House Library, Oxford University

Mabel Shaw Papers, MSS.AFR.S.1502.

3. DEMOCRATIC REPUBLIC OF THE CONGO (DRC)

Archives in Katanga at the regional and provincial level were destroyed in the
late 1980s and early 1990s. Archives at the sub-regional and district or zone and
territoire level were looted during the year 1996–97. Fortunately, valuable documentation could be found at the *Archives Africaines* in Belgium. Mémoires written by students at the Université de Lubumbashi (UNILU) during the 1980s
were also helpful. These mémoires can be found in the respective departments
at the UNILU. Government departments permitted me to view the documents
that remain in their files.

Mémoires, UNILU

Bilonda, Lwamba. "Pour une histoire sociale du Haut Shaba: Le Fonds d'archives du Rassorts Administratif de Kambove." Mémoire, UNILU, 1974.

Cembe, Mbolyo. "La production et commercialisation du poisson au Luapula-Moëro, 1920–59." Mémoire, UNILU, 1986.

Egala, Lissanga. "L'impact du MPR sur l'administration publique Zairoise." Mémoire, UNILU, 1975.

Ka'mpeng, Kabundi-Mpenga. "La problématique du développement rural au Zaire: Réflexion sur les conditions de vie des masses rurales dans la zone de Kasenga." Mémoire, UNILU, 1975–76.

Kapambu-Kabaswa-Kutuswa, Kadiebwe. "Monographie socio-économique du Territoire de Kasenga, 1933–1958." Mémoire, UNILU, 1976–77.

Mankunga Waba Sebent, Kalungwe. "Les Babwile du lac Moëro: Essai d'histoire politique precolonial." Mémoire, UNILU, 1973–74.

Mulamba, Kitoto. "Histoire de la population du Territoire de Kasenga, 1939–1958." Mémoire, UNILU, 1984–85.

Mutombo, Ilunga Saloum-Ya. "Politique colonial et commerce au Katanga (1940–1959)." Mémoire, UNILU, 1980.

Mwindi, Kalombo. "Histoire politico-administratif du Territoire de Sakania, 1940–1960." Mémoire, UNILU, 1979.

Mwitwa pa Kakola, Katanti. "Pweto et Lukanzolwa: Premières capitales du Katanga." Mémoire, UNILU, 1976–77.

Nyembo wa Kalombo Mutaka, Leyka Moussa. "Les frontières africaines: source d'instabilité politique: Essai d'analyse anthropologie sur les peuples Bemba du Zaire et de la Zambie." Mémoire, UNILU, 1985.

Nzuzi wasala ha Kanda. "La politique et la chanson, Congo, 1959–65." Mémoire, UNILU, 1982.

Pelenge, Kwete, "Système de ravitaillements en produits vivriers et amélioration des conditions de vie des travailleurs (cas de la Gécamines)." Mémoire, UNILU, 1988.

Wembolua-Olenya-Kadima. "Organisation et fonctionnement de Conseil de Province du Katanga, 1945–1960." Mémoire, UNILU, 1976.

Service de l'environnement et conservation: Section pêche, Lubumbashi

Rapport de la mission de programmation FAO vol. 2, Annexe 2, Les Pêcheurs du Zaire.

Statistics on Luapula-Mweru prepared by coordinateur provinciale de pêche.

Service de l'environnement et conservation: Section pêche, Kipushi

Assorted Files and Documents.

4. BELGIUM

Archives Africaines (AA), Brussels
Affaires Étrangères

AE/I 271/332 Rapport sur la Marche du Parquet Lukafu, n.d. Rapport Jennigè sur influence anglaise dans le Katanga, 1904. Affaire Rabinek.

AE/I 272/332 Incidents à la frontière du côté des lacs, 1900–1908.

AE/I 273/334 Incidents à la frontière Katanga-Rhodésie, 1908–12.

AE/I 274/336 Travaux de la commission mixte de délimitation Katanga-Rhod ésie, 1911–14.

AE/II 2909/347 Collaboration Anglo-Belge, 1947–52.

AE/II 2962–65/852–57 Délimitation Katanga-Rhodésie, 1921–25.

AE/II 2965/853 Affaire Rabinek, 1902–3, 1910.

AE/II 2967/863 Incidents divers de frontière avec la Grande Bretagne, 1919–33.

Affaires Indigènes et Main d'Oeuvre

AIMO 1697 to AIMO 1737 Haut-Luapula and Katanga AIMO Reports.

RA/AIMO 86 to RA/AIMO 165 Luapula and Katanga AIMO Reports.

Cartographie

CART 2071/343–51 Mission de délimitation Moëro-Tanganyika.

CART 2072/349 Mweru-Tanganyika Survey, 1918.

Fonds du Bien-Être Indigène

FBEI 1/ to FBEI 42/ Luapula and Katanga FBEI Documentation.

Inventaire Provisoire Archives Venant du Congo belge (IPAC)

Documents of *Fonds du Gouverneur Général de Léopoldville* ordered according to the provisional inventory detailed below.

IPAC Boîte 9.590 Rapport d'Inspection: Territoire de Kasenga, 1939.

IPAC Boîte 10.751 Rapports d'Inspection: Territoire de Pweto, 1950, 1953–55.

IPAC Boîte 10.881 Rapports d'Inspection: Territoire de Kasenga, 1956–59.

IPAC Boîte 12.764 Monographies Agricoles des Chefferies, District du Haut-Luapula.

IPAC Boîte 13.013 Rapport Aron Ngwashi, 1953.

IPAC Boîte 13.039 Pêche—Territoire Kasenga, Pweto, 1948–58.

IPAC Boîte 13.042 Pisciculture Katanga, 1944–57.

IPAC Boîte 13.043 Rapports mensuels: agents de pêche, Haut-Katanga, 1957.

IPAC Boîte 13.047 Pêche—Elisabethville, 1946–56.

IPAC Boîte 13.283 Rapport d'inspection: Territoire de Pweto, 1959.

IPAC Boîte 13.348 UMHK List des chefferies, 1957.

IPAC Boîte 13.447 Policiers chefferies.

IPAC Boîte 13.477 Chefferies divers, 1936–57.

IPAC Boîte 13.579 Rapport d'inspection: Territoires Pweto, Kasenga, 1956–57.

IPAC Boîte 14.160 Chefferies Luapula-Moëro, Dossiers: Kasenga, Pweto.

IPAC Boîte 14.205 Mission piscicole, Elisabethville, divers.

IPAC Boîte 14.210 Mission piscicole Elisabethville: divers, 1945–48.

IPAC Boîte 14.211 Mission piscicole Elisabethville: divers.

IPAC Boîte 14.219 Mission piscicole: documentation, photos.

IPAC Boîte 14.220 Mission piscicole: protection pêche, 1935–45.

IPAC Boîte 14.221 Mission piscicole: divers, 1947.

IPAC Boîte 14.222 Mission piscicole: étude—évolution législation pêche, 1947–51.

IPAC Boîte 14.223 Mission piscicole: divers, 1946–50.

IPAC Boîte 14.224 Mission piscicole: difficultés de ravitaillement, 1949.

IPAC Boîte 14.225 Mission piscicole: migration des Pumbu (Kapata), 1949.

IPAC Boîte 14.228 Mission piscicole: divers, 1946–48.

IPAC Boîte AGRI75 Mission piscicole, 1946–51.

IPAC Boîte AGRI51 Mission piscicole, 1947–55.

IPAC Boîte RA/AGRI Rapports annuels: Service de l'agriculture, 1952–58.

Bibliothèque Africaine (BA), Brussels

Congo belge. *Bulletin administratif.* Bruxelles, 1930–59.

Congo belge, *Bulletin des juridictions indigènes et droit coutumier congolais,* Elisabethville, 1933–63.

Congo belge. *Bulletin des juridictions tribunaux.* Bruxelles, 1933–59.

Congo belge, Katanga. *Conseil de Province.* Bruxelles, 1949–59.

Congo belge, Katanga. *Rapport annuel des AIMO.* Elisabethville, 1950–59.

Congo belge, Katanga. *Service de l'agriculture.* Elisabethville, 1950–59.

Congo (Dem. Rep.). *Revue juridique du Congo.* Leopoldville, 1960–64.

5. INTERVIEWS

Interviews are listed according to location and then alphabetically. Where the individual has both name and a title, I have indicated the name followed by the title in brackets (except if the individual requested only to be referred to by his or her title). Transcripts are in the author's possession.

Zambia
Nchelenge and northern Mweru fishing camps

Chansa, Mika. Kashikishi, 23 July 1998, trans. Topsy Mwewa.

Chasekwa, Lista Kanokelya (Bana Kasali). Sindone, 24 July 1998, trans. Topsy Mwewa.

Chilufya, Holis. Kafulwe, 26 July 1998, trans. Abraham Musonda.

Chisakula, Celestine (Bana Chisakula). Kashikishi, 24 July 1998, trans. Topsy Mwewa.

Chisakula, Paul Kapasa. Kashikishi, 21 Oct. 1997.

Chiwale, Augustus. Kashikishi, 13 Jan. 1998.

Chungu, Elizabeth. Kashikishi, 22 July 1998, trans. Topsy Mwewa.

Daka, Patrick. Kashikishi, 21 July 1998.

Kabinda, Prosper. Kashikishi, 12 Jan. 1998.

Kabwebwe, James (Kambwali) and Councilors. Kambwali's Palace, 13 Jan. 1998.

Kalumbwa, Mumba Judith. Kashikishi, 23 July 1998, trans. Topsy Mwewa.

Kamuchoma, Daniel. Kashikishi, 16 Oct. 1997.

Kaoma, Kabel. Kashikishi, 11 Jan. 1998.

Kombe, Joyce. Kashikishi, 23 July 1998, trans. Topsy Mwewa.

Kulaba, Daud Samuel. Kashikishi, 12 Jan. 1998.

Kunda, Gabriel. Kashikishi, 14 Aug. 1998.

Mboba, Alice. Kashikishi, 22 July 1998, trans. Topsy Mwewa.

Mufya, Osia. Kashikishi, 22 July 1998, trans. Topsy Mwewa.

Mukembi, Kabongo. Lupiya, 27 July 1998.

Mulenga, Goodhope. Shishibeti, 20 Oct. 1997.

Mulenga, James Musenga. Shishibeti, 14 Aug. 1997.

Mulenga, Rebecca. Kashikishi, 23 July 1998, trans. Topsy Mwewa.

Mumba, Benedict. Kashikishi, 22 July 1998, trans. Topsy Mwewa.

Mununga and Councilors. Mununga's Palace, 26 July 1998, trans. Abraham Musonda.

Mwaba, Aida Katuta. Kashikishi, 25 July 1998, trans. Topsy Mwewa.

Mwaba, Hello. Kashikishi, 12 Jan. 1998.

Mwaba, Sela. Kashikishi, 22 July 1998, trans. Topsy Mwewa.

Mwewa, Josephine. Kashikishi, 22 July 1998.

Mwembya, Moses. Kaseketi, 20 July 1998, trans. Abaham Musonda.

Mwila, John, and Mwanda Mulenga. Mukwakwa, 25 July 1998.

Puta and Councilors. Puta's Palace, 27 July 1998, trans. Abraham Musonda.

Shala, Albertina. Kashikishi, 23 July 1998, trans. Topsy Mwewa.

Mwense

Bwangu, Jackson, and Joshua Lumbule. Mambilima, 31 Dec. 1997, trans. Joseph Choma.

Chabala, Victor. Kashiba, 24 Dec. 1997.

Chalawila, Andrew. Mbereshi, 29 Oct. 1997.

Chelembi, Mwewa. Mwansabombwe, 29 Dec. 2000.

Chema, Gersham Mulonda (Chilalo). Chilalo, 15 Jan. 2001.

Chibwalwe, Elijah S. M. Kashiba, 22 Dec. 1997 and 3 Jan. 1998.

Chibwe, Emily (Bana Chisenga). Kashiba, 17 July 1998, trans. Mike Kolala.

Chibwidi. Chibwidi, 10 Jan. 2001.

Chikwa, Bonwell. Kashiba, 30 Dec. 1997, trans. Chileshe Kaoma.

Chilapa, Rosemary, and Kasama Kalumbi. Kashiba, 19 Aug. 1998, trans. Mike Kolala.

Chinkonkole, Cosmos Ngoi Kaniembo (Chisami). Mbereshi, 2 Jan. 2001.

Chisenga, Gerald. Kashiba, 2 Nov. 1997.

Chishala, William Katwe. Makandwe River, 30 Dec. 2000.

Chola, Beauty, Diwell Kapya, and Lilya Kabwita. Nkomba, 30 July 1998.

Gosam, Derek (Chipepa). Mwansabombwe 31 Dec. 2000.

Ilunga, John. Chilalo, 15 Jan. 2001.

Kabaso, Achim (Kanyemba). Kanyemba, 6 Jan. 2001.

Kabaso, Jonathan. Mwense, 8 Oct. 1997.

Kafimbwa, Phillip Chona Yatemwa. Kashiba, 26 Dec. 1997, trans. Bruce Mubita.

Kamanga, Howard. Mwansabombwe, 15 Oct. 1997.

Kamweka, Muteba. Mwansabombwe, 13 Jan. 2001.

Kankomba, Elliot Mwitwa, Charles Muyembe, and Joshua Chama. Mambilima, 5 Jan. 1998.

Kanyembo. Kanyembo's Palace, 28 Oct. 1997.

Kapala Lubuli. Kabalenge, 5 Jan. 2001.

Kapongwe, Evelyn (Bana Kapapula). Lubunda, 2 Aug. 1998, trans. Bruce Mubita.

Kapungwe, Janet. Mwansabombwe, 13 Jan. 2001.

Kasau, Moses Mwelwa. Kasau, 30 Dec. 2000.

Kashobwe, Lafwe. Mwansabombwe, 1 Jan. 2001.

Kasonga, Chola, William Mukate, Barnabas Kanyenda. Nkomba, 4 Nov. 1997.

Katongola, Joshua C. Mulundu, 17 July 1998.

Kaunda, Anesia (Bana Chisuku). Lubunda, 17 July, 1998, trans. Mike Kolala.

Kaunda, Margeret, and Robam Kaunda. Mwense, 17 July 1998, trans. Mike Kolala.

Kolala, Mike. Kashiba, 4 Nov. 1997.

Lukwesa, Alam. Musanda, 16 Jan. 2001.

Lukwesa, Daniel. Chimba, 19 Jan. 1998.

Lukwesa. Lukwesa's Palace, 13 Oct. 1997.

Lumbule, Chibale. Mambilima, 14 Oct. 1997.

Lunde Grave Ceremony. Lunde, 22–23 Oct. 1997, trans. Andrew Chalawila.

Luwenga, Fani (Bana Kalifungwe). Kashiba, 19 July 1998, trans. Bruce Mubita.

Mpanga, Dalas (Bana Kamweka). Mwansabombwe, 13 Jan. 2001.

Mukamba, Edward. Kabalenge, 5 Jan. 2001.

Mukobe, Amon (Shanyemba). Shanyemba, 16 Jan. 2001.

Mulalami, James. Mulalami, 15 Jan. 2001.

Mulenga, Lucy Mukolwe. Kabalenge, 5 Jan. 2001.

Mulewambola, Goodson. Kashiba, 19 July 1998, trans. Bruce Mubita.

Mulewambola, Goodson. Kashiba, 30 Dec. 1997, trans. Mike Kolala.

Mulundu, Nshinka, and Councilors. Mulundu's Palace, 9 Jan. 1998, trans. Joseph Choma.

Musonda, Steven. Mwansabombwe, 29 Dec. 2000.

Mutobola, Daniel. Lunde, 27 Oct. 1997.

Muyape, Joseph (Lubunda). Lubunda's Palace, 8 Oct. 1997.
Mwata Kazembe XVIII Munona Chinyanta. Mwansabombwe, 29 Oct. 1997.
Mwelwa, Gosam (Koni). Koni, 2 Feb. 2001.
Mwenso, Harry Kazembe. Mwense, 26 Dec. 1997.
Mwewa, Godwin (Dyulu Kabeya). Mwansabombwe, 12 Dec. 200 and 30 Dec. 2000.
Senika, Malama Mukolwe. Kabalenge, 5 Jan. 2001.
Shakalyata, Mwinempanda, and Kalandala (Mwata Kazembe's Councilors and former aristocrats). Mwansabombwe, 15 Jan. 1998, trans. Andrew Chalawila.

Mansa and southern Luapula
Chilefwaya, Axon. Mansa, 3 Oct. 1997.
Chinga, Luka. Mansa, 6 Oct. 1997.
Kapapula, Booker C. Mansa, 2 Oct. 1997.
Kapapula, Brian. Mansa, 7 Nov. 1997.
Mumba, Bright. Mansa, 6 Oct. 1997.
Mwewa, Enoch. Mansa, 3 Oct. 1997.
Ngandu, Pauline. Mansa, 7 July 1998, trans. Brian Kapapula.

Lusaka
Bwanga, Roda. Soweto Market, Lusaka, 29 June 1998, trans. Chisanga Lungu.
Chama, Grace. Kamwala Market, Lusaka, 30 June 1998.
Chisunka, Queen. Soweto Market, Lusaka, 29 June 1998, trans. Chisanga Lungu.
Kancepa, Tita. Soweto Market, Lusaka, 29 June 1998, trans. Chisanga Lungu.
Kanyembo, Chinyanta. Soweto Market, Lusaka, 29 June 1998, trans. Chisanga Lungu.
Miyambo, Josephine. Soweto Market, Lusaka, 29 June 1998, trans. Chisanga Lungu.
Sillitoe, Alexander J., with Percy and Molly Sillitoe. Lusaka, 31 May 1998.

Democratic Republic of Congo
Kasenga
Cabalala, Kasanda. Kasenga, 15 July 1998, trans. André Kabaso.
Came, Bupe. Kasenga, 16 July 1998, trans. André Kabaso.
Kanyembo, Musunga Pashi (Kikungu). Kasenga, 20 Dec. 1997, trans. André Kabaso.
Kibwe, Mushibwe. Kasenga, 16 July 1998, trans. André Kabaso.
Kiuma, Kisabi Honoré. Kasenga, 15 July 1998, trans. André Kabaso.
Lupandula, David Katuna Funda. Kasenga, 17 Dec. 1997, trans. André Kabaso.
Macris, Antonio. Kasenga, 28 Dec. 1997, trans. André Kabaso.

Matobo, Stefani. Kasenga, 15 July 1998, trans. André Kabaso.
Mwaba, Muteba. Kasenga, 15 July 1998, trans. André Kabaso.

Pweto

Kabwe, Sande, and Bupe Manda. Pweto, 12 July 1998, trans. André Kabaso.
Kavunda, Hilbert, and Claude Kisamba. Pweto, 12 July 1998, trans. André Kabaso.

Lubumbashi

Ilunga, Celine. Lubumbashi, 9 June 1998, trans. André Kabaso.
Kalenga, Françoise. Lubumbashi, 9 June 1998, trans. André Kabaso.
Kashiba, David. Lubumbashi, 15 June 1998.
Kisimba, Alexandre. Kipushi, 17 June 1998.
Lupanzula, Salima. Lubumbashi, 16 June 1998.
Mukeki, Musumbi. Lubumbashi, 10 June 1998, trans. André Kabaso.
Mutombo, Panye. Lubumbashi, 15 June 1998.
Mwila, Helene. Lubumbashi, 9 June 1998, trans. André Kabaso.
Nyombo, Kilufya. Lubumbashi, 10 June 1998, trans. André Kabaso.
Paraskevas, Nicholas. Lubumbashi, 16 June 1998.
Soriano, Abraham. Lubumbashi, 16 June 1998.

INDEX

abacanuma (family behind the king), 37, 38, 40

abakankâla (big men), 20, 86–89; as capitalists, 98–100; church membership and, 108–9; *ulupwa* families and, 191, 195; witchcraft allegations, 110, 195

abanonshi (those who travel to receive remuneration), 87; chisense fishing and, 177, 178; church membership and, 106, 109; as "greedy," 194; kinship and, 189; migrant laborers, 95; witchcraft accusations, 195

Abatwa, 12

access to resources: clans-based tenure systems and, 18; cultivated agricultural land, 59, 144; "open access" regimes, 6–7, 176, 196; ownership and control of, 52

adultery. *See* infidelity, marital

African Fisheries and Marketers Union (AFMU), 152

African Lakes Corporation, 94

African National Congress, 131

agriculture: access to cultivated land, 59, 144; cassava, 12, 56–59, 101, 144, 188; crops cultivated, 12, 56; *vs.* fishing, 51; market controls, 151; nutrient level increase in Lake Mweru and, 174; trade in agricultural commodities, 88; as women's domain, 56

anthropology: historical anthropology, 29; perspectives on property, 9–10

aristocrats: agency of, 35; *amayanga* colonies and, 41–43, 45; Kazembe network of, 36–42; matrilineality and, 37; as "owners" of the king, 30, 35

Arnot, Frederick Stanley, 104

Association des Péchers du Zaire (Apeza), 157

autochthones: *vs.* conquerors, 13–14; intermarriage with the conquering people, 59–60; as owners of land and lagoons, 30–31; political alliances with conquerors, 14–15. *See also specific peoples*

bamunyama (vampire men), 73, 107, 114–15

Baptista, P., 13

Bates Robert, 180

beer, 57

Belgian Congo: chiefs and, 63–64, 68–69; conservation and fishing regulations in, 124–25; economic policies, 89–91; "paternalism," 65–66, 124, 131–32; trade administration during, 93

Belinga, Samuel Eno, 10

Berry, Sara, 7–8, 17

"big men" *(abakankâla)*, 20, 54–55, 86–89, 98–100, 109, 191, 195

"big women," 88–89, 102, 188, 193–96, 198

Bisa, 36

Booth, Harold, 94

boundaries, narratives and definition of, 45, 50–51

AFRICA AND THE DIASPORA
History, Politics, Culture
